DATE DUE

~~29 '99~~			
~~DE 18'99~~			
~~12~~			
~~DE 700~~			
~~MY '01~~			
~~DE 17 05~~			
~~JE 2 0~~			
~~JE 2 06~~			
~~JE 7 06~~			

DEMCO 38-296

The Information Age
Economy, Society and Culture

Volume II
The Power of Identity

Para Irene Castells Oliván,
historiadora de utopías

R

The Power of Identity

Manuel Castells

BLACKWELL
Publishers

HM 221 .C366 1997

Castells, Manuel.

The power of identity

as author of this work has been asserted in Patents Act 1988.

Maiden, MA 02148
USA

Blackwell Publishers Ltd
108 Cowley Road
Oxford OX4 1JF
UK

Library of Congress Cataloging in Publication Data

Castells, Manuel.
    The power of identity / Manuel Castells.
       p. cm. — (Information age ; v. 2)
    Includes bibliographical references and index.
    ISBN 1–55786–873–5 — ISBN 1–55786–874–3 (pbk.)
    1. Information society. 2. Social movements. 3. Information technology—Social aspects. 4. Information technology—Political aspects. 5. Identity. I. Title. II. Series: Castells, Manuel. Information age ; 2
    HM221.C366 1997
    303.48'33—dc20   96-36317
                                          CIP

British Library Cataloguing in Publication Data

A CIP catalogue record for this book is available from the British Library.

Printed in Great Britain by T.J. International Limited, Padstow, Cornwall
This book is printed on acid-free paper

Contents

Figures

Tables

Charts

Acknowledgments

The ideas and analyses presented in this volume have grown out of 25 years of study which I have conducted on social movements and political processes in various areas of the world, although they are now re-elaborated and integrated in a broader theory of the Information Age, as presented in the three volumes of this book. A number of academic institutions were essential environments for the development of my work in this specific area of inquiry. Foremost among them was the Centre d'Étude des Mouvements Sociaux, École des Hautes Etudes en Sciences Sociales, Paris, founded and directed by Alain Touraine, where I was a researcher between 1965 and 1979. Other research institutions that helped my work on social movements and politics were: Centro Interdisciplinario de Desarrollo Urbano, Universidad Catolica de Chile; Instituto de Investigaciones Sociales, Universidad Nacional Autonoma de Mexico; Center for Urban Studies, University of Hong Kong; Instituto de Sociologia de Nuevas Tecnologias, Universidad Autonoma de Madrid; Faculty of Social Sciences, Hitotsubashi University, Tokyo. The final elaboration and writing of the material presented here took place in the 1990s in what has been, since 1979, my intellectual home, the University of California at Berkeley. Many of the ideas were discussed and refined in my graduate seminar on "Sociology of the Information Society." For this, I thank my students, a constant source of inspiration for and criticism of my work. This volume has benefited from exceptional research assistance by Sandra Moog, a sociology graduate student at Berkeley, and a future outstanding scholar. Additional valuable research assistance was provided by Lan-chih Po, a doctoral student in city and regional planning, also at Berkeley. As with the other volumes of this book, Emma Kiselyova considerably helped my research by facilitating access to languages that I do not know, as well as by assessing and commenting on various sections of the volume.

Several colleagues read drafts of the whole volume, or of specific chapters, and commented extensively, helping me to correct some mistakes and to tighten up the analysis, although I obviously take full responsibility for the final interpretation. My gratitude goes to: Ira Katznelson, Ida Susser, Alain Touraine, Anthony Giddens, Martin Carnoy, Stephen Cohen, Alejandra Moreno Toscano, Roberto Laserna, Fernando Calderon, Rula Sadik, You-tien Hsing, Shujiro Yazawa, Chu-joe Hsia, Nancy Whittier, Barbara Epstein, David Hooson, Irene Castells, Eva Serra, Tim Duane, and Elsie Harper-Anderson. I wish to express my special thanks to John Davey, Blackwell's editorial director, who provided his expert insight, as well as careful suggestions on substance in several key sections of the volume.

This is to say that, as with the other volumes of this book, the process of thinking and writing is largely a collective endeavor, albeit ultimately assumed in the solitude of authorship.

November 1996   Berkeley, California

The author and publishers gratefully acknowledge permission from the following to reproduce copyright material:

Professor Ines Alberdi: for figures 4.2 and 4.5.
The Economist: for figures 5.1 and 5.2, both copyright © The Economist, London 1996.
The Journal of Politics: for figure 6.2.
The Southern Poverty Law Center, Alabama: for figure 2.1 obtained from their Klanwatch Militia Task Force Programs.
The University of Chicago Press: for figures 4.10 and 4.14 from E. O. Laumann et al., *The Social Organization of Sexuality: Sexual Practices in the United States* (1994), copyright © 1994 by Edward O. Laumann, Robert T. Michael, CSG Enterprises, Inc., and Stuart Michaels. All rights reserved.
Westview Press, Inc.: for figure 4.1 from *The New Role of Women: Family Formation in Modern Societies* by Hans-Peter Blossfeld et al. (1995), copyright © 1995 by Westview Press.

Our World, our Lives

Lift up your faces, you have a piercing need
For this bright morning dawning for you.
History, despite its wrenching pain,
Cannot be unlived, and if faced
With courage, need not be lived again.

Lift up your eyes upon
This day breaking for you.
Give birth again
To the dream.

Maya Angelou, "On the Pulse of Morning"[1]

Our world, and our lives, are being shaped by the conflicting trends of globalization and identity. The information technology revolution, and the restructuring of capitalism, have induced a new form of society, the network society. It is characterized by the globalization of strategically decisive economic activities. By the networking form of organization. By the flexibility and instability of work, and the individualization of labor. By a culture of real virtuality constructed by a pervasive, interconnected, and diversified media system. And by the transformation of material foundations of life, space and time, through the constitution of a space of flows and of timeless time, as expressions of dominant activities and controlling elites. This new form of social organization, in its pervasive globality, is diffusing throughout the world, as industrial capitalism and its twin enemy, industrial statism, did in the twentieth century, shaking institutions, transforming cultures, creating wealth and inducing poverty, spurring greed, innovation, and hope, while simultaneously

---

[1] Poem on the inauguration of the US President, January 22, 1993.

imposing hardship and instilling despair. It is indeed, brave or not, a new world.

But this is not the whole story. Along with the technological revolution, the transformation of capitalism, and the demise of statism, we have experienced, in the last quarter of the century, the widespread surge of powerful expressions of collective identity that challenge globalization and cosmopolitanism on behalf of cultural singularity and people's control over their lives and environment. These expressions are multiple, highly diversified, following the contours of each culture, and of historical sources of formation of each identity. They include proactive movements, aiming at transforming human relationships at their most fundamental level, such as feminism and environmentalism. But they also include a whole array of reactive movements that build trenches of resistance on behalf of God, nation, ethnicity, family, locality, that is, the fundamental categories of millennial existence now threatened under the combined, contradictory assault of techno-economic forces and transformative social movements. Caught between these opposing trends, the nation-state is called into question, drawing into its crisis the very notion of political democracy, predicated upon the historical construction of a sovereign, representative nation-state. More often than not, new, powerful technological media, such as worldwide, interactive telecommunication networks, are used by various contenders, amplifying and sharpening their struggle, as, for instance, when the Internet becomes an instrument of international environmentalists, Mexican *Zapatistas,* or American militia, responding in kind to computerized globalization of financial markets and information processing.

This is the world explored in this volume, focusing primarily on social movements and politics, as they result from the interplay between technology-induced globalization, the power of identity (gender, religious, national, ethnic, territorial, socio-biological), and the institutions of the state. Inviting the reader to this intellectual journey through the landscapes of contemporary social struggles and political conflicts, I will start with a few remarks that may help the voyage.

This is not a book about books. Thus, I will not discuss existing theories on each topic, or cite every possible source on the issues presented here. Indeed, it would be pretentious to attempt setting, even superficially, the scholarly record on the whole realm of themes covered in this book. The sources and authors that I do use for each topic are materials that I consider relevant to construct the hypotheses I am proposing on each theme, as well as on the meaning of these analyses for a broader theory of social change in the network society. Readers interested in bibliography, and in critical evaluations of such a bibliography, should consult the many available good textbooks on each matter.

The method I have followed aims at communicating theory by analyzing practice, in successive waves of observation of social movements in various cultural and institutional contexts. Thus, empirical analysis is mainly used as a communication device, and as a method of disciplining my theoretical discourse, of making it difficult, if not impossible, to say something that observed collective action rejects in practice. However, I have tried to provide a few empirical elements, within the space constraints of this volume, to make my interpretation plausible, and to allow the reader to judge for her/himself.

There is in this book a deliberate obsession with multiculturalism, with scanning the planet, in its diverse social and political manifestations. This approach stems from my view that the process of techno-economic globalization shaping our world is being challenged, and will eventually be transformed, from a multiplicity of sources, according to different cultures, histories, and geographies. Thus, moving thematically between the United States, Western Europe, Russia, Mexico, Bolivia, the Islamic world, China or Japan, as I do in this volume, has the specific purpose of using the same analytical framework to understand very different social processes that are, none the less, interrelated in their meaning. I would also like, within the obvious limits of my knowledge and experience, to break the ethnocentric approach still dominating much social science at the very moment when our societies have become globally interconnected and culturally intertwined.

One word about theory. The sociological theory informing this book is diluted for your convenience in the presentation of themes in each chapter. It is also blended with empirical analysis as far as it could be done. Only when it is unavoidable will I submit the reader to a brief theoretical excursus, since for me social theory is a tool to understand the world, not an end for intellectual self-enjoyment. I shall try, in the conclusion to this volume, to tighten up the analysis in a more formal, systematic manner, bringing together the various threads woven in each chapter. However, since the book focuses on social movements, and since there is a great deal of disagreement on the meaning of the concept, I advance my definition of social movements as being: purposive collective actions whose outcome, in victory as in defeat, transforms the values and institutions of society. Since there is no sense of history other than the history we sense, *from an analytical perspective* there are no "good" and "bad," progressive and regressive social movements. They are all symptoms of who we are, and avenues of our transformation, since transformation may equally lead to a whole range of heavens, hells, or heavenly hells. This is not an incidental remark, since processes of social change in our world often take forms of fanaticism and violence that we do not usually associate with positive social change. And yet, this is our world, this is us, in our contradictory plurality, and this is what we have to understand, if necessarily to face it, and to overcome it. As for the meaning of *this* and *us*, please dare to read on.

— 1 —

Communal Heavens: Identity and Meaning in the Network Society

The capital is established near Zhong Mountain;
The palaces and thresholds are brilliant and shining;
The forests and gardens are fragrant and flourishing;
Epidendrums and cassia complement each other in beauty.
The forbidden palace is magnificent;
Buildings and pavilions a hundred stories high.
Halls and gates are beautiful and lustrous;
Bells and chimes sound musically.
The towers reach up to the sky;
Upon altars sacrificial animals are burned.
Cleansed and purified,
We fast and bathe.
We are respectful and devout in worship,
Dignified and serene in prayer.
Supplicating with fervor,
Each seeks happiness and joy.
The uncivilized and border people offer tribute,
And all the barbarians are submissive.
No matter how vast the territory,
All will be eventually under our rule.

Hong Xiuquan

Such were the words of the "Imperially Written Tale of a Thousand Words," composed by Hong Xiuquan, the guide and prophet of the Taiping Rebellion, after establishing his heavenly kingdom in Nanjing in 1853.[1] The insurgency of Taiping Tao (Way of Great

---

[1] Cited by Spence (1996: 190–1).

Peace) aimed at creating a communal, neo-Christian fundamentalist kingdom in China. The kingdom was organized, for more than a decade, in conformity with the revelation of the Bible that, by his own account, Hong Xiuquan received from his elder brother, Jesus Christ, after being initiated into Christianity by evangelical missionaries. Between 1845 and 1864, Hong's prayers, teachings, and armies shook up China, and the world, as they interfered with the growing foreign control of the Middle Kingdom. The Taiping Kingdom perished, as it lived, in blood and fire, taking the lives of 20 million Chinese. It longed to establish an earthly paradise by fighting the demons that had taken over China, so that "all people may live together in perpetual joy, until at last they are raised to Heaven to greet their Father."[2] It was a time of crisis for state bureaucracies and moral traditions, of globalization of trade, of profitable drug traffic, of rapid industrialization spreading in the world, of religious missions, of impoverished peasants, of the shaking of families and communities, of local bandits and international armies, of the diffusion of printing and mass illiteracy, a time of uncertainty and hopelessness, of identity crisis. It was another time. Or was it?

The Construction of Identity

Identity is people's source of meaning and experience. As Calhoun writes:

> We know of no people without names, no languages or cultures in which some manner of distinctions between self and other, we and they, are not made . . . Self-knowledge – always a construction no matter how much it feels like a discovery – is never altogether separable from claims to be known in specific ways by others.[3]

By identity, as it refers to social actors, I understand the process of construction of meaning on the basis of a cultural attribute, or related set of cultural attributes, that is/are given priority over other sources of meaning. For a given individual, or for a collective actor, there may be a plurality of identities. Yet, such a plurality is a source of stress and contradiction in both self-representation and social action. This is because identity must be distinguished from what, traditionally, sociologists have called roles, and role-sets. Roles (for example, to be a worker, a mother, a neighbor, a socialist militant, a union member,

---

[2]   Spence (1996: 172).
[3]   Calhoun (1994: 9–10).

a basketball player, a churchgoer, and a smoker, at the same time) are defined by norms structured by the institutions and organizations of society. Their relative weight in influencing people's behavior depend upon negotiations and arrangements between individuals and these institutions and organizations. Identities are sources of meaning for the actors themselves, and by themselves, constructed through a process of individuation.[4] Although, as I will argue below, identities can also be originated from dominant institutions, they become identities only when and if social actors internalize them, and construct their meaning around this internalization. To be sure, some self-definitions can also coincide with social roles, for instance when to be a father is the most important self-definition from the point of view of the actor. Yet, identities are stronger sources of meaning than roles, because of the process of self-construction and individuation that they involve. In simple terms, identities organize the meaning while roles organize the functions. I define *meaning* as the symbolic identification by a social actor of the purpose of her/his action. I also propose the idea that, *in the network society*, for reasons that I will develop below, for most social actors, meaning is organized around a primary identity (that is an identity that frames the others), that is self-sustaining across time and space. While this approach is close to Erikson's formulation of identity, my focus here will be primarily on collective, rather than on individual, identity. However, individualism (different from individual identity) may also be a form of "collective identity," as analyzed in Lasch's "culture of narcissism."[5]

It is easy to agree on the fact that, from a sociological perspective, all identities are constructed. The real issue is how, from what, by whom, and for what. The construction of identities uses building materials from history, from geography, from biology, from productive and reproductive institutions, from collective memory and from personal fantasies, from power apparatuses and religious revelations. But individuals, social groups, and societies process all these materials, and rearrange their meaning, according to social determinations and cultural projects that are rooted in their social structure, and in their space/time framework. I propose, as a hypothesis, that, in general terms, who constructs collective identity, and for what, largely determines the symbolic content of this identity, and its meaning for those identifying with it or placing themselves outside of it. Since the social construction of identity always takes place in a context marked by power relationships, I propose a distinction between three forms and origins of identity building:

[4]   Giddens (1991).
[5]   Lasch (1980).

- *Legitimizing identity*: introduced by the dominant institutions of society to extend and rationalize their domination *vis à vis* social actors, a theme that is at the heart of Sennett's theory of authority and domination,[6] but also fits with various theories of nationalism.[7]
- *Resistance identity*: generated by those actors that are in positions/conditions devalued and/or stigmatized by the logic of domination, thus building trenches of resistance and survival on the basis of principles different from, or opposed to, those permeating the institutions of society, as Calhoun proposes when explaining the emergence of identity politics.[8]
- *Project identity*: when social actors, on the basis of whichever cultural materials are available to them, build a new identity that redefines their position in society and, by so doing, seek the transformation of overall social structure. This is the case, for instance, when feminism moves out from the trenches of resistance of women's identity and women's rights, to challenge patriarchalism, thus the patriarchal family, thus the entire structure of production, reproduction, sexuality, and personality on which societies have been historically based.

Naturally, identities that start as resistance may induce projects, and may also, along the course of history, become dominant in the institutions of society, thus becoming legitimizing identities to rationalize their domination. Indeed, the dynamics of identities along this sequence shows that, from the point of view of social theory, no identity can be an essence, and no identity has, *per se*, progressive or regressive value outside its historical context. A different, and very important matter, is the benefits of each identity for the people who belong.

In my view, each type of identity-building process leads to a different outcome in constituting society. *Legitimizing identity generates a civil society*; that is, a set of organizations and institutions, as well as a series of structured and organized social actors, which reproduce, albeit sometimes in a conflictive manner, the identity that rationalizes the sources of structural domination. This statement may come as a surprise to some readers, since civil society generally suggests a positive connotation of democratic social change. However, this is in fact the original conception of civil society, as formulated by Gramsci, the intellectual father of this ambiguous concept. Indeed, in Gramsci's conception, civil society is formed by a series of "apparatuses," such as the Church(es), unions, parties, cooperatives, civic associations and

[6]   Sennett (1986).
[7]   Anderson (1983); Gellner (1983).
[8]   Calhoun (1994: 17).

so on, which, on the one hand, prolong the dynamics of the state, but, on the other hand, are deeply rooted among people.[9] It is precisely this double character of civil society that makes it a privileged terrain of political change by making it possible to seize the state without launching a direct, violent assault. The conquest of the state by the forces of change (let's say the forces of socialism, in Gramsci's ideology), present in the civil society, is made possible exactly because of the continuity between civil society's institutions and the power apparatuses of the state, organized around a similar identity (citizenship, democracy, the politicization of social change, the confinement of power to the state and its ramifications, and the like). Where Gramsci, and de Tocqueville, see democracy and civility, Foucault or Sennett, and before them Horkheimer or Marcuse, see internalized domination and legitimation of an over-imposed, undifferentiated, normalizing identity.

The second type of identity-building, *identity for resistance*, leads to the formation of *communes*, or *communities*, in Etzioni's formulation.[10] This may be the most important type of identity-building in our society. It constructs forms of collective resistance against otherwise unbearable oppression, usually on the basis of identities that were, apparently, clearly defined by history, geography, or biology, making it easier to essentialize the boundaries of resistance. For instance, ethnically based nationalism, as Scheff proposes, often "arises out of a sense of alienation, on the one hand, and resentment against unfair exclusion, whether political, economic or social."[11] Religious fundamentalism, territorial communities, nationalist self-affirmation, or even the pride of self-denigration, inverting the terms of oppressive discourse (as in the "queer culture" of some tendencies in the gay movement), are all expressions of what I name *the exclusion of the excluders by the excluded.* That is, the building of defensive identity in the terms of dominant institutions/ideologies, reversing the value judgment while reinforcing the boundary. In such a case, the issue arises of the reciprocal communicability between these excluded/exclusionary identities. The answer to this question, that can only be empirical and historical, determines whether societies remain as societies or else fragment into a constellation of tribes, some times euphemistically renamed communities.

The third process of constructing identity, that is *project identity*, produces *subjects*, as defined by Alain Touraine:

[9]   Buci-Glucksman (1978).
[10]   Etzioni (1993).
[11]   Scheff (1994: 281).

> I name subject the desire of being an individual, of creating a
> personal history, of giving meaning to the whole realm of expe-
> riences of individual life . . . The transformation of individuals
> into subjects results from the necessary combination of two affir-
> mations: that of individuals against communities, and that of
> individuals against the market.[12]

Subjects are not individuals, even if they are made by and in individuals. They are the collective social actor through which individuals
reach holistic meaning in their experience.[13] In this case, the building
of identity is a project of a different life, perhaps on the basis of an
oppressed identity, but expanding toward the transformation of
society as the prolongation of this project of identity, as in the above-
mentioned example of a post-patriarchal society, liberating women,
men, and children, through the realization of women's identity. Or,
in a very different perspective, the final reconciliation of all human
beings as believers, brothers and sisters, under the guidance of God's
law, be it Allah or Jesus, as a result of the religious conversion of
godless, anti-family, materialist societies, otherwise unable to fufill
human needs and God's design.

How, and by whom, different types of identities are constructed,
and with what outcomes, cannot be addressed in general, abstract
terms: it is a matter of social context. Identity politics, as Zaretsky
writes, "must be situated historically."[14]

Thus, our discussion must refer to a specific context, the rise of the
network society. The dynamics of identity in this context can be better
understood by contrasting it with Giddens' characterization of identity in "late modernity," a historical period which, I believe, is an era
reaching its end – by which I do not mean to suggest that we are in
some way reaching the "end of history" as posited in some postmodern vagaries. In a powerful theorization whose main lines I share,
Giddens states that "self-identity is not a distinctive trait possessed by
the individual. It is the self as reflexively understood by the person in
terms of her/his biography." Indeed, "to be a human being is to
know . . . both what one is doing and why one is doing it . . . In the
context of post-traditional order, the self becomes a reflexive
project."[15]

How does "late modernity" impact this reflexive project? In
Giddens' terms,

---

[12]   Touraine (1995: 29–30); my translation.
[13]   Touraine (1992).
[14]   Zaretsky (1994: 198).
[15]   Giddens (1991: 53, 35, 32).

one of the distinctive features of modernity is an increasing inter-
connection between the two extremes of extensionality and
intentionality: globalising influences on the one hand and
personal dispositions on the other . . . The more tradition loses
its hold, and the more daily life is reconstituted in terms of the
dialectical interplay of the local and the global, the more individuals are forced to negotiate lifestyle choices among a diversity
of options . . . Reflexively organized life-planning . . . becomes a
central feature of the structuring of self-identity."[16]

While agreeing with Giddens' theoretical characterization of
identity-building in the period of "late modernity," I argue, on the
basis of analyses presented in volume I of this book, that the rise of
the network society calls into question the processes of construction
of identity during that period, thus inducing new forms of social
change. This is because the network society is based on the systemic
disjunction between the local and the global for most individuals and
social groups. And, I will add, by the separation in different
time–space frames between power and experience (volume I, chapters 6 and 7). Therefore, reflexive life-planning becomes impossible,
except for the elite inhabiting the timeless space of flows of global networks and their ancillary locales. And the building of intimacy on the
basis of trust requires a redefinition of identity fully autonomous *vis à
vis* the networking logic of dominant institutions and organizations.

Under such new conditions, civil societies shrink and disarticulate
because there is no longer continuity between the logic of power-
making in the global network and the logic of association and
representation in specific societies and cultures. The search for
meaning takes place then in the reconstruction of defensive identities around communal principles. Most of social action becomes
organized in the opposition between unidentified flows and secluded
identities. As for the emergence of project identities, it still happens,
or may happen, depending on societies. But, I propose the hypothesis
that the constitution of subjects, at the heart of the process of social
change, takes a different route to the one we knew during modernity,
and late modernity: namely, *subjects, if and when constructed, are not built
any longer on the basis of civil societies, that are in the process of disintegration, but as prolongation of communal resistance.* While in modernity
(early or late) project identity was constituted from civil society (as in
the case of socialism on the basis of the labor movement), in the
network society, project identity, if it develops at all, grows from
communal resistance. This is the actual meaning of the new primacy
of identity politics in the network society. The analysis of processes,

[16]   Giddens (1991: 1, 5).

conditions, and outcomes of the transformation of communal resistance into transformative subjects is the precise realm for a theory of social change in the information age.

Having reached a tentative formulation of my hypotheses, it would be against the methodological principles of this book to go any further down the path of abstract theorizing that could quickly divert into bibliographical commentary. I shall try to suggest the precise implications of my analysis by focusing on a number of key processes in the construction of collective identity selected by their particular relevance to the process of social change in the network society. I will start with *religious fundamentalism*, both in its Islamic and Christian versions, although this does not imply that other religions (for example, Hinduism, Buddhism, Judaism) are less important or less prone to fundamentalism. I shall continue with *nationalism*, considering, after some overview of the issue, two very different, but significant processes: the role of nationalism in the disintegration of the Soviet Union, and in post-Soviet republics; and the formation, and re-emergence of Catalan nationalism. I will then turn to *ethnic identity*, focusing on contemporary African-American identity. And I will end by considering, briefly, *territorial identity*, on the basis of my observation of urban movements and local communities around the world. In conclusion, I shall try a succinct synthesis of major lines of inquiry that will emerge from examining various contemporary processes of the (re)construction of identity on the basis of communal resistance.

God's Heavens: Religious Fundamentalism and Cultural Identity

It is an attribute of society, and I would dare to say of human nature if such an entity were to exist, to find solace and refuge in religion. The fear of death, the pain of life, need God, and faith in God, whichever of God's manifestations, for people just to go on. Indeed, outside us God would become homeless.

Religious fundamentalism is something else. And I contend that this "something else" is a most important source of constructing identity in the network society for reasons that will become clearer, I hope, in the following pages. As for its actual content, experiences, opinions, history, and theories are so diverse as to defy synthesis. Fortunately, the American Academy of Arts and Sciences undertook, in the late 1980s, a major comparative project aimed at observing fundamentalisms in various social and institutional contexts.[17] Thus,

---

[17]   Marty and Appleby (1991).

we know that "fundamentalists are always reactive, reactionary,"[18] and that:

> fundamentalists are selective. They may well consider that they are adopting the whole of the pure past, but their energies go into employing those features which will best reinforce their identity, keep their movement together, build defenses around its boundaries, and keep others at a distance . . . Fundamentalists fight under God – in the case of theistic religion – or under the signs of some transcendent reference.[19]

To be more precise, I believe, to be consistent with the collection of essays gathered in the "Fundamentalism Observed" Project, in defining *fundamentalism*, in my own understanding, as *the construction of collective identity under the identification of individual behavior and society's institutions to the norms derived from God's law, interpreted by a definite authority that intermediates between God and humanity.* Thus, as Marty writes, "It is impossible for fundamentalists to argue or settle anything with people who do not share their commitment to an authority, whether it be an inerrant Bible, an infallible Pope, the *Shari'a* codes in Islam, or the implications of *halacha* in Judaism."[20]

Religious fundamentalism has, of course, existed throughout the whole of human history, but it appears to be surprisingly strong and influential as a source of identity in this end of millennium. Why so? My analyses of Islamic fundamentalism, and of Christian fundamentalism, in this section, will try to propose some clues to understand one of the most defining trends in the making of our historical epoch.[21]

Umma versus *Jahiliya*: Islamic fundamentalism

> *The only way to accede to modernity is by our own path, that which has been traced for us by our religion, our history and our civilization.*
> Rached Gannouchi[22]

The 1970s, the birthdate of the information technology revolution in Silicon Valley, and the starting point of global capitalist restructuring, had a different meaning for the Muslim world: it marked the

---

18   Marty (1988: 20).
19   Marty and Appleby (1991: ix–x).
20   Marty (1988: 22).
21   See also Misztal and Shupe (1992a).
22   Rached Gannouchi, interview with *Jeune Afrique,* July 1990. Gannouchi is a leading intellectual in the Tunisian Islamist movement.

beginning of the fourteenth century of the *Hegira*, a period of Islamic revival, purification, and strengthening, as at the onset of each new century. Indeed, in the next two decades an authentic cultural/religious revolution spread throughout Muslim lands, sometimes victorious, as in Iran, sometimes subdued, as in Egypt, sometimes triggering civil war, as in Algeria, sometimes formally acknowledged in the institutions of the state, as in the Sudan or Bangladesh, most times establishing an uneasy coexistence with a formally Islamic nation-state, fully integrated in global capitalism, as in Saudi Arabia, Indonesia, or Morocco. Overall, the cultural identity and political fate of almost a billion people were being fought for in the mosques and in the wards of Muslim cities, crowded by accelerated urbanization, and disintegrated by failed modernization. Islamic fundamentalism, as a reconstructed identity, and as a political project, is at the center of a most decisive process, largely conditioning the world's future.[23]

But, what is Islamic fundamentalism? Islam, in Arabic, means state of submission, and a Muslim is one who has submitted to Allah. Thus, according to the definition of fundamentalism I presented above, it would appear that all Islam is fundamentalist: societies, and their state institutions, must be organized around uncontested religious principles. However, a number of distinguished scholars[24] argue that, while the primacy of religious principles as formulated in the Qur'ān is common to all of Islam, Islamic societies and institutions are also based on multivocal interpretation. Furthermore, in most traditional Islamic societies, the pre-eminence of religious principles over political authority was purely formal. Indeed, the *shari'a* (divine law, formed by the Qur'ān and the *Hadiths*) relates in classic Arabic language to the verb *shara'a*, to walk toward a source. Thus, for most Muslims, *shari'a* is not an invariable, rigid command, but a guide to walk toward God, with the adaptations required by each historical and social context.[25] In contrast to this openness of Islam, Islamic fundamentalism implies the fusion of *shari'a* with *fiqh*, or interpretation and application by jurists and authorities, under the absolute domination of *shari'a*. Naturally, the actual meaning depends on the process of interpretation, and on who interprets. Thus, there is a wide range of variation between conservative fundamentalism, such as the one represented by the House of Saud, and radical fundamentalism, as elaborated in the writings of al-Mawdudi or Sayyid Qtub in the 1950s

---

[23]   Hiro (1989); Balta (1991); Sisk (1992); Choueri (1993); Juergensmayer (1993); Dekmejian (1995).
[24]   See, for example, Bassam Tibi (1988, 1992a); Aziz Al-Azmeh (1993); Farhad Khosrokhavar (1995), among others.
[25]   Garaudy (1990).

and 1960s.[26] There are also considerable differences between the Shia tradition, the one inspiring Khomeini, and the Sunni tradition which constitutes the faith for about 85 percent of Muslims, including revolutionary movements such as Algeria's *Front Islamique de Salvation* (FIS), or Egypt's *Takfir wal-Hijrah*. Yet, in the vision of writers who constitute Islamist thought in this century, such as Egypt's Hassan al Banna and Sayyid Qtub, India's Ali al-Nadawi, or Pakistan's Sayyid Abul al-Mawdudi, the history of Islam is reconstructed to show the perennial submission of state to religion.[27] For a Muslim, the fundamental attachment is not to the *watan* (homeland), but to the *umma*, or community of believers, all made equal in their submission to Allah. This universal confraternity supersedes the institutions of the nation-state, which is seen as a source of division among believers.[28] For the *umma* to live, and expand, until embracing the whole of humanity, it has to accomplish a godly task: to undertake, anew, the fight against *Jahiliya* (the state of ignorance of God, or of lack of observance of God's teachings), in which societies have fallen again. To regenerate humanity, Islamization must proceed first in the Muslim societies that have secularized and departed from the strict obedience of God's law, then in the entire world. This process must start with a spiritual rebirth based on *al-sirat al-mustaqin* (straight path), modeled after the community organized by the Prophet Muhammad in Medina. Yet, to overcome impious forces, it may be necessary to proceed through *jihad* (struggle on behalf of Islam) against the infidels, which may include, in extreme cases, the resort to holy war. In the Shia tradition, martyrdom, re-enacting Imam Ali's sacrifice in 681, is indeed at the heart of religious purity. But the whole of Islam shares the praise for the necessary sacrifices implied by the call of God (*al-da'wah*). As stated by Hassan al Banna, the founder and leader of Muslim Brotherhood, assassinated in 1949: "The Qur'ān is our constitution, the Prophet is our Guide; death for the glory of Allah is our greatest ambition."[29] The ultimate goal of all human actions must be the establishment of God's law over the whole of humankind, thus ending the current opposition between *Dar al-Islam* (the Muslim world), and *Dar al-Harb* (the non-Muslim world).

In this cultural/religious/political framework, Islamic identity is constructed on the basis of a double deconstruction, by the social actors, and by the institutions of society.

Social actors must deconstruct themselves as subjects, be it as indi-

[26]   Carre (1984); Choueri (1993).
[27]   Hiro (1989); Al-Azmeh (1993); Choueri (1993); Dekmejian (1995).
[28]   Oumlil (1992).
[29]   Cited by Hiro (1989: 63).

viduals, as members of an ethnic group, or as citizens of a nation. In addition, women must submit to their guardian men, as they are encouraged to fulfill themselves primarily in the framework of the family: "Men are the protectors and maintainers of women, because God has given the one more (strength) than the other, and because they support them from their means."[30] As Bassam Tibi writes, "Habermas' principle of subjectivity is a heresy for Islamic fundamentalists."[31] Only in the *umma* can the individual be fully himself/herself, as part of the confraternity of believers, a basic equalizing mechanism that provides mutual support, solidarity, and shared meaning. On the other hand, the nation-state itself must negate its identity: *al-dawla islamiiyya* (Islamic state), based on the *Shari'a*, takes precedence over the nation-state (*al-dawla qawmiyya)*. This proposition is particularly effective in the Middle East, a region where, according to Tibi, "the nation-state is alien and is virtually imposed on its parts . . . The political culture of secular nationalism is not only a novelty in the Middle East, but also remains on the surface of involved societies."[32]

However, and this is essential, Islamic fundamentalism is not a traditionalist movement. For all the efforts of exegesis to root Islamic identity in history and the holy texts, Islamists proceeded, for the sake of social resistance and political insurgency, with a reconstruction of cultural identity that is in fact hypermodern.[33] As Al-Azmeh writes: "The politicization of the sacred, the sacralization of politics, and the transformation of Islamic pseudo-legal institutes into 'social devotions', are all means of realizing the politics of the authentic ego, a politics of identity, and therefore the means for the very formation, indeed the invention, of this identity."[34]

But, if Islamism (although rooted in the writings of nineteenth-century Islamic reformers and revivalists, such as al-Afghani) is essentially a contemporary identity, why now? Why has it exploded in the past two decades, after being repeatedly subdued by nationalism in the post-colonial period, as exemplified by the repression of the Muslim Brothers in Egypt and Syria (including the execution of Qtub in 1966), the rise of Sukarno in Indonesia or of the *Front de Liberation Nationale* in Algeria?[35]

[30] Qur'ān, surah IV, v. 34 (trans. Abdullah Yusuf Ali, 1988). See Hiro (1989: 202); Delcroix (1995); Gerami (1996).
[31] Tibi (1992b: 8).
[32] Tibi (1992b: 5).
[33] Gole (1995).
[34] Al-Azmeh (1993: 31).
[35] Piscatori (1986); Moen and Gustafson (1992); Tibi (1992a); Burgat and Dowell (1993); Juergensmayer (1993); Dekmejian (1995).

For Tibi, "the rise of Islamic fundamentalism in the Middle East is inter-related with the exposure of this part of the world of Islam, which perceives itself as a collective entity, to the processes of globalization, to nationalism and the nation-state as globalized principles of organization."[36]

Indeed, the explosion of Islamic movements seems to be related to both the disruption of traditional societies (including the undermining of the power of traditional clergy), and to the failure of the nation-state, created by nationalist movements, to accomplish modernization, develop the economy, and/or to distribute the benefits of economic growth among the population at large. Thus, Islamic identity is (re)constructed by fundamentalists in opposition to capitalism, to socialism, and to nationalism, Arab or otherwise, which are, in their view, all failing ideologies of the post-colonial order.

A case in point is, of course, Iran.[37] The Shah's White Revolution, launched in 1963, was a most ambitious attempt to modernize the economy and society, with the support of the United States, and with the deliberate project of linking up with new global capitalism in the making. So doing, it undermined basic structures of traditional society, from agriculture to the calendar. Indeed, a major conflict between the Shah and the *ulemas* concerned control over time, when, on April 24, 1976, the Shah changed the Islamic calendar to the pre-Islamic Achemenian dynasty calendar. When Khomeini landed in Tehran on February 1, 1979, to lead the revolution, he returned as representative of Imam Nacoste, Lord of Time (*wali al-zaman*) to assert the pre-eminence of religious principles. The Islamic revolution opposed simultaneously the institution of monarchy (Khomeini: "Islam is fundamentally opposed to the whole notion of monarchy");[38] the nation-state (article 10 of the new Iranian Constitution: "All Muslims form a single nation"); and modernization as an expression of Westernization (article 43 of the Iranian Constitution asserts the "prohibition of extravagance and wastefulness in all matters related to the economy, including consumption, investment, production, distribution, and services"). The power of the *ulemas*, the main targets of the Shah's institutional reforms, became enshrined as the intermediary between the *shari'a* and society. The radicalization of the Islamic regime, after Iraq's attack in 1980 and the atrocious war that followed, led to the purification of society, and the setting up of special religious judges to repress impious acts, such as "adultery, homosexuality, gambling, hypocrisy, sympathy for atheists and

---

[36] Tibi (1992b: 7).
[37] Hiro (1989); Bakhash (1990); Esposito (1990); Khosrokhavar (1995).
[38] Hiro (1989: 161).

hypocrites, and treason."[39] There followed thousands of imprison-
ments, flagellations, and executions, on different grounds. The cycle
of terror, particularly aimed at leftist critics and Marxist guerrillas,
closed the circle of fundamentalist logic in Iran.

What are the social bases of fundamentalism? In Iran, where other
revolutionary forces participated in the long, hard-fought mobilizations to topple the Pahlavis' bloody dictatorship, the leaders were
the clerics, and mosques were the sites of revolutionary committees
that organized popular insurgency. As for the social actors, the
strength of the movement was in Tehran and other large cities, particularly among the students, intellectuals, bazaar merchants and
artisans. When the movement came onto the streets, it was joined by
the masses of recent rural immigrants that populated Tehran's
sprawling shanty towns in the 1970s, after the modernization of agriculture expelled them from their villages.

Islamists in Algeria and Tunisia seem to present a similar social
profile, according to some scattered data: support for FIS originated
in a heterogeneous group of educated intellectuals, university
teachers, and low-level civil servants, joined by small merchants and
artisans. However, these movements, taking place in the 1980s, also
had their social roots in rural exodus. Thus, a survey in Tunisia found
that 48 percent of fathers of militants were illiterate, as they migrated
to the cities in the 1970s, from impoverished rural areas. The militants themselves were young: in Tunisia, the average age of 72
militants sentenced in a major trial in 1987 was 32 years.[40] In Egypt,
Islamism is predominant among university students (most student
unions have been under Islamic fundamentalist leadership since the
mid-1980s), and receives support from government employees, particularly teachers, with a growing influence in the police and the
army.[41]

The social roots of radical fundamentalism appear to derive from
the combination of successful state-led modernization in the 1950s
and 1960s and the failure of economic modernization in most Muslim
countries during the 1970s and 1980s, as their economies could not
adapt to the new conditions of global competition and technological
revolution in the latter period. Thus, a young, urban population, with
a high level of education as a result of the first wave of modernization,
was frustrated in its expectations, as the economy faltered and new
forms of cultural dependency settled in. It was joined in its discontent
by impoverished masses expelled from rural areas to cities by the

[39]   Official documents reported in the press, quoted by Hiro (1989: 190)
[40]   Data reported by Burgat and Dowell (1993).
[41]   Hiro (1989); Dekmejian (1995).

unbalanced modernization of agriculture. This social mixture was made explosive by the crisis of the nation-state, whose employees, including military personnel, suffered declining living standards, and lost faith in the nationalist project. The crisis of legitimacy of the nation-state was the result of its widespread corruption, inefficiency, dependency upon foreign powers, and, in the Middle East, repeated military humiliation by Israel, followed by accommodation with the Zionist enemy. The construction of contemporary Islamic identity proceeds as a reaction against unreachable modernization (be it capitalist or socialist), the evil consequences of globalization, and the collapse of the post-colonial nationalist project. This is why the differential development of fundamentalism in the Muslim world seems to be linked to variations in the capacity of the nation-state to integrate in its project both the urban masses, through economic welfare, and the Muslim clergy, through official sanction of their religious power under the aegis of the state, as had been the case in the Ummayyad caliphate or the Ottoman Empire.[42] Thus, while Saudi Arabia is formally an Islamic monarchy, the *ulemas* are on the payroll of the House of Saud, which succeeded in being, at the same time, guardian of the holy sites and guardian of Western oil. Indonesia and Malaysia seem to be able to integrate Islamist pressures within their authoritarian nation-states by ensuring fast economic growth, thus providing some promising prospects to their subjects, although Indonesian cities are accumulating social tensions. On the other hand, the nationalist projects of Egypt, Algeria, and Tunisia, some of the most Westernized Muslim countries, collapsed by and large in the 1980s, thus ushering in social tensions that were predominantly captured by Islamists under moderate (Muslim Brotherhood), radical (*Jama'ah al-Islamiyya*), or democratic-radical versions (Algeria's FIS).[43] In the 1990s, the challenge by Hamas to the proto-Palestinian state constituted around the leadership of Yasser Arafat, in cooperation with Israel, may constitute one of the most dramatic schisms between Arab nationalism (of which the Palestinian movement is the epitome) and radical Islamic fundamentalism.

When Islamist electoral victories, such as in Algeria in December 1991, were voided by military repression, widespread violence and civil war ensued.[44] Even in the most Westernized Muslim country, Turkey, Kemal Atatürk's secular, nationalist heritage came under historical challenge when, in the elections of 1995, Islamists became the country's first political force, relying on the vote of radicalized

---

[42] Balta (1991).
[43] Sisk (1992).
[44] Nair (1996).

intellectuals and the urban poor, and formed the government in 1996.

Political Islamism, and Islamic fundamentalist identity, seem to be expanding in the 1990s in a variety of social and institutional contexts, always related to the dynamics of social exclusion and/or the crisis of the nation-state. Thus, social segregation, discrimination, and unemployment among French youth of Maghrebian origin, among young Turks born in Germany, among Pakistanis in Britain, or among African-Americans, induces the emergence of a new Islamic identity among disaffected youth, in a dramatic transference of radical Islamism to the socially excluded areas of advanced capitalist societies.[45] On the other hand, the collapse of the Soviet state triggered the emergence of Islamic movements in the Caucasus and Central Asia, and even the formation of an Islamic Revival Party in Russia, threatening to realize the fears of a spread of Islamic revolutions in Afghanistan and Iran into the former Soviet republics.[46]

Through a variety of political processes, depending upon the dynamics of each nation-state, and the form of global articulation of each economy, an Islamic fundamentalist project has emerged in all Muslim societies, and among Muslim minorities in non-Muslim societies. A new identity is being constructed, not by returning to tradition, but by working on traditional materials in the formation of a new godly, communal world, where deprived masses and disaffected intellectuals may reconstruct meaning in a global alternative to the exclusionary global order.[47] Furthermore, as Khosrokhavar writes:

> When the project of constituting individuals fully participating in modernity reveals its absurdity in the actual experience of everyday life, violence becomes the only form of self-affirmation of the new subject . . . The neo-community becomes then a necro-community. The exclusion from modernity takes a religious meaning: thus, self-immolation becomes the way to fight against exclusion.[48]

Through the negation of exclusion, even in the extreme form of self-sacrifice, a new Islamic identity emerges in the historical process of building the *umma*, the communal heaven for the true believers.

[45] Luecke (1993); Kepel (1995).
[46] Mikulsky (1992).
[47] Tibi (1992a, b); Gole (1995).
[48] Khosrokhavar (1995: 249–50); my translation.

God Save Me! American Christian fundamentalism

We have come into an electronic dark age, in which the new pagan hordes, with all the power of technology at their command, are on the verge of obliterating the last strongholds of civilized humanity. A vision of death lies before us. As we leave the shores of Christian western man behind, only a dark and turbulent sea of despair stretches endlessly ahead . . . unless we fight!

Francis Schaeffer, *Time for Anger*[49]

Christian fundamentalism is a perennial feature of American history, from the ideas of post-revolutionary federalists, like Timothy Dwight and Jedidiah Morse, to the pre-millennial eschatology of Pat Robertson, through the 1900 revivalists, such as Dwight L. Moody, and the 1970s reconstructionists inspired by Rousas J. Rushdoony.[50] A society relentlessly at the frontier of social change and individual mobility is bound to doubt periodically the benefits of modernity and secularization, yearning for the security of traditional values and institutions rooted in God's eternal truth. Indeed, the very term "fundamentalism," widely used around the world, originated in America, in reference to a series of ten volumes entitled *The Fundamentals*, privately published by two businessmen brothers between 1910 and 1915, to collect holy texts edited by conservative evangelical theologians at the turn of the century. While fundamentalist influence has varied in different historical periods, it has never faded away. In the 1980s and 1990s it certainly surged. While the disintegration of Jerry Falwell's Moral Majority in 1989 led some observers to announce the decline of fundamentalism (parallel to the end of the Communist Satan whose opposition was a major source of legitimacy and funding for fundamentalists), it quickly became obvious that it was the crisis of an organization, and of a political ploy, rather than that of fundamentalist identity.[51] In the 1990s, in the wake of Clinton's presidential victory in 1992, fundamentalism came to the forefront of the political scene, this time in the form of the Christian Coalition, led by Pat Robertson and Ralph Reed, claiming 1.5 million organized members, and marshalling considerable political influence

---

[49]   Schaeffer (1982: 122). Francis Schaeffer is one of the leading inspirations of contemporary American Christian fundamentalism. His *Christian Manifesto*, published in 1981, shortly after his death, was the most influential pamphlet in the 1980s' anti-abortion movement in America.

[50]   Marsden (1980); Ammerman (1987); Misztal and Shupe (1992b); Wilcox (1992).

[51]   Lawton (1989); Moen (1992); Wilcox (1992).

among the Republican electorate. Furthermore, the ideas and world vision of fundamentalists seem to find considerable echo in *fin-de-siècle* America. For instance, according to a Gallup poll on a national sample in 1979, one in three adults declared they had had an experience of religious conversion; almost half of them believed that the Bible was inerrant; and more than 80 percent thought that Jesus Christ was divine.[52] To be sure, America has always been, and still is, a very religious society, much more so, for instance, than Western Europe or Japan. But, this religious sentiment seems to take increasingly a revivalist tone, drifting toward a powerful fundamentalist current. According to Simpson:

> fundamentalism, in its original sense is a set of Christian beliefs and experiences that include (1) subscription to the verbal, plenary inspiration of the Bible and its inerrancy; (2) individual salvation through and acceptance of Christ as a personal Saviour (being born-again) on account of Christ's efficacious, substitutionary atonement for sin in his death and resurrection; (3) the expectation of Christ's premillennial return to earth from heaven; (4) the endorsement of such Protestant orthodox Christian doctrines as the Virgin birth and the trinity.[53]

Yet, Christian fundamentalism is such a wide, diversified trend that it defies a simple definition cutting across the cleavages between pentecostal and charismatic evangelicals, pre-millennial or post-millennial, pietists and activists. Fortunately, we can rely on an excellent, well-documented, scholarly synthesis of American fundamentalist writings and doctrines by Michael Lienesch, on the basis of which, and with the support of other sources that confirm, in general terms, his record and arguments, I will attempt to reconstruct the main traits of Christian fundamentalist identity.[54]

As Lienesch writes, "at the center of Christian conservative thinking, shaping its sense of the self, lies the concept of Conversion, the act of faith and forgiveness through which sinners are brought from sin into a state of everlasting salvation."[55] Through this personal experience of being born again, the whole personality is reconstructed, and becomes "the starting place for constructing a sense not only of autonomy and identity, but also of social order and political purpose."[56] The linkage between personality and society goes through

[52] Lienesch (1993: 1).
[53] Simpson (1992: 26).
[54] Zeskind (1986); Jelen (1989, 1991); Barron and Shupe (1992); Lienesch (1993); Riesebrodt (1993); Hicks (1994).
[55] Lienesch (1993: 23).
[56] Lienesch (1993: 23).

the reconstruction of the family, the central institution of society, that used to be the refuge against a harsh, hostile world, and is now crumbling in our society. This "fortress of Christian life" has to be reconstructed by asserting patriarchalism, that is the sanctity of marriage (excluding divorce and adultery) and, above all, the authority of men over women (as established in biblical literality: Genesis 1; Ephesians 5, 22–23), and the strict obedience of children, if necessary enforced by spanking. Indeed, children are born in sin: "it is of great benefit to the parent when he realizes that it is natural for his child to have desire for evil."[57] Thus, it is essential for the family to educate children in God's fear and in respect for parental authority, and to count on the full support of a Christian education in school. As an obvious consequence of this vision, public schools become the battleground between good and evil, between the Christian family and the institutions of secularism.

A bounty of earthly rewards awaits the Christian who dares to stand up for these principles, and chooses God's plans over his/her own, imperfect, life planning. To start with, a great sex life in marriage. Best-selling authors Tim and Beverly La Haye propose their sex manual as "fully biblical and highly practical,"[58] and show, with the support of illustrations, all the joys of sexuality that, once sanctified and channeled toward procreation, are in strict accordance with Christianity. Under such conditions, men can be men again: instead of current "Christianettes," men should look and act like men, another Christian tradition: "Jesus was not sissified."[59] Indeed, the channeling of male aggressive sexuality in a fulfilling marriage is essential for society, both for the control of violence, and because it is the source of the "Protestant work ethic," and thus of economic productivity. In this view, sexual sublimation is the foundation of civilization. As for women, they are biologically determined to be mothers, and to be the emotional complement of rational men (as per Phyllis Schlafly). Their submission will help them to achieve a sense of self-esteem. It is through sacrifice that women assert their identity as independent from men. Thus, as Beverly La Haye writes "Don't be afraid to give, and give, and give."[60] The result will be the salvation of the family, "this little commonwealth, the foundation on which all of society stands."[61]

With salvation guaranteed, as long as a Christian strictly observes the Bible, and with a stable patriarchal family as a solid footing for life,

---

[57] Beverly La Haye, quoted in Lienesch (1993: 78).
[58] Quoted in Lienesch (1993: 56).
[59] Edwin L. Cole, quoted in Lienesch (1993: 63).
[60] Beverly La Haye, quoted in Lienesch (1993: 77).
[61] Lienesch (1993: 77).

business will also be good, provided that government does not interfere with the economy, leaves alone the undeserving poor, and brings
taxes within reasonable limits (at about 10 percent of income).
Indeed, Christian fundamentalists do not seem to be bothered by the
contradiction between being moral theocratists and economic libertarians.[62] Furthermore, God will help the good Christian in his
business life: after all he has to provide for the family. A living proof
is offered, by his own account, by the very leader of the Christian
Coalition, Pat Robertson, a noted tele-evangelist. After his conversion,
armed with his newborn self-assurance, he went to his business: "God
has sent me here to buy your television station," and he offered a sum,
based on "God's figure": "The Lord spoke: 'Don't go over two and a
half million.'"[63] Overall, it turned out to be an excellent deal, for
which Pat Robertson weekly thanked God in his "700 Club" television
show.

Yet, the Christian way cannot be fulfilled individually because institutions of society, and particularly government, the media, and the
public school system, are controlled by humanists of various origins,
associated, in different fundamentalist versions, with communists,
bankers, heretics, and Jews. The most insidious and dangerous
enemies are feminists and homosexuals because they are the ones
undermining the family, the main source of social stability, Christian
life, and personal fulfillment. (Phyllis Schlafly referred to "the disease
called women's liberation.")[64] The fight against abortion symbolizes
all the struggles to preserve family, life, and Christianity, bridging over
to other Christian faiths. This is why the pro-life movement is the most
militant and influential expression of Christian fundamentalism in
America.

The struggle must be intensified, and the necessary political
compromises with institutional politics must be achieved, because
time is becoming short. The "end of times" is approaching, and we
must repent, and clean up our society, to be ready for Jesus Christ's
Second Coming, which will open a new era, a new millennium of
unprecedented peace and prosperity. Yet, there is a dangerous
passage because we will have to go through the atrocious Battle of
Armageddon, originating in the Middle East, then expanding to the
whole world. Israel, and the New Israel (America), will finally prevail
over their enemies, but at a terrible cost, and only counting on the
capacity of our society to regenerate. This is why the transformation
of society (through grassroots Christian politics), and the regener-

---

[62]   Hicks (1994).
[63]   Reported by Pat Robertson and quoted in Lienesch (1993: 40).
[64]   Quoted by Lienesch (1993: 71).

ation of the self (through a pious, family life), are both necessary and complementary.

Who are the contemporary American fundamentalists? Clyde Wilcox provides some interesting data on the demographic characteristics of evangelicals, as compared to the whole population, in 1988.[65] Taking into account the characteristics of the doctrinal evangelicals, it would seem that they are less educated, poorer, more influential among housewives, more often residents of the South, significantly more religious, and 100 percent of them consider the Bible to be inerrant (as compared to 27 percent for the population at large). According to other sources,[66] the recent expansion of Christian fundamentalism is particularly strong in the suburbs of the new South, South West, and Southern California, among low-middle class and service workers, recently migrated to the new suburbs of fast-expanding metropolitan areas. This prompts Lienesch to hypothesize that they may represent "the first modernized generation of traditional people of recent immigration maintaining rural values in a secular urban society."[67] However, it appears that values, beliefs, and political stands are more important than demographic, occupational, or residential characteristics in spurring Christian fundamentalism. After reviewing a substantial body of available evidence on the matter, Wilcox concludes that "the data demonstrate that the best predictors of support for the Christian Right are religious identities, doctrines, behaviors, affiliations, and political beliefs."[68] Fundamentalism does not appear to be a rationalization of class interests, or territorial positioning. Rather, it acts on the political process in the defense of moral, Christian values.[69] It is, as most fundamentalisms in history, a reactive movement, aiming at constructing social and personal identity on the basis of images of the past and projecting them into a utopian future, to overcome unbearable present times.

But a reaction to what? What is unbearable? Two seem to be the most immediate sources of Christian fundamentalism: the threat of globalization, and the crisis of patriarchalism.

As Misztal and Shupe write, "the dynamics of globalization have promoted the dynamics of fundamentalism in a dialectical fashion."[70] Lechner elaborates further the reasons for this dialectic:

---

[65]   Wilcox (1992).
[66]   Cited by Lienesch (1993).
[67]   Lienesch (1993: 10).
[68]   Wilcox (1992: 223).
[69]   Jelen (1991).
[70]   Misztal and Shupe (1992a: 8).

> In the process of globalization societies have become institutionalized as global facts. As organizations, they operate in secular terms; in their relations, they follow secular rules; hardly any religious tradition attributes transcendent significance to worldly societies in their present form . . . By the standards of most religious traditions, institutionalized societalism amounts to idolatry. But this means that life within society also has become a challenge for traditional religion . . . Precisely because global order is an institutionalized normative order it is plausible that there emerges some search for an "ultimate" foundation, for some transcendent reality beyond this world in relation to which the latter could be more clearly defined.[71]

Furthermore, while the communist threat provided ground for identification between the interests of the US government, Christianity, and America as the chosen nation, the collapse of the Soviet Union, and the emergence of a new global order, creates a threatening uncertainty over the control of America's destiny. A recurrent theme of Christian fundamentalism in the US in the 1990s is opposition to the control of the country by a "world government," superseding the US federal government (which it believes complicit in this development), enacted by the United Nations, the International Monetary Fund, and the World Trade Organization, among other international bodies. In some eschatological writings, this new "world government" is assimilated to the Anti-Christ, and its symbols, including the microchip, are the Mark of the Beast that announces the "end of times." The construction of Christian fundamentalist identity seems to be an attempt to reassert control over life, and over the country, in direct response to uncontrollable processes of globalization that are increasingly sensed in the economy and in the media.

Yet, probably the most important source of Christian fundamentalism in the 1980s and 1990s is the reaction against the challenge to patriarchalism, issued from the 1960s revolts, and expressed in women's, lesbian, and gay movements.[72] Furthermore, the battle is not just ideological. American patriarchal family is indeed in crisis, according to all indicators of divorce, separation, violence in the family, children born out of wedlock, delayed marriages, shrinking motherhood, single lifestyles, gay and lesbian couples, and widespread rejection of patriarchal authority (see chapter 4). There is an obvious reaction by men to defend their privileges, which is better suited to divine legitimacy, after their diminishing role as sole bread-

---

[71]   Lechner (1991: 276–7).
[72]   Lamberts-Bendroth (1993).

winners undermined the material and ideological bases of patriarchalism. But there is something else, shared by men, women, and children. A deep-seated fear of the unknown, particularly scary when the unknown concerns the everyday basis of personal life. Unable to live under secular patriarchalism, but terrified of solitude and uncertainty in a wildly competitive, individualistic society, where family, as a myth and a reality, represented the only safe haven, many men, women, and children, pray God to return them to the state of innocence where they could be content with benevolent patriarchalism under God's rules. And by praying together they become able to live together again. This is why American Christian fundamentalism is deeply marked by the characteristics of American culture, by its familistic individualism, by its pragmatism, and by the personalized relationship to God, and to God's design, as a methodology for solving personal problems in an increasingly unpredictable and uncontrollable life. As if the fundamental prayer were to receive from God's mercy the restoration of the lost American Way of Life in exchange for the sinner's commitment to repentance and Christian testimony.

Nations and Nationalisms in the Age of Globalization: Imagined Communities or Communal Images?

Only when all of us – all of us – recover our memory, will we be able, we and them, to stop being nationalists.
                                    Rubert de Ventos, *Nacionalismos*[73]

The age of globalization is also the age of nationalist resurgence, expressed both in the challenge to established nation-states and in the widespread (re)construction of identity on the basis of nationality, always affirmed against the alien. This historical trend has surprised some observers, after nationalism had been declared deceased from a triple death: the globalization of economy and the internationalization of political institutions; the universalism of a largely shared culture, diffused by electronic media, education, literacy, urbanization, and modernization; and the scholarly assault on the very concept of nations, declared to be "imagined communities"[74] in the mild version of anti-nationalist theory, or even "arbitrary historical inventions," in Gellner's forceful formulation,[75] arising from

---

[73] Rubert de Ventos (1994: 241); my translation.
[74] Anderson (1983).
[75] Gellner (1983: 56).

elite-dominated nationalist movements in their way to build the modern nation-state. Indeed, for Gellner, "nationalisms are simply those tribalisms, or for that matter any other kind of groups, which through luck, effort or circumstance succeed in becoming an effective force under modern circumstances."[76] Success means, both for Gellner and for Hobsbawm,[77] the construction of a modern, sovereign nation-state. Thus, in this view, nationalist movements, as rationalizers of interests of a certain elite, invent a national identity that, if successful, is enshrined by the nation-state, and then diffused by propaganda among its subjects, to the point that "nationals" will then become ready to die for their nation. Hobsbawm does accept the historical evidence of nationalism that emerged from the bottom up (from sharing linguistic, territorial, ethnic, religious, and historical political attributes), but he labels it "proto-nationalism," since only when the nation-state is constituted, do nations and nationalism come into existence, either as an expression of this nation-state or as a challenge to it on behalf of a future state. The explosion of nationalisms in this late millennium, in close relationship to the weakening of existing nation-states, does not fit well into this theoretical model that assimilates nations and nationalism to the emergence and consolidation of the modern nation-state after the French Revolution, which operated in much of the world as its founding mold. Never mind. For Hobsbawm, this apparent resurgence is in fact the historical product of unsolved national problems, created in the territorial restructuring of Europe between 1918 and 1921.[78] However, as David Hooson writes, in his introduction to the global survey he edited, *Geography and National Identity*:

> the last half of the twentieth century will go down in history as a new age of rampant and proliferating nationalisms of a more durable nature than the dreadful but now banished tyrannies which have also characterized our century... The urge to express one's identity, and to have it recognized tangibly by others, is increasingly contagious and has to be recognized as an elemental force even in the shrunken, apparently homogenizing, high-tech world of the end of the twentieth century. [79]

And, as Eley and Suny write, in the introduction to their most insightful reader, *Becoming National*:

---

[76]   Gellner (1983: 87).
[77]   Hobsbawm (1992).
[78]   Hobsbawm (1992: 173–202).
[79]   Hooson (1994b: 2–3).

Does the stress on subjectivity and consciousness rule out any "objective" basis for the existence of nationality? Clearly, such a radically subjectivist view would be absurd. Most successful nationalisms presume some prior community of territory, language, or culture, which provide the raw material for the intellectual project of nationality. Yet, those prior communities should not be "naturalized", as if they had always existed in some essential way, or have simply prefigured a history yet to come . . . Culture is more often not what people share, but what they choose to fight over.[80]

In my view, the incongruence between some social theory and contemporary practice comes from the fact that nationalism, and nations, have a life of their own, independent from statehood, albeit embedded in cultural constructs and political projects. However attractive the influential notion of "imagined communities" may be, it is either obvious or empirically inadequate. Obvious for a social scientist if it is to say that all feelings of belonging, all worshipping of icons, is culturally constructed. Nations would not be an exception to this. The opposition between "real" and "imagined" communities is of little analytical use beyond the laudable effort at demystifying ideologies of essentialist nationalism à la Michelet. But if the meaning of the statement is, as it is explicit in Gellner's theory, that nations are pure ideological artefacts, constructed through arbitrary manipulation of historical myths by intellectuals for the interests of social and economic elites, then the historical record seems to belie such an excessive deconstructionism.[81] To be sure, ethnicity, religion, language, territory, *per se*, do not suffice to build nations, and induce nationalism. Shared experience does: both the United States and Japan are countries of strong national identity, and most of their nationals do feel, and express, strong patriotic feelings. Yet, Japan is one of the most ethnically homogeneous nations on earth, and the United States one of the most ethnically heterogeneous. But in both cases there is a shared history and a shared project, and their historical narratives build on an experience, socially, ethnically, territorially, and genderly diversified, but common to the people of each country on many grounds. Other nations, and nationalisms did not reach modern nation-statehood (for example, Scotland, Catalonia, Quebec, Kurdistan, Palestine), and yet they display, and some have displayed

[80]   Eley and Suny (1996: 9).
[81]   Moser (1985); Smith (1986); Johnston et al. (1988); Touraine (1988); Perez-Argote (1989); Chatterjee (1993); Blas Guerrero (1994); Hooson (1994b); Rubert de Ventos (1994); Eley and Suny (1996).

for several centuries, a strong cultural/territorial identity that expresses itself as a national character.

Thus, four major analytical points must be emphasized when discussing contemporary nationalism with regard to social theories of nationalism. First, contemporary nationalism may or may not be oriented toward the construction of a sovereign nation-state, and thus nations are, historically and analytically, entities independent from the state.[82] Secondly, nations, and nation-states, are not historically limited to the modern nation-state as constituted in Europe in the two hundred years following the French Revolution. Current political experience seems to reject the idea that nationalism is exclusively linked to the period of formation of the modern nation-state, with its climax in the nineteenth century, replicated in the decolonization process of the mid-twentieth century by the import of the Western nation-state into the Third World.[83] To assert so, as it has become fashionable, is simply Euro-centrism, as argued by Chatterjee.[84] As Panarin writes:

> The misunderstanding of the century was the confusion of self-determination of people with the self-determination of nation. The mechanical transference of certain West European principles to the soil of non-European cultures often spawns monsters. One of these monsters was the concept of national sovereignty transplanted to non-European soil . . . The syncretism of the concept of nation in the political lexicon of Europe prevents Europeans from making extremely important differentiations touching on the "sovereignty of people", "national sovereignty", and "rights of an ethnos."[85]

Indeed, Panarin's analysis is vindicated by the development of nationalist movements in many areas of the world, following a wide variety of cultural orientations and political projects, toward the end of the twentieth century.

Thirdly, nationalism is not necessarily an elite phenomenon, and, in fact, nationalism nowadays is more often than not a reaction against the global elites. To be sure, as in all social movements, the leadership tends to be more educated and literate (or computer literate in our time) than the popular masses that mobilize around nationalist goals, but this does not reduce the appeal and significance of nationalism to the manipulation of the masses by elites for the self-interest of these elites. As Smith writes, with obvious regret:

[82]   Keating (1995).
[83]   Badie (1992).
[84]   Chatterjee (1993).
[85]   Panarin (1994/1996: 37).

Through a community of history and destiny, memories may be kept alive and actions retain their glory. For only in the chain of generations of those who share an historic and quasi-familial bond, can individuals hope to achieve a sense of immortality in eras of purely terrestrial horizons. In this sense, the formation of nations and the rise of ethnic nationalisms appears more like the institutionalization of "surrogate religion" than a political ideology, and therefore far more durable and potent than we care to admit.[86]

Fourthly, because contemporary nationalism is more reactive than proactive, it tends to be more cultural than political, and thus more oriented toward the defense of an already institutionalized culture than toward the construction or defense of a state. When new political institutions are created, or recreated, they are defensive trenches of identity, rather than launching platforms of political sovereignty. This is why I think that a more appropriate point of theoretical departure for understanding contemporary nationalism is Kosaku Yoshino's analysis of cultural nationalism in Japan:

> Cultural nationalism aims to regenerate the national community by creating, preserving, or strengthening a people's cultural identity when it is felt to be lacking or threatened. The cultural nationalist regards the nation as a product of its unique history and culture, and as a collective solidarity endowed with unique attributes. In short, cultural nationalism is concerned with the distinctiveness of the cultural community as the essence of a nation.[87]

Thus, nationalism is constructed by social action and reaction, both by elites and by the masses, as Hobsbawm argues, countering Gellner's emphasis on "high culture" as the exclusive origin of nationalism. But, against Hobsbawm's or Anderson's views, nationalism as a source of identity cannot be reduced to a particular historical period and to the exclusive workings of the modern nation-state. To reduce nations and nationalisms to the process of construction of the nation-state makes it impossible to explain the simultaneous rise of postmodern nationalism and decline of the modern state.

Rubert de Ventos, in an updated, refined version of Deutsch's classical perspective,[88] has suggested a more complex theory that sees the emergence of national identity through the historical interaction of four series of factors: *primary factors*, such as ethnicity, territory,

---

[86]   Smith (1989/1996: 125).

[87]   Yoshino (1992: 1).

[88]   Deutsch (1953); Rubert de Ventos (1994).

language, religion, and the like; *generative factors*, such as the development of communications and technology, the formation of cities, the emergence of modern armies and centralized monarchies; *induced factors*, such as the codification of language in official grammars, the growth of bureaucracies, and the establishment of a national education system; and *reactive factors*, that is the defense of oppressed identities and subdued interests by a dominant social group or institutional apparatus, triggering the search for alternative identities in the collective memory of people.[89] Which factors play which role in the formation of each nationalism, and of each nation, depends on historical contexts, on the materials available to collective memory, and on the interaction between conflicting power strategies. Thus, nationalism is indeed culturally, and politically, constructed, but what really matters, both theoretically and practically, is, as for all identities, how, from what, by whom, and for what it is constructed.

In this *fin de siècle*, the explosion of nationalisms, some of them deconstructing multinational states, others constructing plurinational entities, is not associated with the formation of classical, sovereign, modern states. Rather, nationalism appears to be a major force behind the constitution of quasi-states; that is, political entities of shared sovereignty, either in stepped-up federalism (as in the Canadian (re)constitution in process, or in the "nation of nationalities," proclaimed in the Spanish Constitution of 1978, and widely expanded in its practice in the 1990s); or in international multilateralism (as in the European Union, or in the renegotiation of the Commonwealth of Independent States of ex-Soviet republics). Centralized nation-states resisting this trend of nationalist movements in search of quasi-statehood as a new historical reality (for example, Indonesia, Nigeria, Sri Lanka, even India) may well fall victim to this fatal error of assimilating the nation to the state, as a state as strong as Pakistan realized after the secession of Bangladesh.

In order to explore the complexity of the (re)construction of national identity in our new historical context, I will briefly elaborate on two cases that represent the two poles of the dialectic I am proposing as characteristic of this period: the deconstruction of a centralized, multinational state, the former Soviet Union, and the subsequent formation of what I consider to be quasi-nation-states; and the national quasi-state emerging in Catalonia through the double movement of federalism in Spain and of confederalism in the European Union. After illustrating the analysis with these two case studies, I shall offer some hints on the new historical avenues of nationalism as a renewed source of collective identity.

[89]   Rubert de Ventos (1994: 139–200).

Nations against the state: the breakup of the Soviet Union and the Commonwealth of Impossible States (*Sojuz Nevozmoznykh Gosudarstv*)

The Russian people of the cities and villages, half-savage beasts, stupid, almost frightening, will die to make room for a new human race.
Maxim Gorki, "On the Russian peasantry"[90]

The revolt of constituent nations against the Soviet state was a major factor, albeit not the only one, in the surprising collapse of the Soviet Union, as argued by Helene Carrere d'Encausse and Ronald Grigor Suny,[91] among other scholars. I shall analyze (in volume III) the complex intertwining of economic, technological, political, and national identity elements that, *together*, explain one of the most extraordinary developments in history, as the Russian Revolutions both opened and closed the political span of the twentieth century. Yet, while discussing the formation of national identity, and its new contours in the 1990s, it is essential to refer to the Soviet experience, and its aftermath, because it is a privileged terrain for observing the interplay between nations and the state, two entities that, in my view, are historically and analytically distinct. Indeed, the nationalist revolt against the Soviet Union was particularly significant because it was one of the few modern states explicitly built as a pluri-national state, with nationalities affirmed both for individuals (every Soviet citizen had an ascribed nationality written in his/her passport), and in the territorial administration of the Soviet Union. The Soviet state was organized in a complex system of 15 federal republics, to which were added autonomous republics within the federal republics, territories (*krai*), and autonomous native districts (*okrag*), each republic comprising also several provinces (*oblasti*). Each federal republic, as well as autonomous republics within the federal republics, was based on a territorial nationality principle. This institutional construction was not a simple fiction. Certainly, autonomous nationalist expressions in contradiction to the will of the Soviet Communist party were ruthlessly repressed, particularly during the Stalinist period, and millions of Ukrainians, Estonians, Latvians, Lithuanians, Volga Germans, Crimean Tatars, Chechens, Mesketyans, Ingushi, Balkars, Karachai, and Kalmyks were deported to Siberia and Central Asia to prevent their cooperation with German invaders, or with other potential enemies, or simply to clear land for strategic projects of the state. But so were millions of Russians, for a variety of reasons, often randomly

---

[90]   1922, in *SSR vnutrennie protivorechiia*, Tchalidze Publications, 1987: 128, as cited by Carrere d'Encausse (1993: 173).
[91]   Carrere d'Encausse (1993); Suny (1993).

assigned. Yet, the reality of nationality-based administrations went beyond token appointments of national elites to leading positions in the republics' administration.[92] Policies of nativization (*korenizatsiya*) were supported by Lenin and Stalin until the 1930s, and renewed in the 1960s. They encouraged native languages and customs, implemented "affirmative action" programs, favoring recruitment and promotion of non-Russian nationalities in the state and party apparatuses of the republics, as well as in educational institutions, and fostered the development of national cultural elites, naturally on the condition of their subservience to Soviet power. As Suny writes:

> Lost in the powerful nationalist rhetoric is any sense of the degree to which the long and difficult years of Communist party rule actually continued the "making of nations" of the pre-revolutionary period ... It thereby increased ethnic solidarity and national consciousness in the non-Russian republics, even as it frustrated full articulation of a national agenda by requiring conformity to an imposed political order.[93]

The reasons for this apparent openness to national self-determination (enshrined in the Soviet Constitution in the right of republics to secede from the Union) lie deep in the history and strategy of the Soviet state.[94] Soviet pluri-national federalism was the result of a compromise following intense political and ideological debates during the revolutionary period. Originally, the Bolshevik position, in line with classical Marxist thought, denied the relevance of nationality as a significant criterion to build the new state: proletarian internationalism was intended to supersede "artificial," or "secondary," national differences between the working classes, manipulated into inter-ethnic bloody confrontations by imperialist interests, as shown by World War I. But in January 1918, the urgency of finding military alliances in the civil war, and in the resistance against foreign invasion, convinced Lenin of the need for support from nationalist forces outside Russia, particularly in Ukraine, after observing the vitality of national consciousness. The Third All-Russian Congress of Soviets adopted the "Declaration of the Rights of Working and Exploited People," transforming the ruins of the Russian Empire into "the fraternal union of Soviet Republics of Russia freely meeting on an internal basis." To this "internal federalization" of Russia, the Bolsheviks added, in April, the call for "external

---

[92]   Slezkine (1994).
[93]   Suny (1993: 101, 130).
[94]   Pipes (1954); Conquest (1967); Carrere d'Encausse (1987); Suny (1993); Slezkine (1994).

federalization" of other nations, explicitly naming the people of Poland, Ukraine, Crimea, Transcaucasia, Turkestan, Kirghiz, "and others."[95] The critical debate concerned the principle under which national identity would be recognized in the new federal state. The Bundists, and other socialist tendencies, wanted national cultures recognized throughout the whole structure of the state, without distinguishing them territorially, since the goal of the revolution was precisely to transcend ancestral bondings of ethnicity and territory on behalf of new, class-based, socialist universalism. To this view, Lenin and Stalin opposed the principle of territoriality as the basis for nationhood. The result was the multilayered national structure of the Soviet state: national identity was recognized in the institutions of governance. However, in application of the principle of democratic centralism, this diversity of territorial subjects would be under the control of the dominant apparatuses of the Soviet Communist party, and of the Soviet state. Thus, the Soviet Union was constructed around a double identity: on the one hand, ethnic/national identi-ties (including Russian); on the other hand, Soviet identity as the foundation of the new society: *sovetskii narod* (the Soviet people) would be the new cultural identity to be achieved in the historical horizon of Communist construction.

There were also strategic reasons in this conversion of proletarian internationalists into territorial nationalists. A. M. Salmin has proposed an interesting model for interpreting the Leninist–Stalinist strategy underlying Soviet federalism.[96] The Soviet Union was a centralized, but flexible institutional system whose structure should remain open and adaptive to receive new countries as members of the Union, as the cause of communism would advance throughout the world. Five concentric circles were designed as both security areas and waves of expansion of the Soviet state as vanguard of the revolution. The first was Russia, and its satellite republics, organized in the RSFSR. Paradoxically Russia, and the Russian Federation, was the only republic with no autonomous Communist party, no President of the republican Supreme Soviet, and with the least developed republican institutions: it was the exclusive domain of the Soviet Communist party. To make safer this bastion, Russia did not have land borders with the potentially aggressive capitalist world. Thus, around Russia, Soviet republics were organized, in the outlying borders of the Soviet Union, so that they would eventually protect, at the same time, Soviet power and their national independence. This is why some ethnically based areas, such as Azerbaijan, became Soviet republics

---

95   Singh (1982: 61).
96   Salmin (1992).

because they were bordering the outside world, while others, equally distinctive in its ethnic composition, like Chechn'ya, were kept in the Russian Federation because they were geographically closer to the core. The third ring of Soviet geopolitics was constituted by people's democracies under Soviet military power: this was originally the case for Khoresm, Bukhara, Mongolia, and Tannu-Tura, and became the precedent for the incorporation of Eastern Europe after World War II. The fourth circle would be formed by distant socialist countries, such as, years later, Cuba, North Korea, or Vietnam. China was never considered to be a part of this category because of deep distrust of future Chinese power. Finally, allied progressive governments and revolutionary movements around the world constituted the fifth circle, and their potential would depend on keeping a balance between their internationalism (meaning their pro-Soviet stand) and their national representativeness. It was this constant tension between the class-based universalism of communist utopia and geopolitical interests based on the ethnic/national concerns of potential allies that determined the schizophrenia of Soviet policy toward the national question.

The result of these contradictions throughout the tormented history of the Soviet Union was an incoherent patchwork of people, nationalities, and state institutions.[97] The more than one hundred nationalities and ethnic groups of the Soviet Union were dispatched all along its immense geography, following geopolitical strategies, collective punishments and rewards, and individual caprices. Thus, Armenian-populated Nagorno-Karabaj was included by Stalin in Azerbaijan to please Turkey by putting its ancestral enemies under Azeri control (Azeris are a Turkic people); Volga Germans ended up in Kazakhstan, in whose northern territory they are now the driving economic force, supported by German subsidies to keep them off Germany; Cossack settlements proliferated in Siberia and in the Far East; Ossetians were split between Russia (North) and Georgia (South), while Ingushis were distributed between Chechn'ya, North Ossetia, and Georgia; Crimea, taken by Russia from Tatars in 1783, and from where the Tatars were deported by Stalin during World War II, was transferred by Khrushchev (himself a Ukrainian) to Ukraine in 1954 to commemorate 300 years of Russian–Ukrainian friendship, reportedly after a night of heavy drinking. Furthermore, Russians were sent all over the territory of the Soviet Union, most often as skilled workers or willing pioneers, sometimes as rulers, sometimes as exiles. Thus, when the Soviet Union disintegrated, the principle of territorial nationality trapped inside the newly independent republics

[97]   Kozlov (1988); Suny (1993); Slezkine (1994).

tens of millions of suddenly "foreign nationals." The problem seems to be particularly acute for the 25 million Russians living outside the new Russian frontiers.

One of the greatest paradoxes of Soviet federalism is that Russia was probably the most discriminated of nationalities. The Russian Federation had much less political autonomy from the central Soviet state than any other republic. Analysis by regional economists showed that, in general terms, there was a net transfer of wealth, resources, and skills from Russia to the other republics (Siberia, which is the most ethnically Russian area of the Russian Federation, was the fundamental source of exports, and thus of hard currency for the Soviet Union).[98] As for national identity, it was Russian history, religion, and traditional identity that became the main target of Soviet cultural repression, as documented in the 1980s by Russian writers and intellectuals, such as Likhachev, Belov, Astafiev, Rasputin, Solukhin, or Zalygin.[99] After all, the new Soviet identity had to be built on the ruins of the historical Russian identity, with some tactical exceptions during World War II, when Stalin needed to mobilize everything against the Germans, including Alexander Nevsky's memory. Thus, while there was indeed a policy of russification of culture throughout the Soviet Union (indeed, contradictory to the parallel trend of *korenizatsiya*), and ethnic Russians kept control of party, army, and KGB (but Stalin was Georgian, and Khrushchev was Ukrainian), Russian identity as a national identity was repressed to a much greater extent than other nationalities, some of which were in fact symbolically revived for the sake of pluri-national federalism.

This paradoxical constitution of the Soviet state expressed itself in the revolt against the Soviet Union, using the breathing space provided by Gorbachev's *glasnost*. The Baltic republics, forcefully annexed in 1940 in defiance of international law, were the first to claim their right to self-determination. But they were closely followed by a strong Russian nationalist movement that was in fact the most potent mobilizing force against the Soviet state. It was the merger of the struggle for democracy, and the recovery of Russian national identity under Yeltsin's leadership in 1989–91, that created the conditions for the demise of Soviet communism and the breakup of the Soviet Union.[100] Indeed, the first democratic election of the head of state in Russian history, with the election of Yeltsin on June 12, 1991, marked the beginning of the new Russia and, with it, the end of the Soviet Union. It was Russia's traditional flag that led the resistance to

---

[98]   Granberg and Spehl (1989); Granberg (1993).
[99]   Carrere d'Encausse (1993: ch. 9).
[100] Castells (1992b); Carrere d'Encausse (1993).

the Communist coup in August 1991. And it was Yeltsin's strategy of dismantling the Soviet state, by concentrating power and resources in the republican institutions, that led to the agreement with other republics, first of all with Ukraine and Belarus, in December 1991, to end the Soviet Union, and to transform the ex-Soviet republics into sovereign states, loosely confederated in the Commonwealth of Independent States (*Sojuz Nezavisimykh Gosudarstv*). The assault on the Soviet state was not conducted only by nationalist movements: it linked up with democrats' demands, and with the interests of political elites in a number of republics, carving their own turf among the ruins of a crumbling empire. But it took a nationalist form, and received popular support on behalf of the nation. The interesting matter is that nationalism was much less active in the most ethnically distinctive republics (for example, in Central Asia) than in the Baltic states, and in Russia.[101]

The first years of existence of this new conglomerate of independent states revealed the fragility of their construction, as well as the durability of historically rooted nationalities, across the borders inherited from the disintegration of the Soviet Union.[102] Russia's most intractable problem became the war in Chechn'ya. The Baltic republics practiced discrimination against their Russian population, inducing new inter-ethnic strife. Ukraine saw the peaceful revolt of the Russian majority in Crimea against Ukrainian rule, and continued to experience the tension between strong nationalist sentiment in western Ukraine, and pan-Slavic feelings in eastern Ukraine. Moldova was torn between its historical Romanian identity and the Russian character of its eastern population that tried to create the Republic of Dniester. Georgia exploded in a bloody confrontation between its multiple nationalities (Georgians, Abkhazians, Armenians, Ossetians, Adzharis, Meshketians, Russians). Azerbaijan continued to fight intermittently with Armenia over Nagorno-Karabaj, and induced pogroms against Armenians in Baku. And the Muslim republics of Central Asia were torn between their historic links with Russia and the perspective of joining the Islamic fundamentalist whirlwind spinning from Iran and Afghanistan. As a result, Tajikistan suffered a full-scale civil war, and other republics Islamized their institutions and education to integrate radical Islamism before it was too late. Thus, the historical record seems to show that artificial, half-hearted, acknowledgment of the national question by Marxism–Leninism not only did not solve historical conflicts, but actually made them more virulent.[103]

---

[101]   Carrere d'Encausse (1993); Starovoytova (1994).
[102]   Hooson (1994b); Lyday (1994); Stebelsky (1994); Khazanov (1995).
[103]   Twinning (1993); Panarin (1994); Khazanov (1995).

Reflecting on this extraordinary episode, and on its aftermath in the 1990s, several key issues of theoretical relevance deserve commentary.

First of all, one of the most powerful states in the history of humankind was not able, after 74 years, to create a new national identity. *Sovetskii narod* was not a myth, in spite of what Carrere d'Encausse says.[104] It did have some reality in the minds and lives of the generations born in the Soviet Union, in the reality of people making families with people from other nationalities, and living and working throughout the whole Soviet territory. Resistance against the Nazi juggernaut rallied people around the Soviet flag. After the Stalinist terror subsided, in the late 1950s, and when material conditions improved, in the 1960s, a certain pride in being part of a superpower nation did develop. And, in spite of widespread cynicism and withdrawal, the ideology of equality and human solidarity took root in the Soviet citizenry, so that, overall, a new Soviet identity started to emerge. However, it was so fragile, and so dependent on the lack of information about the real situation of the country and of the world, that it did not resist the shocks of economic stagnation and the learning of the truth. In the 1980s, Russians who dared to proclaim themselves as "Soviet citizens" were derided as *Sovoks* by their compatriots. While *sovetskii narod* was not necessarily a failing identity project, it disintegrated before it could settle in the minds and lives of the people of the Soviet Union. Thus, the Soviet experience belies the theory according to which the state can construct national identity by itself. The most powerful state, using the most comprehensive ideological apparatus in history for more than seven decades, failed in recombining historical materials and projected myths into the making of a new identity. Communities may be imagined, but not necessarily believed.

Secondly, the formal acknowledgment of national identities in the territorial administration of the Soviet state, as well as policies of "nativization," did not succeed in integrating these nationalities into the Soviet system, with one significant exception: the Muslim republics of Central Asia, precisely those that were most distinctive from the dominant Slavic culture. These republics were so dependent on central power for their daily survival that only in the last moments of the disintegration of the Soviet Union did their elites dare to lead the drive for independence. In the rest of the Soviet Union, national identities could not find themselves expressed in the artificially constructed institutions of Soviet federalism. A case in point is Georgia, a multi-ethnic puzzle constructed on the basis of a historic kingdom. Georgians represent about 70 percent of the 5.5 million

[104]   Carrere d'Encausse (1993: 234).

population. They generally belong to the Georgian Orthodox Church. But they had to coexist with Ossetians, primarily Russian Orthodox, whose population is split between North Ossetia Autonomous Republic (in Russia) and South Ossetia Autonomous Oblast (in Georgia). In the north-western corner of Georgia, the Abkhaz, a Sunni Muslim Turkic people, number only about 80,000, but they constituted 17 percent of the Abkhaz Autonomous Soviet Socialist Republic, created inside Georgia as a counterpoint to Georgian nationalism. It did succeed: in the 1990s, the Abkhaz, with support from Russia, fought to obtain quasi-independence in their territory, in spite of being a minority of the population. Georgia's second autonomous republic, Adzharia, is also Sunni Muslim, but from ethnic Georgians, thus supporting Georgia, while seeking their autonomy. Muslim Ingushis are in conflict with Ossetians in the border areas between Georgia, Ossetia, and Chechn'ya-Ingushetia. In addition, Meshketian Turks, deported by Stalin, are returning to Georgia, and Turkey has expressed its willingness to protect them, inducing distrust in Georgia's Armenian population. The net result of this territorially entangled history was that, in 1990–91, when Gamsakhurdia led a radical Georgian nationalist movement, and proclaimed independence without considering the interests of Georgia's national minorities, and without respecting civil liberties, he triggered a civil war (in which he died), both between his forces and Georgian democrats, and between Georgian forces, Abkhazians, and Ossetians. The intervention of Russia, and the pacifying role of Shevernadze, elected president in 1991 as a last resort to save the country, brought an unstable peace to the region, only to see neighboring Chechn'ya explode in an atrocious, protracted, debilitating guerrilla war. Thus, the failure of integrating national identities into the Soviet Union did not come from their recognition, but from the fact that their artificial institutionalization, following a bureaucratic and geopolitical logic, did not pay attention to the actual history and cultural/religious identity of each national community, and their geographical specificity. This is what authorizes Suny to speak of "the revenge of the past,"[105] or David Hooson to write:

> The question of identity is clearly the most insistent to have surfaced after the long freeze [in the former Soviet Union]. But it is not enough to treat it as a purely ethnic or cultural question. What is involved here is a re-search for the real regions of cultures, economies *and* environment which mean something (or in some cases everything) to the peoples who inhabit them.

[105]   Suny (1993).

The process of crystallization of these regions, beyond the bald and flawed "Republic" boundaries of today, promises to be long and painful but inevitable and ultimately right.[106]

Thirdly, the ideological emptiness created by the failure of Marxism–Leninism to actually indoctrinate the masses was replaced, in the 1980s, when people were able to express themselves, by the only source of identity that was kept in the collective memory: *national identity.* This is why most anti-Soviet mobilizations, including democratic movements, were carried under the respective national flag. It is true, as it has been argued, and as I have argued, that political elites, in Russia, and in the federal republics, utilized nationalism as the ultimate weapon against failing communist ideology, to undermine the Soviet state, and seize power in the institutions of each republic.[107] However, the elites used this strategy because it was effective, because nationalist ideology resonated more in people's minds than abstract appeals to democracy, or to the virtues of the market, often assimilated to speculation in people's personal experience. Thus, the resurgence of nationalism cannot be explained by political manipulation: rather, its use by the elites is a proof of the resilience and vitality of national identity as a mobilizing principle. When, after 74 years of endless repetition of official socialist ideology, people discovered that the king was naked, the reconstruction of their identity could only take place around basic institutions of their collective memory: family, community, the rural past, sometimes religion, and, above all, the nation. But the nation was not meant as the equivalent of statehood and officialdom, but as personal self-identification in this now confusing world: I am Ukrainian, I am Russian, I am Armenian, became the rallying cry, the perennial foundation from which to reconstruct life in collectivity. This is why the Soviet experience is a testimony to the perdurability of nations beyond, and despite, the state.

Perhaps the greatest paradox of all is that when, at the end of this historical *parcours,* new nation-states emerged to assert their suppressed identities, *it is unlikely that they could really function as fully sovereign states.* This is, first of all, because of the intertwining of a mosaic of nationalities and historical identities within the current boundaries of independent states.[108] The most obvious issue refers to the 25 million Russians living under a different flag. But the Russian Federation (although currently populated by 82 percent of ethnic

---

[106]   Hooson (1994a: 140).
[107]   Castells (1992b); Hobsbawm (1994).
[108]   Twinning (1993); Hooson (1994b).

Russians) is also made up of 60 different ethnic/national groups, some of which are sitting on top of a wealth of natural and mineral resources, as in Sakha-Yakutia, or Tatarstan. As for the other republics, besides the illustrative case of Georgia, Kazakhs are only a minority in Kazakhstan; Tajikistan has 62 percent of Tajiks, and 24 percent Uzbeks; Kyrgyz make up only 52 percent of Kyrgyztan's population; Uzbekistan has 72 percent of Uzbeks, and a wide diversity of different nationalities; 14 percent of Moldova's residents are Ukrainian, and 13 percent Russian. Ukrainians account for only 73 percent of Ukraine's population. Latvians are 52 percent of Latvia, and Estonians 62 percent of Estonia. Thus, any strict definition of national interests around the institutionally dominant nationality would lead to intractable conflicts in the whole Eurasian continent, as Shevernadze conceded, explaining his willingness to cooperate with Russia, after his initial hostility. Furthermore, the interpenetration of the economies, and the sharing of infrastructure, from the electrical grid to pipelines and water supply, makes extremely costly the disentanglement of the territories of the former Soviet Union, and puts a decisive premium on cooperation. More so in a process of multilateral integration in the global economy that requires inter-regional linkages to operate efficiently. Naturally, the deep-seated fears of a new form of Russian imperialism will loom large in the future evolution of these new states. This is why there will be no reconstruction of the Soviet Union, regardless of who is in power in Russia. Yet, the full recognition of national identity cannot be expressed in the full independence of the new states, *precisely because of the strength of identities that cut across state borders.* This is why I propose, as the most likely, and indeed promising future, the notion of the Commonwealth of Inseparable States (*Sojuz Nerazdelimykh Gosudarstv*); that is, of a web of institutions flexible and dynamic enough to articulate the autonomy of national identity and the sharing of political instrumentality in the context of the global economy. Otherwise, the affirmation of sheer state power over a fragmented map of historical identities will be a caricature of nineteenth-century European nationalism: it will lead in fact to a Commonwealth of Impossible States (*Sojuz Nevozmoznykh Gosudarstv*).

Nations without a state: *Catalunya*

The State must be fundamentally differentiated from the Nation because the State is a political organization, an independent power externally, a supreme power internally, with material forces in manpower and money to maintain its independence and authority. We cannot identify the one with the other, as it was usual, even by Catalan patriots themselves who

were speaking or writing of a Catalan nation in the sense of an inde-
pendent Catalan state . . . Catalunya continued to be Catalunya after
centuries of having lost its self-government. Thus, we have reached a clear,
distinct idea of nationality, the concept of a primary, fundamental social
unit, destined to be in the world society, in Humanity, what man is for
the civil society.

Enric Prat de la Riba, *La nacionalitat catalana*[109]

If the analysis of the Soviet Union shows the possibility of states, however powerful, failing to produce nations, the experience of Catalonia (or *Catalunya*, in Catalan) allows us to reflect on the conditions under which nations exist, and (re)construct themselves over history, without a nation-state, and without searching to establish one.[110] Indeed, as stated by the current president, and national leader of *Catalunya* in the last quarter of the twentieth century, Jordi Pujol: "*Catalunya* is a nation without a state. We belong to the Spanish state, but we do not have secessionist ambitions. This must be clearly affirmed . . . The case of *Catalunya* is peculiar: we have our own language, and culture, we are a nation without a state."[111] To clarify this statement, and to elaborate on its broader, analytical implications, a brief historical reminder is necessary. Since not every reader is familiar with Catalonian history, I shall put forward, succinctly, the historical elements that authorize one to speak of the continuity of *Catalunya* as a materially lived, distinctive, national reality, of which the persistence of its language, and its contemporary widespread use against all odds, is a powerful indicator.[112]

Catalunya's official birthday as a nation is generally dated to 988, when Count Borrell finally severed links with the remnants of the Carolingian Empire that, around 800, had taken the lands and inhabitants of this southern frontier of the empire under its protection to counteract the threat from Arab invaders to Occitania. By the end of the ninth century, Count Guifrè el Pelòs, who had fought successfully against Arab domination, received from the French king the counties of Barcelona, Urgell, Cerdanya-Conflent, and Girona. His heirs became counts in their own right, without needing to be appointed by the French kings, assuring the hegemony of the Casal

---

[109]   Originally published 1906; this edition 1978: 49–50.
[110]   Keating (1995).
[111]   1986; quoted in Pi (1996: 254).
[112]   For historical sources, see the compendium of Catalan history in Vilar (1987–90); and the special issue of *L'Avenc: Revista d'Historia* (1996). See also Vicens Vives and Llorens (1958); Vicens Vives (1959); Vilar (1964); Jutglar (1966); Sole-Tura (1967); McDonogh (1986); Rovira i Virgili (1988); Azevedo (1991); Garcia-Ramon and Nogue-Font (1994); Keating (1995); Salrach (1996).

de Barcelona over the borderlands that would be called *Catalunya* in the twelfth century. Thus, while most of Christian Spain was engaged in the "Reconquest" against the Arabs for eight centuries, building in the process the kingdom of Castile and Leon, *Catalunya*, after a period of Arab domination in the eighth and ninth centuries, evolved from its Carolingian origins to become, between the early thirteenth and mid-fifteenth centuries, a Mediterranean empire. It extended to Mallorca (1229), Valencia (1238), Sicily (1282), part of Greece, with Athens (1303), Sardinia (1323), and Naples (1442), including, as well, French territories beyond the Pyrénées, particularly Roussillon and Cerdagne. Although *Catalunya* had a significant rural hinterland, it was primarily a commercial empire, governed by the alliance of nobility and urban merchant elites, along lines similar to those of the merchant republics of northern Italy. Concerned with the military power of Castile, the prudent Catalans accepted the merger proposed by the small, but conveniently located, kingdom of Aragon in 1137. It was only in the late fifteenth century, after the voluntary merger with proto-imperial Castile, through the marriage of Fernando, king of *Catalunya*, Valencia and Aragon, with Isabel, queen of Castile, in application of the Compromiso de Caspe (1412), that *Catalunya* ceased to be a sovereign political entity. The marriage of the two nations was supposed to respect language, customs, and institutions, as well as sharing wealth. Yet, the power and wealth of the Spanish Crown and of its landowning nobility, as well as the influence of the fundamentalist Church built around the Counter-Reformation, steered the historical course in a different direction, subjugating non-Castilian peoples, in Europe, and in the Iberian peninsula, as well as in America. *Catalunya*, as the rest of Europe, was excluded from commerce with the American colonies, a major source of wealth in the Spanish kingdom. It reacted by developing its own consumer goods industry and by trading in its regional environment, triggering a process of incipient industrialization and capital accumulation from the second half of the sixteenth century. In the meantime Castile, after crushing, in 1520–23, the free Castilian cities (*Comunidades*) where an artisan class and a proto-bourgeoisie were emerging, went on to build a *rentier* economy to finance a warrior-theocratic state with proceeds from its American colonies and from heavy taxation on its subjects. The clash of culture and institutions accelerated in the seventeenth century when Philip IV, in need of additional fiscal revenues, tightened up centralism, leading to the insurrection of both Portugal and *Catalunya* (where the Revolt of the Reapers took place) in 1640. Portugal, with the support of England, regained its independence. *Catalunya* was defeated, and most of its freedoms were taken away. Again, between 1705 and 1714, *Catalunya* fought for its autonomy, supporting the cause of the Austrians against Philip V, from the Bourbon dynasty, in the Spanish War of Succession. It is a mark of the Catalan character that its defeat, and the entry of Philip V's armies into Barcelona on September 11, 1714, is now celebrated as *Catalunya*'s national day. *Catalunya* lost all its political institutions of self-government, established since the Middle Ages: the municipal government based on democratic councils, the parliament, the Catalan sovereign government (*Generalitat*). The new institutions, established by the *Decreto de nueva planta*, issued by Philip V, concentrated authority in the hands of the military commander, or General Captain of Catalunya. It followed a long period of outright institutional and cultural repression from central powers, that, as documented by historians, deliberately aimed at the gradual elimination of the Catalan language, which was first banned in the administration, then in commercial transactions, and, finally, in the schools, reducing its practice to the domains of family and Church.[113] Again, Catalans reacted by closing themselves off from state matters, and going back to work, reportedly just two days after the occupation of Barcelona, in a concerted attitude. Thus, *Catalunya* industrialized by the end of the eighteenth century, and was, for more than a century, the only truly industrial area of Spain.

The economic strength of the Catalan bourgeoisie, and the relatively high educational and cultural level of the society at large, contrasted throughout the nineteenth century with its political marginality. Then, when trade policies from Madrid began to threaten the still fragile Catalan industry, which required protectionism, a strong Catalan nationalist movement developed from the late nineteenth century, inspired by articulate ideologues, such as pragmatic nationalist Enric Prat de la Riba, or the federalists Valenti Almirall and Francesc Pi i Margall, sung by national poets, such as Joan Maragall, chronicled by historians, such as Rovira i Virgili, and supported by the work of philologists, such as Pompeu Fabra, who codified the modern Catalan language in the twentieth century. Yet, the Madrid political class never really accepted the alliance with Catalan nationalists, not even with the Lliga Regionalista, a clearly conservative party, probably the first modern political party in Spain, created in 1901 as a reaction to the control of elections by local bosses (*caciques*) on behalf of the central government. On the other hand, the growth of a powerful working-class movement, mainly anarcho-syndicalist, in *Catalunya* in the first third of the twentieth century, pushed Catalan nationalists, by and large dominated by their conservative wing until the 1920s, to rely on Madrid's

---

[113]   Ferrer i Girones (1985).

protection against workers' demands, and threats of social revolution.[114] However, when in 1931 the Republic was proclaimed in Spain, the left-wing republicans (*Esquerra republicana de Catalunya*) were able to establish a bridge between the Catalan working class, the petty bourgeoisie, and the nationalist ideals, and they became the dominant force in Catalan nationalism. Under the leadership of Lluis Companys, a labor lawyer elected president of the restored *Generalitat*, *Esquerra* made a Spain-wide alliance with the Spanish Republicans, the Socialists, the Communists, and the labor unions (Anarchists, and Socialists). In 1932, under popular pressure expressed in a referendum, the Spanish government approved a Statute of Autonomy that re-stated liberties, self-government, and cultural/linguistic autonomy to *Catalunya*. Indeed, the satisfaction of nationalist demands from *Catalunya* and the Basque Country by the Spanish Republic was one of the most powerful triggers of the military insurrection that provoked the 1936–9 Civil War. Consequently, after the Civil War, the systematic repression of Catalan institutions, language, culture, identity, and political leaders (starting with the execution of Companys in 1940, after being delivered to Franco by the Gestapo) became a distinctive mark of Franco's dictatorship. It included the deliberate elimination of Catalan-speaking teachers from schools, so as to make impossible the teaching of Catalan. In a corresponding movement, nationalism became a rallying cry for the anti-Franco forces in *Catalunya*, as it was in the Basque Country, to the point that all democratic political forces, from Christian Democrats and Liberals to Socialists and Communists, were Catalan nationalists as well. This meant, for instance, that all political parties in *Catalunya*, both during the anti-Franco resistance and since the establishment of Spanish democracy in 1977, were and are Catalan, not Spanish, although they are federated in most cases with similar parties in Spain, while keeping their autonomy as parties (for example, the Catalan Socialist Party is linked to the Spanish PSOE; the Unified Socialist Party of Catalunya to the Communists, and so on). In 1978, Article 2 of the new Spanish Constitution, declared Spain a "nation of nationalities," and, in 1979, the Statute of Autonomy of Catalunya provided the institutional basis for Catalan autonomy, within the framework of Spain, including the declaration of official bilingualism, with Catalan being enshrined as "Cataluña's own language." In the regional elections of *Catalunya*, the Catalan nationalist coalition (*Convergencia i Unio*), led by *Catalunya*'s contemporary leader, an educated, cosmopolitan, medical doctor of modest background, Jordi Pujol, obtained a majority five consecutive times, still

[114]   Sole-Tura (1967).

being in power in 1996. The *Generalitat* (Catalan government) was strengthened, and became a dynamic institution, pursuing autonomous policies on all fronts, including the international arena. In the 1990s, Jordi Pujol is the president of the Association of European Regions. The city of Barcelona mobilized on its own, led by another charismatic figure, Catalan Socialist mayor Pasqual Maragall, a professor of urban economics, and the grandson of *Catalunya*'s national poet. Barcelona projected itself into the world, skillfully using the 1992 Summer Olympic Games to emerge internationally as a major metropolitan center, linking up historical identity and informational modernity. In the 1990s, the Catalan Nationalist party came to play a major role in Spanish politics. The inability of either the Socialist Party (in 1993) or the Conservative Partido Popular (in 1996) to win a majority of seats in the Spanish general elections made Jordi Pujol the indispensable partner of any parliamentary coalition to govern. He supported the Socialists first, the Conservatives later – at a price. *Catalunya* received the management of 30 percent of its income taxes, as well as exclusive competence in education (that is conducted in Catalan, at all levels), health, environment, communications, tourism, culture, social services, and most police functions. Slowly, but surely, *Catalunya*, together with the Basque Country, are forcing Spain to become, unwillingly, a highly decentralized federal state, as the other regions claim the same level of autonomy and resources that Catalans and Basques obtain. And yet, with the exception of a small, democratic, and peaceful pro-independence movement, mainly supported by young intellectuals, the Catalans, and the Catalan nationalist coalition, reject the idea of separatism, claiming they simply need institutions to exist as a nation, not to become a sovereign nation-state.[115]

What is, then, this Catalan nation, able to survive centuries of denial, and yet to refrain from entering the cycle of building a state against another nation, Spain, which became also part of *Catalunya*'s historical identity? For Prat de la Riba, probably the most lucid ideologist of conservative Catalan nationalism in its formative stage, "Catalunya is the long chain of generations, united by the Catalan language and tradition, that succeed to each other in the territory where we live."[116] Jordi Pujol also insists on the language as the foundation of Catalan identity, and so do most observers: "The identity of Catalunya is, to a very large extent, linguistic and cultural. Catalunya has never claimed ethnic or religious specificity, nor has insisted on geography, or being strictly political. There are many components of

---

[115]   Keating (1995).
[116]   Prat de la Riba (1894), cited by Sole-Tura (1967: 187); my translation.

our identity, but language and culture are its backbone."[117] Indeed, *Catalunya* was, for more than 2,000 years, a land of passage and migrations, between various European and Mediterranean peoples, thus forging its sovereign institutions in interaction with several cultures, from which it became clearly differentiated by the beginning of the twelfth century, when the name of *Catalunya* appears for the first time.[118] According to the leading French historian of *Catalunya*, Pierre Vilar, what made Catalans distinctive as a people, from an early age (as early as the thirteenth and fourteenth centuries), was the language, clearly distinct from Spanish or French, with a developed literature already in the thirteenth century, exemplified in the writings of Raimon Llull (1235–1315), using the *Catalanesc*, that evolved from Latin in parallel to Provençal and Spanish. Language as identity became particularly relevant in the last half of the twentieth century when a traditionally low birth rate of Catalans in modern times, coupled with the differential industrialization of *Catalunya*, led to massive migration from impoverished Southern Spain, thus submerging Catalan speakers, still fighting against the prohibition of their language, with wave after wave of Spanish-speaking workers, who set up their life and families in *Catalunya*, particularly in the Barcelona suburbs. Thus, after *Catalunya* recovered its autonomy under the 1978 Spanish Constitution, in 1983 the Catalan Parliament voted unanimously a "Law of Linguistic Normalization," introducing teaching in Catalan in all public schools and universities, as well as the Catalan language in the administration, in public places, streets and roads, and in public television.[119] The explicit policy was to reach, over time, full integration of the non-Catalan population into the Catalan culture, so as not to create cultural ghettos that would fracture the society probably along class lines. So, in this strategy, the state is used to reinforce/produce the nation, without claiming sovereignty from the Spanish state.

Why is language so important in the definition of Catalan identity? One answer is historical: it is, over hundreds of years, what has been the sign of identification of being Catalan, together with democratic political institutions of self-government when they were not suppressed. Although Catalan nationalists define as a Catalan whoever lives and works in *Catalunya*, they also add "and wants to be a Catalan." And the sign of "wanting to be" is speaking the language, or trying to (in fact, "trying to" is even better because it is a real sign of willingness to be). Another answer is political: it is the easiest way

---

[117]   Pujol (1995), quoted in Pi (1996: 176); my translation.
[118]   Salrach (1996).
[119]   Puiggene i Riera et al. (1991).

to expand, and reproduce, the Catalan population without resorting to criteria of territorial sovereignty that would then necessarily collide with the territoriality of the Spanish state. Yet, an additional, and more fundamental answer, may be linked to what language represents, as a system of codes, crystallizing historically a cultural configuration that allows for symbolic sharing without worshipping of icons other than those emerging in everyday life's communication. It may well be that nations without states are organized around linguistic communities – an idea on which I will elaborate below – although, obviously, a common language does not make a nation. Latin American nations would certainly object to this approach, as would the UK and the US. But, for the moment, let us stay in *Catalunya*.

I hope that, after this historical reminder, it can be conceded that it is not an invented identity. For at least over 1,000 years, a given human community, mainly organized around language, but with a great deal of territorial continuity as well, and with a tradition of indigenous political democracy and self-government, has identified itself as a nation, in different contexts, against different adversaries, being part of different states, having its own state, searching for autonomy without challenging the Spanish state, integrating immigrants, enduring humiliation (indeed, commemorating it every year), and yet existing as *Catalunya*. An effort has been made by some analysts to identify Catalanism with the historical aspirations of a frustrated industrial bourgeoisie asphyxiated by a pre-capitalist, bureaucratic Spanish monarchy.[120] This was certainly a major element present in the Catalanist movement of the late nineteenth century, and in the formation of the Lliga.[121] But class analysis cannot account for the continuity of explicit discourse of Catalan identity throughout history, in spite of all the efforts of Spanish centralism to eradicate it. Prat de la Riba denied that *Catalunya* was reducible to class interests, and he was right, although his Lliga was primarily a bourgeois party.[122] Catalanism has been often associated with nineteenth-century romanticism, but it was also connected to the modernist movement of the turn of the century, oriented toward Europe and the international movement of ideas, and away from traditional Spanish regenerationism searching for a new source of transcendent values after the loss of the remnants of the empire in 1898. A cultural community, organized around language and a shared history, *Catalunya* is not an imagined entity, but a constantly renewed historical product, even if nationalist movements construct/reconstruct

---

[120] Jutglar (1966).
[121] Sole-Tura (1967).
[122] Prat de le Riba (1906).

their icons of self-identification with codes specific to each historical context, and relative to their political projects.

A decisive characterization of Catalan nationalism concerns its relationship to the nation-state.[123] Declaring *Catalunya* at the same time European, Mediterranean, and Hispanic, Catalan nationalists, while rejecting separatism from Spain, search for a new kind of state. It would be a state of variable geometry, bringing together respect for the historically inherited Spanish state with the growing autonomy of Catalan institutions in conducting public affairs, and the integration of both Spain and *Catalunya* in a broader entity, Europe, that translates not only into the European Union, but into various networks of regional and municipal governments, as well as of civic associations, that multiply horizontal relationships throughout Europe under the tenuous shell of modern nation-states. This is not simply clever tactics in the 1990s. It comes from the centuries-old, pro-European standing of Catalan elites, in contrast with the splendid cultural isolationism practiced by most Castilian elites in most historical periods. It is explicit also in the thinking of some of the most universal Catalan writers or philosophers, such as Josep Ferrater Mora, who could write in 1960: "The catalanization of Catalunya may be the last historical opportunity to make Catalans 'good Spaniards', and to make Spaniards 'good Europeans.'"[124] This is because only a Spain that could accept its plural identity – *Catalunya* being one of its most distinctive – could be fully open to a democratic, tolerant Europe. And, for this to happen, Catalans have first to feel at home within the territorial sovereignty of the Spanish state, being able to think, and speak, in Catalan, thus creating their commune within a broader network. This differentiation between cultural identity and the power of the state, between the undisputed sovereignty of apparatuses and the networking of power-sharing institutions, is a historical innovation in relation to most processes of construction of nation-states, solidly planted in historically shaky soil. It seems to relate better than traditional notions of sovereignty to a society based on flexibility and adaptability, to a global economy, to networking of media, to the variation and interpenetration of cultures. By not searching for a new state but fighting to preserve their nation, Catalans may have come full circle to their origins as people of borderless trade, cultural/linguistic identity, and flexible government institutions, all features that seem to characterize the information age.

---

[123] Keating (1995); Pi (1996); Trias (1996).
[124] Ferrater Mora (1960: 120).

Nations of the information age

Our excursus at the two opposite extremes of Europe yields some knowledge of the new significance of nations and nationalism as a source of meaning in the information age. For the sake of clarity, I shall define nations, in line with the arguments and elaborations presented above, as *cultural communes constructed in people's minds and collective memory by the sharing of history and political projects.* How much history must be shared for a collectivity to become a nation varies with contexts and periods, as are also variable the ingredients that pre-dispose the formation of such communes. Thus, Catalan nationality was distilled over a thousand years of sharing, while the United States of America forged a very strong national identity, in spite of, or because of, its multi-ethnicity, in a mere two centuries. What is essential is the historical distinction between nations and states, which only came to merge, and not for all nations, in the modern age. Thus, from the vantage point of our end of millennium perspective, we know of nations without states (for example, Catalonia, the Basque Country, Scotland, or Quebec), of states without nations (Singapore, Taiwan, or South Africa), of pluri-national states (the former Soviet Union, Belgium, Spain, or the United Kingdom), of uni-national states (Japan), of shared-nation states (South Korea and North Korea), and of nations sharing states (Swedes in Sweden and Finland, Irish in Ireland and the United Kingdom, maybe Serbs, Croats, and Bosnian Muslims in a future Bosnia-Herzegovina). What is clear is that citizenship does not equate nationality, at least exclusive nationality, as Catalans feel Catalan first of all, yet, at the same time, most declare themselves Spanish, and even "European," as well. So, the assimilation of nations and states to the composite nation-state, beyond a given historical context, is simply contradicted by observation when the record is constructed over the long haul and in a global perspective. It seems that the rationalist reaction (Marxist or otherwise) against German idealism (Herder, Fichte), and against French nationalistic hagiography (Michelet, Renan), obscured the understanding of the "national question," thus inducing bewilderment when confronted with the power and influence of nationalism at the end of this century.

Two phenomena, as illustrated in this section, appear to be characteristic of the current historical period: first, the disintegration of pluri-national states that try to remain fully sovereign or to deny the plurality of their national constituents. This was the case of the former Soviet Union, of the former Yugoslavia, of the former Ethiopia, of Czechoslovakia, and maybe it could be the case, in the future, of Sri Lanka, India, Indonesia, Nigeria, and other countries. The result of this disintegration is the formation of *quasi-nation-states.* They are nation-states because they receive the attributes of sovereignty on the basis of a historically constituted national identity (for example, Ukraine). But they are "quasi" because the entangled set of relationships with their historical matrix forces them to share sovereignty with either their former state or a broader configuration (for example, the CIS; Eastern European republics associated with the European Union). Secondly, we observe the development of nations that stop at the threshold of statehood, but force their parent state to adapt, and cede sovereignty, as in the case of *Catalunya*, the Basque Country, Flanders, Wallonie, Scotland, Quebec, and, potentially, Kurdistan, Kashmir, Punjab, or East Timor. I label these entities *national quasi-states*, because they are not fully fledged states, but win a share of political autonomy on the basis of their national identity.

The attributes that reinforce national identity in this historical period vary, although, in all cases, they presuppose the sharing of history over time. However, *I would make the hypothesis that language, and particularly a fully developed language, is a fundamental attribute of self-recognition, and of the establishment of an invisible national boundary less arbitrary than territoriality, and less exclusive than ethnicity.* This is, in a historical perspective, because language provides the linkage between the private and the public sphere, and between the past and the present, regardless of the actual acknowledgment of a cultural community by the institutions of the state. And it is not because Fichte used this argument to build pan-German nationalism that the historical record should be discarded. But there is also a powerful reason for the emergence of language-based nationalism in our societies. If nationalism is, most often, a reaction against a threatened autonomous identity, then, in a world submitted to cultural homogenization by the ideology of modernization and the power of global media, language, as the direct expression of culture, becomes the trench of cultural resistance, the last bastion of self-control, the refuge of identifiable meaning. Thus, after all, nations do not seem to be "imagined communities" constructed at the service of power apparatuses. Rather, they are produced through the labors of shared history, and then spoken in the images of communal languages whose first word is *we*, the second is *us*, and, unfortunately, the third is *them*.

Ethnic Unbonding: Race, Class, and Identity in the Network Society

See you 100 Black Men. . . . See you jailed. See you caged. See you tamed. See you pain. See you fronting. See you lamping. See you want. See you need. See you dissed. See you Blood. See you Crip. See you Brother.

See you sober. See you loved. See you peace. See you home. See you listen. See you love. See you on it. See you faithful. See you chumped. See you challenged. See you change. See you. See you. See you . . . I definitely wanna be you.

Peter J. Harris, "Praisesong for the Anonymous Brothers"[125]

Do *you* want, as well? Really? Ethnicity has been a fundamental source of meaning and recognition throughout human history. It is a founding structure of social differentiation, and social recognition, as well as of discrimination, in many contemporary societies, from the United States to Sub-Saharan Africa. It has been, and it is, the basis for uprisings in search of social justice, as for Mexican Indians in Chiapas in 1994, as well as the irrational rationale for ethnic cleansing, as practiced by Bosnian Serbs in 1994. And it is, to a large extent, the cultural basis that induces networking and trust-based transactions in the new business world, from Chinese business networks (volume I, chapter 3) to the ethnic "tribes" that determine success in the new global economy. Indeed, as Cornel West writes: "In this age of globalization, with its impressive scientific and technological innovations in information, communication, and applied biology, a focus on the lingering effects of racism seems outdated and antiquated . . . Yet race – in the coded language of welfare reform, immigration policy, criminal punishment, affirmative action, and suburban privatization – remains a central signifier in the political debate."[126] However, if race and ethnicity are central – to America, as to other societies' dynamics – their manifestations seem to be deeply altered by current societal trends.[127] I contend that while race matters, probably more than ever as a source of oppression and discrimination,[128] ethnicity is being specified as a source of meaning and identity, to be melted not with other ethnicities, but under broader principles of cultural self-definition, such as religion, nation, or gender. To convey the arguments in support of this hypothesis I shall discuss, briefly, the evolution of African-American identity in the United States.

The contemporary condition of African-Americans has been transformed in the past three decades by a fundamental phenomenon: their profound division along class lines, as shown in the pioneering work of William Julius Wilson,[129] the implications of which shattered for ever the way America sees African-Americans, and, even more

---

[125] From Wideman and Preston (1995: xxi).
[126] West (1996: 107–8).
[127] Appiah and Gates (1995).
[128] Wieviorka (1993); West (1995).
[129] Wilson (1987).

importantly, the way African-Americans see themselves. Supported by a stream of research in the past decade, Wilson's thesis, and its development, points at a dramatic polarization among African-Americans. On the one hand, spurred by the civil rights movement of the 1960s, particularly thanks to affirmative action programs, a large, well-educated, and relatively comfortable African-American middle class has emerged, making significant inroads into the political power structure, from mayoral offices to chairmanship of the Joint Chiefs of Staff, and, to some extent, in the corporate world. Thus, about a third of African-Americans are now part of the American middle class, although men, unlike women, still make much less money than their white counterparts. On the other hand, about a third of African-Americans, comprising 45 percent of African-American children at or below the poverty level, are much worse off in the 1990s than they were in the 1960s. Wilson, joined by other researchers, such as Blakely and Goldsmith, or Gans, attributes the formation of this "underclass" to the combined effect of an unbalanced information economy, of spatial segregation, and of misled public policy. The growth of an information economy emphasizes education, and reduces the availability of stable manual jobs, disadvantaging blacks at the entry level of the job market. Middle-class blacks escape the inner city, leaving behind, entrapped, the masses of the urban poor. To close the circle, the new black political elite finds support among the urban poor voters, but only as long as they can deliver social programs, which is a function of how worrisome, morally or politically, urban poor are for the white majority. Thus, new black political leadership is based on its ability to be the intermediary between the corporate world, the political establishment, and the ghettoized, unpredictable poor. Between these two groups, the final third of African-Americans strives not to fall into the poverty hell, hanging onto service jobs, disproportionately in the public sector, and to educational and vocational training programs that provide some skills to survive in a deindustrializing economy.[130] The punishment for those who do not succeed is increasingly atrocious. Among poorly educated, central-city black male residents in 1992, barely one-third held full-time jobs. And even among those who do work, 15 percent are below the poverty line. The average net worth of assets of the poorest fifth of blacks in 1995 was exactly zero. One-third of poor black households lives in substandard housing, meaning, among other criteria, "to show evidence of rats." The ratio of urban crime rate over suburban crime rate has grown from 1.2 to 1.6 between 1973 and 1992. And, of course, inner-

[130]   Wilson (1987); Blakely and Goldsmith (1993); Carnoy (1994); Wacquant (1994); Gans (1995); Hochschild (1995); Gates (1996).

city residents are those who suffer most from these crimes. Furthermore, the poor male black population is subjected to massive incarceration, or lives under the control of the penal system (awaiting trial, probation). While blacks are about 12 percent of the American population, in the 1990s they account for more than 50 percent of prison inmates.[131] The overall incarceration rate for black Americans in 1990 was 1,860 per 100,000, that is 6.4 times higher than for whites. And, yes, African-Americans are better educated, but in 1993 23,000 black men received a college diploma, while 2.3 million were incarcerated.[132] If we add all persons under supervision of the penal system in America in the 1996, we reach 5.4 million people. Blacks represented 53 percent of inmates in 1991.[133] The ratios of incarceration and surveillance are much higher among poor blacks, and staggering among black young males. In cities such as Washington DC, for age groups 18–30, the majority of black males are in prison or on probation. Women, and families, have to adjust to this situation. The notorious argument of the absent male in the poor African-American family has to account for the fact that many poor men spend considerable periods of their life in prison, so that women have to be prepared to raise children by themselves, or to give birth on their own responsibility.

These are well-known facts, whose social roots in the new techno-logical and economic context I shall try to analyze in volume III. But I am concerned, at this point in my analysis, with the consequences of such a deep class divide on the transformation of African-American identity.

To comprehend this transformation since the 1960s, we must go back to the historical roots of this identity: as Cornel West argues, blacks in America are precisely African and American. Their identity was constituted as kidnapped, enslaved people under the freest society of the time. Thus, to conciliate the obvious contradiction between the ideals of freedom, and the highly productive, slavery-based economy, America had to deny the humanity of blacks because only non-humans could be denied freedom in a society constituted on the principle that "all men are born equal." As Cornel West writes: "This unrelenting assault on black humanity produced the funda-mental condition of black culture – that of *black invisibility* and *namelessness.*"[134] Thus, black culture, following Cornel's analysis, had to learn to cope with its negation without falling into self-annihilation.

[131]   Tonry (1995: 59).
[132]   Gates (1996: 25).
[133]   See volume III, chapter 2.
[134]   West (1996: 80).

It did. From songs to art, from communal churches to brotherhood, black society emerged with a deep sense of collective meaning, not lost during the massive rural exodus to the Northern ghettos, translated into extraordinary creativity in art, music, and literature, and into a powerful, multifaceted political movement, whose dreams and potential were personified by Martin Luther King Jr in the 1960s.

Yet, the fundamental divide introduced among blacks by the partial success of the civil rights movement has transformed this cultural landscape. But, how exactly? At first sight, it would seem that the black middle class, building on its relative economic affluence and political influence, could be assimilated into the mainstream, constituting itself under a new identity, as African-Americans, moving toward a position similar to that of Italian-Americans, or Chinese-Americans. After all, Chinese-Americans were highly discriminated against for most of California's history, yet they have reached in recent years a rather respected social status. Thus, in this perspective, African-Americans could become another, distinctive segment in the multi-ethnic quilt of American society. While, on the other hand, the "underclass" would become more poor than black.

Yet, this thesis of a dual cultural evolution does not seem to hold when checked against available data. Jennifer Hochschild's powerful study of the cultural transformation of blacks and whites in their relationship to the "American Dream" of equal opportunity and individual mobility shows exactly the contrary.[135] Middle-class blacks are precisely those who feel bitter about the frustrated illusion of the American Dream, and feel most discriminated against by the permanence of racism, while a majority of whites feel that blacks are being unduly favored by affirmative action policies, and complain about reverse discrimination. On the other hand, poor blacks, while fully conscious of racism, seem to believe in the American Dream to a greater extent than middle-class blacks, and, in any case, are more fatalistic and/or individualistic about their fate (it always was like this), although a temporal perspective in the evolution of opinion polls seems to indicate that poor blacks, too, are losing whatever faith in the system they had. Still, the major fact that clearly stands out from Hochschild's effort to bring to the analysis a wealth of empirical data is that, by and large, affluent African-Americans do not feel welcome in mainstream society. Indeed, they are not. Not only racial hostility among whites continues to be pervasive, but gains by middle-class black males still leave them way behind whites in education, occupation, and income, as shown by Martin Carnoy.[136]

[135]   Hochschild (1995).
[136]   Carnoy (1994).

So, race matters a lot.[137] But, at the same time, the class divide among blacks has created such fundamentally different living conditions that there is growing hostility among the poor against those former brothers that left them out.[138] Most middle-class blacks strive to get ahead not only from the reality of the ghetto, but from the stigma that the echoes from the dying ghetto project on them through their skin. They do so, particularly, by insulating their children from the poor black communities (moving to suburbs, integrating them into white-dominated private schools), while, at the same time, reinventing an African-American identity that revives the themes of the past, African or American, while keeping silent on the plight of the present.

In a parallel move, end-of-millennium ghettos develop a new culture, made out of affliction, rage, and individual reaction against collective exclusion, where blackness matters less than the situations of exclusion that create new sources of bonding, for instance, territorial gangs, started in the streets, and consolidated in and from the prisons.[139] Rap, not jazz, emerges from this culture. This new culture expresses identity, as well, and it is also rooted in black history, and in the venerable American tradition of racism and racial oppression, but it incorporates new elements: the police and penal system as central institutions, the criminal economy as a shop floor, the schools as contested terrain, churches as islands of conciliation, mother-centered families, rundown environments, gang-based social organization, violence as a way of life. These are the themes of new black art and literature emerging from the new ghetto experience.[140] But it is not the same identity, by any means, as the identity emerging in middle-class African-America through the careful reconstruction of the humanity of the race.

Yet, even accepting their cultural split, both sets of identities face what appear to be insuperable difficulties in their constitution. This is, for affluent African-Americans, because of the following contradiction:[141] they feel the rejection of institutional racism, so that they can only integrate into the American mainstream as leaders of their kin, as the "Talented Tenth" that Du Bois, the leading black intellectual at the turn of the century, considered to be the necessary saviors of "the negro race," as for all races.[142] But the social, economic, and

---

[137] West (1996).
[138] Hochschild (1995); Gates (1996).
[139] Sanchez Jankowski (1991, 1996).
[140] Wideman and Preston (1995); Giroux (1996).
[141] Hochschild (1995).
[142] Gates and West (1996: 133).

cultural divide between the "Talented Tenth" and a significant, growing proportion of black America is such that they would have to deny themselves, and their children, accomplishing such a role, to become part of a pluri-class, multiracial coalition of progressive social change. In their superb little book debating this question, Henry Louis Gates Jr and Cornel West seem to think, on the one hand, that there is no other alternative, and yet, they do have reasonable doubts of the feasibility of such an option. Gates: "The real crisis of black leadership is that the very idea of black leadership is in crisis."[143] West:

> Since a multi-racial alliance of progressive middlers, liberal slices of the corporate elite, and subversive energy from below is the only vehicle by which some form of radical democratic account-ability can redistribute resources and wealth and restructure the economy and government so that all benefit, the significant secondary efforts of the black Talented Tenth alone in the twenty-first century will be woefully inadequate and thoroughly frustrating.[144]

Indeed, Du Bois himself left America for Ghana in 1961 because, he said, "I just cannot take any more of this country's treatment . . . Chin up, and fight on, but realize that American Negroes can't win."[145]

Will this failure of full integration efforts lead to a revival of black separatism in America? Could this be the new basis for identity, in direct line with the radical 1960s movements, as exemplified by the Black Panthers? It would seem so, at least among the militant youth, if we were to pay attention to the renewed cult of Malcolm X, the growing influence of Farrakhan's Nation of Islam, or, even more so, the extraordinary impact of the 1995 "Million Men March" in Washington DC, built around atonement, morality, and black male pride. Yet, these new manifestations of cultural–political identity reveal further cleavages among African-Americans, and they are actually organized around principles of self-identification that are not ethnic but religious (Islam, black churches), and strongly gendered (male pride, male responsibility, subordination of females). The impact of the "Million Men March," and its foreseeable development in the future, cuts across class lines, but shrinks the gender basis of African-American identity, and blurs the lines between religious, racial, and class self-identification. In other words, it was not based on identity but on the reflection of a disappearing identity. How can it be that, while society is reminding blacks every minute that they are

---

[143]   Gates (1996: 38).
[144]   West (1996: 110).
[145]   Gates and West (1996: 111).

black (thus, a different, stigmatized human kind, coming in a long journey from non-humanity), blacks themselves are living so many different lives, so as not to be able to share, and, instead, being increasingly violent against each other? It is this yearning for the lost community that is emerging in black America in the 1990s – because perhaps the deepest wound inflicted on African-Americans in the past decade has been the gradual loss of collective identity, leading to individual drifting while still bearing a collective stigma.

This is not a necessary process. Socio-political movements such as Jessie Jackson's "Rainbow Coalition," among others, continue to try hard to bring together black churches, minorities, communities, unions, and women, under a common banner to fight politically for social justice and racial equality. Yet, this is a process of building a political identity that only if fully successful in the long term could create a collective, cultural identity that would be necessarily new for both whites and blacks, if it is to overcome racism while maintaining historical, cultural differences. Cornel West, while acknowledging a "hope not hopeless but unhopeful," calls for "radical democracy" to transcend both racial divisions and black nationalism.[146] But in the ghetto trenches, and in the corporate boardrooms, historical African-American identity is being fragmented, and individualized, without yet being integrated into a multiracial, open society.

Thus, I formulate the hypothesis that ethnicity does not provide the basis for communal heavens in the network society, because it is based on primary bonds that lose significance, when cut from their historical context, as a basis for reconstruction of meaning in a world of flows and networks, of recombination of images, and reassignment of meaning. Ethnic materials are integrated into cultural communes that are more powerful, and more broadly defined than ethnicity, such as religion or nationalism, as statements of cultural autonomy in a world of symbols. Or else, ethnicity becomes the foundation for defensive trenches, then territorialized in local communities, or even gangs, defending their turf. Between cultural communes and self-defense territorial units, ethnic roots are twisted, divided, reprocessed, mixed, differentially stigmatized or rewarded, according to a new logic of informationalization/globalization of cultures and economies that makes symbolic composites out of blurred identities. Race matters, but it hardly constructs meaning any longer.

[146] West (1996: 112).

Territorial Identities: the Local Community

One of the oldest debates in urban sociology refers to the loss of community as a result of urbanization first, and of suburbanization later. Empirical research some time ago, most notably by Claude Fischer and by Barry Wellman,[147] seems to have put to rest the simplistic notion of a systematic co-variation between space and culture. People socialize and interact in their local environment, be it in the village, in the city, or in the suburb, and they build social networks among their neighbors. On the other hand, locally based identities intersect with other sources of meaning and social recognition, in a highly diversified pattern that allows for alternative interpretations. So, where, in recent years, Etzioni sees the revival of community to a large extent on a local basis, Putnam watches the disintegration of the Tocquevillian vision of an intense civil society in America, with membership and activity in voluntary associations dropping substantially in the 1980s.[148] Reports from other areas of the world are equally conflicting in their estimates. However, I do not think it would be inaccurate to say that local environments, *per se*, do not induce a specific pattern of behavior, or, for that matter, a distinctive identity. Yet, what communalist authors would argue, and what is consistent with my own cross-cultural observation, is that people resist the process of individualization and social atomization, and tend to cluster in community organizations that, over time, generate a feeling of belonging, and ultimately, in many cases, a communal, cultural identity. I introduce the hypothesis that for this to happen, a process of social mobilization is necessary. That is, people must engage in urban movements (not quite revolutionary), through which common interests are discovered, and defended, life is shared somehow, and new meaning may be produced.

I know something about this subject, having spent a decade of my life studying urban social movements around the world.[149] Summarizing my findings, as well as the relevant literature, I proposed that urban movements (processes of purposive social mobilization, organized in a given territory, oriented toward urban-related goals) were focused on three main sets of goals: urban demands on living conditions and collective consumption; the affirmation of local cultural identity; and the conquest of local political autonomy and citizen participation. Different movements combined these three sets of goals in various proportions, and the outcomes of their efforts were

---

[147]   Wellman (1979); Fischer (1982).
[148]   Etzioni (1993); Putnam (1995).
[149]   Castells (1983).

equally diversified. Yet, in many instances, regardless of the explicit achievements of the movement, its very existence produced meaning, not only for the movement's participants, but for the community at large. And not only during the lifespan of the movement (usually brief), but in the collective memory of the locality. Indeed, I argued, and I argue, that this production of meaning is an essential component of cities, throughout history, as the built environment, and its meaning, is constructed through a conflictive process between the interests and values of opposing social actors.

I added something else, referring to the historical moment of my observation (the late 1970s, early 1980s), but projecting my view toward the future: urban movements were becoming critical sources of resistance to the one-sided logic of capitalism, statism, and informationalism. This was, essentially, because the failure of proactive movements and politics (for example, the labor movement, political parties) to counter economic exploitation, cultural domination, and political oppression had left people with no other choice than either to surrender or to react on the basis of the most immediate source of self-recognition and autonomous organization: their locality. Thus, so emerged the paradox of increasingly local politics in a world structured by increasingly global processes. There was production of meaning and identity: my neighborhood, my community, my city, my school, my tree, my river, my beach, my chapel, my peace, my environment. But it was a defensive identity, an identity of retrenchment of the known against the unpredictability of the unknown and uncontrollable. Suddenly defenseless against a global whirlwind, people stuck to themselves: whatever they had, and whatever they were, became their identity. I wrote in 1983:

> Urban movements do address the real issues of our time, although neither on the scale nor terms that are adequate to the task. And yet they do not have any choice since they are the last reaction to the domination and renewed exploitation that submerges our world. But they are more than a last symbolic stand and a desperate cry: they are symptoms of our own contradictions, and therefore potentially capable of superseding these contradictions . . . They do produce new historical meaning – in the twilight zone of pretending to build within the walls of a local community a new society they know unattainable. And they do so by nurturing the embryos of tomorrow's social movements within the local utopias that urban movements have constructed in order never to surrender to barbarism."[150]

---

[150] Castells (1983: 331).

What has happened since then? The empirical answer is, of course, extraordinarily diverse, particularly if we look across cultures and areas of the world.[151] I would, however, venture, for the sake of the analysis, to synthetize urban movements' main trajectories in the 1980s and 1990s under four headings.

First, in many cases, urban movements, and their discourses, actors, and organizations, have been integrated in the structure and practice of local government, either directly or indirectly, through a diversified system of citizen participation, and community development. This trend, while liquidating urban movements as sources of alternative social change, has considerably reinforced local government, and introduced the possibility of the local state as a significant instance of reconstruction of political control and social meaning. I will return to this fundamental development in chapter 5, when analyzing the overall transformation of the state.

Secondly, local communities, and their organizations, have indeed nurtured the grassroots of a widespread, and influential, environmental movement, particularly in middle-class neighborhoods, and in the suburbs, exurbia, and urbanized countryside (see chapter 3). However, these movements are often defensive and reactive, focusing on the strictest conservation of their space and immediate environment, as exemplified, in the United States, by the "not in my backyard" attitude, mixing in the same rejection toxic waste, nuclear plants, public housing projects, prisons, and mobile home settlements. I will make a major distinction, which I will develop in chapter 3 when analyzing the environmental movement, between the search for controlling space (a defensive reaction), and the search for controlling time; that is, for the preservation of nature, and of the planet, for future generations, in a very long term, thus adopting cosmological time, and rejecting the instant time approach of instrumentalist development. Identities emerging from these two perspectives are quite different, as defensive spaces lead to collective individualism, and offensive timing opens up the reconciliation between culture and nature, thus introducing a new, holistic philosophy of life.

Thirdly, a vast number of poor communities around the world have engaged in collective survival, as with the communal kitchens that flourished in Santiago de Chile or Lima during the 1980s. Be it in squatter settlements in Latin America, in American inner cities, or in working-class neighborhoods in Asian cities, communities have built their own "welfare states" (in the absence of responsible public policies) on the basis of networks of solidarity and reciprocity, often

[151]   Massolo (1992); Fisher and Kling (1993); Calderon (1995); Judge et al. (1995); Tanaka (1995); Borja and Castells (1996); Hsia (1996); Yazawa (forthcoming).

around churches, or supported by internationally funded non-governmental organizations (NGOs); sometimes with the help of leftist intellectuals. These organized, local communities have played, and continue to play, a major role in the daily survival of a significant proportion of the world's urban population, at the threshold of famine and epidemic. This trend was illustrated, for instance, by the experience of community associations organized by the Catholic Church in São Paulo in the 1980s,[152] or by internationally sponsored NGOs in Bogota in the 1990s.[153] In most of these cases, a communal identity does emerge, although very often it is absorbed into a religious faith, to the point that I would risk the hypothesis that this kind of communalism is, essentially, a religious commune, linked to the consciousness of being the exploited and/or the excluded. Thus, people organizing in poor local communities may feel revitalized, and acknowledged as human beings, by and through religious deliverance.

Fourthly, there is a darker side of the story, concerning the evolution of urban movements, particularly in segregated urban areas, a trend that I foresaw some time ago:

> If urban movements' appeals are not heard, if the new political avenues remain closed, if the new central social movements (feminism, new labor, self-management, alternative communication) do not develop fully, then the urban movements – reactive utopias that tried to illuminate the path they could not walk – will return, but this time as urban shadows eager to destroy the closed walls of their captive city.[154]

Fortunately, the failure was not total, and the diversified expression of organized local communities did provide avenues of reform, survival, and self-identification, in spite of the lack of major social movements able to articulate change in the new society emerging in the past two decades. Yet, harsh policies of economic adjustment in the 1980s, a widespread crisis of political legitimacy, and the exclusionary impact of the space of flows over the space of places (see volume I), took their toll on social life and organization in poor local communities. In American cities, gangs emerged as a major form of association, work, and identity for hundreds of thousands of youths. Indeed, as Sanchez Jankowski has showed in his first-hand, comprehensive study of gangs,[155] they play a structuring role in many areas,

---

[152]   Cardoso de Leite (1983); Gohn (1991).
[153]   Espinosa and Useche (1992).
[154]   Castells (1983: 327).
[155]   Sanchez Jankowski (1991).

which explains the ambiguous feeling of local residents toward them, partly fearful, yet partly feeling able to relate to the gang society better than to mainstream institutions, which are usually present only in their repressive manifestation. Gangs, or their functional equivalent, are not, by any means, an American graffiti. The *pandillas* in most Latin American cities are a key element of sociability in poor neighborhoods, and so are they in Jakarta, in Bangkok, in Manila, in Mantes-la-Jolie (Paris), or in Meseta de Orcasitas (Madrid). Gangs are, however, an old story in many societies, particularly in America (remember William White's *Street Corner Society*). Yet there is something new in the gangs of the 1990s, characterizing the construction of identity as the twisted mirror of informational culture. It is what Magaly Sanchez and Yves Pedrazzini, on the basis of their study of the *malandros* (bad boys) of Caracas, call the *culture of urgency*.[156] It is a culture of the immediate end of life, not of its negation, but of its celebration. Thus, everything has to be tried, felt, experimented, accomplished, before it is too late, since there is no tomorrow. Is this really so different from the culture of consumerist narcissism *à la* Lasch? Have the bad boys of Caracas, or elsewhere, understood faster than the rest of us what our new society is all about? Is the new gang identity the culture of communal hyper-individualism? Individualism because, in the immediate gratification pattern, only the individual can be a proper accounting unit. Communalism because, for this hyper-individualism to be an identity – that is, to be socialized as value not just as senseless consumption – it needs a milieu of appreciation and reciprocal support: a commune, as in White's times. But, unlike White's, this commune is ready to explode at any time, it is a commune of the end of time, it is a commune of timeless time, characterizing the network society. And it exists, and explodes, territorially. Local cultures of urgency are the reverse expression of global timelessness.

Thus, local communities, constructed through collective action and preserved through collective memory, are specific sources of identities. But these identities, in most cases, are defensive reactions against the impositions of global disorder and uncontrollable, fast-paced change. They do build havens, but not heavens.

---

[156] Sanchez and Pedrazzini (1996).

Conclusion: the Cultural Communes of the Information Age

The transformation of our culture and our society would have to happen at a number of levels. If it occurred only in the minds of individuals (as to some degree it already has), it would be powerless. If it came only from the initiative of the state, it would be tyrannical. Personal transformation among large numbers is essential, and it must not only be a transformation of consciousness but must also involve individual action. But individuals need the nurture of groups that carry a moral tradition reinforcing their own aspirations.

Robert Bellah et al., *Habits of the Heart*[157]

Our intellectual journey through communal landscapes provides some preliminary answers to the questions raised at the beginning of this chapter on the construction of identity in the network society.

For those social actors excluded from or resisting the individualization of identity attached to life in the global networks of power and wealth, cultural communes of religious, national, or territorial foundation seem to provide the main alternative for the construction of meaning in our society. These cultural communes are characterized by three main features. They appear as reactions to prevailing social trends, which are resisted on behalf of autonomous sources of meaning. They are, at their onset, defensive identities that function as refuge and solidarity, to protect against a hostile, outside world. They are culturally constituted; that is, organized around a specific set of values whose meaning and sharing are marked by specific codes of self-identification: the community of believers, the icons of nationalism, the geography of locality.

Ethnicity, while being a fundamental feature of our societies, especially as a source of discrimination and stigma, may not induce communes on its own. Rather, it is likely to be processed by religion, nation, and locality, whose specificity it tends to reinforce.

The constitution of these cultural communes is not arbitrary. It works on raw materials from history, geography, language, and environment. So, they are constructed, but materially constructed, around reactions and projects historically/geographically determined.

Religious fundamentalism, cultural nationalism, territorial communes are, by and large, defensive reactions. Reactions against three fundamental threats, perceived in all societies, by the majority of humankind, in this end of millennium. Reaction against

---

[157]   Bellah et al. (1985: 286).

globalization, which dissolves the autonomy of institutions, organizations, and communication systems where people live. Reaction against networking and flexibility, which blur the boundaries of membership and involvement, individualize social relationships of production, and induce the structural instability of work, space, and time. And reaction against the crisis of the patriarchal family, at the roots of the transformation of mechanisms of security-building, socialization, sexuality, and, therefore, of personality systems. When the world becomes too large to be controlled, social actors aim at shrinking it back to their size and reach. When networks dissolve time and space, people anchor themselves in places, and recall their historic memory. When the patriarchal sustainment of personality breaks down, people affirm the transcendent value of family and community, as God's will.

These defensive reactions become sources of meaning and identity by constructing new cultural codes out of historical materials. Because the new processes of domination to which people react are embedded in information flows, the building of autonomy has to rely on reverse information flows. God, nation, family, and community will provide unbreakable, eternal codes, around which a counter-offensive will be mounted against the culture of real virtuality. Eternal truth cannot be virtualized. It is embodied in us. Thus, against the informationalization of culture, bodies are informationalized. That is, individuals bear their gods in their heart. They do not reason, they believe. They are the bodily manifestation of God's eternal values, and as such, they cannot be dissolved, lost in the whirlwind of information flows and cross-organizational networks. This is why language, and communal images, are so essential to restore communication between the autonomized bodies, escaping the domination of a-historical flows, yet trying to restore new patterns of meaningful communication among the believers.

This form of identity-building revolves essentially around the principle of *resistance identity*, as defined at the beginning of this chapter. *Legitimizing identity* seems to have entered a fundamental crisis because of the fast disintegration of civil society inherited from the industrial era, and because of the fading away of the nation-state, the main source of legitimacy (see chapter 5). Indeed, cultural communes organizing the new resistance emerge as sources of identity by breaking away from civil societies and state institutions from which they originate, as is the case with Islamic fundamentalism breaking away from economic modernization (Iran), and/or from Arab states' nationalism; or with nationalist movements, challenging the nation-state and the state institutions of societies where they come into existence. This negation of civil societies and political institutions where cultural communes emerge leads to the closing of the boundaries of the commune. In contrast to pluralistic, differentiated civil societies, cultural communes display little internal differentiation. Indeed, their strength, and their ability to provide refuge, solace, certainty, and protection, comes precisely from their communal character, from their collective responsibility, cancelling individual projects. Thus, in the first stage of reaction, the (re)construction of meaning by defensive identities breaks away from the institutions of society, and promises to rebuild from the bottom up, while retrenching themselves in a communal heaven.

It is possible that from such communes, new subjects – that is collective agents of social transformation – may emerge, thus constructing new meaning around *project identity*. Indeed, I would argue that, given the structural crisis of civil society and the nation-state, this may be the main potential source of social change in the network society. As for how and why these new proactive subjects could be formed from these reactive, cultural communes, this will be the core of my analysis of social movements in the network society to be elaborated throughout this volume.

But we can already say something on the basis of the observations and discussions presented in this chapter. The emergence of project identities of different kinds is not a historical necessity. It may well be that cultural resistance will remain enclosed in the boundaries of communes. If this is the case, and where and when this is the case, communalism will close the circle of its latent fundamentalism on its own components, inducing a process that might transform communal heavens into heavenly hells.

— 2 —

The Other Face of the Earth: Social Movements against the New Global Order

Your problem is the same as many people have. It relates to the social and economic doctrine known as "neo-liberalism". This is a meta-theoretical problem. I am telling you. You start from the assumption that "neo-liberalism" is a doctrine. And by you I refer to all those with schemes as rigid and square as their head. You think that "neo-liberalism" is a capitalist doctrine to confront economic crises that capitalism charges are caused by "populism". Well, in fact "neo-classicism" is not a theory to explain crises or to confront them. It is the crisis itself, made theory and economic doctrine! This is to say that "neo-liberalism" does not have the slightest coherence, neither has plans or historical perspective. I mean, it's pure theoretical shit.

Durito, talking to Subcomandante Marcos in the Lacandon Forest, 1994[1]

Globalization, Informationalization, and Social Movements[2]

Globalization and informationalization, enacted by networks of wealth, technology, and power, are transforming our world. They are enhancing our productive capacity, cultural creativity, and communication potential. At the same time, they are disfranchising

[1] *Durito* is a usual character in the writings of Subcomandante Marcos, the *Zapatista* spokesperson. He is a beetle, but a very clever one: indeed, he is Marcos' intellectual adviser. The problem is he always fears being crushed by the too numerous guerrillas around him, so he begs Marcos to keep the movement small. This text by *Durito* is cited from *Ejercito Zapatista de Liberacion Nacional*/Subcomandante Marcos (1995: 58–9); my translation, with *Durito's* benevolence.

[2] This chapter has benefited from valuable intellectual exchanges at the

societies. As institutions of state and organizations of civil society are based on culture, history, and geography, the sudden acceleration of the historical tempo, and the abstraction of power in a web of computers, are disintegrating existing mechanisms of social control and political representation. With the exception of a small elite of *globapolitans* (half beings, half flows), people all over the world resent loss of control over their lives, over their environment, over their jobs, over their economies, over their governments, over their countries, and, ultimately, over the fate of the Earth. Thus, following an old law of social evolution, resistance confronts domination, empowerment reacts against powerlessness, and alternative projects challenge the logic embedded in the new global order, increasingly sensed as disorder by people around the planet. However, these reactions and mobilizations, as is often the case in history, come in unusual formats and proceed through unexpected ways. This chapter, and the next one, explore these ways.

To broaden the empirical scope of my inquiry, while keeping its analytical focus, I will compare three movements that explicitly oppose the new global order of the 1990s, coming from extremely different cultural, economic, and institutional contexts, through sharply contrasting ideologies: the Zapatistas in Chiapas, Mexico; the American militia; and *Aum Shinrikyo*, a Japanese cult.

In the next chapter I will analyze the environmental movement, arguably the most comprehensive, influential movement of our time. In its own way, and through the creative cacophony of its multiple voices, environmentalism also challenges global ecological disorder, indeed the risk of eco-suicide, brought about by uncontrolled global development, and by the unleashing of unprecedented technological forces without checking their social and environmental sustainability. But its cultural and political specificity, and its character as a pro-active, rather than reactive, social movement, advise a separate analytical treatment of the environmental movement, as distinct from defensive movements built around the trenches of specific identities.

Before proceeding into the heart of the matter, let me introduce three brief methodological remarks that are necessary for understanding the analyses to be presented in the following pages.[3]

First, *social movements* must be understood in their own terms:

International Seminar on Globalization and Social Movements organized by the International Sociological Association's Research Committee on Social Movements, held at Santa Cruz, California, April 16–19, 1996. I thank the organizers of the seminar, Barbara Epstein and Louis Maheu, for their kind invitation.
[3] For a theoretical discussion of social movements directly relevant to the inquiry presented here, see Castells (1983); Dalton and Kuechler (1990); Epstein (1991); Riechmann and Fernandez Buey (1994); Calderon (1995); Dubet and

namely, *they are what they say they are*. Their practices (and foremost their discursive practices) are their self-definition. This approach takes us away from the hazardous task of interpreting the "true" consciousness of movements, as if they could only exist by revealing the "real" structural contradictions. As if, in order to come to life, they would necessarily have to bear these contradictions, as they bear their weapons and brandish their flags. A different, and necessary, research operation is to establish the relationship between the movements, as defined by their practice, their values, and their discourse, and the social processes to which they seem to be associated: for example, globalization, informationalization, the crisis of representative democracy, and the dominance of symbolic politics in the space of media. In my analysis I will try to conduct both operations: the characterization of each movement, in terms of its own specific dynamics; and its interaction with the broader processes that induce its existence, and become modified by this very existence. The importance I give to the movement's discourse will be reflected in my writing. When presenting and analyzing the movements, I will follow very closely their own *words*, not just ideas, as recorded in documents on which I have worked. However, in order to spare the reader from the minute details of reference citation, I have opted for giving generic references to the materials from which the discourses have been obtained, leaving the interested reader to find in these materials the precise words reported in my writing.

Secondly, social movements may be socially conservative, socially revolutionary, or both, or none. After all, we now have concluded (I hope for ever) that there is no predetermined directionality in social evolution, that the only sense of history is the history we sense. Therefore, from an analytical perspective, there are no "bad" and "good" social movements. They are all symptoms of our societies, and all impact social structures, with variable intensities and outcomes that must be established by research. Thus, I like the *Zapatistas*, I dislike the American militia, and I am horrified by *Aum Shinrikyo*. Yet, they are all, as I will argue, meaningful signs of new social conflicts, and embryos of social resistance and, in some cases, social change. Only by scanning with an open mind the new historical landscape will we be able to find shining paths, dark abysses, and muddled breakthroughs into the new society emerging from current crises.

Thirdly, to put some order into a mass of disparate material on the social movements to be examined in this and following chapters, I

Wieviorka (1995); Maheu (1995); Melucci (1995); Touraine (1995); Touraine et al. (1996); Yazawa (forthcoming).

find it useful to categorize them in terms of Alain Touraine's classic typology that defines a social movement by three principles: the movement's *identity*, the movement's *adversary*, and the movement's vision or social model, which I call *societal goal*.[4] In my personal adaptation (which I believe to be consistent with Touraine's theory), *identity* refers to the self-definition of the movement of what it is, on behalf of whom it speaks. *Adversary* refers to the movement's principal enemy, as explicitly identified by the movement. *Societal goal* refers to the movement's vision of the kind of social order, or social organization, it would wish to attain in the historical horizon of its collective action.

Having clarified the point of departure, let's depart for this voyage to the other face of the Earth, the one refusing globalization for the sake of capital and informationalization for the sake of technology. And where dreams of the past, and nightmares of the future, inhabit a chaotic world of passion, generosity, prejudice, fear, fantasy, violence, flawed strategies, and lucky strikes. Humanity, after all.

The three movements I have selected to understand insurgency against globalization are extremely different in their identity, in their goals, in their ideology, and in their relationship to society.[5] This is precisely the interest of the comparison because they are similar, however, in their explicit opposition to the new global order, identified as the enemy in their discourse and in their practice. And all of them are likely to have significant impacts on their societies, directly or indirectly. The *Zapatistas* have already transformed Mexico, inducing a crisis in the corrupt politics and unjust economy prevailing in Mexico, while putting forward proposals for democratic reconstruction that are being widely debated in Mexico, and throughout the world. The American militia, the most militant component of a broader socio-political movement self-identified as *The Patriots* (or *False Patriots*, as their critics call them), has much deeper roots in American society than is usually acknowledged, and may induce unpredictable, significant outcomes in America's tense political scene, as I will argue below. *Aum Shinrikyo*, while remaining a marginal cult in Japanese society, has dominated media attention and public debate for more than a year (in 1995–96), and it has acted as a

---

[4]   Touraine (1965, 1966). Touraine's formulation in fact uses a slightly different terminology, in French: *principe d'identité, principe d'opposition; principe de totalité*. I decided that it would be clearer for an international audience to use more plain words to say the same thing, at the risk of losing the authentic French flavor.
[5]   This comparative analysis is based on a joint study with Shujiro Yazawa and Emma Kiselyova, conducted in 1995. For a first elaboration of this study, see Castells et al. (1996).

symptom of unseen injuries, and unfolding dramas, behind the curtains of Japanese serenity. The point I am trying to make by bringing together these different, powerful insurgencies, is precisely the diversity of sources of resistance to the new global order. Together with the reminder that the neo-liberal illusion of the end of history is over, as historically specific societies take their revenge against their domination by global flows.

Mexico's *Zapatistas*: the First Informational Guerrilla Movement[6]

The Movimiento Civil Zapatista *is a movement that opposes social solidarity to organized crime from the power of money and government.*
Manifesto of *Movimiento Civil Zapatista*, August 1995

The novelty in Mexico's political history was the inversion of the control process against the powers that be, on the basis of alternative communication . . . The newness in Chiapas' political war was the emergence of various senders of information that interpreted events in very different ways.

The flow of public information reaching society, through the media, and through new technological means, was much greater than what conventional communication strategies could control. Marcos gave his opinion, the Church gave its opinion, and independent journalists, NGOs, and intellectuals, from the forest, from Ciudad de Mexico, from

---

[6]   The analysis of the *Zapatista* movement presented here is greatly indebted, as is often the case in this book, to contributions by two women. Professor Alejandra Moreno Toscano, a distinguished urban historian at the Universidad Nacional Autonoma de Mexico, and a former Secretary of Social Welfare of Mexico DF, was deputy to Manuel Camacho, the President's representative, during the critical period of negotiations between the Mexican government and the *Zapatistas* in the first months of 1994. She provided me with documents, opinion, and insights, and decisively helped my understanding of the overall process of Mexican politics in 1994–96. For her analysis (the most intelligent approach that I have read), see Moreno Toscano (1996). Secondly, Maria Elena Martinez Torres, one of my doctoral students at Berkeley, was a thorough observer of Chiapas peasantry. During our intellectual interaction, she provided me with her own analyses (Martinez Torres, 1994, 1996). Naturally, I bear exclusive responsibility for the interpretation, and possible mistakes, in the conclusions presented in this book. Additional sources used on the *Zapatista* movement are: Garcia de Leon (1985); Arquilla and Rondfeldt (1993); Collier and Lowery Quaratiello (1994); *Ejercito Zapatista de Liberacion Nacional* (1994, 1995); Trejo Delarbre (1994a, b); Collier (1995); Hernandez Navarro (1995); Nash et al. (1995); Rojas (1995); Rondfeldt (1995); Tello Diaz (1995); Woldenberg (1995).

the world's financial and political capitals, all gave their own opinion. These alternative opinions, made possible by open media, or by closed media that felt the pinch from open media, called into question forms of construction of "the truth", and induced, within the political regime as well, a variety of opinions. The view from power became fragmented.
                                    Moreno Toscano, *Turbulencia politica*, p. 82

Mexico, the nation that generated the prototype of social revolution of the 20th century, is now the scene of a prototype transnational social netwar of the 21st century.
                                    Rondfeldt, Rand Corporation, 1995

On January 1, 1994, the first day of the North American Free Trade Agreement (NAFTA), about 3,000 men and women, organized in the *Ejercito Zapatista de Liberacion Nacional,* lightly armed, took control of the main municipalities adjacent to the Lacandon Forest, in the Southern Mexican state of Chiapas: San Cristobal de las Casas, Altamirano, Ocosingo and Las Margaritas. Most of them were Indians from various ethnic groups, although there were also *mestizos,* and some of their leaders, and particularly their spokesperson, Subcomandante Marcos, were urban intellectuals. The leaders had their faces hidden behind ski masks. When the Mexican Army dispatched reinforcements, the guerrillas withdrew to the rainforest in good order. However, several dozen of them as well as civilians, and a number of soldiers and policemen, died in the confrontation or were summarily executed by soldiers in the aftermath. The impact of the uprising in Mexico, and the widespread sympathy that the *Zapatistas'* cause immediately inspired in the country, and in the world, convinced the Mexican president, Carlos Salinas de Gortari, to negotiate. On January 12, Salinas announced a unilateral ceasefire, and appointed as his "peace representative," Manuel Camacho, a respected Mexican politician, once considered his likely successor, who had just resigned from government after his presidential hopes were frustrated by Salinas (see my analysis of the Mexican political crisis in chapter 5). Manuel Camacho, and his trusted intellectual adviser, Alejandra Moreno Toscano, traveled to Chiapas, met with the influential Catholic Bishop Samuel Ruiz, and were able to engage in serious peace talks with the *Zapatistas* who quickly acknowledged the sincerity of the dialogue, although they remained justifiably wary of potential repression and/or manipulation. Camacho read to the insurgents a text in *tzotzil,* also broadcast in *tzeltal* and *chol:* the first time ever a leading Mexican official had acknowledged Indian languages. On January 27, an agreement was signed, setting a ceasefire, freeing prisoners on both sides, and engaging a process of negotiation on a broad agenda of political reform, Indian rights, and social demands.

Who are the *Zapatistas*?

Who were these insurgents, unknown until then to the rest of the world, in spite of two decades of widespread peasant mobilizations in the communities of Chiapas and Oaxaca? They were peasants, most of them Indians, *tzeltales*, *tzotziles*, and *choles*, generally from the communities established since the 1940s in the Lacandon rainforest, on the Guatemalan border. These communities were created with government support in order to find a way out of the social crisis created by the expulsion of *acasillados* (landless peasants working for landowners) from the *fincas* (farms), and ranches, owned by middle and large landowners, generally *mestizos*. For centuries, Indians and peasants have been abused by colonizers, bureaucrats, and settlers. And for decades they have been kept in constant insecurity, as the status of their settlements constantly changed, in accordance with the interests of government and landowners. In 1972, President Echeverria decided to create the "bioreserve" of Montes Azul, and to return most of the forest to 66 families of the original Lacandon tribe, thus ordering the relocation of 4,000 families that had resettled in this area, after their expulsion from their original communities. Behind the Lacandon tribes and the sudden love of nature, there were the interests of the forestry company Cofolasa, supported by the government development corporation, NAFINSA, which received logging rights. Most settlers refused to relocate, and started a 20-year struggle for their right to land, which was still lingering on when Salinas assumed the Presidency in 1988. Salinas finally accepted the rights of some colonists, but restricted his generosity to those few supporting the PRI (*Partido Revolucionario Institucional*), the government party. In 1992, a new decree abolished the legal rights of the Indian communities that had resettled for the second time. This time the pretext was the Rio Conference on the Environment, and the need to protect the rainforest. Cattle feeding in the area was also curtailed in order to help Chiapas ranchers, competing with cattle smuggling from Guatemala. The final blow to the fragile economy of peasant communities came when Mexican liberalization policies in the 1990s, in preparation for NAFTA, ended restrictions of imports of corn, and eliminated protection on the price of coffee. The local economy, based on forestry, cattle, coffee, and corn, was dismantled. Furthermore, the status of communal land became uncertain after Salinas' reform of the historic article 27 of the Mexican Constitution, which ended communal possession of agricultural property by the villagers (*ejidos*), in favor of full commercialization of individual property, another measure directly related to Mexico's alignment with privatization in accordance with NAFTA. In 1992 and 1993, peasants mobilized peacefully against these policies. But, after their powerful march of Xi' Nich, which brought thousands of peasants from Palenque to Ciudad de Mexico, was left without answer, they changed tactics. By the middle of 1993, in most communities of Lacandon, corn was not planted, coffee was left in the bushes, children withdrew from schools, and cattle were sold to buy weapons. The headline of the insurgents' Manifesto on January 1, 1994 read: "*Hoy decimos BASTA!*" (Today, we say ENOUGH!)

These peasant communities, mostly Indian, joined by other settlements from the Los Altos area, were not alone in the social struggles they had undertaken since the early 1970s. They were supported, and to some extent organized, by the Catholic Church, under the initiative of San Cristobal de las Casas' Bishop Samuel Ruiz, somewhat associated with liberation theology. Not only did the priests support and legitimize Indian claims, but they helped to form hundreds of cadres of peasants' unions. These cadres shared membership of the Church and of the unions. There were over one hundred *tuhuneles* (aides of priests), and over one thousand catechists, who provided the backbone of the movement, which developed in the form of peasant unions, each one of them based in a community (*ejido*). Strong religious feeling among Indian peasants was reinforced by education, information, and support from the Church, leading to frequent conflicts between the local Church, on the one hand, and Chiapas ranchers and Chiapas PRI apparatus, on the other hand. Yet, while the Church was decisive in educating, organizing, and mobilizing Indian peasant communities for many years, Samuel Ruiz and his aides strongly opposed armed struggle and were not among the insurgents, contrary to accusations by Chiapas ranchers. The cadres who organized the armed insurrection came, in their majority, from the Indian communities themselves, particularly from the ranks of young men and women who had grown up in the new climate of economic distress and social struggle. Other cadres came from Maoist groups formed in urban Mexico (particularly in Ciudad de Mexico, and in Monterrey) in the 1970s, in the aftermath of the student movement of 1968 crushed in the Tlatelolco massacre. The *Fuerzas de Liberacion Nacional* seem to have been active in the area for a long time, although accounts diverge on this point. In any case, whatever the origin, it seems that, after a series of setbacks in urban areas, a few revolutionaries, men and women, undertook the long march of establishing their credibility among the most oppressed sectors of the country, through patient work and daily sharing of their hardship and struggles. Marcos seems to have been one of these militants, coming to the region in the early 1980s, according to government sources, after completing studies in sociology and communication in Mexico and Paris, and teaching social sciences in one of the best universities in Mexico DF.[7] He is clearly a very learned intellectual, who speaks several languages, writes well, is extraordinarily imaginative, has a wonderful sense of humor, and is at ease in his relationship with the media. These revolutionary intellectuals, because of their honesty and dedication, were welcomed by the priests and, for a long time, in spite of ideological differences, they worked together in organizing peasant communities, and in supporting their struggles. It was only after 1992, when promises of reforms continued to go unfulfilled, and when the situation in the Lacandon communities become more dire because of the overall process of economic modernization in Mexico, that *Zapatista* militants set up their own structure and initiated preparations for guerrilla warfare. In May 1993 a first skirmish with the army took place, but the Mexican government downplayed the incident to avoid problems in the ratification of NAFTA by the US Congress. It should, however, be emphasized that the leadership of the *Zapatistas* is genuinely peasant, and mainly Indian. Marcos, and other urban militants, could not act on their own.[8] The process of deliberation, as well as negotiation with the government, consisted of lengthy procedures with the full participation of the communities. This was critical since, once a decision had been made, the whole community had to follow the common decision, to the extent that, in a few instances, villagers were expelled because of their refusal to participate in the uprising. Yet, during the two and a half years of the open insurgency process, the overwhelming majority of Lacandon communities, and a majority of Indians in Chiapas, showed their support for the insurgents, following them to the forest when the army took over their villages in February 1995.

The value structure of the *Zapatistas*: identity, adversaries, and goals

The deep causes of the rebellion are obvious. *But what are the insurgents' demands, goals, and values? How do they see themselves and how do*

---

[7]   The Mexican government claims to have identified Subcomandante Marcos and the main leaders of the *Zapatistas*, and its claim appears to be plausible. It has been widely reported in the media. However, since the *Zapatistas* are still insurgents at the time of writing, I do not feel it is proper to accept these claims as a matter of fact.

[8]   Moreno Toscano (1996).

they identify their enemy? On the one hand, they place themselves in historical continuity with five hundred years of struggle against colonization and oppression. Indeed, the turning point of the peasant movement was the massive demonstration in San Cristobal de las Casas on October 12, 1992, protesting the fifth centenary of the Spanish conquest of America by destroying the statue of Chiapas' conqueror, Diego de Mazariegos. On the other hand, they see the reincarnation of this oppression in the current form of the new global order: NAFTA, and the liberalizing reforms undertaken by President Salinas, which fail to include peasants and Indians in the modernization process. The changes in the historic article 27 of the Mexican Constitution, which had given formal satisfaction to the demands of agrarian revolutionaries championed by Emiliano Zapata, became the symbol of the exclusion of peasant communities by the new order of free traders. To this critique, shared by the whole movement, Marcos and others added their own challenge to the new global order: the projection of the socialist revolutionary dream beyond the end of communism and the demise of guerrilla movements in Central America. As Marcos wrote with irony:

> There is nothing to fight for any longer. Socialism is dead. Long life to conformism, to reform, to modernity, to capitalism and to all kind of cruel etceteras. Let's be reasonable. That nothing happens in the city, or in the countryside, that everything continues the same. Socialism is dead. Long life to capital. Radio, press, and television repeat it. Some socialists, now reasonably repentant, also repeat the same.[9]

Thus, the *Zapatistas*' opposition to the new global order is twofold: they fight against the exclusionary consequences of economic modernization; but they also challenge the inevitability of a new geopolitical order under which capitalism becomes universally accepted.

The insurgents affirmed their Indian pride, and fought for the recognition of Indian rights in the Mexican Constitution. However, it does not seem that the defense of ethnic identity was a dominant element in the movement. Indeed, the Lacandon communities have been created by forced resettlement which broke up original identities from different communities and brought them together as peasants. Furthermore, it seems that, as Collier writes,

> Ethnic identity once *divided* indigenous communities from one another in the Chiapas central highlands. Recent events

---

[9]   EZLN (1994: 61); my translation.

underscore a transformation: now, in the wake of the Zapatista rebellion, peoples of diverse indigenous background are emphasizing what they share with one another in revindication of economic, social, and political exploitation.[10]

Thus, this new Indian identity was constructed through their struggle, and came to include various ethnic groups: "What is common to us is the land that gave us life and struggle."[11]

The *Zapatistas* are not subversives, but legitimate rebels. They are *Mexican patriots*, up in arms against new forms of foreign domination by American imperialism. And they are *democrats*, appealing to article 39 of the Mexican Constitution which proclaims "the right of the people to alter or modify its form of government." Thus, they call upon Mexicans to support democracy, ending *de facto* rule of one-party government based on electoral fraud. This call, coming from Chiapas, the Mexican state with the largest vote for PRI candidates, traditionally imposed by local *caciques*, elicited a strong echo in the urban middle-class sectors of a Mexican society craving freedom, and tired of systemic corruption. That the uprising took place precisely in the year of the presidential election, and in an election that was supposed to liberalize the PRI's hold on the state, is a sign of the tactical ability of the *Zapatistas*, and it was a major factor in protecting them from outright repression. President Salinas wanted to establish his legacy as both economic modernizer and political liberalizer, not only for his place in history, but for his next job: his candidacy to become the first secretary general of the newly constituted World Trade Organization, precisely the institution articulating the new world economic order. Under these circumstances, a Harvard-educated economist could hardly launch all-out military repression against a genuine peasant, Indian movement fighting against social exclusion.

[10]   Collier (1995: 1); a similar argument is put forward by Martinez Torres (1994). In the Manifesto issued by the *Zapatistas* over the Internet in November 1995, to commemorate the twelfth anniversary of the founding of their organization, they strongly emphasized their character as a Mexican movement for justice and democracy, beyond the defense of Indian identity: "The country we want, we want it for all the Mexicans, and not only for the Indians. The Democracy, Liberty, and Justice we want, we want for all Mexicans, and not only for the Indians. We do not want to separate from the Mexican Nation, we want to be part of it, we want to be accepted as equal, as persons with dignity, as human beings ... Here we are brothers, the dead of always. Dying again, but now to live" (EZLN, *Comunicado* on Internet, 17 November 1995; my translation).
[11]   *Zapatista* declaration, January 25, 1994; cited by Moreno Toscano (1996: 92).

The communication strategy of the *Zapatistas*: the Internet and the media

The success of the *Zapatistas* was largely due to their communication strategy, to the point that they can be called the *first informational guerrilla movement*. They created a media event in order to diffuse their message, while desperately trying not to be brought into a bloody war. There were, of course, real deaths, and real weapons, and Marcos, and his comrades, were ready to die. Yet, actual warfare was not their strategy. The *Zapatistas* used arms to make a statement, then parlayed the possibility of their sacrifice in front of the world media to force a negotiation and advance a number of reasonable demands which, as opinion polls seem to indicate, found widespread support in Mexican society at large.[12] Autonomous communication was a paramount objective for the *Zapatistas*:

> When the bombs were falling over the mountains south of San Cristobal, when our combatants were resisting attacks from federal troops, when the air smelled with powder and blood, the "Comite Clandestino Revolucionario Indigena del EZLN" called and told me, more or less: We must say our word and be heard. If we do not do it now, others will take our voice and lies will come out from our mouth without us wanting it. Look for a way to speak our word to those who would like to listen.[13]

The *Zapatistas'* ability to communicate with the world, and with Mexican society, and to capture the imagination of people and of intellectuals, propelled a local, weak insurgent group to the forefront of world politics. In this sense Marcos was essential. He did not have organizational control of a movement that was rooted in the Indian communities, and he did not show any signs of being a great military strategist, although he was wise in ordering retreat every time the army was to engage them. But he was extraordinarily able in establishing a communication bridge with the media, through his well-constructed writings, and by his *mise-en-scène* (the mask, the pipe, the setting of the interviews), somehow serendipitously found, as in the case of the mask that played such an important role in popularizing the revolutionaries' image: all over the world, everybody could become *Zapatista* by wearing a mask. Furthermore (although this may be an

---

[12]   According to a poll conducted on December 8 and 9, 1994, 59 percent of Mexico City residents had a "good opinion" of the *Zapatistas*, and 78 percent thought that their demands were justified (published in the newspaper *Reforma*, December 11, 1994).

[13]   Marcos, February 11, 1994; cited by Moreno Toscano (1996: 90).

over-theorization), masks are a recurrent ritual in pre-Colombian Mexican Indian cultures, so that rebellion, equalization of faces, and historical flashback played into each other in a most innovative theatrics of revolution. Essential in this strategy was the *Zapatistas'* use of telecommunications, videos, and of computer-mediated communication, both to diffuse their messages from Chiapas to the world (although probably not transmitted from the forest), and to organize a worldwide network of solidarity groups that literally encircled the repressive intentions of the Mexican government; for instance, during the army invasion of insurgent areas on February 9, 1995. It is interesting to underline that at the origins of the *Zapatistas'* use of the Internet are two developments of the 1990s: the creation of *La Neta*, an alternative computer communication network in Mexico and Chiapas; and its use by women's groups (particularly by *"De mujer a mujer"*) to link up Chiapas' NGOs with other Mexican women, as well as with women's networks in the US. *La Neta*.[14] originated in the link-up in 1989–93 between Mexican NGOs, supported by the Catholic Church, and the Institute for Global Communication in San Francisco, supported by skilled computer experts donating their time and expertise to good causes. In 1994, with the help of a grant from the Ford Foundation, *La Neta* was able to establish a node in Mexico with a private Internet provider. In 1993 *La Neta* had been established in Chiapas, with the purpose of getting local NGOs on line, including the Center for Human Rights "Bartolome de las Casas," and a dozen other organizations, which came to play a major role in informing the world during the *Zapatista* uprising. Extensive use of the Internet allowed the *Zapatistas* to diffuse information and their call throughout the world instantly, and to create a network of support groups which helped to produce an international public opinion movement that made it literally impossible for the Mexican government to use repression on a large scale. Images and information from and around the *Zapatistas* acted powerfully on the Mexican economy and politics. As Martinez Torres writes:

> Ex-President Salinas created a "bubble economy" which for several years permitted the illusion of prosperity based on a massive inflow of speculative investments in high-interest government bonds, that via a spiraling trade deficit and debt allowed the middle and working classes to enjoy for a while a multitude of imported consumer goods. Yet, as easy as it was to lure investors

---

[14] It seems necessary to clarify the multiple meaning of *La Neta* for non-Mexican readers. Besides being the figurative Spanish feminine of The Net, *la neta* is Mexican slang for "the real story."

in, any loss of investor confidence could potentially spiral into panic and run on Mexican bonds, with the possibility of causing a collapse of the system. In effect, the Mexican economy [in 1994] was an enormous confidence game. Since confidence is basically created by manipulation of information it can be destroyed in exactly the same way. In the new world order where information is the most valuable commodity, that same information can be much more powerful than bullets.[15]

This was the key to the *Zapatistas'* success. Not that they deliberately sabotaged the economy. But they were protected by their relentless media connection, and by their Internet-based worldwide alliances, from outright repression, forcing negotiation, and raising the issue of social exclusion and political corruption to the eyes and ears of world public opinion.

Indeed, experts of the Rand Corporation concur with this analysis,[16] having forecasted the eventuality of *Zapatista*-type "netwars" since 1993: "The revolutionary forces of the future may consist increasingly of widespread multi-organizational networks that have no particular national identity, claim to arise from civil society, and include aggressive groups and individuals who are keenly adept at using advanced technology for communications, as well as munitions."[17] The *Zapatistas* seem to have realized the worst nightmares of experts of the new global order.

The contradictory relationship between social movement and political institution

However, while the impact of the *Zapatistas'* demands shook up the Mexican political system, and even the Mexican economy, they became entangled in their own contradictory relationship to the political system. On the one hand, the *Zapatistas* called for the democratization of the political system, reinforcing similar demands being made within Mexican society. But they were never able to make precise the meaning of their political project, besides the obvious condemnation of electoral fraud. In the meantime, the PRI had been irreversibly shaken, divided into groups that were literally killing each other (see chapter 5). The presidential elections of August 1994 were reasonably clean, giving Zedillo, an obscure PRI candidate brought into the limelight by accidental circumstances, a triumph fueled by

---

[15] Martinez Torres (1996: 5).
[16] Rondfeldt (1995).
[17] Arquilla and Rondfeldt (1993).

fear of the unknown. Ironically, political reforms in the election process, partly as a result of *Zapatista* pressure, contributed to the legitimacy of the election, after the agreement on January 27, 1994 between all presidential candidates. The leftist opposition party, whose leader had been rebuffed by the *Zapatistas*, suffered electorally for having sought Marcos' support. In August 1994, the *Zapatistas* called a National Democratic Convention in a site of the Lacandon Forest that they named Aguascalientes, the name of the historic site where, in 1915, revolutionary leaders (Villa, Zapata, Orozco) met to establish the Revolutionary Convention. In spite of massive participation from grassroots organizations, leftist parties, intellectuals, and media, Aguascalientes exhausted itself in the symbolism of the event, this ephemeral gathering being unable to translate the new *Zapatista* language into conventional, leftist politics. Thus, in May 1995, in the midst of protracted negotiations with the government in San Andres Larrainzar, the *Zapatistas* organized a popular consultation on the possibility of becoming a civilian political force. In spite of the obvious difficulties (they were still an insurgent organization), almost 2 million people participated in the consultation throughout Mexico, supporting the proposal in their vast majority. Thus, in January 1996, to commemorate two years of their uprising, the *Zapatistas* decided to transform themselves into a political party, seeking full participation in the political process. They also decided, however, to keep their weapons until an agreement could be reached with the government on all points of contention. In January 1996 an important agreement on a future constitutional acknowledgment of Indian rights was reached, but negotiations were in process at the time of writing (in October 1996) concerning political reform, and economic matters. A difficult issue seemed to be the claim by the Indian communities to keep ownership of their land, including of their underground resources, a demand adamantly rejected by the Mexican government since it is widely believed that Chiapas is rich in hydrocarbons underground. As for political reform, the unwillingness of the PRI to release its hold on power made agreement very difficult.

The future potential of a *Zapatista* political party is uncertain. On the one hand, Marcos remains, by the end of 1996, one of the most popular leaders in Mexico. On the other hand, much of his popularity is linked to his status as a revolutionary myth. Marcos as a compromising *politico* might lose much of his appeal, something that he seems to be aware of. Thus, he and his *companeros*, were, at the time of writing, hesitant to proceed with full institutionalization of their political standing, although this is a likely outcome of their insurgency, albeit in the context of a still uncertain transformation of the Mexican political system.

Yet, regardless of the *Zapatistas'* fate, their insurgency did change Mexico, challenging the one-sided logic of modernization, characteristic of the new global order. Acting on the powerful contradictions existing inside the PRI between modernizers and the interests of a corrupt party apparatus, the debate triggered by the *Zapatistas* helped considerably to break PRI's hold on Mexico. The Mexican economy, buoyant and euphoric in 1993, was exposed in all its weakness, prompting US critics of NAFTA to claim vindication. An absent actor in the current Latin American modernization processes, the Indian peasantry (about 10 percent of the Mexican population) suddenly came to life. A constitutional reform, in the process of approval in November 1996, acknowledged the pluri-cultural character of Mexico, and gave new rights to the Indians, including the publication of textbooks in 30 Indian languages, to be used in public schools. Health and education services improved in many Indian communities, and limited self-government was in the process of implementation.

The affirmation of Indian cultural identity, albeit in a reconstructed manner, was connected to their revolt against outrageous abuse. But their fight for dignity was decisively helped by religious affiliation expressed in the deep current of populist Catholicism in Latin America, as well as by the last stand for the Marxist left in Mexico. That this left, built on the idea of the proletariat fighting for socialism with its guns, was transformed into an Indian, peasant movement of the excluded fighting for democracy, on behalf of constitutional rights, via the Internet and the mass media, shows the depth of the transformation of liberation avenues in Latin America. It also shows that the new global order induces multiple local disorder, caused by historically rooted sources of resistance to the logic of global capital flows. Chiapas Indians fighting against NAFTA by means of their alliance with ex-Maoist militants and liberation theologists are a distinctive expression of the old search for social justice under new historical conditions.

Up in Arms against the New World Order: the American Militia and the Patriot Movement in the 1990s[18]

In brief, the New World Order is a utopian system in which the US economy (along with the economy of every other nation) will be "globalized"; the wage levels of all US and European workers will be brought down to those of workers in the Third World; national boundaries will for all practical purposes cease to exist; an increased flow of Third World immigrants into the United States and Europe will have produced a non-White majority everywhere in the formerly White areas of the world; an elite consisting of international financiers, the masters of mass media, and managers of multinational corporations will call the shots; and the United Nations peacekeeping forces will be used to keep anyone from opting out of the system.

William Pierce, *National Vanguard*[19]

The Internet was one of the major reasons the militia movement expanded faster than any hate group in history. The militia's lack of an organized center was more than made up for by the instant communication and rumor potential of this new medium. Any militia member in remote Montana who had a computer and a modem could be part of an entire

---

[18]   The main source of information on the American militia and the "Patriots" is the Southern Poverty Law Center, headquartered in Montgomery, Alabama. This remarkable organization has displayed extraordinary courage and effectiveness in protecting citizens against hate groups in America since its foundation in 1979. As part of its program, it has established a Klanwatch/Militia Task Force which provides accurate information and analysis to understand and counteract new and old, anti-government and anti-people extremist groups. For most recent information, used in my analysis, see Klanwatch/Militia Task Force (1996, subsequently cited as KMTF). A well-documented account of the American militia in the 1990s is Stern (1996). I have also used the excellent analysis provided by my doctoral student Matthew Zook on militia groups and the Internet in 1996 (Zook, 1996). Additional sources specifically used in the analysis presented in this chapter are J. Cooper (1995); Anti-Defamation League (1994, 1995); Armond (1995); Armstrong (1995); Bennett (1995); Berlet and Lyons (1995); *Broadcasting and Cable* (1995); *Business Week* (1995d); Coalition for Human Dignity (1995); Cooper (1995); Heard (1995); Helvarg (1995); Jordan (1995); Ivins (1995); Maxwell and Tapia (1995); Sheps (1995); *The Nation* (1995); Orr (1995); Pollith (1995); Ross (1995); *The Gallup Poll Monthly* (1995); *The New Republic* (1995); *The New York Times Sunday* (1995a, b); *The Progressive* (1995); *Time* (1995); WEPIN Store (1995); Dees and Corcoran (1996); Winerip (1996).

[19]   Quote from White supremacist William Pierce's article in the March 1994 issue of his journal *National Vanguard*, cited by KMTF (1996: 37). Pierce is head of the National Alliance and author of the best-selling novel *The Turner Diaries*.

worldwide network that shared his or her thoughts, aspirations, organizing strategies and fears – a global family.
Kenneth Stern, *A Force upon the Plain*, p. 228

The blast of a truck loaded with fertilizer-based explosives in Oklahoma City on April 19, 1995 not only blew up a federal government building, killing 169 people, but it also exposed a powerful undercurrent of American society, until then relegated to traditional hate groups and political marginality. Timothy McVeigh, the main suspect in the bombing, used to carry with him William Pierce's novel about an underground cell, *The Patriots*, that bombs a federal building: McVeigh reportedly called Pierce's private number hours before the actual Oklahoma bombing. McVeigh, and his army buddy, Terry Nichols (both awaiting trial at the time of writing) were found to be loosely related to the Michigan Militia. The bombing occurred on the second anniversary of the Waco assault, in which most members of the Davidian cult, and their children, were killed in a siege by federal agents, an event denounced, as a rallying cry, by militia groups all around the United States.[20]

The militia groups are not terrorist, but some of their members may well be, organized in a different, but ideologically related form of movement, the "underground patriots." These are constituted on the basis of autonomous, clandestine cells, which set up their own targets in accordance with views pervasive throughout the movement. In 1994–6 a number of bombings, bank robberies, railroad sabotage, and other violent acts are believed to have been committed by such groups, and the intensity and lethality of their actions are increasing. Tons of explosives have been stolen from commercial sites, and stocks of military weaponry, including Stinger portable missiles, have disappeared from military arsenals. Attempts to develop bacteriological weapons have been discovered. And tens of thousands of "Patriots" around the United States are armed with war weapons, and undergo regular training in guerrilla tactics.[21]

The militia are the most militant, and organized, wing of a much broader, self-proclaimed "Patriot movement,"[22] whose ideological galaxy encompasses established, extreme conservative organizations,

---

[20]   The Texas Militia issued the following appeal a few days before April 19, 1995, the second anniversary of the Waco incident: "All able-bodied citizens are to assemble with their arms to celebrate their right to keep and bear arms and to assemble as militias in defense of the Republic" (cited in the editorial of *The Nation*, 1995: 656).
[21]   KMTF (1996).
[22]   KMTF (1996); Stern (1996).

such as the John Birch Society; a whole array of traditional, white supremacist, neo-nazi, and anti-semitic groups, including the Ku-Klux-Klan, and the Posse Comitatus; fanatic religious groups such as Christian Identity, an anti-semitic sect emanating from Victorian England's British Israelism; anti-federal government groups, such as the Counties' Rights Movements, Wise Use anti-environmental coalition, the National Taxpayers' Union, and defenders of "Common Law" courts. The Patriots' galaxy also extends, in loose forms, to the powerful Christian Coalition, as well as to a number of militant "Right to Life" groups, and counts on the sympathy of many members of the National Rifle Association, and pro-gun advocates. The direct appeal of the Patriots may reach to as many as 5 million people in America, according to well-informed sources,[23] although the very character of the movement, with its blurred boundaries, and the lack of organized membership, makes impossible an accurate statistical estimate. Still, its influence can be counted in millions, not thousands, of supporters. What these disparate groups, formerly un-related, came to share in the 1990s, and what broadens their appeal, is their common, declared enemy: the US federal government, as representative of the "New World Order," being set up against the will of American citizens. According to views pervasive throughout the Patriot movement, this "New World Order," aimed at destroying American sovereignty, is enacted by a conspiracy of global financial interests and global bureaucrats that have captured the US federal government. At the core of this new system are the World Trade Organization, the Trilateral Commission, the International Monetary Fund, and, above all, the United Nations, whose "peacekeeping forces" are seen as an international, mercenary army, spearheaded by Hong Kong policemen and Gurkha units, ready to suppress people's sovereignty. Four events seemed to confirm this conspiracy for the Patriots: the passing of NAFTA in 1993; the approval by Clinton of the Brady Bill in 1994, establishing limited controls on the sale of some types of automatic weapons; the siege of white supremacist Randy Weaver in Idaho, resulting in the killing of his wife by the FBI, in 1992; and the tragic siege of Waco, leading to the death of David Koresh and his followers in 1993. A paranoid reading of these events led to the conviction that the government was proceeding to disarm citizens, to subdue them later, submitting Americans to surveillance from hidden cameras, and black helicopters, and implanting bio-chips in the newborn. To this global threat, on jobs, on privacy, on liberty, on the American way of life, they oppose the Bible and the original American Constitution, expunged of its Amendments. In

---

[23]   Berlet and Lyons (1995); KMTF (1996); Winerip (1996).

accordance with these texts, both received from God, they affirm the sovereignty of citizens and its direct expression in county govern-ments, not acknowledging the authority of federal government, its laws, its courts, as well as the validity of the Federal Reserve Bank. The choice is dramatic. In the words of the Militia of Montana, created in February 1994, and an organizational inspiration for the whole move-ment: "Join the Army and Serve the UN or Join America and Serve the Militia" (Motto of WWW home page of the Montana Militia). Federal agents, particularly those from the Bureau of Alcohol, Tobacco, and Firearms, are considered to be in the frontline of the repression against Americans on behalf of the emerging world government. This, in the view of the militia, justifies making federal agents potential targets of the movement. Thus, as popular broad-caster Gordon Liddy put it in one of his talk shows: "They've got a big target [on their chest]: ATF. Don't shoot at that because they've got a vest on underneath that. Head shots, head shots. Kill the sons of bitches!"[24] In some segments of this highly diverse Patriot movement there is also a powerful mythology rooted in eschatological views of the world and End of Times prophecies (see chapter 1). Following the Book of Revelations, chapter 13, preachers such as tele-evangelist Pat Robertson, the leader of the Christian Coalition, remind Christians that they may be asked to submit to the satanic "Mark of the Beast," variously identified as new codes on paper money, supermarket bar codes, or microchip technology.[25] Resisting the new global, ungodly order, coming at the End of Times, is seen as a Christian duty and an American citizen's right. Yet, the sinister colorfulness of the move-ment's mythology sometimes obscures its profile, and actually downplays its political and social significance. This is why it is im-portant to pay attention to the diversity of the movement, while still emphasizing its underlying commonality.

The militias and the Patriots: a multi-thematic information network

Militias, self-organized citizens armed to defend their country, religion, and freedom, are institutions that played an important role during the first century of America's existence.[26] The state militias were replaced by state national guards in 1900. However, in the 1990s, starting with the Montana Militia, right-wing populist groups have formed "unorganized militias," using some legal ambiguity in federal

---

[24]   Stern (1996: 221).
[25]   Berlet and Lyons (1995).
[26]   Whisker (1992); J. Cooper (1995).

laws to circumvent the legal prohibition to form military units outside of government control. The most distinctive feature of militia groups is that they are armed, sometimes with war weapons, and are structured in a military-style chain of command. By the end of 1995, KMTF could count 441 active militias in all 50 states, with paramilitary training sites in at least 23 states (see figure 2.1). Numbers of militia members are difficult to estimate. Berlet and Lyons ventured to evaluate them, in 1995, at between 15,000 and 40,000.[27] By all accounts they are growing rapidly. There is no national organization. Each state's militia is independent, and there are sometimes several, unrelated militia groups in the same state: 33 in Ohio, with about 1,000 members, and hundreds of thousands of sympathizers, according to police sources.[28] The Militia of Montana is the founding example, but the largest is the Michigan Militia, with several thousand active members. Their ideology, beyond the common opposition to the new world order and to the federal government, is highly diversified. Their membership is overwhelmingly white, Christian, and predominantly male. They certainly include a significant number of racists, anti-semites, and sexists among their ranks. Yet, most militia groups do not define themselves as racist or sexist, and some of them (for instance the Michigan Militia) make an explicit anti-racist statement in their propaganda. In Zook's analysis of militia pages in the World Wide Web, focusing on 11 of the most popular militia, seven of the home pages made anti-racist statements, four made no mention of race, and none contained overt racism.[29] Two pages took anti-sexist stands, two welcomed women, and the others did not mention sex. Indeed, the Michigan Militia refused to support the "Montana freemen," during their 1996 siege in a ranch, because they were racist. And one of the Militia Home Pages "E Pluribus Unum," part of the Ohio Militia, is run by an African-American Christian fundamentalist couple. To be sure, these statements could be faked, but given the importance of Internet posting to contact new members, it would be inconsistent to misrepresent the ideology on which new recruits are attracted. It seems that the militia and the Patriots, while including traditional racist, anti-semitic, hate groups, have a much broader ideological constituency, and this is exactly one of the reasons for their new success. Namely, their ability to reach out across the ideological spectrum to unite all sources of disaffection against the federal government. As KMTF's report says:

[27] Berlet and Lyons (1995).
[28] Winerip (1996).
[29] Zook (1996).

Figure. 2.1 Geographical distribution of Patriot groups in the US by number of groups and paramilitary training sites in each state, 1996

Source: Southern Poverty Law Center, Klanwatch/Militia Task Force, Montgomery, Alabama, 1996

Level of Patriot activity indicated by number of groups in each state

- 5 and under
- 6–10
- 11–20
- 21–30
- over 30
- state with paramilitary training site

Unlike their factious white supremacist predecessors, Patriots
have been able to bridge minor ideological differences in favor
of a broad unity on the anti-government agenda. As a result, they
have created the most inviting insurgent force in recent history,
home to a wide variety of anti-government groups whose organizational roles may differ dramatically.[30]

Two fast-expanding components of the Patriot movement are the
Counties' Rights movement, and the "Common Law" courts. The first
is a militant wing of the Wise Use coalition, which has growing influence in the Western states. The coalition opposes environmental
regulation enforced by the federal government and appeals to the
"customs and culture" of logging, mining, and grazing on public land.
Land-use zoning is equated with socialism, and management of the
ecosystem is considered to be a part of the new world order.[31]
Consequently, the movement asserts the right of county sheriffs to
arrest federal land managers, which prompted a number of violent
incidents. People and communities are urged to acknowledge exclusively the authority of their elected officials at the municipal and
county level, rejecting the federal government's right to legislate on
their property. Seventy counties have passed Wise Use ordinances
claiming local control over public land, and violent actions have
intimidated environmentalists and federal land managers from New
Mexico and Nevada to northern Idaho and Washington. Common
Law courts have been established in 40 states, supported by an array
of books and videos that claim to provide a legal basis for people to
reject the judicial system, setting up their own "judges," "trials," and
"juries." They have even established a national "Supreme Court of
Common Law" with 23 justices, based on the Bible and on their own
interpretation of law. Common Law followers declare themselves
"sovereign," that is freemen, and refuse accordingly to pay taxes and
social security, to comply with driving licensing, and to submit to all
other government controls not contemplated in the original
American legal body. To protect their sovereignty, and retaliate
against public officials, they often file commercial liens against
targeted public officials and judges, creating a nightmarish confusion
in a number of county courts. As an extension of the Common Law
movement, a rapidly expanding network of people, from Montana to
California, refuse the authority of the Federal Reserve Bank to print
money, and they issue their own bank documents, including cashier
checks, with such good reproduction technology that they have often

[30]   KMTF (1996: 14).
[31]   Helvarg (1995).

been cashed, prompting a number of arrests for forgery and fraud. These practices are making the Common Law movement the most confrontational of all the Patriot groups, and were at the root of the three-month stand-off between "freemen" and the FBI in a ranch in Jordan, Montana, in 1996.

Such a diverse, almost chaotic, movement cannot have a stable organization, or even a coordinating instance. Yet, the homogeneity of its core world vision and, particularly, its identification of a common enemy are remarkable. This is because linkages between groups and individuals do exist, but they are carried out through the media (radio, mainly), through books, pamphlets, speaking tours, and alternative press, by Fax, and, mainly, through the Internet.[32] According to KMTF, "the computer is the most vital piece of equipment in the Patriot movement's arsenal."[33] On the Internet there are numerous militia bulletin board systems, home pages, and chat groups; for instance, the Usenet group MAM, established in 1995. Several reasons have been proposed for the widespread use of the Internet by militiamen. One is that, as Stern writes, "Internet was the perfect culture in which to grow the virus of conspiracy theory. Messages appeared on the screen with no easy way to separate junk from credible . . . For conspiracy enthusiasts like militia members, unverified statements from cyberspace reaffirmed their set conclusions by providing an endless stream of additional 'evidence.'"[34] Also, the frontier spirit characteristic of the Internet fits well with the freemen, expressing themselves, and making their statement without mediation or government control. More importantly, the network structure of the Internet reproduces exactly the autonomous, spontaneous networking of militia groups, and of the Patriots at large, without boundaries, and without definite plan, but sharing a purpose, a feeling, and, most of all, an enemy. It is mainly on the Internet (backed up by Fax and direct mailing) that the movement thrives and organizes itself. It was through the Associated Electronic Network News, organized by the Thompsons in Indianapolis, that a conspiracy theory was diffused according to which the Oklahoma bombing was a provocation by the federal government similar to Hitler's arson of the Reichstag in order to crack down on the militia. Other bulletin board systems, such as the "Paul Revere Net," link up groups around the country, exchange information, circulate rumors, and coordinate actions. For example, confidential reports inform browsers that Gorbachev, after giving a speech in California saying that "we are now

---

[32] KMTF (1996); Stern (1996); Zook (1996).
[33] KMTF (1996: 16).
[34] Stern (1996: 228).

entering the new world order," went on to hide in a Southern California naval base to oversee the dismantling of America's armed forces in preparation for the arrival of the world order's army. Indeed, its arrival took place in May 1996, when a permanent base was established in New Mexico to train hundreds of German pilots in cooperation with the US Air Force. Or so thought the thousands of callers that submerged the Pentagon's switchboard after CNN reported the opening of such a base.

Radio talk shows are also important. Rush Limbaugh's audience of 20 million on 600 stations around the country is an instrument of political influence without parallel in 1990s America. While he is not a militia supporter, his themes ("femi-nazis," "eco-wacos") resonate in the movement. Other popular radio programs are more directly in tune with the Patriots: Gordon Liddy's call-in show, or *The Intelligence Report*, hosted by white supremacist Mark Koernke. Alternative cable channels, broadcasting similar topics to similar audiences, include National Empowerment Television, Jones Intercable, and Time–Warner-owned Paragon Cable in Florida, which features *Race&Reason*, an anti-semitic, racist show. A myriad of newspapers and bulletins, such as Washington DC's *Spotlight*, or the white supremacist tract *The Turner Diaries*, add to a highly decentralized, extensive network of alternative media. This network diffuses targeted information, airs people's resentment, publicizes right, extremist ideas, spreads rumors of conspiracies, and purveys the eschatological mythology that has become the cultural background for end-of-millennium right-wing populism. Thus, while the FBI looks in vain for proof of an organized conspiracy to overturn the government by force, the actual conspiracy, with no names (or multiple names), and with no organization (or hundreds of them), flows in the information networks, feeding paranoia, connecting anger, and maybe spilling blood.

The Patriots' banners

In spite of its diversity, the Patriot movement, with the militia at its forefront, does share some common goals, beliefs, and foes. It is this set of values and purposes that constructs a world vision and, ultimately, defines the movement itself.

There is an underlying, simple, but powerful view of the world and society which is expressed in different forms in the Patriot movement. According to this vision, America is divided into two kinds of people: producers and parasites. Producers, working people, are oppressed between two layers of parasites: corrupt government officials, wealthy corporate elites, and bankers, at the top; and stupid and lazy people, undeserving of the welfare they receive of society, at the bottom. The situation is being made worse by the current process of globalization, steered by the United Nations and international financial institutions, on behalf of corporate elites and government bureaucracies, which threatens to transform ordinary people into mere slaves of a world-wide plantation-like economy. God will prevail, but for this citizens must take up their guns to fight for "the future of America itself."[35] From this world vision emerges a specific set of targets for the move-ment, which organize its practice.

First of all, the militia, and the Patriots in general, are an extreme libertarian movement (and, in this sense, very different from tra-ditional Nazis or fascists who call for a strong state). Their enemy is the federal government. In their view, the basic units of society are the individual, the family, and the local community. Beyond that immediate level of face-to-face acknowledgment, government is only tolerated as the direct expression of the citizens' will; for example, county governments, with elected officials who can be known and controlled on a personal basis. Higher levels of government are suspected, and the federal government is denounced outright as illegitimate, as having usurped citizens' rights and manipulated the Constitution to overstep the original mandate of the founding fathers of America. For militiamen, Thomas Jefferson and Patrick Henry are the heroes, and Alexander Hamilton the obvious villain. This rejec-tion of the legitimacy of federal government expresses itself in very concrete, powerful attitudes and actions: rejection of federal taxes, refusal of environmental regulation and land-use planning, sovereignty of common law courts, jury nullification (namely deciding as jurors in court cases not in accordance with the law but according to their consciences), pre-eminence of county governments over higher authorities, and hatred of federal law-enforcement agencies. At the limit, the movement calls for civil disobedience against the government, backing it up, if and when necessary, with the guns of "natural law"-abiding citizens.

While the federal government and its enforcement agencies are the immediate enemies, and the immediate cause of the mobilization of the Patriots, a more ominous threat looms on the horizon: the new world order. The new world order, a notion popularized by tele-evangelist Pat Robertson, extrapolating from Bush's post-Cold War end-of-history ideology, implies that the federal government is actively working toward the goal of one world government in collaboration with Russia (particularly with Gorbachev, considered to be a key strategist in the plot). This project is supposedly being carried out by

[35]   M. Cooper (1995).

the intermediary of international organizations: the United Nations, the new World Trade Organization, and the International Monetary Fund. The placement of American military troops under the command of the United Nations, and the signing of NAFTA, are considered but the first steps toward such a new order, often explicitly associated with the coming of the Information Age. The actual impact on the American people is seen as their economic impoverishment for the benefit of multinational corporations and banks, and their political disfranchisement for the sake of global political bureaucracies.

Together with these localist, libertarian strands, a third major theme runs through the movement: a backlash against feminists (not against women as long as they remain in their traditional role), gays, and minorities (as beneficiaries of government protection). There is one clearly predominant characteristic in the Patriot movement: in a large majority, they are white, heterosexual males. The "Angry White Male" (actually the name of one Patriot organization) seem to have come together in this mixture of reactions to economic deprivation, reaffirmation of traditional values and privileges, and cultural backlash. Traditional national and family values (that is, patriarchalism) are affirmed against what are considered to be excessive privileges accorded by society to gender, cultural, and ethnic minorities, as exemplified by affirmative action and anti-discrimination legislation. While this theme does connect with a much older rejection of racial equality by white supremacist groups and anti-immigrant coalitions, it is new in its comprehensiveness, particularly because of the explicit rejection of women's rights, and in its hostile targeting of liberal values diffused by the mainstream media.

A fourth theme present in most of the movement is the intolerant affirmation of the superiority of Christian values, so linking up closely with the Christian fundamentalist movement, analyzed in chapter 1. Most Patriots seem to subscribe to the pretension that Christian values and rituals, as interpreted by their defenders, must be enforced through the institutions of society; for example, mandatory prayer in public schools and the screening of libraries and the media to censor what would be considered anti-Christian or anti-family values. The widespread anti-abortion movement, with fanatic assassins at its fringes, is its most notorious organizational instrument. Christian fundamentalism seems to be pervasive throughout the whole movement. It might seem paradoxical, this connection between an extreme libertarian movement, such as the militia, and Christian fundamentalism, a movement that aims at theocracy and therefore would seek government imposition of moral and religious values on its citizens. However, this is only a contradiction in the historical horizon, since in 1990s America both fundamentalists and libertarians converge on the destruction of a federal government that is perceived as being apart from both God and The People.

Guns and Bibles could well be the movement's motto.[36] Guns were the rallying point around which the militia came together in 1994 in response to the Brady Bill. A vast coalition was formed against this, and subsequent attempts at gun control. Around the powerful lobby of the National Rifle Association, controlling many votes in Congress, coalesced rural folks around the country, gun shop owners, extreme libertarians, and militia groups, to make the defense of the constitutional right to bear arms the last line of defense for America as it ought to be. Guns equal freedom. The Wild West rides again, on the streets of Los Angeles as on the Michigan farms. Two of the deepest features of American culture, its rugged individualism and its mistrust of despotic governments, from which many immigrants escape to come to America, provide the seal of authenticity to the resistance against threats generated by the informationalization of society, the globalization of economy, and the professionalization of politics.

Who are the Patriots?

A component of the movement is certainly made up of disaffected farmers in the Midwest and in the West, supported by a miscellaneous cast of small town societies, from coffeeshop owners to traditionalist pastors. But it would be inaccurate to consider that the appeal of the movement is limited to a rural world phased out by technological modernization. There are no demographic data on the movement's composition, but a simple look at the geographical distribution of the militia (figure 2.1) shows its territorial, thus social, diversity. The groups of states with the highest numbers of militia activity include such diverse areas as Pennsylvania, Michigan, Florida, Texas, Colorado, and California, more or less following the most populous states (minus New York, plus Colorado), but this is precisely the point: militia seem to be where people are, all over the country, not just in Montana. If we consider the Christian Coalition to be a part of the movement, then Patriots are present in the suburbs of most large metropolitan areas (there are about 1.5 million members of the Christian Coalition). Some militia groups, for instance in New Hampshire, and in California, seem to recruit among computer professionals. Thus, it does not seem that the Patriots are a class-based, or territorially specific movement. Rather, they are, fundamentally, a cultural and political movement, defenders of the

[36] Maxwell and Tapia (1995).

traditions of the country against cosmopolitan values, and of self-rule of local people against the imposition of global order. However, if class is not relevant in the composition of the movement, it is relevant in the identification of its enemies. Corporate elites; bankers; the wealthy, powerful and arrogant big firms, and their lawyers; and scientists and researchers, are their enemies. Not as a class, but as representatives of an un-American world order. Indeed, the ideology is not anti-capitalist, but is, rather, an ideology in defense of free capitalism, opposed to a corporate manifestation of state capitalism that appears to be close to socialism. Thus, a class analysis of the Patriots does not seem to address the essence of the movement. It is a political insurgency that cuts across class lines and regional differentiation. And it relates to the social and political evolution of American society at large.

The militia, the Patriots, and American society in the 1990s

Right-wing populism is hardly a novelty in the United States; indeed, it is a phenomenon that has played an important role in American politics throughout the country's history.[37] Furthermore, angry popular reactions to economic distress have occurred in both America and Europe in different forms, from classic fascism and Nazism to the xenophobic and ultra-nationalist movements of recent years. One of the conditions that can help explain the fast spread of the militia, besides the Internet, is growing economic hardship and social inequality in America. Men's average income has deteriorated substantially in the past two decades, particularly during the 1980s. Families are barely maintaining the living standards of a quarter of a century ago by putting in the contribution of two wage earners instead of one. On the other hand, the top 1 percent of households increased its average income from $327,000 to about $567,000 between 1976 and 1993, while average family income remains at about $31,000. CEO's pay is 190 times higher than that of their average worker.[38] For the American worker and small entrepreneur, the age of globalization and informationalization has been the age of a relative, and often an absolute, decline in their standard of living, reversing the historical trend of the improvement of each generation's material well-being over that of previous generations. Occasionally, the culture of the new global rich adds insult to injury. For instance, Montana, the seedbed of the new militia, is also one of the favorite destinations of the new billionaires, fond of acquiring thousands of acres of pristine land to

[37]   Lipset and Raab (1978).
[38]   *The New York Times* (1995b).

build ranches from which to run their global networks. Ranchers in the area resented these moves.[39]

Furthermore, at the moment when the traditional family becomes indispensable as an instrument of both financial and psychological security, it has been falling apart, in the wake of the gender war ignited by the resistance of patriarchalism to women's rights (see chapter 4). Cultural challenges to sexism and to heterosexual orthodoxy confuse masculinity. In addition, a new wave of immigration, this time from Latin America and Asia, and the growing multi-ethnicity of America, although in continuity with the country's history, add to the feeling of loss of control. The shifts from agriculture and manufacturing to services, and from goods handling to information processing, undermine acquired skills and work subcultures. And the end of the Cold War, with the collapse of communism, eliminates the easy indentification of the external enemy, hampering the chances of bringing America together in a common cause. The age of information becomes the age of confusion, and thus the age of fundamental affirmation of traditional values and uncompromising rights. Bureaucratic, and sometimes violent, reactions by law-enforcement agencies to various forms of protest deepen the anger, sharpen the feelings, and seem to justify the call to arms, bringing the new American militia in direct confrontation with the emerging global order.

The Lamas of Apocalypse: Japan's *Aum Shinrikyo*[40]

The final goal of body techniques that Aum tries to develop by yoga and austerity is a mode of communication without any medium. Communication can be obtained by having resonance with others' bodies without relying on consciousness of identity as self, without using the medium of language.

Masachi Osawa, *Gendai*, October 1995[41]

---

[39]   Stevens (1995).

[40]   The analysis of *Aum Shinrikyo* presented here essentially reproduces the contribution to our joint study, and article, by Shujiro Yazawa, who conducted most of the research on *Aum*, although I also studied the movement, in cooperation with Yazawa, in Tokyo in 1995. Sources directly used in the analysis, besides reports in newspapers and magazines, are Aoyama (1991); Asahara (1994, 1995); *Vajrayana Sacca* (1994); Drew (1995); Fujita (1995); *Mainichi Shinbun* (1995); Miyadai (1995); Ohama (1995); Osawa (1995); Nakazawa et al. (1995); Shimazono (1995); Yazawa (forthcoming).

[41]   Translated by Yazawa.

On March 20, 1995, an attack with sarin gas in three different trains on the Tokyo subway killed 12 people, injured over 5,000, and shook the foundations of the apparently stable Japanese society. The police, using information from a similar incident which had occurred in Matsumoto in June 1994, determined that the attack had been carried out by members of *Aum Shinrikyo*, a religious cult at the core of a network of business activities, political organizations, and paramilitary units. The ultimate goal of *Aum Shinrikyo*, according to its own discourse, was to survive the coming apocalypse, to save Japan, and eventually the world, from the war of extermination that would inevitably result from the competing efforts by Japanese corporations and American imperialism to establish a new world order and a united world government. To overcome Armageddon, *Aum* would prepare a new kind of human being, rooted in spirituality and self-improvement through meditation and exercise. Yet, to face the aggression of world powers that be, *Aum* had to defend itself by taking up the challenge of new weapons of extermination. The challenge came quickly indeed. The cult's founder and guru, Shoko Asahara, was arrested and put on trial (probably to be sentenced to death), along with the most prominent members of the cult. The cult itself continues to exist, albeit with a reduced constituency.

The debate over the origins, development, and goals of *Aum* went on for months in the Japanese media, and has not receded more than one and a half years later, at the time of writing. It prompted fundamental questions about the actual state of Japanese society. How could such acts be possible in one of the wealthiest, least unequal, safest, most ethnically homogeneous, and most culturally integrated societies in the world? Specially striking for the public was the fact that the cult had recruited particularly among scientists and engineers from some of the best Japanese universities. Coming in a period of political uncertainty, after the crisis of the LDP, Japan's governing party for almost five decades, the apparently senseless act was seen as a symptom. But a symptom of what? To understand a very complex development, with fundamental, but not so obvious, implications, we must reconstruct the evolution of the cult, starting with the biography of its founder, who played a crucial role in this development.

Asahara and the development of *Aum Shinrikyo*

Asahara was born blind in a poor family in Kumamoto Prefecture. He attended a special school for the blind, and, after completing his studies there, prepared for admission examinations into Tokyo University. His explicit project was to become Prime Minister. After failing the exam, he opened a pharmacy and specialized in the sale of traditional Chinese medicine. Some of these medicines were of questionable use, and his lack of a license eventually led to his arrest. After marrying and having a child, in 1977 he shifted his interest to religion. He educated himself in Sento, and tried to develop a spiritual health care method based on Taoism. The decisive change in his life came when he joined the Agon cult, a religious group preaching perfection through the practice of austerity.[42] Meditation, physical exercise, yoga, and esoteric Buddhism were essential practices of the group. Asahara combined Agon's teaching with his own ideas about creating a new religious world. In 1984, he opened a yoga school in Shibuya, Tokyo. At the same time, he established *Aum* as a corporation (*Aum* is a Sanskrit word meaning "deep wisdom"). He developed his yoga school's reputation by making claims in the media about his own supernatural powers, as shown by his ability to float in the air (a claim he backed up with photos showing himself in action, a first venture in special visual effects, which signaled *Aum*'s future emphasis on media technology). Stating that God had ordered him to build a utopia with a few elected ones, in 1985 the yoga master became a religious leader, and instructed his disciples at the school in search of perfection through the hard practice of austerity. In 1986 Asahara created the formal religious cult *Aum Shinsen*, with about 350 members. Most of them were inducted as priests, unlike other cults where only a small minority of members can devote themselves fully to the practice of austerity and meditation. This high ratio of priesthood was very important for the future of *Aum*, since it had to find substantial means of financial support for such a large number of priests. Thus, *Aum* requested donations of all assets from its recruits (sometimes by force), priced teachings and training seminars, and invested in various businesses. Among these business activities, it created a very profitable commercial chain of stores (*Mahaposha*), selling personal computers at discount price, and specializing in distribution of pirate software. With the profits from these computer stores, *Aum* financed a number of eating and drinking outlets, and other miscellaneous businesses. In 1987, the name was changed to *Aum Shinrikyo* (the Japanese word for "truth"). A year later, as a step to utopia, *Aum* built its headquarters in a village in the foothills of Mount Fuji. In spite of some resistance from the authorities, it finally obtained recognition as a non-profit, tax-exempt, religious corporation. Having consolidated Aum's position, and with the support of about 10,000 members, Asahara decided to enter politics in order to transform society. In

---

[42]   Austerity implies strenuous physical exercise and privation of food and bodily pleasure as a regular form of existence.

1990, he and 25 other *Aum* members ran for Congress but obtained almost no votes. They claimed their votes had been stolen. This political disappointment was a turning point for the ideology of *Aum*, which abandoned its attempts to participate in the political process. Future efforts would be directed toward confrontation with government. Shortly afterwards, an attempt to build a new hall for the cult in Naminomura was fiercely opposed by local residents, and, after a few incidents, *Aum* members were arrested. The media echoed rumors of kidnapping and extortions of former cult members. When a group of victims of *Aum* formed an association, their lawyer disappeared. The cult went into a paranoiac frenzy, feeling harassed by police, government, and the media.

In this context, Asahara started to emphasize the eschatological line of thinking that had been present in the cult's themes from its inception. Asahara, referring to the prophecies of Nostradamus, predicted that, around the year 2000, nuclear war between the US and the USSR would break out, and that, as a result, 90 percent of urban dwellers would die. Thus, the very best should prepare themselves to survive the disaster. To do so, hard physical exercise, austerity, and meditation, following the teachings of Asahara, would be needed in order to create a superhuman race. *Aum*'s meditation halls would be the birth places of a new civilization after Armageddon. Yet spiritual perfection would not be enough. The enemy would use all kinds of new weapons: nuclear, chemical, bacteriological. Therefore, *Aum*, as the last chance for humankind's survival, should be prepared for this terrible warfare at the End of Times. Consequently, *Aum* established several companies to buy and process materials for development of chemical and biological weapons. It imported one helicopter and several armored vehicles, bought on Russia's black market, and started to learn how to design and produce high-technology weapons, included laser-guided guns.[43]

In a logical development, in 1994, *Aum* decided to become a counter-state. It formed ministries and bureaux, mirroring the structure of the Japanese state, and appointed members to each ministry and agency, to constitute a shadow government, with Asahara at the top of this holy counter-state. The role of this organization would be to lead the cult and the few elected survivors in the final battle against the forces of evil, namely the united world government (dominated by multinational corporations) and its direct agents: American imperialists and Japanese police. In June 1994, a first experiment with nerve gas was carried out in Matsumoto, killing seven people. Police investigations of the cult, and reports in the media, prompted the

[43]   Drew (1995).

sense among cult members that confrontation was inevitable, and that the first episodes leading to the prophecy were taking place. The attack on Tokyo's subway, a few months later, propelled the cult, Japan, and maybe the world, into a new era of messianic critique potentially backed by weapons of mass extermination.

Aum's beliefs and methodology

The beliefs and teachings of *Aum Shinrikyo* are complex, and have been changing somewhat throughout the cult's evolution. Yet it is possible to reconstruct the essence of its vision and practice on the basis of available documents and reports. At the root of its purpose and method, *Aum* stresses the notion of deliverance (*gedatsu*), that is, according to Osawa, one of *Aum's* best observers:

> Dissolving the integrity of the body as individual to overcome the locality of the body. Believers must transcend the boundary between the body and its external world by differentiating the body endlessly. By continual exercise, it is possible to reach the point where the body can be felt as fluid, gas, or wave of energy. The body tries to integrate itself as individual because we have self consciousness in the inner side of the integrated body. It is this inner side of the body that organizes the self. Therefore, to disintegrate our bodies to the extent that we feel our bodies as fluid or gas, means the disorganization of ourselves. This is deliverance.[44]

Deliverance means true freedom and happiness. Indeed, humans have lost their selves and become impure. The real world is in fact an illusion, and life as usually lived by people is full of burdens and pains. Realizing and accepting this harsh reality enables one to face death in truth. To reach this truth, through deliverance, *Aum* developed a technology of meditation and austerity (*Mahayana*), with precise indicators of the stage of perfection achieved by every believer at various stages.

However, for most followers, deliverance is uncertain at best. Thus, two additional elements provide coherence to *Aum's* method and vision: on the one hand, faith in the guru's superpowers, guaranteeing salvation after a certain stage of perfection is achieved; on the other hand, a sense of urgency derived from the coming catastrophic crisis of civilization. In *Aum's* view, there is a direct link between the end of the world and the salvation of believers, who are preparing for the apocalypse by acquiring supernatural powers. In this sense, *Aum*

[44]   Osawa (1995).

is at the same time a mystical cult and a practical corporation providing survival training for doomsday 2000 – at a price.

Aum and Japanese society

Most *Aum* priests were young university graduates. In 1995, 47.5 percent of its priests were in their twenties, and 28 percent in their thirties; 40 percent were women. Indeed, an explicit goal of *Aum* was "to solve gender differences" by changing "the inner world of gender." In the absence of a powerful feminist movement in Japan (as yet), *Aum* gained some influence among college-educated women frustrated by an extremely patriarchal society. A high proportion of the men were graduates in the natural sciences from distinguished universities.[45] *Aum*'s appeal to highly educated youth came as a shock to the Japanese public. According to Yazawa,[46] this appeal can be better understood by the alienation of Japanese youth, in the aftermath of the defeat of the powerful Japanese social movements of the 1960s. Instead of transformative social values, the "Information Society" was promised. But this promise fell short of cultural innovation and spiritual fulfillment. In a society with no mobilized social challengers, and without values of cultural transformation, a new generation has grown up since the 1970s in material affluence, but without spiritual meaning. It was seduced at the same time by technology and esotericism. Many *Aum* believers were people who could not find a place for their desires for change and meaningfulness in the bureaucratized structure of schools, administrations, and corporations, and were revolting against traditional, authoritarian family structures. They had no purpose in their lives, and not even enough physical space to express themselves in the congested conurbation of Japanese cities. The only thing left for them was their own bodies. For many of these youths, their desire was to live in a different world by using science and technology to help their bodies transcend natural and social limits. In Yazawa's concept, theirs was a desire based on the "informationalization of the body," meaning the transformation of human physical potential by the power of ideas, beliefs, and meditation. This is where *Aum*'s methodology of deliverance fitted particularly well. The promise of deliverance was that people could feel themselves and others at the same time. Community and belonging was restored, but as an expression of the self, through perfection and control of the body's own limits, not as a result of external imposition, enabling communication without a medium by directly connecting to other bodies. This new form of com-

[45]   *Mainichi Shinbun* (1995).
[46]   Castells et al. (1996); Yazawa (forthcoming).

munication was only considered to be possible among bodies that had already overcome their locality. Asahara's body, by having already escaped from his body's locality, would be the catalyst to induce the deliverance of others. As a result, a virtual community of communicating bodies was gradually formed, with Asahara as the sole center of this community.[47]

Some of these ideas and practices are not unusual in yoga and in Tibetan Buddhism. What was specific to *Aum*'s version of disembodied communication through yoga and meditation was, on the one hand, its technological implementation (for instance, through the extensive use of training videos, and of electronically stimulating devices), and, on the other hand, its political instrumentation. In some instances, experiments were carried out by means of electronic helmets attached to the followers' heads, to enable them to receive communication waves directly from the guru's brain (a little technological push to the theory of disembodied communication). Asahara's ideas developed finally into the identity of his self or "true self," in which the selves of all disciples were to be ultimately dissolved. Communication channels with the outside world were closed off, as it was declared the enemy, heading toward Armageddon. The inside network was structured in a hierarchical organization, in which communication came from the top, with no horizontal channels of communication among the believers. In this view, the outside world was unreal, and the virtual reality generated by a combination of technology and yoga techniques was the real world. The outside, unreal world was evolving toward its apocalypse. The inner, virtual reality, internally communicated world, was the fundamental reality, preparing itself for salvation.

In the latest stage of the discourse of *Aum*, a more precise social prediction took shape: future social change would be caused by a cycle of economic recession, then depression, followed by war and death. Natural disasters and economic depression would overtake Japan in the last years of the millennium. The reason: stepped up competition from other Asian countries using their comparative advantage of lower labor costs. To answer this challenge, Japan would develop its military industry and try to impose its will on Asia, in the interests of Japanese corporations striving to create a world government under the control of multinational corporations. In response, the United States would enter the war against Japan to protect its Asian vassals, and to advance its own project of world government. The war would linger on, and all kinds of high-technology weapons would be used. This would be a war of extermination, which could lead to the end of

47   Osawa (1995).

humankind. In this account, *Aum*'s vision reflected, in a distorted and schematic way, the fears of Japanese society about losing its competitive edge in the world economy, about a potential conflict with the United States, and about the catastrophic consequences of uncontrolled new technologies.

What distinguished *Aum* was its response to these threats. To be ready for such a war, and to survive it (as in some popular science fiction movies of the 1990s), would require both the rebirth of spirituality and the mastery of advanced weapons technology, particularly biological, chemical, and laser-guided weapons. As mentioned above, *Aum* did indeed try to acquire these weapons and hire scientists able to develop them in the United States, Israel, and Russia. While pursuing spiritual perfection, and uniting its members in a collective, spiritual body, *Aum* equipped itself to fight the survival war, and declared such a war in advance, against the supporters of the united world government looming on the horizon.

In a distorted way, *Aum*'s fears and ideas were similar to those found in many of the youth subcultures of Japan. According to Shinji Miyadai, two perceptions of the world could be found among them.[48] The first one was that of an "endless everyday life" without purpose, goals, or happiness. The second was that of possible commonality only in the case of a nuclear war that would force the survivors to unite. By building on both ideas – that is, by finding happiness in the inner self and preparing for the post-nuclear war commune – *Aum* directly connected with these expressions of cultural despair from youth alienated in an over-organized society. In this sense, *Aum* was not an act of collective madness, but the hyperbolic, amplified manifestation of educated rebels, manipulated by a messianic guru at the cross-roads between meditation and electronics, business and spirituality, informational politics and high-tech warfare. *Aum* appears to have been a horror caricature of Japanese Information Society, mirroring its government structure, its corporate behavior, and its worship of advanced technology mixed with traditional spiritualism. Perhaps the reason Japan became obsessed with *Aum* was because of the recognition of how truly Japanese this close-up vision of apocalypse was.

The Meaning of Insurgencies against the New Global Order

After analyzing three movements against globalization, in their practices, in their discourses, and in their contexts, I will venture their

---

[48]   Miyadai (1995).

comparison, seeking to draw conclusions for the broader analysis of social change in the network society. I will use my adaptation of Alain Touraine's typology as a way to read the movements in relation to the same analytical categories. Seen from this perspective, the three movements analyzed here coincide in the identification of their adversary: it is the new global order, designated by the *Zapatistas* as the conjunction of American imperialism and corrupt, illegitimate PRI government in NAFTA; incarnated by international institutions, most notably the United Nations, and the US federal government in the view of American militia; while for *Aum* the global threat comes from a unified world government representing the interests of multi-national corporations, US imperialism and Japanese police. Thus, the three movements are primarily organized around their opposition to an adversary that is, by and large, the same: the agents of the new global order, seeking to establish a world government that will subdue the sovereignty of all countries and all people.

To such an enemy, each movement opposes a specific principle of identity, reflecting the sharp differences between the three societies where they come from: in the case of the *Zapatistas*, they see themselves as Indians and oppressed Mexicans fighting for their dignity, their rights, their land, and the Mexican nation; in the case of the militia, American citizens fighting for their sovereignty, and for their liberties, as expressed in the original, godly American Constitution. As for *Aum*, their identity principle is more complex: it is in fact their individual identity, expressed in their bodies, although such bodies

Chart 2.1   Structure of values and beliefs of insurgent movements against globalization

Movement	Identity	Adversary	Goal
Zapatistas	Oppressed, excluded Indians/Mexicans	Global capitalism (NAFTA), illegal PRI government	Dignity, democracy, land
American militia	Original American citizens	New world order, US federal government	Liberty and sovereignty of citizens and local communities
Aum Shinrikyo	Spiritual community of delivered bodies of believers	United world government, Japanese police	Survival of apocalypse

share each other in the guru's mind – it is the combination of physical individuality and reconstructed spiritual community. In each of the three cases, there is an appeal to authenticity in their identity principle, but with different manifestations: a historically rooted, broad community (the Indians of Mexico, as part of Mexicans); local/county communities of free citizens; and a spiritual community of individuals freed from dependence on their bodies. These identities are based on cultural specificity and on desire for control over their own destiny. And they are opposed to the global adversary on behalf of a higher societal goal, which in all three cases leads to integration between their specific identity and the well-being of society at large: Mexico, America, the surviving Humankind. Yet, this integration is sought through the fulfillment of different values for each movement: social justice and democracy for all Mexicans; individual freedom from government domination for all American citizens; and transcendence of materiality through spiritual liberation in the case of *Aum*. These societal goals, however, are the weakest element in each one of the three movements: they are primarily identity-based mobilizations in reaction to a clearly identified adversary. They are reactive, and defensive, rather than purveyors of a societal project, even if they do propose visions of an alternative society. Chart 2.1 lists the elements defining each movement.

The powerful impact of each of these movements has come, to a large extent, from their media presence and from their effective use of information technology. Media attention is sought, or found, by performing in the French anarchist tradition, briefly revived in May 1968, of *l'action exemplaire*: a spectacular action is undertaken which, by its powerful appeal, even through sacrifice, calls people's attention to the movement's claims, and is ultimately intended to wake up the masses, manipulated by propaganda and subdued by repression. Forcing a debate on their claims, and inducing people to participate, movements expect to put pressure on governments and institutions, reversing the course of submission to the new world order.

This is why weapons are essential in the three movements, not as a goal, but as a sign of freedom, and as an event-trigger device, calling media attention. This media-oriented strategy was particularly explicit, and skillfully executed, in the case of the *Zapatistas*, who tried carefully to minimize violence and to work via the media and the Internet to reach out to the world. But the paramilitary theatrics of the militia, and the deliberate exploitation of violent tactics, or the threat of it, to attract media attention are also a key component of American Patriots. Even *Aum*, distrustful of the media, did pay considerable attention to debates on television, and to press reports, dedicating some of its best members to such tasks. And its gas attacks seem to have had the double purpose of verifying the doomsday prophecy, and of diffusing in the world their warning, through the media. It would seem that the new protest movements cast their messages and project their claims in the form of symbolic politics characteristic of informational society (see chapter 6). Their media skills are fundamental fighting tools, while their manifestos and their weapons are means to create an event worth reporting.

New communication technologies are fundamental for these movements to exist: indeed, they are their organizational infrastructure. Without the Internet, Fax, and alternative media, the Patriots would not be an influential network, but a disconnected, powerless series of reactions. Without the communication capacity enabling the *Zapatistas* to reach urban Mexico, and the world, in real time, they may have remained an isolated, localized guerrilla force, as many of those still fighting in Latin America. *Aum* did not make much use of the Internet, simply because the Internet was hardly present in Japan in the early 1990s. But they did use extensively Fax, and video, and computers, as crucial tools in building a highly controlled, yet decentralized organizational network. Besides, they were trying a technological breakthrough (admittedly esoteric) by developing electronically stimulated, direct communication from brain to brain. The revolutionary cells of the information age are built on flows of electrons.

Alongside their similarity, the three movements also display profound differences, linked to their historical/cultural origins, and to the level of technological development of their societies. A sharp distinction must be drawn between the articulate political project of the *Zapatistas*, the confusion and paranoia of most militia groups, and the apocalyptic logic of *Aum*. This also relates to the difference between the eschatological component in both the militia and *Aum*, and the absence of such views of the End of Time in the *Zapatistas*. Thus, specific social contexts, cultures, historical processes, and levels of political consciousness do determine substantial differences in the processes of insurgency, even triggered by a similar cause.

The three movements have interacted closely with the political processes of the societies in which they take place. The *Zapatistas* deliberately launched their attack in the year of the Mexican presidential election, and they played a fundamental role in deepening the contradictions within the PRI, and in forcing the opening up of the Mexican political system (see chapter 5). *Aum* surged during a period when, in 1993, the formerly stable Japanese political system was crumbling down. By voicing, spectacularly, the alienation of a new generation of professionals and scientists, *Aum* amplified and accelerated the debate in Japan about the social model of the post-hypergrowth period, in which material affluence had been reached and threats of foreign domination had been superseded. After decades of accelerated modernization by waves of state intervention and national mobilization, Japan had to confront itself as a society, after the public realization that alienation, violence, and terrorism, could also be suffered and performed by Japanese against Japanese.

The American militia also grew in a context of widespread political disaffection and anti-government sentiment in the United States, a sentiment that was also expressed in electoral politics through the Republican Party's exploitation of the "neo-conservative revolution" (see chapter 5). A significant part of this new conservative vote has its origin in Christian fundamentalism, and other sectors of opinion related to the Patriot movement, as it manifested itself in the Republican congressional landslide victory in 1994, and in the relative impact of the Buchanan campaign during the Republican presidential primaries of 1996. There is indeed a loose connection between the deterioration of living conditions in America, the erosion of traditional party politics, the rise of right-wing libertarianism and populism within mainstream politics, the backlash of traditional values against processes of social change and family disintegration, and the emergence of the Patriot movement. These linkages are crucial to understanding the new relationship between American society and its political system.[49]

Thus, new social movements, in their diversity, react against globalization, and against its political agents, and act upon the continuing process of informationalization by changing the cultural codes at the root of new social institutions. In this sense, they surge from the depths of historically exhausted social forms, but decisively affect, in a complex pattern, the society in the making.

Conclusion: the Challenge to Globalization

The social movements I have analyzed in this chapter are very different. And yet, under different forms, reflecting their diverse social and cultural roots, they all challenge current processes of globalization, on behalf of their constructed identities, in some instances claiming to represent the interests of their country, or of humankind, as well.

The movements I have studied, in this and other chapters of this volume, are not the only ones opposing the social, economic, cultural,

[49]   Balz and Brownstein (1996).

and environmental consequences of globalization. In other areas of the world, for instance in Europe, similar challenges rise against capitalist restructuring, and against the imposition of new rules in the name of global competition, on the basis of the labor movement. For instance, the French strike of December 1995 was a powerful manifestation of such opposition, in the most classic French ritual of labor unions leading workers and students in the streets on behalf of the nation. Opinion polls showed strong support for the strike among the population at large, in spite of the daily inconvenience caused by the lack of public transportation. Yet, since there is an excellent sociological analysis available on this movement,[50] whose main lines of interpretation I share, I refer the reader to this analysis in order to diversify even further the cross-cultural picture of refusal of the process of globalization. These, and other movements spreading throughout the world, are ending the neo-liberal fantasy of creating a new global economy independent of society by using computer architecture. The grand exclusionary scheme (explicit or implicit) of concentrating information, production, and markets in a valuable segment of population, disposing of the rest in different forms, more or less humane according to each society's temper, is triggering, in Touraine's expression, a *"grand refus."* But the transformation of this rejection into the reconstruction of new forms of social control over new forms of capitalism, globalized and informationalized, requires the processing of social movements' demands by the political system and the institutions of the state. The ability, or inability, of the state to cope with the conflicting logics of global capitalism, identity-based social movements, and defensive movements from workers and consumers, will largely condition the future of society in the twenty-first century. Yet, before examining the dynamics of the state in the information age, we must analyze the recent development of different kinds of powerful social movements that are proactive rather than reactive: environmentalism and feminism.

[50]   Touraine et al. (1996).

— 3 —

The Greening of the Self: the Environmental Movement

The Green approach to politics is a kind of celebration. We recognize that each of us is part of the world's problems, and we are also part of the solution. The dangers and potentials for healing are not just outside us. We begin to work exactly where we are. There is no need to wait until conditions become ideal. We can simplify our lives and live in ways that affirm ecological and human values. Better conditions will come because we have begun . . . It can therefore be said that the primary goal of Green politics is an inner revolution, "the greening of the self."
                                        Petra Kelly, *Thinking Green*[1]

If we are to appraise social movements by their historical productivity, namely, by their impact on cultural values and society's institutions, the environmental movement of the last quarter of this century has earned a distinctive place in the landscape of human adventure. In the 1990s, 80 percent of Americans, and over two-thirds of Europeans consider themselves environmentalists; party and candidates can hardly be elected to office without "greening" their platform; governments and international institutions alike multiply programs, special agencies, and legislation to protect nature, improve the quality of life and, ultimately, save the Earth in the long term and ourselves in the short term. Corporations, including some notorious polluters, have included environmentalism in their public relations agenda, as well as among their most promising new markets. And throughout the globe, the old, simplistic opposition between development for the poor and conservation for the rich has been transformed into a multi-layered debate over the actual content of sustainable development for each country, city, and region. To be sure, most of our funda-

---

[1]   *In Essays by Petra Kelly (1947–1992)* (Kelly, 1994: 39–40). In this quote, she refers to Joanna Macy's "the greening of the self" (Macy, 1991).

fundamental problems concerning the environment remain, since their treatment requires a transformation of modes of production and consumption, as well as of our social organization and personal lives. Global warming looms as a lethal threat, the rain forest still burns, toxic chemicals are deeply into the food chain, a sea of poverty denies life, and governments play games with people's health, as exemplified by Major's madness with British cows. Yet, the fact that all these issues, and many others, are in the public debate, and that a growing awareness has emerged of their interdependent, global character, creates the foundation for their treatment, and, maybe, for a reorientation of institutions and policies toward an environmentally responsible socio-economic system. The multifaceted environmental movement that emerged from the late 1960s in most of the world, with its strong points in the United States and Northern Europe, is to a large extent at the root of a dramatic reversal in the ways in which we think about the relationship between economy, society, and nature, thus inducing a new culture.[2]

It is somewhat arbitrary, however, to speak of the environmental movement, since it is so diverse in its composition, and varies so much in its expressions from country to country, and between cultures. Thus, before assessing its transformative potential, I will attempt a typological differentiation of various components of environmentalism, and use examples for each type, to bring the argument down to earth. Then, I shall proceed to a broader elaboration on the relationship between environmentalists' themes, and fundamental dimensions on which structural transformation takes place in our society: the struggles over the role of science and technology, over the control of space and time, and over the construction of new identities. Having characterized the environmental movements in their social diversity and in their cultural sharing, I shall analyze their means and ways of acting on society at large, thus exploring the issue of their institutionalization, and their relationship to the state. Finally, consideration will be given to the growing linkage between environmental movements and social struggles, both locally and globally, along the increasingly popular perspective of environmental justice.

[2] For an overview of the environmental movement, see (among other sources) Holliman (1990); Gottlieb (1993); Kaminiecki (1993); Shabecoff (1993); Dalton (1994); Alley et al. (1995); Diani (1995); Brulle (1996); Wapner (1996).

The Creative Cacophony of Environmentalism: a Typology

Collective action, politics, and discourses grouped under the name of environmentalism are so diverse as to challenge the idea of a movement. And, yet, I argue that it is precisely this cacophony of theory and practice that characterizes environmentalism as a new form of decentralized, multiform, network-oriented, pervasive social movement. Besides, as I will try to show, there are some fundamental themes that run across most, if not all, environmentally related collective action. However, for the sake of clarity, it seems helpful to proceed in the analysis of this movement on the basis of one distinction and one typology.

The distinction is between environmentalism and ecology. By *environmentalism* I refer to all forms of collective behavior that, in their discourse and in their practice, aim at correcting destructive forms of relationship between human action and its natural environment, in opposition to the prevailing structural and institutional logic. By *ecology*, in my sociological approach, I understand a set of beliefs,

Chart 3.1 Typology of Environmental Movements			
Type (Example)	*Identity*	*Adversary*	*Goal*
Conservation of nature (Group of Ten, USA)	Nature lovers	Uncontrolled development	Wilderness
Defense of own space (Not in my Back Yard)	Local community	Polluters	Quality of life/health
Counter-culture, deep ecology (Earth first!, ecofeminism)	The green self	Industrialism, technocracy, and patriarchalism	Ecotopia
Save the planet (Greenpeace)	Internationalist eco-warriors	Unfettered global development	Sustainability
Green politics (*Die Grünen*)	Concerned citizens	Political establishment	Counter-power

theories, and projects that consider humankind as a component of a broader ecosystem and wish to maintain the system's balance in a dynamic, evolutionary perspective. In my view, environmentalism is ecology in practice, and ecology is environmentalism in theory, but in the following pages I will restrict the use of the term "ecology" to explicit, conscious manifestations of this holistic, evolutionary perspective.

As for the typology, I shall again call upon Alain Touraine's useful characterization of social movements, as presented in chapter 2, to differentiate five major varieties of environmental movement, *as they have manifested themselves in observed practices* in the past two decades, at the international level. I suggest that this typology has general value, although most of the examples are drawn from North American and German experiences because they are the most developed environmental movements in the world, and because I had easier access to this information. Please accept the usual disclaimer about the inevitable reductionism of this, and all typologies, which I hope will be compensated for by examples that will bring the blood and flesh of actual movements into this somewhat abstract characterization.

To undertake our brief journey across the kaleidoscope of environmentalism by means of the proposed typology, you need a map. Chart 3.1 provides it, and requires some explanation. Each type is defined, analytically, by a specific combination of the three characteristics defining a social movement: *identity*, *adversary*, and *goal*. For each type, I identify the precise content of the three characteristics, resulting from observation, using several sources, to which I refer. Accordingly, I give a name to each type, and provide examples of movements that best fit each type. Naturally, in any given movement or organization there may be a mixture of characteristics, but I select, for analytical purposes, those movements that seem to be closer to the ideal type in their actual practice and discourse. After looking at Chart 3.1, you are invited to a brief description of each one of the examples that illustrate the five types, so that distinct voices of the movement can be heard through its cacophony.

The *conservation of nature*, under its different forms, was at the origin of the environmentalist movement in America, as enacted by organizations such as the Sierra Club (founded in San Francisco in 1891 by John Muir), the Audubon Society, or the Wilderness Society.[3] In the early 1980s, old and new mainstream environmental organizations came together in an alliance, known as the Group of Ten, that included, besides the above-cited organizations, the National Parks

---

[3]   Allen (1987); Scarce (1990); Gottlieb (1993); Shabecoff (1993).

and Conservation Association, the National Wildlife Federation, the Natural Resources Defense Council, Izaak Walton League, Defenders of Wildlife, Environmental Defense Fund, and the Environmental Policy Institute. In spite of differences in approach and in their specific field of intervention, what brings together these organizations, and many others created along similar lines, is their pragmatic defense of conservationist causes through the institutional system. In the words of Michael McCloskey, Sierra Club Chairman, their approach can be characterized as "muddling through": "We come out of a mountaineering tradition where you first decide that you're going to climb the mountain. You have a notion of a general route, but you find handholds and the footholds as you go along and you have to adapt and keep changing."[4] Their summit to be climbed is the preservation of wilderness, in its different forms, within reasonable parameters of what can be achieved in the present economic and institutional system. Their adversaries are uncontrolled development, and unresponsive bureaucracies such as the US Bureau of Reclamation, not caring to protect our natural preserve. They define themselves as nature lovers, and appeal to this feeling in all of us, regardless of social differences. They work through and by the institutions, using lobbying very often with great skill and political muscle. They rely on widespread popular support, as well as on donations from well-wishing, wealthy elites, and from corporations. Some organizations, such as the Sierra Club, are very large (about 600,000 members) and are organized in local chapters, whose actions and ideologies vary considerably, and do not always fit with the image of "mainstream environmentalism." Most others, such as the Environmental Defense Fund, focus on lobbying, analyzing, and diffusing information. They often practice coalition politics, but they are careful not to be carried away from their environmental focus, distrusting radical ideologies and spectacular action out of step with the majority of public opinion. However, it would be a mistake to oppose mainstream conservationists to the true, radical environmentalists. For instance, one of the historic leaders of the Sierra Club, David Brower, became a source of inspiration for radical environmentalists. Reciprocally, Dave Foreman, from Earth First!, was, in 1996, on the Board of Directors of the Sierra Club. There is a great deal of osmosis in the relationships between conservationists and radical ecologists, as ideologies tend to take second place to their shared concern about the relentless, multiform destruction of nature. This, in spite of sharp debates and conflicts within a large, diversified movement.

---

[4]   Quoted in Scarce (1990: 15).

The *mobilization of local communities in defense of their space*, against
intrusion of undesirable uses, constitutes the fastest-growing form of
environmental action, and the one that perhaps most directly links
people's immediate concerns to broader issues of environmental
deterioration.[5] Often labeled, somewhat maliciously, the *"Not in my
Back Yard" movement*, it developed in the United States first of all under
the form of the toxics movement, originated in 1978 during the in-
famous Love Canal incident of industrial toxic waste dumping in
Niagara Falls, New York. Lois Gibbs, the homeowner who gained
notoriety because of her fight to defend the health of her son, as well
as the value of her home, went on to establish, in 1981, the Citizen's
Clearinghouse for Hazardous Wastes. According to the Clearinghouse's counting, in 1984 there were 600 local groups fighting against
toxic dumping in the United States, which increased to 4,687 in 1988.
Over time, communities mobilized also against freeway construction,
excessive development, and location of hazardous facilities in their
proximity. While the movement is local, it is not necessarily localistic,
since it often affirms residents' right to the quality of their life in opposition to business or bureaucratic interests. To be sure, life in society is
made up of trade-offs among people themselves, as residents, workers,
consumers, commuters, and travelers. But what is questioned by
these movements is, on the one hand, the bias of location of undesirable materials or activities toward low-income communities and
minority inhabited areas; on the other hand, the lack of transparency
and participation in decision-making about the uses of space. Thus,
citizens call for extended local democracy, for responsible city planning, and for fairness in sharing the burdens of urban/industrial
development, while avoiding exposure to hazardous dumping or
utilities. As Epstein concludes in her analysis of the movement:

> The demand of the toxics/environmental justice movement for
> a state that has more power to regulate corporations, a state that
> is accountable to the public rather than the corporations, seems
> entirely appropriate, and possibly a basis for a broader demand
> that state power over corporations be reasserted and expanded,
> and that state power be exercised on behalf of public welfare and
> especially the welfare of those who are most vulnerable.[6]

In other instances, in middle-class suburbs, residents' mobilizations
were more focused on preserving their status quo against non-desired
development. Yet, regardless of their class content, all forms of protest

---

[5]   Gottlieb (1993); Szasz (1994); Epstein (1995).
[6]   Epstein (1995: 20).

aimed at establishing control over the living environment on behalf of the local community, and in this sense, defensive local mobilizations are certainly a major component of broader environmental movement.

Environmentalism has also nurtured some of the counter-cultures that sprang from the 1960s and 1970s movements. By counter-culture, I understand the deliberate attempt to live according to norms different, and to some extent contradictory, from those institutionally enforced by society, and to oppose those institutions on the ground of alternative principles and beliefs. Some of the most powerful counter-cultural currents in our societies express themselves under the form of abiding only by the laws of nature, and thus affirming the priority of respect for nature over any other human institution. This is why I think it makes sense to include under the notion of *counter-cultural environmentalism* expressions as apparently distinct as radical environmentalists (such as *Earth First!* or the *Sea Shepherds*), the Animal Liberation movement, and ecofeminism.[7] In fact, in spite of their diversity and lack of coordination, most of these movements share the ideas of "deep ecology" thinkers, as represented, for instance, by Norwegian writer Arne Naess. According to Arne Naess and George Sessions, the basic principles of "deep ecology" are:

(1) The well-being and flourishing of human and non-human Life on Earth have value in themselves. These values are independent of the usefulness of the non-human world for human purposes. (2) Richness and diversity of life forms contribute to the realization of these values and are also values in themselves. (3) Humans have no right to reduce this richness and diversity except to satisfy vital needs. (4) The flourishing of human life and cultures is compatible with a substantial decrease of the human population. The flourishing of non-human life requires such a decrease. (5) Present human interference with the non-human world is excessive, and the situation is rapidly worsening. (6) Policies must therefore be changed. These policies affect basic economic, technological, and ideological structures. The resulting state of affairs will be deeply different from the present. (7) The ideological change is mainly that of appreciating life quality (dwelling in situations of inherent value) rather than adhering to an increasingly high standard of living. There will be profound awareness of the difference between big and great. (8) Those who subscribe to the foregoing points have an

---

[7]   For sources, see Adler (1979); Spretnak (1982); Manes (1990); Scarce (1990); Davis (1991); Dobson (1991); Epstein (1991); Moog (1995).

obligation directly or indirectly to try to implement the necessary changes.[8]

To respond to such an obligation, in the late 1970s a number of radical ecologists, led by David Foreman, an ex-Marine turned eco-warrior, created in New Mexico and Arizona *Earth First!*, an uncompromising movement that engaged in civil disobedience and even "ecotage" against dam construction, logging, and other aggressions to nature, thus facing prosecution and jail. The movement, and a number of other organizations that followed suit, were completely decentralized, formed by autonomous "tribes," that would meet periodically, according to the rites and dates of Native American Indians, and decide their own actions. Deep ecology was the ideological foundation of the movement, and it figures prominently in *The Earth First! Reader*, published with a foreword by David Foreman.[9] But equally, if not more, influential was Abbey's novel *The Monkey Wrench Gang*, about a counter-cultural group of eco-guerrillas, who became role models for many radical ecologists. Indeed, "monkeywrenching" became a synonym for eco-sabotage. In the 1990s, the animal liberation movement, focusing on outright opposition to experimentation with animals, seems to be the most militant wing of ecological fundamentalism.

Ecofeminism is clearly distant from the "macho-tactics" of some of these movements. And yet, ecofeminists share the principle of absolute respect for nature as the foundation of liberation from both patriarchalism and industrialism. They see women as victims of the same patriarchal violence that is inflicted upon nature. And so, the restoration of natural rights is inseparable from women's liberation. In the words of Judith Plant:

> Historically, women have had no real power in the outside world, no place in decision-making. Intellectual life, the work of the mind, has traditionally not been accessible to women. Women have been generally passive, as has been nature. Today, however, ecology speaks for the earth, for the "other" in human/environmental relations. And ecofeminism, by speaking for the original others, seeks to understand the interconnected roots of all domination, and ways to resist to change.[10]

Some ecofeminists were also inspired by Carolyn Merchant's controversial historical reconstruction, going back to prehistoric, natural

---

[8]   Naess and Sessions (1984), reproduced in Davis (1991: 157–8).
[9]   Davis (1991).
[10] Plant (1991:101).

societies, free of male domination, a matriarchal Golden Age, where there was harmony between nature and culture, and where both men and women worshipped nature in the form of the goddess.[11] There has also been, particularly during the 1970s, an interesting connection between environmentalism, spiritual feminism, and neo-paganism, sometimes expressed in ecofeminist and non-violent direct action militancy by witches belonging to the craft.[12]

Thus, through a variety of forms, from eco-guerrilla tactics, to spiritualism, going through deep ecology and ecofeminism, radical ecologists link up environmental action and cultural revolution, broadening the scope of an all-encompassing environmental movement, in their construction of *ecotopia*.

Greenpeace is the world's largest environmental organization, and probably the one that has most popularized global environmental issues, by its media-oriented, non-violent direct actions.[13] Founded in Vancouver in 1971, around an anti-nuclear protest off the coast of Alaska, and later headquartered in Amsterdam, it has grown into a transnational, networked organization that, as of 1994, had 6 million members worldwide and annual revenues in excess of $100 million. Its highly distinctive profile as an environmental movement derives from three major components. First, a sense of urgency regarding the imminent demise of life on the planet, inspired by a North American Indian legend: "When the earth is sick and the animals have disappeared, there will come a tribe of peoples from all creeds, colours and cultures who believe in deeds not words and who will restore the Earth to its former beauty. The tribe will be called 'Warriors of Rainbow.'"[14] Secondly, a Quaker-inspired attitude of bearing witness, both as a principle for action, and as a strategy of communication. Thirdly, a business-like, pragmatic attitude, largely influenced by Greenpeace's historic leader and chairman of the board, David McTaggart, "to get things done." No time for philosophical discussions: key issues must be identified by using knowledge and investigative techniques throughout the planet; specific campaigns must be organized on visible targets; spectacular actions geared toward media attention will follow, thus raising a given issue in the public eye, and forcing companies, governments, and international institutions to take action or face further unwarranted publicity. Greenpeace is at the same time a highly centralized organization, and

[11]   Merchant (1980); see also Spretnak (1982); Moog (1995).
[12]   Adler (1979); Epstein (1991).
[13]   Hunter (1979); Eyerman and Jamison (1989); DeMont (1991); Horton (1991); Ostertag (1991); Melchett (1995); Wapner (1995, 1996).
[14]   Greenpeace Environmental Fund, cited in Eyerman and Jamison (1989: 110).

a globally decentralized network. It is controlled by a council of country's representatives, a small executive board, and regional trustees for North America, Latin America, Europe, and the Pacific. Its resources are organized in campaigns, each one of them subdivided by issues. In the mid-1990s, major campaigns were: toxic substances, energy and atmosphere, nuclear issues, and ocean/terrestrial ecology. Offices in 30 countries in the world serve to coordinate global campaigns, and raise funds and support, on a national/local basis, but most of the action aims at a global impact since main environmental problems are global. Greenpeace sees as its adversary a model of development characterized by a lack of concern with its consequences on life on the planet. Accordingly, it mobilizes to enforce the principle of environmental sustainability as the overarching principle to which all other policies and activities must be subordinated. Because of the importance of their mission, the "rainbow warriors" are not inclined to engage in debates with other environmental groups, and do not indulge in counter-culture, regardless of individual variation in the attitudes of their huge membership. They are resolutely internationalists, and see the nation-state as the major obstacle to accomplishing control over currently unfettered, destructive development. They are at war against an eco-suicidal model of development, and they aim to deliver immediate results on each front of action, from converting the German refrigeration industry to "green-freeze" technology, thus helping to protect the ozone layer, to influencing the restriction of whaling, and the creation of a whales sanctuary in Antarctica. The "rainbow warriors" are at the crossroads of science for life, global networking, communication technology, and intergenerational solidarity.

Green politics does not appear, at first sight, to be a type of movement by itself but, rather, a specific strategy, namely entering the realm of electoral politics on behalf of environmentalism. Yet, a close up of the most important example of green politics, *Die Grünen*, clearly shows that, originally, it was not politics as usual.[15] The German Green party, constituted on January 13, 1980, on the basis of a coalition of grassroots movements, is not strictly speaking an environmental movement, even if it has probably been more effective in advancing the environmental cause in Germany than any other European movement in its country. The major force underlying its formation was the Citizen Initiatives of the late 1970s, mainly organized around the peace and anti-nuclear mobilizations. It uniquely brought

[15]   See, among an ocean of sources on the German Green party, Langguth (1984); Hulsberg (1988); Wiesenthal (1993); Scharf (1994); and, particularly, Poguntke (1993) and Frankland (1995).

together veterans of the 1960s movements with feminists who discovered themselves as such by reflecting precisely on the sexism of
1960s revolutionaries, and with youth and educated middle classes
concerned with peace, nuclear power, the environment (the forest
disease, *waldsterben*), the state of the world, individual freedom, and
grassroots democracy.

The creation and rapid success of the Greens (they entered the
national parliament in 1983) stemmed from very exceptional circumstances. First of all, there were really no political expressions for social
protest in Germany beyond the three main parties that had alternated
in power, and even formed a coalition in the 1960s: in 1976, over 99
percent of the vote went to the three parties (Christian Democrats,
Social Democrats, and Liberals). Thus, there was a potential disaffected vote, particularly among the youth, waiting for the possibility
of expressing itself. Financial political scandals (the Flick affair) had
rocked the reputation of all political parties and suggested their
reliance on industry's contributions. Furthermore, what political
scientists call the "political opportunity structure" supported the
strategy of forming a party, and keeping unity among its constituents:
among other elements, significant government funds were made
available to the movement, and the German electoral law requiring
at least 5 percent of the national vote to enter parliament disciplined
the otherwise fractious Greens. Most Green voters were young,
students, teachers, or members of other categories distant from industrial production, either unemployed (but supported by
government), or working for the government. Their agenda included
ecology, peace, defense of liberties, protection of minorities and
immigrants, feminism, and participatory democracy. Two-thirds of
Green party leaders were active participants in various social movements in the 1980s. Indeed, *Die Grünen* presented themselves, in Petra
Kelly's words, as an "anti-party party," aimed at "politics based on a
new understanding of power, a 'counter-power' that is natural and
common to all, to be shared by all, and used by all for all."[16]
Accordingly, they rotated representatives elected to office, and took
most of the decisions in assemblies, following the anarchist tradition
that inspired the Greens more than the Greens would accept. The
acid test of real politics by and large dissolved these experiments after
a few years, particularly after the 1990 electoral débâcle, mainly motivated by the Greens' total misunderstanding of the relevance of
German unification, in an attitude coherent with their opposition to
nationalism. The latent conflict between the *realos* (pragmatic leaders
trying to advance the Green agenda through institutions) and the

[16]   Kelly (1994: 37).

fundis (loyal to the basic principles of grassroots democracy and ecologism) exploded into the open in 1991, leaving an alliance of centrists and pragmatics in control of the party. Reoriented, and reorganized, the German Green party recovered its strength in the 1990s, entered Parliament again, and won strong positions in regional and local governments, particularly in Berlin, Frankfurt, Bremen, and Hamburg, sometimes governing in alliance with the Social Democrats. Yet, it was not the same party. That is, it had indeed become a political party. Besides, this party had no longer the monopoly of environmental agenda since the Social Democrats, and even the Liberals, became much more open to new ideas put forward by the social movements. Furthermore, Germany in the 1990s was a very different country. There was no danger of war, but of economic decay. Widespread youth unemployment, and the retrenchment of the welfare state became more pressing issues for the "greying" green voters than cultural revolution. The murder of Petra Kelly in 1992, probably by her male companion, who then committed suicide, struck a dramatic chord, suggesting the limits of escaping society in everyday life while leaving untouched fundamental economic, political, and psychological structures. However, through green politics, the Green party became consolidated as the consistent left of *fin-de-siècle* Germany, and the 1970s rebellious generation still kept most of their values when ageing, and transmitted them to their children through the way they lived their lives. Thus, a very different Germany emerged from the green politics experiment, both culturally and politically. But the impossibility of integrating party and movement without inducing either totalitarianism (Leninism), or reformism at the expense of the movement (social democracy), received another historical confirmation as the iron law of social change.

The Meaning of Greening: Societal Issues and the Ecologists' Challenge

The conservation of nature, the search for environmental quality, and an ecological approach to life are nineteenth-century ideas that, in their distinct expression, remained for a long time confined to enlightened elites of dominant countries.[17] Often they were the preserve of a gentry overwhelmed by industrialization, as for the origins of the Audubon Society in the United States. In other instances, a communal, utopian component was the nest of early political ecologists, as in the case of Kropotkin, that linked for ever

[17] Bramwell (1989, 1994).

anarchism and ecology, in a tradition best represented in our time by Murray Bookchin. But in all cases, and for almost one century, it remained a restricted intellectual trend, aimed primarily at influencing the consciousness of powerful individuals, who would foster conservationist legislation or donate their wealth to the good cause of nature. Even when social alliances were forged (for example, between Robert Marshall and Catherine Bauer in the United States in the 1930s), their policy outcome was packaged in a way in which economic and social welfare concerns were paramount.[18] Although there were influential, courageous pioneers, such as Alice Hamilton and Rachel Carson in the United States, it was only in the late 1960s that, in the United States, in Germany, in Western Europe, then rapidly diffusing to the entire world, North and South, West and East, a mass movement emerged, both at the grassroots and in public opinion. Why so? Why did ecological ideas suddenly catch fire in the planet's dried prairies of senselessness? I propose the hypothesis that there is a direct correspondence between the themes put forward by the environmental movement and the fundamental dimensions of the new social structure, the network society, emerging from the 1970s onwards: science and technology as the basic means and goals of economy and society; the transformation of space; the transformation of time; and the domination of cultural identity by abstract, global flows of wealth, power, and information constructing real virtuality through media networks. To be sure, in the chaotic universe of environmentalism we can find all these themes and, at the same time, none of them in specific cases. However, I contend that there is an implicit, coherent ecological discourse that cuts across various political orientations and social origins within the movement, and that provides the framework from which different themes are emphasized at different moments and for different purposes.[19] There are, naturally, sharp conflicts and strong disagreements in and between components of the environmental movement. Yet, these disagreements are more frequently about tactics, priorities, and language, than about the basic thrust in linking up the defense of specific environments to new human values. At the risk of oversimplification, I will synthesize the main lines of discourse present in the environmental movement in four major themes.

[18]   Gottlieb (1993).
[19]   For evidence of the presence, and relevance, of these themes in the environmental movements of several countries, see Dickens (1990); Dobson (1990); Scarce (1990); Epstein (1991); Zisk (1992); Coleman and Coleman (1993); Gottlieb (1993); Shabecoff (1993); Bramwell (1994); Porrit (1994); Riechmann and Fernandez Buey (1994); Moog (1995).

First, *an ambiguous, deep connection with science and technology.* As Bramwell writes: "the development of Green ideas was the revolt of science against science that occurred towards the end of the 19th century in Europe and North America."[20] This revolt intensified and diffused, in the 1970s, simultaneously with the information technology revolution, and with the extraordinary development of biological knowledge through computer modeling, that took place in the aftermath. Indeed, science and technology play a fundamental, albeit contradictory role in the environmental movement. On the one hand, there is a profound distrust of the goodness of advanced technology, leading in some extreme manifestations to neo-Luddite ideologies, as represented by Kirpatrick Sale. On the other hand, the movement largely relies on gathering, analyzing, interpreting, and diffusing scientific information about the interaction between man-made artifacts and the environment, sometimes with a high degree of sophistication. Major environmental organizations usually have scientists on their staff, and in most countries there is a tight connection between scientists and academics, and environmental activists.

Environmentalism is a science-based movement. Sometimes it is bad science, but it none the less pretends to know what happens to nature, and to humans, revealing the truth hidden by vested interests of industrialism, capitalism, technocracy, and bureaucracy. While criticizing the domination of life by science, ecologists use science to oppose science on behalf of life. The advocated principle is not the negation of knowledge, but superior knowledge: the wisdom of a holistic vision, able to reach beyond piecemeal approaches and short-sighted strategies geared toward the satisfaction of basic instincts. In this sense, environmentalism aims at retaking social control over the products of the human mind before science and technology take on a life of their own, with machines finally imposing their will on us, and on nature, a humankind's ancestral fear.

Struggles over structural transformation are tantamount to fighting for historical redefinition of the two fundamental, material expressions of society: space and time. And, indeed, *control over space, and the emphasis on locality* is another major, recurrent theme of various components of the environmental movement. I proposed, in volume I, chapter 6, the idea of a fundamental opposition emerging in the network society between two spatial logics, that of the space of flows and that of the space of places. The space of flows organizes the simultaneity of social practices at a distance, by means of telecommunications and information systems. The space of places privileges social interaction and institutional organization on the basis of physical contiguity.

---

[20]   Bramwell (1994: vii).

What is distinctive of new social structure, the network society, is that most dominant processes, concentrating power, wealth, and information, are organized in the space of flows. Most human experience, and meaning, are still locally based. The disjunction between the two spatial logics is a fundamental mechanism of domination in our societies, because it shifts the core economic, symbolic, and political processes away from the realm where social meaning can be constructed and political control can be exercised. Thus, the emphasis of ecologists on locality, and on the control by people of their living spaces, is a challenge to a basic lever of the new power system. Even in the most defensive expressions, such as in the struggles labeled "Not in my Back Yard," to assert the priority of local living over the uses of a given space by "outside interests," such as companies dumping toxics or airports extending their runways, bears the profound meaning of denying abstract priorities of technical or economic interests over actual experiences of actual uses by actual people. What is challenged by environmental localism is the loss of connection between these different functions or interests under the principle of mediated representation by abstract, technical rationality exercised by uncontrolled business interests and unaccountable technocracies. Thus, the logic of the argument develops into yearning for small-scale government, privileging the local community and citizen participation: *grassroots democracy is the political model implicit in most ecological movements.* In the most elaborated alternatives, the control over space, the assertion of place as source of meaning, and the emphasis on local government, is linked up to the self-management ideals of the anarchist tradition, including small-scale production, and emphasis on self-sufficiency, which leads to assumed austerity, the critique of conspicuous consumption, and the substitution of use value of life for exchange value of money. To be sure, people protesting against toxic dumping in their neighborhood are not anarchists, and few of them would actually be ready to transform the entire fabric of their lives as they are. But the internal logic of the argument, the connection between the defense of one's place against the imperatives of the space of flows, and the strengthening of economic and political bases of locality, allow for the sudden identification of some of these linkages in the public awareness when a symbolic event takes place (such as the building of a nuclear power plant). So are created the conditions for convergence between everyday life's problems and projects for alternative society: this is how social movements are made.

Alongside space, *the control over time is at stake in the network society, and the environmental movement is probably the most important actor in projecting a new, revolutionary temporality.* This matter is as important as complex, and requires slow-pace elaboration. In volume I, chapter 7, I proposed a distinction (on the basis of current debates in sociology and history, as well as of Leibniz's and Innis's philosophies of time and space) between three forms of temporality: clock time, timeless time, and glacial time. *Clock time*, characteristic of industrialism, for both capitalism and statism, was/is characterized by the chronological sequencing of events, and by the discipline of human behavior to a predetermined schedule creating scarcity of experience out of institutionalized measurement. *Timeless time*, characterizing dominant processes in our societies, occurs when the characteristics of a given context, namely, the informational paradigm and the network society, induce systemic perturbation in the sequential order of phenomena performed in that context. This perturbation may take the form of compressing the occurrence of phenomena, aiming at instantaneity (as in "instant wars" or split-second financial transactions), or else by introducing random discontinuity in the sequence (as in the hypertext of integrated, electronic media communication). Elimination of sequencing creates undifferentiated timing, thus annihilating time. In our societies, most dominant, core processes are structured in timeless time, yet most people are dominated by and through clock time.

There is still another form of time, as conceived and proposed in social practice: *glacial time.* In Lash and Urry's original formulation, the notion of glacial time implies that "the relation between humans and nature is very long-term and evolutionary. It moves back out of immediate human history and forwards into a wholly unspecifiable future."[21] Developing their elaboration, I propose the idea that the environmental movement is precisely characterized by the project of introducing a "glacial time" perspective in our temporality, in terms of both consciousness and policy. Ecological thinking considers interaction between all forms of matter in an evolutionary perspective. The idea of limiting the use of resources to renewable resources, central to environmentalism, is predicated precisely on the notion that alteration of basic balances in the planet, and in the universe, may, *over time,* undo a delicate ecological equilibrium, with catastrophic consequences. The holistic notion of integration between humans and nature, as presented in "deep ecology" writers, does not refer to a naive worshipping of pristine natural landscapes, but to the fundamental consideration that the relevant unit of experience is not each individual, or for that matter, historically existing human communities. To merge ourselves with our cosmological self we need first to change the notion of time, to feel "glacial time" running through our

---

[21]   Lash and Urry (1994: 243).

lives, to sense the energy of stars flowing in our blood, and to assume the rivers of our thoughts endlessly merging in the boundless oceans of multiformed living matter. In very direct, personal terms, glacial time means to measure our life by the life of our children, and of the children of the children of our children. Thus, managing our lives and institutions for them, as much as for us, is not a New Age cult, but old-fashioned care-taking of our descendants, that is of our own flesh and blood. To propose sustainable development as intergenerational solidarity brings together healthy selfishness and systemic thinking in an evolutionary perspective. The anti-nuclear movement, one of the most potent sources of the environmental movement, based its radical critique of nuclear power on the long-term effects of radioactive waste, besides immediate safety problems, thus bridging to the safety of generations thousands of years from us. To some extent, interest in the preservation of and respect for indigenous cultures extends backwards the concern for all forms of human existence coming from different times, and affirming that we are them, and they are us. It is this *unity of the species, then of matter as a whole, and of its spatiotemporal evolution*, that is called upon implicitly by the environmental move-ment, and explicitly by deep ecologist and ecofeminist thinkers.[22] The material expression unifying different claims and themes of environ-mentalism is their alternative temporality, demanding the assumption by society's institutions of the slow-pace evolution of our species in its environment, with no end to our cosmological being, as long as the universe keeps expanding from the moment/place of its shared beginning. Beyond the time-bounded shores of subdued clock time, still experienced by most people in the world, the historical struggle over new temporality takes place between the annihilation of time in the recurrent flows of computer networks, and the realization of glacial time in the conscious assumption of our cosmological self.

Through these fundamental struggles over the appropriation of science, space, and time, ecologists induce *the creation of a new identity*, a biological identity, *a culture of the human species as a component of nature*. This socio-biological identity does not imply denial of histor-ical cultures. Ecologists bear respect for folk cultures, and indulge in cultural authenticity from various traditions. Yet, their objective enemy is state nationalism. This is because the nation-state, by defin-ition, is bound to assert its power over a given territory. Thus, it breaks the unity of humankind, as well as the interrelation between terri-tories, undermining the sharing of our global ecosystem. In the words of David McTaggart, the historic leader of Greenpeace International: "The biggest threat we must address is nationalism. In the next

---

[22]   Diamond and Orenstein (1990); McLaughlin (1993).

century we are going to be faced with issues which simply cannot be addressed on a nation-by-nation basis. What we are trying to do is work together internationally, despite centuries of nationalist prejudice."[23] In what is only an apparent contradiction, ecologists are, at the same time, localists and globalists: globalists in the management of time, localists in the defense of space. Evolutionary thinking and policy require a global perspective. People's harmony with their environment starts in their local community.

This *new identity as a species*, that is a socio-biological identity, can be easily superimposed on multifaceted, historical traditions, languages, and cultural symbols, but it will hardly mix with state-nationalist identity. Thus, to some extent, environmentalism supersedes the opposition between the culture of real virtuality, underlying global flows of wealth and power, and the expression of fundamentalist cultural or religious identities. It is the only global identity put forward on behalf of all human beings, regardless of their specific social, historical, or gender attachments, or of their religious faith. However, since most people do not live their lives cosmologically, and the assumption of our shared nature with mosquitoes still poses some tactical problems, the critical matter for the influence of new ecological culture is its ability to weave threads of singular cultures into a human hypertext, made out of historical diversity and biological commonality. I call this culture *green culture* (why invent another term when millions of people already name it like this), and I define it in Petra Kelly's terms: "We must learn to think and act from our hearts, to recognize the interconnectedness of all living creatures, and to respect the value of each thread in the vast web of life. This is a spiritual perspective, and it is the foundation of all Green politics... Green politics requires us to be both tender and subversive."[24] The tenderness of subversion, the subversion of tenderness: we are a long way from the instrumentalist perspective that has dominated the industrial era, in both its capitalist and statist versions. And we are in direct contradiction with the dissolution of meaning in the flows of faceless power that constitute the network society. Green culture, as proposed in and by a multifaceted environmental movement, is the antidote to the culture of real virtuality characterizing dominant processes in our societies.

Thus, the science of life versus life under science; local control over places versus an uncontrollable space of flows; realization of glacial time versus annihilation of time, and continued slavery to clock time; green culture versus real virtuality. These are the fundamental

---

[23]   Interview in Ostertag (1991: 33).
[24]   Kelly (1994: 37).

challenges of the environmental movement to dominant structures of the network society. And this is why it addresses the issues that people perceive vaguely as being the stuff of which their new lives are made. It remains that between this "fierce green fire" and people's hearths, the tenements of society stand tall, forcing environmentalism to a long march through the institutions from which, as with all social movements, it does not emerge unscathed.

Environmentalism in Action: Reaching Minds, Taming Capital, Courting the State, Tap-dancing with the Media

Much of the success of the environmental movement comes from the fact that, more than any other social force, it has been able to best adapt to the conditions of communication and mobilization in the new technological paradigm.[25] Although much of the movement relies on grassroots organizations, environmental action works on the basis of media events. By creating events that call media attention, environmentalists are able to reach a much broader audience than their direct constituency. Furthermore, the constant presence of environmental themes in the media has lent them a legitimacy higher than that of any other cause. Media orientation is obvious in the cases of global environmental activism such as Greenpeace, whose entire logic is geared toward creating events to mobilize public opinion on specific issues in order to put pressure on the powers that be. But it is also the daily staple of environmental struggles at the local level. Local TV news, radio, and newspapers are the voice of environmentalists, to the point that corporations and politicians often complain that it is the media rather than ecologists who are responsible for environmental mobilization. The symbiotic relationship between media and environmentalism stems from several sources. First of all, the non-violent direct action tactics, which permeated the movement from the early 1970s, provided good reporting material, particularly when news requires fresh images. Many environmental activists have imaginatively practiced the traditional French anarchist tactics of *l'action exemplaire*, a spectacular act that strikes minds, provokes debate, and induces mobilization. Self-sacrifice, such as enduring arrests and jail, risking their lives in the ocean, chaining themselves to trees, using their bodies as blocking devices against undesirable construction or evil convoys, disrupting official ceremonies, and so many other direct

---

[25]   See Epstein (1991); Horton (1991); Ostertag (1991); Costain and Costain (1992); Gottlieb (1993); Kanagy et al. (1994).

actions, coupled with self-restraint and manifest non-violence, introduce a witness-bearing attitude that restores trust and enhances ethical values in an age of widespread cynicism. Secondly, the legitimacy of the issues raised by environmentalists, directly connecting to the basic humanistic values cherished by most people, and often distant from partisan politics, provided a good terrain for the media to assume the role of the voice of the people, thus increasing their own legitimacy, and making journalists feel good about it. Furthermore, in local news, the reporting of health hazards or the environmental disruption of people's lives brings home systemic problems in a more powerful way than any traditional ideological discourses. Often, environmentalists themselves feed the media with precious images that say more than a thick report. Thus, American environmental groups have distributed video cameras to grassroots groups around the world, from Connecticut to Amazonia, for them to film explicit violations of environmental laws, then using the technological infrastructure of the group to process, and diffuse, accusatory images.

Environmentalists have also been at the cutting edge of new communication technologies as organizing and mobilizing tools, particularly in the use of the Internet.[26] For instance, a coalition of environmental groups in the United States, Canada, and Chile, formed around Friends of the Earth, the Sierra Club, Greenpeace, Defenders of Wildlife, the Canadian Environmental Law Association, and others, mobilized against approval of the North American Free Trade Agreement (NAFTA) because of the lack of sufficient environmental protection provisions in it. They used the Internet to coordinate actions and information, and they built a permanent network that draws the battle lines of transnational environmental action in the Americas in the 1990s. World Wide Web sites are becoming rallying points for environmentalists around the world, as with the sites established in 1996 by organizations such as *Conservation International* and *Rainforest Action Network* to defend the cause of indigenous people in tropical forests. *Food First*, a California-based organization, has linked up with a network of environmental groups in developing countries, connecting environmental and poverty issues. Thus, through the Net, it was able to coordinate its action with *Global South*, a Thailand-based organization that provides the environmental perspective from newly industrializing Asia. Through these networks, grassroots groups around the world become suddenly able to act globally, at the level where main problems are created. It seems that a computer-literate elite is emerging as the global, coordinating

[26]   Bartz (1996).

core of grassroots environmental action groups around the world, a phenomenon not entirely dissimilar to the role played by artisan printers and journalists at the beginning of the labor movement, orienting, through information to which they had access, the illiterate masses that formed the working class of early industrialization.

Environmentalism is not merely a consciousness-raising movement. Since its beginnings, it has focused on making a difference in legislation and governance. Indeed, the core of environmental organizations (such as the so-called Group of Ten in the United States) gears its efforts to lobby for legislation, and to support, or oppose, political candidates on the basis of their stand on certain issues. Even non-traditional, action-oriented organizations, such as Greenpeace, have increasingly shifted their focus to put pressure on governments, and on international institutions, to obtain laws, decisions, and implementation of decisions on specific issues. Similarly, at the local and regional level, environmentalists have campaigned for new forms of city and regional planning, for public health measures, for control of excessive development. It is this pragmatism, this issue-oriented attitude, that has given environmentalism an edge over traditional politics: people feel that they can make a difference right now and here, without mediation or delay. There is no distinction between means and goals.

In some countries, particularly in Europe, environmentalists have entered political competition, running candidates for office, with mixed success.[27] Evidence shows that green parties do much better in local elections, where there is still a direct linkage between the movement and its political representatives. They also perform relatively well in international elections, for example, the elections to the European Parliament, because, being an institution that holds only symbolic power, citizens feel comfortable about seeing their principles represented, with little cost in losing influence on decision-making. In national politics, political scientists have shown that chances for green parties are influenced less by people's environmental beliefs than by specific institutional structures framing the opportunities for political competition.[28] In a nutshell, the greater the accessibility of environmental themes and/or protest vote to mainstream parties, the lower the chances for the Greens; the greater the chances for a symbolic vote, without consequences for holding office, the better the performance by Green candidates. Indeed, it seems that Germany was the exception, not the rule, in the

[27]   Poguntke (1993); Dalton (1994); Diani (1995); Richardson and Rootes (1995).
[28]   Richardson and Rootes (1995).

development of green politics, as I argued above. Overall, it seems that there is a worldwide trend toward the greening of mainstream politics, albeit often in a very pale green, together with the sustained autonomy of the environmental movement. As for the movement itself, its relationship to politics increasingly mixes lobbying, targeted campaigning for or against candidates, and influencing voters through issue-oriented mobilizations. Through these diverse tactics, environmentalism has become a major public opinion force with which parties and candidates have to reckon in many countries. On the other hand, most environmental organizations have become largely institutionalized, that is, they have accepted the need to act in the framework of existing institutions, and within the rules of productivism and a global, market economy. Thus, cooperation with large corporations has become the rule rather than the exception. Corporations often fund a variety of environmental activities, and have become extremely aware of green self-presentation, to the point that environmental themes are now standard images in corporate advertising. But not all is manipulation. Corporations around the world have also been influenced by environmentalism, and have tried to adapt their processes and their products to new legislation, new tastes, and new values, naturally trying to make a profit out of it at the same time. However, because the actual production units in our economy are no longer individual corporations, but transnational networks made up of various components (see volume 1, chapter 3), environmental transgression has been decentralized to small business, and to newly industrializing countries, thus modifying the geography and topology of environmental action in the coming years.

Overall, with the extraordinary growth of environmental consciousness, influence, and organization, the movement has become increasingly diversified, socially and thematically, reaching from the corporate boardrooms to the fringe alleys of counter-cultures, passing through city halls and parliamentary houses. In the process, themes have been distorted, and in some cases manipulated. But this is the mark of any major social movement. Environmentalism is indeed a major social movement of our time, as it reaches out to a variety of social causes under the comprehensive banner of environmental justice.

Environmental Justice: Ecologists' New Frontier

Since the 1960s environmentalism has not been solely concerned with watching birds, saving forests, and cleaning the air. Campaigns against toxic waste dumping, consumers' rights, anti-nuclear protests, pacifism, feminism, and a number of other issues have merged with the defense of nature to root the movement in a wide landscape of rights and claims. Even counter-cultural trends, such as New Age meditation and neo-paganism, mingled with other components of the environmental movement in the 1970s and 1980s.

In the 1990s, while some major issues, such as peace and anti-nuclear protest, have receded into the background, partly because of the success of protests, partly because of the end of the Cold War, a variety of social issues have come to be a part of an increasingly diversified movement.[29] Poor communities and ethnic minorities have mobilized against being the target of environmental discrimination, submitted more often than the population at large to toxic substances, pollution, health hazards, and degradation of their living quarters. Workers have revolted against the source of occupational injuries, old and new, from chemical poisoning to computer-induced stress. Women's groups have shown that, being more often than not the managers of everyday family life, they are the ones that suffer most directly the consequences of pollution, of deteriorating public facilities, and of uncontrolled development. Homelessness is a major cause of declining quality of urban life. And, throughout the world, poverty has been shown, again and again, to be a cause of environmental degradation, from the burning of forests, to pollution of rivers, lakes, and oceans, to rampaging epidemics. Indeed, in many industrializing countries, particularly in Latin America, environmental groups have blossomed, and have linked up with human rights groups, women's groups, and non-governmental organizations, forming powerful coalitions that go beyond, but do not ignore, institutional politics.[30]

Thus, the concept of environmental justice, as an all-encompassing notion that affirms the use value of life, of all forms of life, against the interests of wealth, power, and technology, is gradually capturing minds and policies, as the environmental movement enters a new stage of development.

At first sight, it would seem to be opportunistic tactics. Given the success and legitimacy of the environmental label, less popular causes wrap themselves in new ideologies to win support and attract attention. And, indeed, some of the conservative, nature groupings of the environmental movement have grown wary of an excessively broad embrace that might take the movement away from its focus. After all, labor unions have fought for occupational health legislation since the onset of industrialization, and poverty is, and was, a major issue in its own right, without having to paint in green its sinister

[29] Gottlieb (1993: 207–320); Szasz (1994); Epstein (1995); Brulle (1996).
[30] Athanasiou (1996); Borja and Castells (1996).

darkness. Yet, what is happening in environmentalism goes beyond tactics. The ecological approach to life, to the economy, and to the institutions of society emphasizes the holistic character of all forms of matter, and of all information processing. Thus, the more we know, the more we sense the possibilities of our technology, and the more we realize the gigantic, dangerous gap between our enhanced productive capacities, and our primitive, unconscious, and ultimately destructive social organization. This is the objective thread that weaves the growing connectedness of social revolts, local and global, defensive and offensive, issue-oriented and value-oriented, emerging in and around the environmental movement. This is not to say that a new international of good-willing, generous citizens has emerged. Yet. As shown in this volume, old and new cleavages of class, gender, ethnicity, religion, and territoriality are at work in dividing and sub-dividing issues, conflicts, and projects. But this is to say that embryonic connections between grassroots movements and symbol-oriented mobilizations on behalf of environmental justice bear the mark of alternative projects. These projects hint at superseding the exhausted social movements of industrial society, to resume, under historically appropriate forms, the old dialectics between domination and resistance, between *realpolitik* and utopia, between cynicism and hope.

— 4 —

The End of Patriarchalism: Social Movements, Family, and Sexuality in the Information Age

> *If all who have begged help*
> *From me in this world,*
> *All the holy innocents,*
> *Broken wives, and cripples,*
> *The imprisoned, the suicidal –*
> *If they had sent me one kopeck*
> *I should have become "richer*
> *Than all Egypt"* . . .
> *But they did not send me kopecks,*
> *Instead they shared with me their strength,*
> *And so nothing in the world*
> *Is stronger than I,*
> *And I can bear anything, even this.*
>
> Anna Akhmatova, Selected Poems [1]

Patriarchalism is a founding structure of all contemporary societies. It is characterized by the institutionally enforced authority of males over females and their children in the family unit. For this authority to be exercised, patriarchalism must permeate the entire organization of society, from production and consumption to politics, law, and culture. Interpersonal relationships, and thus personality, are marked, as well, by domination and violence originating from the culture and institutions of patriarchalism. Yet, it is analytically, and politically, essential not to forget the rooting of patriarchalism in the family structure, and in the socio-biological reproduction of the species, as historically (culturally) framed. Without the patriarchal family, patriarchalism would be exposed as sheer domination, and

---

[1]   Akhmatova (1985: 84).

thus eventually overrun by the uprising of the "half of the heaven" historically kept under submission.

The patriarchal family, the cornerstone of patriarchalism, is being challenged in this end of millennium by the inseparably related processes of the transformation of women's work and the transformation of women's consciousness. Driving forces behind these processes are the rise of an informational, global economy, technological changes in the reproduction of the human species, and the powerful surge of women's struggles, and of a multifaceted feminist movement, three trends that have developed since the late 1960s. The massive incorporation of women into *paid* work increased women's bargaining power *vis à vis* men, and undermined the legitimacy of men's domination as providers of the family. Besides, it put an unbearable burden on women's lives by their daily, quadruple shift (paid work, homemaking, child rearing, and night shift for the husband). Contraception first, *in vitro* fertilization later, and genetic manipulation looming on the horizon, are giving women, and society, growing control over the timing and frequency of child bearing. As for women's struggles, they did not wait until this end of millennium to manifest themselves. They have characterized the entire span of human experience, albeit in a diversity of forms, most often absent from history books and from the written record altogether.[2] I have argued that many historical, and contemporary, urban struggles were, in fact, women's movements dealing with the demands and management of everyday life.[3] And feminism as such has an old history, as exemplified by the suffragists in the United States. Yet, I think it is fair to say that only in the last quarter of this century have we witnessed what amounts to a mass insurrection of women against their oppression throughout the world, albeit with different intensity depending on culture and country. The impact of such movements has been felt deeply in the institutions of society, and, more fundamentally, in the consciousness of women. In industrialized countries, a large majority of women consider themselves equal to men, entitled to their rights, and to women's control over their bodies and their lives. Such a consciousness is rapidly extending throughout the planet. This is the most important revolution because it goes to the roots of society and to the heart of who we are.[4] And it is irreversible. To say so does not mean that problems of discrimination, oppression, and abuse of women, and of their children, have disappeared, or even substantially diminished in their intensity. In fact,

[2] Rowbotham (1974).
[3] Castells (1983).
[4] Mitchell (1966).

while legal discrimination has been somewhat curtailed, and the labor market place shows equalizing trends as women's education soars, interpersonal violence and psychological abuse are widespread, precisely because of male anger, individual and collective, in losing power. This is not, and will not be, a velvet revolution. The human landscape of women's liberation and men's defense of their privileges is littered with corpses of broken lives, as is the case with all true revolutions. None the less, in spite of the sharpness of conflict, the transformation of women's consciousness, and of societal values in most societies, in less than three decades, is staggering, and it yields fundamental consequences for the entire human experience, from political power to the structure of personality.

I argue that the process that summarizes and concentrates this transformation is the undoing of the patriarchal family. If the patriarchal family crumbles, the whole system of patriarchalism, gradually but surely, and the whole of our lives, will be transformed. This is a scary perspective, and not only for men. This is why the challenge to patriarchalism is one of the most powerful factors presently inducing fundamentalist movements aimed at restoring the patriarchal order, as those studied in the previous chapters of this volume. Their backlash could indeed alter current processes of cultural change, since no history is pre-scripted. Yet, current indicators point to a substantial decline of traditional forms of patriarchal family. I will start my analysis by focusing on some of these indicators. Not that statistics, by themselves, can tell the story of the crisis of patriarchalism. But when changes are so widespread as to be reflected in national and comparative statistics, we can safely assume the depth and speed of these changes.

Then, we still have to account for the timing of this transformation. Why now? Feminist ideas have been present at least for a century, if not longer, albeit in their specific historical translation. Why did they catch fire in our time? I propose the hypothesis that the reason lies in a combination of four elements: first, the transformation of the economy, and of the labor market, in close association with the opening of educational opportunities to women.[5] Thus, I will try to present some of the data displaying such a transformation, linking them to the characteristics of the informational, global economy, and of the network enterprise, as presented in volume I. Secondly, there is the technological transformation in biology, pharmacology, and medicine that has allowed a growing control over child bearing, and over the reproduction of the human species, as argued in volume I, chapter 7. Thirdly, against this background of

[5]   Saltzman-Chafetz (1995).

economic and technological transformation, patriarchalism has been impacted by the development of the feminist movement, in the aftermath of the 1960s social movements. Not that feminism was a distinctive component of these movements. In fact, it started afterwards, in the late 1960s and/or early 1970s, among women who had been part of the movement, as a reaction to the sexism, and even abuse (see below) that they had had to suffer in the movement. But the context of social movement formation, with emphasis on the "personal as political," and with its multidimensional themes, freed the possibility of thinking away from the instrumental avenues of male-dominated movements (such as the labor movement, or revolutionary politics), and drifting toward a more experimental approach to the actual sources of oppression as felt, before they could be tamed by the discourse of rationality. The fourth element inducing the challenge to patriarchalism is the rapid diffusion of ideas in a globalized culture, and in an interrelated world, where people and experience travel and mingle, quickly weaving a hyperquilt of women's voices throughout most of the planet. Thus, after surveying the transformation of women's work, I will analyze the formation of a highly diversified feminist movement, and the debates emerging from the collective experience of constructing/reconstructing women's identity.

The impact of social movements, and particularly of feminism, on gender relations triggered a powerful shock wave: the calling into question of heterosexuality as the norm. For lesbians, separation from men as the subjects of their oppression was the logical, if not inevitable, consequence of their view of male domination as the source of women's plight. For gay men, the questioning of the traditional family, and the conflictive relationships between men and women, provided an opening to explore other forms of interpersonal relationships, including new forms of families, gay families. For all, sexual liberation, without institutional limits, became the new frontier of self-expression. Not in the homophobic image of endless cruising, but in the affirmation of the self, and in the experimentation with sexuality and love. The impact of gay and lesbian movements on patriarchalism is, of course, devastating. Not that forms of interpersonal domination cease to exist. Domination, as exploitation, always renews itself in history. But patriarchalism, as it has probably existed since the dawn of human times (Carolyn Merchant notwithstanding) is definitively shaken by undermining of the heterosexual norm. Thus, I will explore the origins and horizon of gay and lesbian movements, bridging from San Francisco to Taipei, to emphasize the growing cultural and geographical diversity of these movements.

Finally, I will address the issue of the transformation of personality in our society, as it results from the transformation of family structure and of sexual norms, since I think it can be argued that families constitute the basic socialization mechanism, and sexuality has something to do with personality. This is how the interaction between structural change and social movements – that is, between the network society and the power of identity – transforms us.

The Crisis of the Patriarchal Family

By the crisis of the patriarchal family I refer to the weakening of a model of family based on the stable exercise of authority/domination over the whole family by the adult male head of the family. It is possible, in the 1990s, to find indicators of such a crisis in most societies, particularly in the most developed countries. It is not obvious to use very rough statistical indicators as evidence of a feature, patriarchalism, that is political, cultural, and psychological. Yet, since a population's behavior and structure usually evolve at a very slow pace, the observation of sizeable trends affecting the structure and dynamics of the patriarchal family in comparative national statistics are, in my view, a powerful sign of change, and, I argue, of crisis of previously stable patriarchal patterns. I will summarize the argument before proceeding with a quick statistical scanning.

Dissolution of households of married couples, by divorce or separation, are a first indicator of disaffection with a model of family that relied on the long-term commitment of family members. To be sure, there can be (and this is the rule, in fact) successive patriarchalism: the reproduction of the same model with different partners. However, structures of domination (and mechanisms of trust) are undermined by the experience, both for women and for children, often caught in conflicting loyalties. Furthermore, with increasing frequency, dissolution of married households leads to the formation of single households and/or single-parent households, in this case ending patriarchal authority in the family, even if the structures of domination reproduce mentally in the new household.

Secondly, the increasing frequency of marital crises, and the growing difficulty of making marriage, work, and life compatible, seem to be associated with two other powerful trends: delaying coupling; and setting up partnerships without marriage. Here, again, the lack of legal sanction weakens patriarchal authority, both institutionally and psychologically.

Thirdly, as a result of these different tendencies, together with demographic factors, such as the aging of population, and the difference in mortality rates between sexes, an increasing variety of household structures emerges, thus diluting the prevalence of the classic nuclear family model (first time married couples and their children), and undermining its social reproduction. Single households, and single-parent households, proliferate.

Fourthly, under the conditions of family instability, and with the increasing autonomy of women in their reproductive behavior, the crisis of the patriarchal family extends into the crisis of social patterns of population replacement.[6] On the one hand, an increasing proportion of children are born out of wedlock, and are usually kept by their mothers (although unmarried couples jointly parenting a child are also part of the statistic). Thus, biological reproduction is assured, but outside traditional family structure. On the other hand, women, with heightened consciousness and facing hardship, limit the number of children they give birth to, and delay their first child. Ultimately, in some small circles, whose size seems to be increasing, women give birth to children for themselves, or adopt children alone.

Altogether, these trends, reinforcing each other, call into question the structure and values of the patriarchal family. It is not necessarily the end of the family, since other family arrangements are being experimented with, and may in the end reconstruct how we live with each other, and how we procreate and educate in different, maybe better, ways.[7] But the trends that I mention point to the end of the family as we have known it until now. Not just the nuclear family (a modern artifact), but the family based on patriarchal domination that has been the rule for millennia.

Let us have a look at some basic statistics. I will emphasize here a comparative approach, while reserving a more systematic overview of the crisis of patriarchal family in the United States, where the process seems to be more advanced, in a later section of this chapter.[8] While the trends indicated are most pronounced in developed countries, there is a general change in the same direction in much of the world. Thus, I will rely to a large extent on the report elaborated in 1995 by the Population Council on the transformation of families in the world,[9] which I will complement with various sources, as cited. I will

[6]   In the European Union in 1995 the birth rate was the lowest in peacetime in the twentieth century: there were only 290,000 more births than deaths. In Germany and Italy, there were more deaths than births. Eastern Europe's population declined even further, particularly in Russia (*The Economist*, November 19, 1996).

[7]   Stacey (1990).

[8]   See United Nations (1970-95, 1995); Saboulin and Thave (1993); Valdes and Gomariz (1993); Cho and Yada (1994); OECD (1994b); Alberdi (1995); Bruce et al. (1995); De Vos (1995); Mason and Jensen (1995).

[9]   Bruce et al. (1995).

The End of Patriarchalism

focus on the 1970–95 period for reasons presented above in this chapter.

Table 4.1 shows, with one exception, a significant increase in the crude rate of divorce for selected countries: more than doubling in

Table 4.1 Rate of change in crude divorce rate in selected countries, 1971–90

Country	1971	1990	Rate of change 1971–90	
			Rate	%
Canada	1.38	2.94	1.56	113
France	0.93	1.86	0.93	100
Italy	0.32	0.48	0.16	50
Japan	0.99	1.27	0.28	28
UK	1.41	2.88	1.47	104
USA	3.72	4.70	0.98	26
USSR	2.63	3.39	0.76	29
Mexico	0.21	0.54	0.33	157
Egypt	2.09	1.42	−0.67	−32

Source: UN, *Demographic Yearbook* (1970–1995)

Table 4.2 Trends in divorce rates per 100 marriages in developed countries

Country	1970	1980	1990
Canada	18.6	32.8	38.3
Czechoslovakia	21.8	26.6	32.0[a]
Denmark	25.1	39.3	44.0
England and Wales	16.2	39.3	41.7[a]
France	12.0	22.2	31.5[a]
Greece	5.0	10.0	12.0
Hungary	25.0	29.4	31.0
Italy	5.0	3.2	8.0
Netherlands	11.0	25.7	28.1
Sweden	23.4	42.2	44.1
United States	42.3	58.9	54.8[b]
(former) West Germany	12.2	22.7	29.2

Note: Rates shown are a synthetic index calculated by summing duration-specific divorce rates in each year. (Original source incorrectly identifies rates as "per 1,000 marriages.")
[a] 1989
[b] 1985
Source: Monnier, Alain and de Guibert-Lantoine, Catherine (1993) "La conjoncture démographique: l'Europe et les pays développés d'outre-mer", *Population* 48(4):1043–67
Compiled and elaborated by Bruce et al. (1995)

the UK, France, Canada, and Mexico between 1971 and 1990. The less pronounced increases in the US (still +26 percent) and in the USSR (+29 percent) over the period are due to the fact that they had the highest rates in 1971. Interestingly enough, the one Muslim country that I selected for purposes of comparison displays a decrease in the divorce rate (probably reflecting trends toward Islamization of society), although it is still higher, in 1990, than that of Italy, Mexico, or Japan.

Table 4.2 shows the divorce rates per 100 marriages for selected, highly industrialized countries. There is a discrepancy between the levels of divorce for each country, but there is a general upward trend between 1970 and 1980, and between 1980 and 1990, with again the exception of the United States in 1990, partly because almost 55 percent of marriages ended up in divorce in this country in 1990.

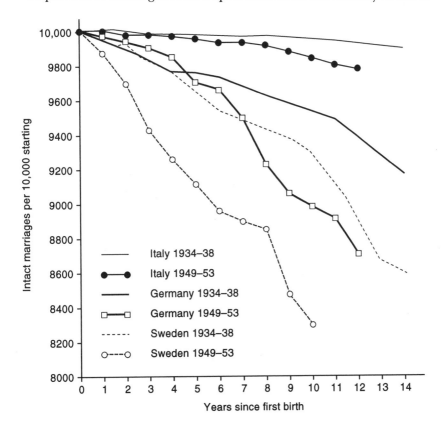

Figure 4.1   Marriage survival curves for Italy, West Germany, and Sweden: mothers born in 1934–38 and 1949–53
Source: Blossfeld et al. (1995)

Table 4.3   Percentage of first marriages dissolved through separation, divorce, or death among women aged 40–49 in less-developed countries

Region/country	Date	%
Asia		
Indonesia	1987	37.3
Sri Lanka	1987	25.6
Thailand	1987	24.8
Latin America/Caribbean		
Colombia	1986	32.5
Dominican Republic	1986	49.5
Ecuador	1987	28.9
Mexico	1987	25.5
Peru	1986	26.1
Middle East/North Africa		
Egypt	1989	22.8
Morocco	1987	31.2
Tunisia	1988	11.1
Sub-Saharan Africa		
Ghana	1988	60.8
Kenya	1989	24.2
Senegal	1986	42.3
Sudan	1989/90	28.2

Sources: United Nations (1987), table 47 in *Fertility Behaviour in the Context of Development: Evidence from the World Fertility Survey* (New York: United Nations), and tabulations from demographic and health surveys
Compiled and elaborated by Bruce et al. (1995)

De facto separations are not included in the statistics, nor are the rates of the ending of cohabitation. However, we know, through survey research, that cohabitation households are more likely to separate than married couples,[10] and that separations correlate with the rate of divorce, thus actually increasing the overall number, and proportion, of termination of households.[11] A global survey of divorce patterns found that a growing proportion of divorces involve couples with young children, thus increasing the likelihood that marital dissolution will lead to single parenthood.[12] Figure 4.1 shows the decreasing rate of marriage survival between older and younger

[10]   Bruce et al. (1995).
[11]   Alberdi (1995).
[12]   Goode (1993).

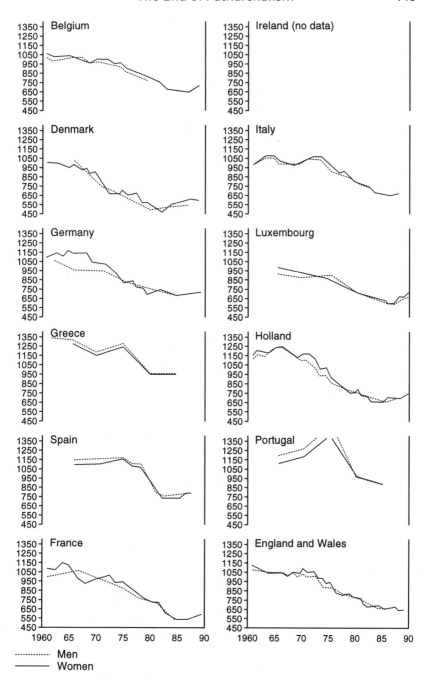

Figure 4.2   Evolution of first marriage in countries of the European
Union since 1960   *Source*: Alberdi (1995)

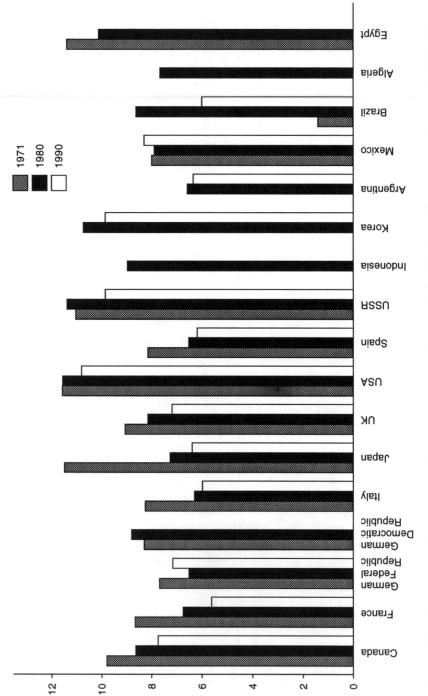

Figure 4.3 Crude marriage rates in selected countries   *Source:* United Nations, *Demographic Yearbook* (1970–95)

Table 4.4   Trends in percentage of women aged 20–24 who have never been married

Region/country	Earlier date	%	Later date	%
Less-developed countries				
Asia				
Indonesia	1976	20	1987	36
Pakistan	1975	22	1990/91	39
Sri Lanka	1975	61	1987	58
Thailand	1975	42	1987	48
Latin America/Caribbean				
Colombia	1976	44	1986	39
Dominican Republic	1975	27	1986	39
Ecuador	1979	43	1987	41
Mexico	1976	34	1987	42
Peru	1978	49	1986	56
Middle East/North Africa				
Egypt	1980	36	1989	40
Morocco	1980	36	1987	56
Tunisia	1978	57	1988	64
Sub-Saharan Africa				
Ghana	1980	15	1988	23
Kenya	1978	21	1989	32
Senegal	1978	14	1986	23
Developed countries				
Czechoslovakia	1970	35	1980	33
Austria	1971	45	1980	57
France	1970	46	1980	52
Spain	1970	68	1981	59
United States	1970	36	1980	51

Sources: Less-developed countries: United Nations (1987), table 43 in *Fertility Behaviour in the Context of Development: Evidence from the World Fertility Survey* (New York: United Nations), and Westoff, Charles F., Blanc, Ann K. and Nyblade, Laura (1994) *Marriage and Entry into Parenthood* (Demographic and Health Surveys Comparative Studies no. 10. Calverton, Maryland: Macro International Inc.); *developed countries*: compiled by the United Nations Statistical Division for: United Nations (1995) *The World's Women 1970–1995: Trends and Statistics* (New York: United Nations) Compiled and elaborated by Bruce et al. (1995)

cohorts of women for Italy, West Germany, and Sweden.[13]

This trend is by no means limited to industrialized countries. Table 4.3, for selected developing countries, displays rates of dissolution, for different causes, of first marriages for women aged 40–49: with the

[13]   Blossfeld (1995).

Table 4.5 Non-marital births as a percentage of all births by region (country averages)

Region/country (no. of countries)	1970	1980	1990
Developed countries			
Canada	n.a.	13.2	21.1[a]
Eastern Europe (6)	7.1	9.0	12.9
Northern Europe (6)	8.8	19.5	33.3
Southern Europe (5)	4.1	5.4	8.7
Western Europe (6)	5.6	8.3	16.3
Japan	1.0[b]	1.0[c]	1.0[d]
Oceania (2)	9.0[b]	13.4[c]	20.2[e]
United States	5.4[b]	14.2[c]	28.0
(former) USSR (14)	8.2	8.8	11.2
Less-developed countries			
Africa (12)	n.a.	4.8[f]	n.a.
Asia (13)	n.a.	0.9[f]	n.a.
Latin America/Caribbean (13)	n.a.	6.5[f]	n.a.

n.a. = not available.
[a] 1989   [c] 1975   [e] 1985
[b] 1965   [d] 1988   [f] 1975–1980 (average)
Sources: Eastern, Northern, Southern, and Western Europe, (former) USSR, and Canada: Council of Europe (1993) *Recent Demographic Developments in Europe and North America, 1992* (Strasbourg: Council of Europe Press); *USA, Oceania, and Japan:* United Nations (1992) *Patterns of Fertility in Low Fertility Settings* (New York: United Nations), and US Department of Health and Human Services (1993) *Monthly Vital Statistics Report* 42(3) supplement; *less-developed countries:* United Nations (1987) *Fertility Behaviour in the Context of Development* (New York: United Nations)
Compiled and elaborated by Bruce et al. (1995)

exception of Tunisia, it oscillates between 22.8 percent and 49.5 percent, with a peak of 60.8 percent in Ghana.

In the 1990s in Europe the number of divorces *vis à vis* marriages has stabilized, but this is mainly due to a reduction in the number of marriages since 1960, so that overall the number, and proportion, of dual-parent married households has decreased substantially.[14] Figure 4.2 displays the general trend toward the reduction of first marriages in countries of the European Union, and figure 4.3 presents the evolution of crude marriage rates for selected countries in different areas in the world. With the exception of Mexico and Germany, there is a decline over the 20-year period, with a significant drop in Japan.

The delay in the age of marriage is also a quasi-universal trend, and

[14] Alberdi (1995).

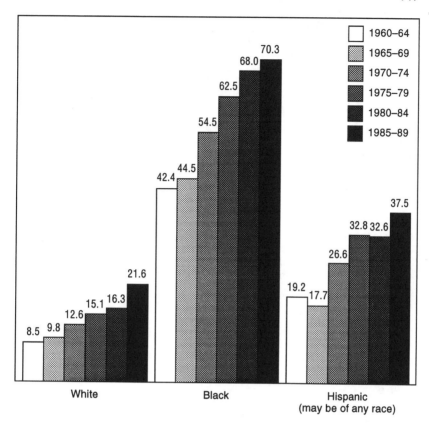

Figure 4.4 Percentage of women (15–34 years) with first birth occurring before first marriage, by race and ethnic origin, in US, 1960–89
Source: US Bureau of the Census (1992a)

a particularly important one in the case of young women. Table 4.4 shows the percentage of women aged 20–24 who have never married. The later dates are very diverse, so it is difficult to compare, but, with the exception of Ghana and Senegal, between one-third and two-thirds of young women are unmarried; with the exception of Spain and Sri Lanka, the proportion of unmarried women 20–24 has increased since 1970. Worldwide, the proportion of married women aged 15 and older declined from 61 percent in 1970 to 56 percent in 1985.[15]

An increasing proportion of children are born out of wedlock in developed countries (table 4.5), and the most important observation concerns the trend: in the United States, the proportion jumped from

[15]   United Nations (1991).

The End of Patriarchalism

Table 4.6 Trends in single-parent households as a percentage of all households with dependent children and at least one resident parent in developed countries

Country	Early 1970s	Mid-1980s
Australia	9.2	14.9
France	9.5	10.2
Japan	3.6	4.1
Sweden	15.0	17.0
United Kingdom	8.0	14.3
United States	13.0	23.9
(former) USSR	10.0	20.0
(former) West Germany	8.0	11.4

Note: Single-parent households are households with dependent children and one resident parent.
Source: Burns, Ailsa (1992) "Mother-headed families: an international perspective and the case of Australia", *Social Policy Report* 6(1)
Compiled and elaborated by Bruce et al. (1995)

Table 4.7 Trends in percentage of households headed by women *de jure*

Region/country	Earlier date	%	Later date	%
Demographic survey data				
Asia				
Indonesia	1976	15.5	1987	13.6
Sri Lanka	1975	15.7	1987	17.8
Thailand	1975	12.5	1987	20.8
Latin America/Caribbean				
Colombia	1976	17.5	1986	18.4
Dominican Republic	1975	20.7	1986	25.7
Ecuador	1979	15.0	1987	14.6
Mexico	1976	13.5	1987	13.3
Peru[a]	1977/78	14.7	1986	19.5
Trinidad and Tobago	1977	22.6	1987	28.6
Middle East/North Africa				
Morocco	1979/80	11.5	1987	17.3
Sub-Saharan Africa				
Ghana	1960	22.0	1987	29.0
Sudan	1978/79	16.7	1989/90	12.6

Table 4.7 contd

Region/country	Earlier date	%	Later date	%
Census data				
Asia				
Hong Kong	1971	23.5	1991	25.7
Indonesia	1971	16.3	1980	14.2
Japan	1980	15.2	1990	17.0
Korea	1980	14.7	1990	15.7
Philippines	1970	10.8	1990	11.3
Latin America/Caribbean				
Brazil	1980	14.4	1989	20.1
Costa Rica	1984	17.5	1992	20.0
Panama	1980	21.5	1990	22.3
Peru	1981	22.1	1991	17.3
Uruguay	1975	21.0	1985	23.0
Venezuela	1981	21.8	1990	21.3
Sub-Saharan Africa				
Burkina Faso	1975	5.1	1985	9.7
Cameroon	1976	13.8	1987	18.5
Mali	1976	15.1	1987	14.0

Note: *de jure* = "usual" household headship.
[a]   *de facto* = headship on day of interview.
Sources: *Demographic surveys*: Ghana: Lloyd, Cynthia B. and Gage-Brandon, Anastasia J. (1993) "Women's role in maintaining households: family welfare and sexual inequality in Ghana", *Population Studies* 47(1): 115–31. Ecuador: Ono-Osaku, Keiko and Themme, A.R. (1993) "Cooperative analysis of recent changes in households in Latin America", in IUSSP *Proceedings of Conference on the Americas, Vera Cruz;* all other countries: Ayad, Mohamed et al. (1994) *Demographic Characteristics of Households* (Demographic and Health Surveys Comparative Studies no. 14. Calverton, Maryland: Macro International Inc.); *censuses*: United Nations (1995) *The World's Women 1970–1995: Trends and Statistics* (New York: United Nations) Compiled and elaborated by Bruce et al. (1995)

5.4 percent of all births in 1970 to 28 percent in 1990. The phenomenon is ethnically differentiated: it reaches 70.3 percent for African-American women in the age group 15–34 (figure 4.4). In Scandinavian countries non-marital child bearing in the 1990s accounts for about 50 percent of all child bearing.[16]

As a result of both separations and single motherhood, the proportion of single-parent households with dependent children (usually female-headed) increased between the early 1970s and the mid-1980s in developed countries (table 4.6), and the upward trend

---

[16]   Alberdi (1995); Bruce et al. (1995).

Table 4.8　Indicators of recent changes in family and household formation: selected Western countries, 1975–90

Region and country	Women 20–24 in cohabitation, c. 1985–90 (%)	Extramarital births, c. 1988 (%)	Rise in extramarital births, 1975–88 (%)	One-parent households with children c. 1985 (%)
Scandinavia				
Iceland	–	52	19	–
Sweden	44	52	19	32
Denmark	43	45	23	26
Norway	28	34	23	23
Finland	26	19	9	15
Northern Europe				
Netherlands	23	11	8	19
United Kingdom	24	25	16	14
France	24	26	18	10
West Germany	18	10	4	13
Austria	–	23	8	15
Switzerland	–	6	2	9
Luxembourg	–	12	8	18
Belgium	18	10	7	15
Ireland	4	13	8	7
Southern Europe				
Portugal	7	14	7	–
Spain	3	8	6	11
Italy	3	6	3	16
Greece	1	2	1	–
Malta	–	2	1	–
Cyprus	–	1	0	–
North America				
United States	8	26	12	28
Canada	15	21	14	26
Oceania				
Australia	6	19	7	15
New Zealand	12	25	9	–

Sources: Council of Europe (various issues); European Values Studies, 1990 Round; Moors and van Nimwegen (1990); United Nations (various years, 1990); personal communications from Larry Bumpass (United States), Peter McDonald, Lincoln Day (Australia), Thomas Burch (Canada), Ian Pool (New Zealand).
Compiled by Lesthaeghe (1995)

Table 4.9 Percentage of one-person households over total number of households for selected countries, 1990–93

Country	Year	Total households (000s)	One-person households (000s)	%
Germany[a]	1993	36,230	12,379	34.2
Belgium	1992	3,969	1,050	26.5
Denmark[b]	1993	2,324	820	35.3
France	1992	22,230	6,230	28.0
Greece	1992	3,567	692	19.4
Great Britain	1992	23,097	6,219	26.9
Ireland	1991	1,029	208	20.2
Italy	1992	19,862	4,305	21.7
Luxembourg	1992	144	34	23.6
Netherlands	1992	6,206	1,867	30.1
Portugal	1992	3,186	399	12.5
Spain	1992	11,708	1,396	11.9
Estimates				
Finland	1993	2,120	716	33.8
Austria	1993	3,058	852	27.9
Sweden	1990	3,830	1,515	39.6
US	1993	96,391	23,642	24.5
Japan	1993	41,826	9,320	22.3

[a] Data from microcensus, April 1993.
[b] Data for Faeroe and Greenland not included.
Source: Statistiches Bundesamt (1995) *Statistisches Jahrbuch 1995 fuer das Ausland* (Wiesbaden: Metzer and Poeschel)

has continued in the 1990s in the US (see below). For developing countries, a similar trend can be detected on the basis of statistics on households headed by women *de jure*. Table 4.7 shows an overall upward trend in the proportion of female-headed households between the mid-1970s and the mid/late-1980s (with some exceptions, e.g. Indonesia), with Brazil showing over 20 percent of its households in this category in 1989, up from 14 percent in 1980.

Bringing together various indicators of household formation, Lesthaeghe constructed table 4.8 for OECD countries, whose data contrast northern Europe and North America with southern Europe, where traditional family structures resist better. Even so, excepting Ireland and Switzerland, the proportion of one-parent households with children in the mid-1980s represented between 11 percent and 32 percent of all households.

Table 4.9 shows the percentage of single households for selected countries in the early 1990s. It deserves a close look: with the exception of southern Europe, it oscillates between 20 percent and 39.6 percent of all households, with 26.9 percent for the UK, 24.5 percent for the US, 22.3 percent for Japan, 28.0 percent for France, and 34.2 percent for Germany. Obviously, most of these households are formed by single elderly, and thus the aging of the population accounts for a good part of the phenomenon. Still, the fact that between one-fifth and over one-third of households are single does call into question the pervasiveness of the patriarchal way of life. Incidentally, the resistance of traditional patriarchal families in Italy and Spain takes its toll: women counteract by not having children, so that both countries are the lowest in the world in fertility rate, way below the replacement rate for the population (1.2 for Italy, 1.3 for Spain).[17] In addition, in Spain the age of emancipation is also the highest in Europe: 27 years for women, 29 for men. Widespread youth unemployment and an acute housing crisis contribute to keep the traditional family together, at the cost of creating fewer families, and stopping the reproduction of Spaniards.[18]

This is, in fact, the most obvious consequence of the crisis of the patriarchal family: the precipitous decline of fertility rates in developed countries, below the rate of replacement of their population (see figure 4.5 for European countries). In Japan, the total fertility rate has been below replacement level since 1975, reaching 1.54 in 1990.[19] In the US, the total fertility rate has declined sharply in the past three decades, from its high historical point in the late 1950s, to reach a level below the replacement rate during the 1970s and 1980s, until stabilizing in the early 1990s at about the replacement level of 2.1. The number of births, however, increased because of the arrival of the baby boomer cohorts to procreation age (figure 4.6). Table 4.10 displays the total fertility rate by main regions of the world, with projections up to the mid-1990s. It has declined overall in the past two decades, and in the more developed regions has slipped below the replacement rate, and stays there. It should be noticed, however, that this is not an iron rule of population. Anna Cabre has shown the relationship between the recuperation of the fertility rate in Scandinavia in the 1980s and the generous social policy, and tolerance of society, in this privileged area of the world.[20] This is exactly why over 50 percent of children were conceived in an extra-marital relationship. Under conditions of psychological and material support, and not being penalized in their jobs, Scandinavian women

17   Alberdi (1995).
18   Leal et al. (1996).
19   Tsuya and Mason (1995).
20   Cabre (1990); Cabre and Domingo (1992).

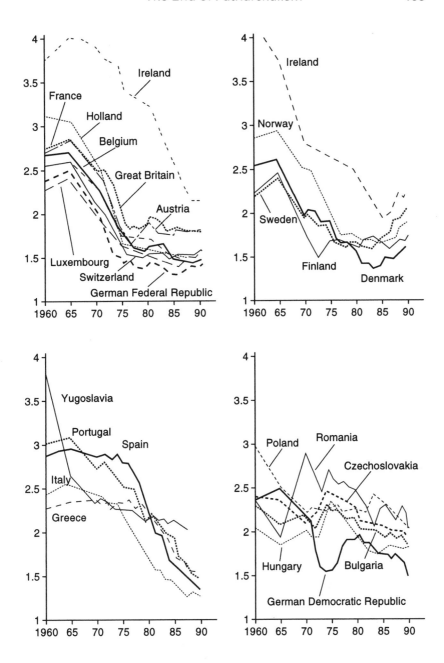

Figure 4.5   Synthetic index of fertility in European countries since 1960
Source: Alberdi (1995)

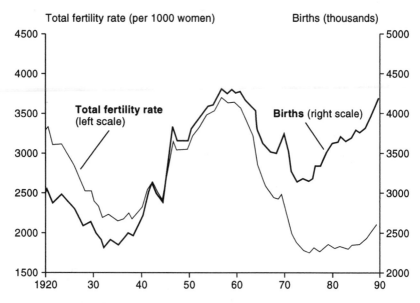

Figure 4.6 Total fertility rate and number of births in US, 1920–90
(total fertility rate = number of children that women would have by
the end of their child-bearing years based on age-specific birth rates
of a single year)
Source: US Bureau of the Census (1992a)

went back to having children, and their countries displayed in the
1980s the highest fertility rate in Europe. However, the recent picture
is not so rosy. Constraints on the Scandinavian welfare state reduced
the amount of support, and, accordingly, in the early 1990s
Scandinavian fertility rates stabilized, at replacement rate levels.[21]
Also, in a number of countries, particularly in the United States, the
total fertility rate is being pushed up by their immigrant population,
thus inducing multi-ethnicity and multiculturalism. One of the most
important socio-cultural differences might be the preservation of
patriarchalism among ethnic minority immigrant communities in
contrast to the disintegration of traditional families among native
ethnic groups (black and white) in industrialized societies. This trend
is, of course, self-reproducing, even accounting for a reduction in the
birth rate of immigrant minorities as soon as they improve their
economy and their education.

Overall, it seems that in most developed countries, with the major
exceptions of Japan and Spain, the patriarchal family is in the process

[21]   Alberdi (1995).

Table 4.10 Total fertility rate by main regions of the world

	1970–75	1980–85	1990–95[a]
World	4.4	3.5	3.3
More-developed regions	2.2	2.0	1.9
Less-developed regions	5.4	4.1	3.6
Africa	6.5	6.3	6.0
Asia	5.1	3.5	3.2
Europe	2.2	1.9	1.7
Americas	3.6	3.1	–
Latin	–	–	3.1
Northern	–	–	2.0
Oceania	3.2	2.7	2.5
USSR	2.4	2.4	2.3

[a] 1990–95 as projections.
Sources: United Nations, *World Population Prospects*, estimates as assessed in 1984; United Nations, *World Population at the Turn of the Century* (1989), p. 9; United Nations Population Fund, *The State of World Population: Choices and Responsibilities* (1994)

of becoming a minority form in the way people live. In the United States, only about one-quarter of all households in the 1990s fits the ideal type of a married couple with children (see below). If we add the qualification "with the couple's children," the proportion drops. Certainly, not all is women's liberation. Demographic structure has something to do with it: another one-quarter of households in the US are one-person households, and the majority of them are elderly people, mainly women outliving their husbands. Yet, a statistical study conducted by Antonella Pinelli on the variables conditioning new demographic behavior in Europe concludes that:

> we see that marital instability, cohabitation, and extramarital births are taking place where there is a high-value on non-material aspects of the quality of life, and where women enjoy economic independence and relatively great political power. The conditions for women should be emphasized. Divorce, cohabitation, and extramarital fertility are the most widespread where women enjoy economic independence and are in a position to face the possibility of being a single mother without becoming, for this reason, a social subject at risk.[22]

Her conclusions must be corrected, however, by the observation that this is only part of the story. Children born out of wedlock in the United States result as much from poverty and lack of education as

[22] Pinelli (1995: 88).

from women's self-affirmation. None the less, the general trend, as shown in a few statistical illustrations, is toward the weakening and potential dissolution of traditional family forms of unchallenged patriarchal domination, with wife and children clustering around the husband/father.

In developing countries similar trends are at work in the urban areas, but national statistics, overwhelmed by traditional rural societies (particularly in Africa and Asia), downplay the phenomenon, in spite of which we still have been able to detect some traces. The Spanish exception is fundamentally linked to youth unemployment, and to a serious housing shortage that precludes the formation of new households in the largest metropolitan areas.[23] As for Japan, cultural trends, such as the shame of non-marital births, help to consolidate patriarchalism, although recent trends seem to be eroding patriarchal ideology and women's relegation to the secondary labor market.[24] But my hypothesis about Japanese exceptionalism in preserving the patriarchal structure concerns mainly the absence of a significant feminist movement. Since such a movement is growing in the 1990s, I dare to forecast that in this matter, as in many others, Japanese uniqueness is to some extent a function of time. Without denying the cultural specificity of Japan, the forces at work, in the structure of society and in the minds of women, are such that Japan too will have to reckon with the challenge to patriarchalism from Japanese working women.[25]

If current trends continue to expand throughout the world, and I contend they will, families as we have known them will become, in a number of societies, a historical relic not too long in the historical horizon. And the fabric of our lives will have been transformed, as we already feel, sometimes painfully, the tremors of this transformation. Let us now turn to analyze the underlying trends at the root of this crisis and, it is to be hoped, at the source of new forms of togetherness between women, children, pets, and even men.

Women at Work

Work, family, and labor markets have been deeply transformed in the last quarter of this century by the massive incorporation of women to *paid labor*, in most cases outside their home.[26] Worldwide, 854 million

[23] Leal et al. (1996).
[24] Tsuya and Mason (1995).
[25] Gelb and Lief-Palley (1994).
[26] Kahne and Giele (1992); Mason and Jensen (1995).

Table 4.11 Labor force participation rates by sex (%)

	Men						Women					
	1973	1979	1983	1992	1993	1994[a]	1973	1979	1983	1992	1993	1994[a]
Australia	91.1	87.6	85.9	85.3	85.0	84.9	47.7	50.3	52.1	62.3	62.3	63.2
Austria	83.0	81.6	82.2	80.7	80.8	..	48.5	49.1	49.7	58.0	58.9	..
Belgium	83.2	79.3	76.8	72.6	..	..	41.3	46.3	48.7	54.1	..	..
Canada	86.1	86.3	84.7	78.9	78.3	..	47.2	55.5	60.0	65.1	65.3	..
Denmark	89.6	89.6	87.6	88.0	86.0	..	61.9	69.9	74.2	79.0	78.3	..
Finland	80.0	82.2	82.0	78.5	77.6	77.1	63.6	68.9	72.7	70.7	70.0	69.8
France	85.2	82.6	78.4	74.7	74.5	..	50.1	54.2	54.3	58.8	59.0	..
Germany	89.6	84.9	82.6	79.0	78.6	..	50.3	52.2	52.5	61.3	61.4	..
Greece	83.2	79.0	80.0	73.0	73.7	..	32.1	32.8	40.4	42.7	43.6	..
Ireland[b]	92.3	88.7	87.1	81.9	..	..	34.1	35.2	37.8	39.9	..	..
Italy	85.1	82.6	80.7	79.1	74.8	..	33.7	38.7	40.3	46.5	43.3	..
Japan	90.1	89.2	89.1	89.7	90.2	90.1	54.0	54.7	57.2	62.0	61.8	61.8
Luxembourg[b]	93.1	88.9	85.1	77.7	..	..	35.9	39.8	41.7	44.8	..	..
Netherlands	85.6	79.0	77.3	80.8	83.3	..	29.2	33.4	40.3	55.5	..	..
New Zealand	89.2	87.3	84.7	83.0	83.3	82.3	39.2	45.0	45.7	63.2	63.2	..
Norway	86.5	89.2	87.2	82.6	82.0	82.8	50.6	61.7	65.5	70.9	70.8	71.3
Portugal[c]	..	90.9	86.9	82.3	82.5	..	..	57.3	56.7	60.6	61.3	62.2
Spain	92.9	83.1	80.2	75.1	74.5	73.9	33.4	32.6	33.2	42.0	42.8	43.9
Sweden	88.1	87.9	85.9	81.8	79.3	78.1	62.6	72.8	76.6	77.7	75.7	74.6
Switzerland	100.0	94.6	93.5	93.7	92.5	91.0	54.1	53.0	55.2	58.5	57.9	56.9
United Kingdom	93.0	90.5	87.5	84.5	83.3	81.8	53.2	58.0	57.2	64.8	64.7	64.5
United States	86.2	85.7	84.6	85.3	84.9	85.4	51.1	58.9	61.8	69.0	69.0	70.5
North America	86.2	85.8	84.6	84.6	84.2	..	50.7	58.6	61.6	68.6	68.7	..
OECD Europe[d]	88.7	84.8	82.3	79.2	80.1	..	44.7	48.6	49.8	56.9	60.6	..
Total OECD[d]	88.2	85.9	84.3	82.9	81.3	..	48.3	53.1	55.1	61.9	61.6	..

a Secretariat estimates.   b 1991 instead of 1992 for Ireland and Luxembourg.   d Above countries only.
c Labor force data include a significant number of persons aged less than 15 years.
Source: OECD *Employment Outlook* (1995)

Table 4.12 Total employment by sex (average annual growth rates in percentages)

	Men						Women					
	1973–75	1975–79	1979–83	1983–91	1992	1993	1973–75	1975–79	1979–83	1983–91	1992	1993
Australia	-0.3	0.6	-0.1	1.5[d]	-0.3	0.0	2.0	1.7	2.0	3.9[d]	0.6	0.8
Austria	-1.1	0.8	0.9	0.7	0.8	..	-1.2	1.0	0.8	2.1	3.3	..
Belgium	-0.4	-0.4	-1.8	0.0	-1.1	..	0.8	0.9	0.2	2.0	0.5	..
Canada	1.9	1.8	-0.6	1.1	-1.2	1.2	4.7	4.5	2.6	2.8	-0.4	1.1
Denmark	-1.8	0.7[b]	-1.7	0.9	..	..	-0.5	3.6[b]	0.9	1.4	..	..
Finland	0.7	-0.6[b]	0.9	-0.5	-7.6	-5.9	2.0	-0.0[b]	1.9	-0.1	-6.5	-6.3
France	-0.4	-0.2	-0.7	-0.1	-1.2	..	0.8	1.6	0.7	1.4	0.5	..
Germany	-2.5	0.3	-0.5	0.8[e]	-0.3	..	-1.0	0.9	-0.0	2.0[e]	1.7	..
Greece	-0.5	0.8	0.6	0.1	..	..	1.6	1.1	4.1	0.7	..	..
Ireland	-0.2	1.5	-1.4	-0.5	..	..	1.6	2.0	1.9	1.1	..	..
Italy	0.6	-0.1	0.0	0.1	-1.1	..[h]	2.4	2.7	1.3	1.6	0.3	-0.3
Japan	0.5	0.7	0.8	1.1	1.1	0.6	-1.7	2.0	1.7	1.7	1.0	..
Luxembourg	1.0	-0.7	-0.7	2.3[f]	..	..	4.6	1.5	1.8	3.3[f]	..	..
Netherlands	-1.5	0.3	-0.8	2.1	1.3	..	2.9	2.7	4.0	5.3	3.2	..
New Zealand	2.1	0.2	-0.3	-1.0[d]	0.4	..	5.2	2.7	0.8	1.3[d]	0.6	..
Norway	0.9	1.1	-0.2	-0.4	-0.5	-0.5	2.9	4.4	1.8	1.40	-0.1	0.5
Portugal	-1.3[a]	0.3	0.4[c]	1.0	..[g]	-2.8	-1.5[a]	0.9	1.1[c]	3.0	..[g]	-1.2
Spain	-0.2	-1.7[b]	-1.8	0.8	-3.2	-5.4	-1.5	-1.3[b]	-1.7	3.0	0.3	-2.4
Sweden	1.0	-0.3	-0.6	0.1[c]	-5.1	-7.9	4.2	2.0	1.3	0.9[c]	-3.5	-6.2
Switzerland	-2.8	-0.5	0.8	0.8	-2.1	-2.5	-1.9	0.6	2.0	1.6	-2.4	-2.5
United Kingdom	-1.0	-0.2	-2.3	0.4	-3.3	-2.8	1.5	1.2	-1.0	2.3	-1.0	-1.3
United States	-0.6	2.5	-0.3	1.3	0.3	1.3	2.0	5.0	1.7	2.4	0.9	1.5
North America	-0.4	2.4	-0.4	1.2	0.2	1.3	2.2	4.9	1.8	2.4	0.8	1.5
OECD Europe[i]	-0.8	-0.2	-0.8	0.4	-2.0	..	1.2	1.4	0.5	2.0	-0.3	..
Total OECD[i]	-0.4	0.9	-0.3	0.9	-1.4	..	1.0	2.8	1.2	2.2	-0.1	..

a Break in series between 1973 and 1974.
d Break in series between 1985 and 1986.
g Break in series between 1991 and 1992.
b Break in series between 1975 and 1976.
e Break in series between 1986 and 1987.
h Break in series between 1992 and 1993.
c Break in series between 1982 and 1983.
f Data refer to 1983-90.
i Above countries only.

Source: OECD *Employment Outlook* (1995)

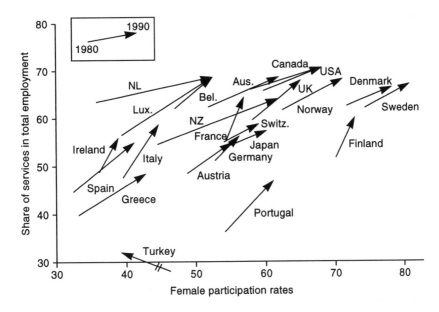

Figure 4.7   Growth in service sector employment and in female participation rates, 1980–90 (Aus., Australia; Bel., Belgium; Lux., Luxembourg; NL, Netherlands; NZ, New Zealand; Switz., Switzerland)
Source: OECD (1994b), Statistical Annex, tables A and D

women were economically active in 1990, accounting for 32.1 percent of the global labor force. Among women aged 15 years and over, 41 percent were economically active.[27] In OECD countries, the average labor force participation rate for women rose from 48.3 percent in 1973 to 61.6 percent in 1993, while for men it declined from 88.2 percent to 81.3 percent (see table 4.11). In the United States, women's labor participation rate went up from 51.1 percent in 1973 to 70.5 percent in 1994. Growth rates of employment for 1973–93 also indicate a general upward trend for women (reversed in some European countries in the 1990s), and a positive differential *vis à vis* men (table 4.12). Similar trends can be observed world-wide. Switching to the United Nations statistical categorization of "economic activity rate" (whose percentages are lower than those of labor force participation), tables 4.13 and 4.14 show a similar upward trend for women's economic activity rate, with the partial exception of Russia which already had a high level in 1970.

    The massive entry of women into the paid labor force is due, on the one hand, to the informationalization, networking, and globalization

[27]   United Nations (1995).

Table 4.13 Economic activity rates, 1970–90

			1970	1975	1980	1985	1990
OECD							
Canada	(15+)	Total	40.9(71)	44.6(76)			
		Men	53.3	55.6			
		Women	28.4	33.8			
France	(15+)	Total	42.0(71)	42.6	43.3	43.4(86)	44.8
		Men	55.2	55.1	54.4	52.6	51.6
		Women	29.4	30.5	32.7	34.6	38.2
Germany	(14+)	Total	43.9	43.4	44.9		49.6
		Men	59.2	57.1	58.4		60.8
		Women	30.0	30.9	32.6		39.2
Italy	(14+)	Total	36.6	35.4	40.2	41.1	42.0
		Men	54.7	52.2	55.2	54.6	54.3
		Women	19.3	19.4	26.0	28.2	30.3
Japan	(15+)	Total	51.0	48.6	48.4	51.5	51.7
		Men	63.4	62.3	60.2	63.6	62.4
		Women	39.1	35.2	36.8	39.8	41.3
UK	(16+)	Total	42.5		47.3(81)		50.3
		Men	51.7		59.4		58.4
		Women	33.0		35.8		42.6
USA	(16+)	Total	41.8	44.5	49.1		
		Men	53.9	55.6	56.8		
		Women	30.2	33.9	41.8		44.4(92)
Russian	(16+)	Total	48.4		51.7(79)		50.2
Federation		Men	52.1		55.7		55.0
		Women	45.3		48.1		45.8
Asia							
China	(15+)	Total			52.3(82)		
		Men			57.3		
		Women	44.25		47.0		
India	(15+)	Total	32.9(71)				37.5(91)
		Men	52.5				51.6
		Women	11.9				22.3
Indonesia	(15+)	Total	34.9(71)		35.5		
		Men	47.3		48.1		
		Women	22.8		23.5		
Korea	(15+)	Total	33.0	38.5	37.9		
		Men	42.8	46.9	46.3		
		Women	23.2	30.0	29.3		
Latin America							
Argentina	(14+)	Total	38.5		38.5	37.5	38.1
		Men	57.9		55.1	55.3	55.4
		Women	19.4		22.0	19.9	21.0
Mexico	(12+)	Total	26.9	27.6	33.0		29.6
		Men	43.6	42.9	48.2		46.2
		Women	10.2	12.0	18.2		13.6

Table 4.13 contd

			1970	1975	1980	1985	1990
Brazil	(10+)	Total	31.7		36.3		41.9
		Men	10.5		53.1		56.3
		Women	13.1		19.8		27.9
Africa							
Algeria	(6+)	Total	21.7(66)				23.6
		Men	42.2				42.4
		Women	1.8				4.4
Nigeria	(14+)	Total					30.3
		Men					40.7
		Women					19.7
Middle East							
Egypt	(6+)	Total	27.9(71)	30.2(76)			31.6
		Men	51.2	54.1			49.3
		Women	4.2	5.5			13.5

Note: Economic activity rate = economically active population/total population.
Source: ILO, *Yearbook of Labour Statistics* (1970–94)

Table 4.14 Growth rate of women's economic activity rate, 1970–90

	1970	1990	Growth rate (%)
France	29.4	38.2	29.9
Germany	30.0	39.2	30.7
Italy	19.3	30.3	57.0
Japan	39.1	41.3	5.6
UK	33.0	42.6	29.1
USA	30.2	44.4	47.0
Russia	45.3	45.8	1.1
India	11.9	22.3	87.4
Argentina	19.4	21.0	8.2
Mexico	10.2	13.6	33.3
Brazil	13.1	27.9	113.0
Algeria	1.8	4.4	144.4
Egypt	4.2	13.5	221.4

Note: Economic activity rate = economically active population/total
population.
Source: ILO, *Yearbook of Labour Statistics* (1970–94)

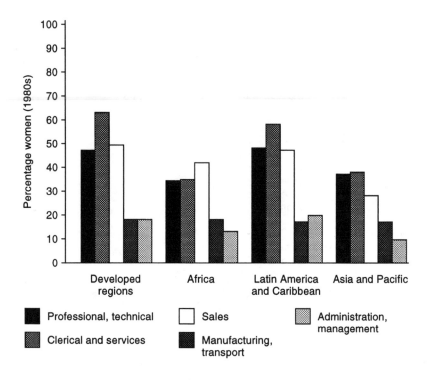

Figure 4.8a   Women as a percentage of the labor force by type of
employment
Source: Prepared by the Statistical Office of the United Nations
Secretariat (1991) from International Labour Office, *Yearbook of Labour
Statistics* (various years)

of the economy; on the other hand, to the gendered segmentation of
the labor market taking advantage of specific social conditions of
women to enhance productivity, management control, and ultimately
profits.[28] Let us look at some statistical indicators.[29]

When analyzing the transformation of employment structure in the
informational economy (volume I, chapter 4), I showed the growth
of service employment, and, within services, the strategic role played
by two distinctive categories of services: business services, and social
services, characteristic of the informational economy, as forecasted by
early theorists of postindustrialism. Figure 4.7 displays the convergence between growth of services and of female employment in

[28]   Kahne and Giele (1992); Rubin and Riney (1994).
[29]   See Blumstein and Schwartz (1983); Cobble (1993); OECD (1993-95, 1994a,
b, 1995); Mason and Jensen (1995); United Nations (1995).

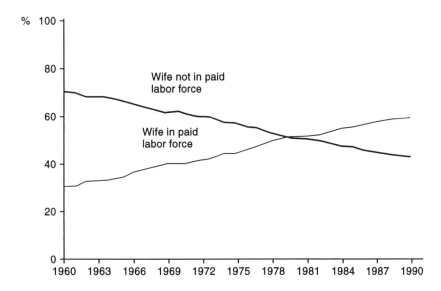

Figure 4.8b   Married couple families with wives in the labor force, in
US, 1960–90 (data for 1983 not available)
Source: US Bureau of the Census (1992a)

1980–90. Figure 4.8a shows the concentration of women in service
employment in different areas of the world. However, it should be
noticed that, in most of the world, the majority of labor is still agricultural (but not for long), and therefore, most women still work in
agriculture: 80 percent of economically active women in sub-Saharan
Africa, and 60 percent in southern Asia. Worldwide, about half of
economically active women are in services.[30] The proportion is much
higher in most developed countries, and has been increasing over
time, to reach about 85 percent of the female labor force in the US
and the UK. However, the most significant aspect is in which kind
of services women work. As shown in table 4.15, in most developed
countries, the bulk of female employment is in social services and
personal services. However, if we calculate the rate of increase of each
type of service in total female employment for the 1973–93 period
(table 4.16), we observe a spectacular increase in business services,
followed at some distance by social/personal services. Trade and
restaurant employment is the least dynamic segment in the evolution
of women's employment in advanced countries. Thus, there is a direct
correspondence between the type of services linked to informationalization of the economy and the expansion of women's employment

[30]   United Nations (1991).

Table 4.15 Female service employment by activities and rank of information intensity of total employment (%), 1973–93

		1 Financing, insurance, real estate, and business services	2 Community, social and personal services	2 Transport, storage and communications	3 Wholesale and retail trade, restaurants and hotels	(Rank of information intensity) Activities not adequately defined	Total
Canada	1975	11.2	40.2	4.0	25.8		81.2
	1983	12.1	40.9	4.2	25.4		82.6
	1993	13.6	43.9	3.7	24.8		86.0
USA	1973	9.1	41.5	3.5	23.9		78.0
	1983	11.9	41.9	3.3	24.5		81.6
	1993	12.6	46.6	3.5	22.7		85.3
Japan	1973	3.4	22.0	2.0	24.7	0.2	52.3
	1983	6.9	24.1	1.9	27.1	0.2	60.3
	1993	9.4	26.9	2.5	27.5	0.4	66.7
Germany	1973						
	1983	8.2	34.2	3.3	22.5		68.2
	1993	10.3	38.4	3.6	22.4		74.6
Italy	1977	1.7	31.0	1.8	18.8		53.3
	1983	3.1	34.6	2.0	21.0		60.6
	1993	8.1	36.4	2.7	22.6		69.8
UK	1973	7.4	36.0	2.8	24.7		70.7
	1983	9.8	42.2	2.8	25.0	0.1	79.9
	1993						84.9
Spain	1977	2.1	28.2	1.5	24.4		56.3
	1983	3.0	35.8	1.7	24.4		64.9
	1993	6.3	41.8	2.2	26.9		77.2

Source: OECD, Labour Force Statistics (1995)

Table 4.16   Rates of growth for each category of female service employment as a percentage of total female employment, 1973–1993[a]

Country	Business services (%)	Social and personal services (%)	Transportation, storage and communication (%)	Trade, hotels and restaurants (%)
USA	38.5	12.2	0	−5.0
Japan	176.5	22.2	25	1.3
Germany (1983–93)	25.6	12.3	9	−0.4
Italy (1977–93)	376.5	17.4	50	−3.9
UK	32.4	17.2	0	1.2
Spain (1977–93)	200.0	48.2	47	10.2

[a]   Unless dates for calculations are otherwise indicated.
Source: Elaboration on data from table 4.15

in advanced countries. A similar conclusion results from observing the changing evolution of female employment by occupation between 1980 and 1989 in selected OECD countries (table 4.17). Overall, professional/technical and administrative/managerial categories have grown faster than others, although clerical workers still account, in general, for the largest group of women workers. Women are not being relegated to the lowest skilled service jobs: they are employed across the entire skills structure, and the growth of women's jobs is higher at the upper end of the occupational structure. This is exactly why there is discrimination: because they perform similarly qualified jobs at lower pay, with greater job insecurity, and with lower chances of careers to the top.

Globalization has also played a major part in involving women in the labor force around the world. The electronics industry, internationalized since the late 1960s, recruited mainly among young, unskilled women in Asia[31] The US *maquiladoras* in northern Mexico rely heavily on female labor. And the newly industrialized economies have brought into paid work underpaid women at almost all levels of the occupational structure[32] At the same time, a substantial share of urban employment for women in developing countries remains in the informal sector, particularly in providing food and services for metropolitan dwellers.[33]

[31]   Salaff (1981, 1988).
[32]   Standing (1990).
[33]   Portes et al. (1989).

Table 4.17 Distribution of female employment by occupation,[a] 1980 and 1989 (%)

Country [b,c]	Professional, technical and related	Administrative and managerial	Clerical and related	Sales workers	Service workers	Agriculture and related	Production and related
Belgium							
1983	25.9	1.4	24.4	13.7	18.6	2.8	13.2
1988	28.2	1.4	27.3	14.6	14.4	2.1	11.6
Index (1983 = 100)	118.0	113.0	122.0	116.0	84.0	86.0	95.0
Canada							
1980	19.1	5.4	34.5	10.0	18.3	2.8	9.9
1989	20.9	10.7	30.5	9.9	17.0	2.2	8.9
Index (1980 = 100)	143.0	185.0	114.0	123.0	122.0	98.0	113.0
Finland							
1980	19.8	1.4	21.8	8.6	22.3	10.5	15.5
1989	31.2	1.9	22.7	11.5	16.2	6.5	10.0
Index (1980 = 100)	172.0	147.0	113.0	145.0	79.0	66.0	70.0
Germany							
1980	14.1	1.3	30.7	12.9	16.3	6.9	15.9
1986	16.2	1.5	29.8	12.8	16.1	5.5	13.3
Index (1980 = 100)	118.0	115.0	99.0	102.0	102.0	83.0	86.0
Greece							
1981	10.7	0 7	12.9	9.0	9.7	41.6	15.5
1989	14.4	0.8	14.6	10.8	11.5	34.0	13.9
Index (1981= 100)	156.0	130.0	131.0	138.0	137.0	95.0	104.0
Japan							
1980	9.6	0.5	23.1	14.3	12.7	13.1	26.5
1989	11.4	0.8	26.4	14.4	11.4	8 8	26.5
Index (1980 = 100)	173.0	132.0	116.0	104.0	77.0	116.0	250.0

Table 4.17 contd

Country[b,c]	Professional, technical and related	Administrative and managerial	Clerical and related	Sales workers	Service workers	Agriculture and related	Production and related
Norway							
1980	23.6	2.2	19.2	12.8	24.9	5.9	11.2
1989	28.3	3.5	19.8	12.4	22.3	3.9	9.4
Index (1980 = 100)	141.0	188.0	121.0	114.0	106.0	78.0	99.0
Spain							
1980	8.7	0.2	13.2	15.4	25.6	18.2	18.7
1989	15.2	0.4	18.2	15.4	25.2	11.1	14.4
Index (1980 = 100)	202.0	280.0	160.0	116.0	114.0	70.0	89.0
Sweden							
1980	30.6	0.8	21.6	8.7	22.8	3.0	12.4
1989	42.0	n.a.	21.9	9.3	13.2	1.8	11.7
Index (1980 = 100)	154.0	n.a.	114.0	120.0	65.0	66.0	106.0
United States							
1980	16.8	6.9	35.1	6.8	19.5	1.2	13.8
1989	18.1	11.1	27.8	13.1	17.7	1.1	11.1
Index (1980 = 100)	136.0	202.0	99.0	243.0	115.0	115.0	101.0

[a] Major groups of the International Standard Classification of Occupations (ISCO).
[b] Not all countries publish data according to ISCO. Countries in which occupational classification systems have changed during the relevant period are omitted.
[c] The index indicates the growth in total numbers employed in the occupation over the decade.
Source: ILO, Yearbook of Labour Statistics (various years)

Why women? First, because, in contrast with the misleading statements printed in the media, overall there has been a sustained job creation in the world in the past three decades, with the exception of Europe (see volume I, chapter 4). But, even in Europe, women's labor participation has increased while men's has declined. So, women's entry into the labor force is not just a response to labor demand. Also, women's unemployment is not always higher than for men: in 1994 it was lower than men's in the United States (6 percent *v.* 6.2 percent), and in Canada (9.8 percent *v.* 10.7 percent); and it was much lower than men's in 1993 in the United Kingdom (7.5 percent *v.* 12.4 percent). On the other hand, it was slightly higher in Japan and Spain, and significantly higher in France and Italy. Thus, the increase in women's labor participation rate goes on independently of their differential in unemployment *vis à vis* men, and of the growth of labor demand.

If labor demand, in purely quantitative terms, does not explain calling upon women, their appeal for employers must be explained by other characteristics. I think it is well established in the literature that it is the social gendering of women's work that makes them, as a whole, an attractive labor pool[34] This has certainly nothing to do with biological characteristics: women have proved that they can be firefighters and dockers around the world, and strenuous factory work by women marked industrialization from its beginning. Nor, for that matter, has young women's employment in electronics anything to do with the myth of their fingers' dexterity, but with the social acceptance of wasting their eyes in 10 years through microscopic assembly. Anthropologists have documented how, at the origins of women's employment in electronic factories in South-east Asia, there was the pattern of patriarchal authority extending from the family household into the factory, under agreement between factory managers and the paterfamilias.[35]

Neither, it seems, is the reason for hiring women to do with their lack of unionization. The causality seems to work the other way around: women are not unionized because they are often employed in sectors where there is little or no unionization, such as private business services or electronics manufacturing. Even so, women constitute 37 percent of union members in the United States, 39 percent in Canada, 51 percent in Sweden, and 30 percent in Africa, on average.[36] Garment workers in the United States and in Spain, women in the Mexican *maquiladoras*, and teachers and nurses

[34]   Spitz (1988); Kahne and Giele (1992); OECD (1994b).
[35]   Salaff (1981).
[36]   United Nations (1991).

throughout the world have mobilized in defense of their demands, with greater vehemence than male-dominated steel or chemical workers' unions in recent times. The supposed submissiveness of women workers is an enduring myth whose fallacy managers have come to realize, at their cost.[37] So, which are the main factors inducing the explosion of women's employment?

The first, and most obvious, factor concerns the possibility of paying less for similar work. With the expansion of universal education, including college education, particularly in most developed countries, women came to constitute a pool of skills that was immediately tapped by employers. Women's wage differential *vis à vis* men persists throughout the world, while, as we have seen, in most advanced countries differences in occupational profile are small. In the US, women earned 60–65 percent of men's earnings in the 1960s, and their share improved somewhat to 72 percent in 1991, but the main reason for this was the decline in men's real wages.[38] In the UK, women's earnings were 69.5 percent of men's in the mid-1980s. They were 73.6 percent in Germany in 1991, up from 72 percent in 1980. For France, the corresponding figures are 80.8 percent, up from 79 percent. Women's average wage is 43 percent of men's in Japan, 51 percent in Korea, 56 percent in Singapore, 70 percent in Hong Kong, and varies in a wide range between 44 percent and 77 percent in Latin America.[39]

I want to emphasize that in most cases women are not being deskilled, or reduced to menial jobs, but, quite the opposite. They are often promoted to multi-skilled jobs that require initiative, and education, as new technologies demand an autonomous labor force able to adapt, and reprogram its own tasks, as in the case studies of insurance and banking that I summarized in volume I, chapter 4. This is in fact the second major reason for hiring women, at a bargain price: their relational skills, increasingly necessary in an informational economy where the administration of things takes second place to the management of people. In this sense, there is an extension of the gendered division of labor between male's traditional production and female's traditional home-making, and social-making, under patriarchalism. It just happens that the new economy requires increasingly the skills that were confined to the private domain of relational work to be brought to the forefront of management and processing of information and people.

But there is something else that I believe is probably the most

---

[37]   Cobble (1993).
[38]   Kim (1993).
[39]   United Nations (1995).

Table 4.18 Size and composition of part-time employment, 1973–94 (%)

Part-time employment as a proportion of employment

	Men						Women					
	1973	1979	1983	1992	1993	1994	1973	1979	1983	1992	1993	1994
Australia	3.7	5.2	6.2	10.6	10.3	10.9	28.2	35.2	36.4	43.3	42.3	42.6
Austria	1.4	1.5	1.5	1.6	1.7	..	15.6	18.0	20.0	20.5	22.8	..
Belgium	1.0	1.0	2.0	2.1	2.3	2.5	10.2	16.5	19.7	28.1	28.5	28.3
Canada	4.7	5.7	7.6	9.3	9.8	9.5	19.4	23.2	26.1	25.8	26.2	26.1
Denmark	..	5.2	6.6	10.1	11.0	..	..	46.3	44.7	36.7	37.3	..
Finland	..	3.2	4.5	5.5	6.2	6.0	..	10.6	12.5	10.4	11.1	11.2
France	1.7	2.4	2.5	3.6	4.1	4.6	12.9	17.0	20.1	24.5	26.3	27.8
Germany[a]	1.8	1.5	1.7	2.6	2.9	..	24.4	27.6	30.0	30.7	32.0	..
Greece	..	..	3.7	2.8	2.6	3.1	..	..	12.1	8.4	7.6	8.0
Iceland	..	..	..	9.2	9.9	..	..	..	..	49.8	47.5	..
Ireland	..	2.1	2.7	3.9	4.8	..	14.0	13.1	15.5	18.6	21.3	..
Italy	3.7	3.0	2.4	2.8	2.5	2.8	25.1	10.6	9.4	11.5	11.0	12.4
Japan	6.8	7.5	7.3	10.6	11.4	11.7	18.4	27.8	29.8	34.8	35.2	35.7
Luxembourg	1.0	1.0	1.0	1.2	1.0	..	..	17.1	17.0	16.5	18.3	..
Mexico[b]	..	..	..	18.7	19.6	..	..	..	..	36.1	36.6	..
Netherlands[c]	4.6	5.5	7.2	13.3	13.6	14.7	24.6	44.0	50.1	62.1	63.0	64.8
New Zealand	8.6	4.9	5.0	10.3	9.7	9.7	47.8	29.1	31.4	35.9	35.7	36.6
Norway[d]	..	10.6	11.5	9.8	9.8	9.5	..	51.7	54.9	47.1	47.6	46.5
Portugal	..	2.5	..	4.1	4.5	4.7	..	16.5	..	11.3	11.1	12.1
Spain	..	..	..	2.0	2.4	2.6	..	..	..	13.7	14.8	15.2
Sweden[e]	..	5.4	6.3	8.4	9.1	9.7	..	46.0	45.9	41.3	41.4	41.0
Switzerland	..	..	..	8.3	8.6	8.8	..	..	..	53.7	54.1	55.4
Turkey	..	..	..	11.3	17.9	..	..	..	..	37.0	40.4	..
United Kingdom	2.3	1.9	3.3	6.2	6.6	7.1	39.1	39.0	42.4	43.5	43.8	44.3
United States[f]	8.6	9.0	10.8	10.8	10.9	11.5	26.8	26.7	28.1	25.4	25.3	27.7

Table 4.18 contd

	Part-time employment as a proportion of total employment						Women's share in part-time employment					
	1973	1979	1983	1992	1993	1994	1973	1979	1983	1992	1993	1994
Australia	11.9	15.9	17.5	24.5	23.9	24.4	79.4	78.7	78.0	75.0	75.3	74.2
Austria	6.4	7.6	8.4	9.0	10.1	..	85.8	87.8	88.4	89.6	89.7	..
Belgium	3.8	6.0	8.1	12.4	12.8	12.8	82.4	88.9	84.0	89.7	89.3	88.1
Canada	9.7	12.5	15.4	16.7	17.2	17.0	68.4	72.1	71.3	69.7	68.9	69.4
Denmark	..	22.7	23.8	22.5	23.3	..	..	86.9	84.7	75.8	74.9	..
Finland	..	6.7	8.3	7.9	8.6	8.5	..	74.7	71.7	64.3	63.1	63.6
France	5.9	8.1	9.6	12.5	13.7	14.9	82.3	82.1	84.3	83.7	83.3	82.7
Germany[a]	10.1	11.4	12.6	14.4	15.1	..	89.0	91.6	91.9	89.3	88.6	..
Greece	..	..	6.5	4.8	4.3	4.8	..	..	61.2	61.3	61.6	58.9
Iceland	..	..	..	27.8	27.3	..	..	..	..	82.1	80.4	..
Ireland	..	5.1	6.6	9.1	10.8	..	..	71.2	71.6	72.5	71.7	..
Italy	6.4	5.3	4.6	5.8	5.4	6.2	58.3	61.4	64.8	68.8	70.5	71.1
Japan	13.9	15.4	16.2	20.5	21.1	21.4	70.0	70.1	72.9	69.3	67.7	67.5
Luxembourg	5.8	5.8	6.3	6.9	7.3	..	87.5	87.5	88.9	88.9	91.2	..
Mexico[b]	..	..	..	24.0	24.9	..	..	..	..	46.3	46.1	..
Netherlands[c]	..	16.6	21.4	32.5	33.4	35.0	..	76.4	77.3	75.2	75.7	75.1
New Zealand	11.2	13.9	15.3	21.6	21.2	21.6	72.3	77.7	79.8	73.3	74.2	74.9
Norway[d]	23.0	27.3	29.6	26.9	27.1	26.5	76.4	77.0	77.3	80.1	80.5	80.6
Portugal	..	7.8	..	7.3	7.4	8.0	..	80.4	..	68.2	66.3	67.1
Spain	..	..	..	5.8	6.6	6.9	..	..	..	77.0	75.6	74.9
Sweden[e]	..	23.6	24.8	24.3	24.9	24.9	..	87.5	86.6	82.3	81.3	80.1
Switzerland	..	..	..	27.8	28.1	28.9	..	..	..	83.1	82.5	82.7
Turkey	..	..	..	19.3	24.8	..	..	..	..	59.3	50.2	..
United Kingdom	16.0	16.4	19.4	22.8	23.3	23.8	90.9	92.8	89.8	84.9	84.5	83.6
United States[f]	15.6	16.4	18.4	17.5	17.5	18.9	66.0	68.0	66.8	66.4	66.2	67.3

[a] Up to 1990 data refer to Western Germany; thereafter, they refer to the whole of Germany. [b] 1991 instead of 1992. [c] Break in series after 1985.
[d] Break in series after 1987. [e] Break in series after 1986 and after 1992. [f] Break in series after 1993.
Source: OECD, Employment Outlook (1995)

Table 4.19 Share of self-employment in total employment, by sex and activity (%)

| | All non-agricultural activities | | | | Service activities (1990) both sexes | | | |
| | Share of female employment | | Share of male employment | | Wholesale and retail trade, restaurants and hotels (ISIC 6) | Transport, storage and communications (ISIC 7) | Financing, insurance, real estate and business services (ISIC 8) | Community, social and personal services (ISIC 9) |
	1979	1990	1979	1990				
Australia	10.0	9.6	13.9	14.4	15.5	14.5	14.0	6.6
Austria	:	:	:	:	13.7	3.6	10.0	5.0
Belgium	8.8	10.3	12.6	16.7	36.0	5.5	21.7	8.2
Canada	6.0	6.4	7.2	8.3	7.2	6.4	10.4	8.5
Denmark	:	2.8	:	10.4	13.3	6.9	9.6	3.2
Finland	4.2	5.6	7.9	11.5	16.0	11.2	10.5	4.0
France	:	5.5	:	11.9	19.2	4.8	9.2	5.3
Germany	4.8	5.4	9.4	9.7	15.7	6.6	17.1	5.5
Greece	25.7	15.4	34.0	32.7	48.0	25.5	35.9	9.4
Ireland	:	6.1	:	16.8	24.4	13.7	13.6	6.8
Italy	12.8	15.1	21.7	25.8	45.8	14.1	8.9	15.5
Japan	12.9	9.3	14.6	12.1	15.0	4.8	8.1	12.0
Luxembourg	:	5.8	:	7.9	17.5	3.8	7.0	3.7
Netherlands	:	7.3	:	9.6	13.4	3.3	11.9	7.8
New Zealand	:	11.8	:	24.0	18.2	11.1	19.2	9.6
Norway	3.4	3.6	8.9	8.8	7.5	9.3	6.7	4.4
Portugal	:	12.3	:	18.3	38.3	8.6	13.7	4.6
Spain	12.5	13.9	17.1	19.2	34.0	26.8	13.7	6.0
Sweden	6.2	3.9	2.5	10.1	13.6	8.8	11.6	3.7
United Kingdom	3.2	7.0	9.0	16.6	15.9	10.5	14.2	7.8
United States	4.9	5.9	8.7	8.7	8.5	4.6	11.4	7.3

Source: OECD, *Employment Outlook* (1991), table 2.12; (1992) tables 4.A.2 and 4.A.8

important factor inducing the expansion of women's employment in the 1990s: their flexibility as workers.[40] Indeed, women account for the bulk of part-time employment and temporary employment, and for a still small but growing share of self-employment (tables 4.18 and 4.19). Relating this observation to the analyses presented in volume I, chapters 3 and 4, concerning the networking of economic activity, and the flexibilization of work as major features of the informational economy, it seems reasonable to argue that there is a fit between women's working flexibility, in schedules, time, and entry and exit to and from the labor market, and the needs of the new economy.[41] This fit is also a gendered condition. Since women's work has traditionally been considered as complementary to men's earnings in the family, and since women are still responsible for their household and, above all, for the rearing of their children, work flexibility fits, as well, survival strategies of coping with both worlds on the edge of a nervous breakdown.[42] Indeed, in the European Union (as everywhere else), marriage and children are the most important factors in inducing women's part-time employment (figure 4.9). Thus, the type of worker required by the informational, networked economy fits the survival interests of women who, under the conditions of patriarchalism, seek to make compatible work and family, with little help from their husbands.

This process of full incorporation of women into the labor market, and into paid work, has important consequences for the family. The first is that more often than not a woman's financial contribution becomes decisive for the household budget. Thus, female bargaining power in the household increases significantly. Under strict patriarchalism, women's domination by men was, to start with, a living matter: home-making was their job. Thus, rebellion against patriarchal authority could be only extreme, often leading to marginality. With women bringing pay home, and with men in many countries (for instance in the United States) seeing their real pay-checks decline, matters of disagreement could be discussed without necessarily escalating to all-out patriarchal repression. Furthermore, the ideology of patriarchalism legitimizing domination on the basis of the family provider's privilege was decisively undermined. Why could husbands not help at home if both members of the couple were equally absent for long hours, and if both were equally contributing to the family budget? The questions became more pressing with the increasing difficulty for women of assuming paid work, home work, child

[40]   Susser (forthcoming).
[41]   Thurman and Trah (1990); Duffy and Pupo (1992).
[42]   Michelson (1985).

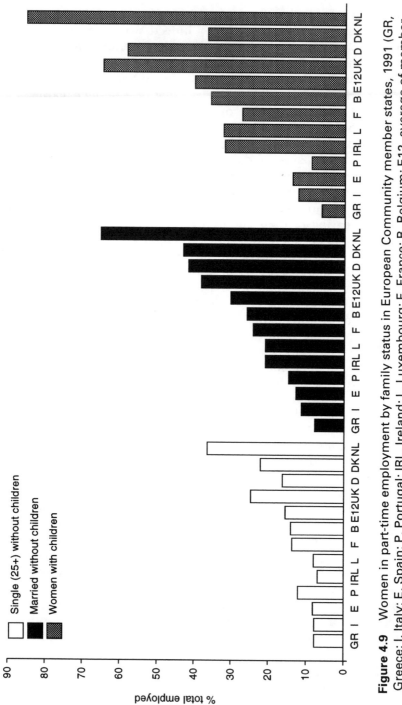

Figure 4.9 Women in part-time employment by family status in European Community member states, 1991 (GR, Greece; I, Italy; E, Spain; P, Portugal; IRL, Ireland; L, Luxembourg; F, France; B, Belgium; E12, average of member states; UK, United Kingdom; D, Germany; DK, Denmark; NL, Netherlands)
Source: European Commission, *Employment in Europe* (1993)

rearing, and management of husbands, while society was still organized on the assumption of the vanishing full-time housewife. With no proper child care, no planning of the spatial connection between residence, jobs, and services, and deteriorating social services,[43] women were confronted with their reality: their beloved husbands/fathers were taking advantage of them. And since their work outside the home opened their world, and broadened their social networks and their experience, often marked by sisterhood against daily harshness, they started to ask questions of themselves, and to give their answers to their daughters. The soil was ready for the seeding of feminist ideas that were *simultaneously* germinating in the fields of cultural social movements.

Sisterhood is Powerful: the Feminist Movement

The feminist movement, as manifested in its practice and discourses, is extraordinarily diverse. Its richness and depth increase as we analyze its contours in a global, comparative perspective, and as feminist historians and theoreticians unearth the hidden record of women's resistance and feminist thinking.[44] I will limit the analysis presented here to the contemporary feminist movement that surged in the late 1960s, first in the United States, then in Europe in the early 1970s, and diffused throughout the world in the next two decades. I will also focus on those features that are common to the movement, and that make it a transformative social movement challenging patriarchalism, while accounting for the diversity of women's struggles and the multiculturalism of their expression. As a preliminary, working definition of feminism, as understood here, I will follow Jane Mansbridge in broadly defining feminism as "the commitment to ending male domination."[45] I also concur with her view of feminism as a "discursively created movement." This does not imply that feminism is just discourse, or that the feminist debate, as expressed in the writings of various women, theorists and academics, is the primordial manifestation of feminism. What I contend, in line with Mansbridge and others,[46] is that the essence of feminism, as practiced and as narrated, is the (re)definition of woman's identity: sometimes by affirming equality between men and women, thus de-gendering biological/cultural differences; in other instances, on the contrary, as affirming

---

[43] Servon and Castells (1996).
[44] Rowbotham (1974, 1992); Kolodny (1984); Spivak (1990); Massolo (1992).
[45] Mansbridge (1995: 29).
[46] Butler (1990); Chodorow (1994); Whittier (1995).

the essential specificity of women, often in association with stating the superiority of women's ways as sources of human fulfillment; or else, claiming the necessity to depart from men's world, and recreate life, and sexuality, in sisterhood. *In all cases, through equality, difference, or separation, what is negated is woman's identity as defined by men, and as enshrined in the patriarchal family.* As Mansbridge writes:

> This discursively created movement is the entity that inspires movement activists and is the entity to which they feel accountable . . . This kind of accountability is an accountability through identity . . . It requires thinking of the collective as a worthy identity and oneself as part of that identity. Feminist identities are usually achieved, not given . . . Today, feminist identities are created and reinforced when feminists get together, act together, and read what other feminists have written. Talking and acting creates street theory and gives it meaning. Reading keeps one in touch and continues to make one think. Both experiences, of personal transformation and continuing interaction, make feminists "internally accountable" to the feminist movement.[47]

Thus, a fundamental commonality underlies the diversity of feminism: the historical effort, individual as well as collective, formal and informal, to redefine womanhood in direct opposition to patriarchalism.

To assess such an effort, and to propose a grounded typology of feminist movements, I will recall, succinctly, the trajectory of feminist movements in the past three decades. To simplify the argument, I will focus mainly on its place of rebirth, the United States, and I will try to correct the potential ethnocentrism of this approach with brief observations on other areas of the world, followed by a commentary on feminism in a comparative perspective.

American feminism: a discontinuous continuity[48]

American feminism has a long history in a country with a short history. From the official birth of organized feminism in 1848 at a village

---

[47]   Mansbridge (1995: 29).

[48]   For an excellent analysis of the evolution and transformation of the American feminist *movement* in the past three decades, see Whittier (1995); for an overview of feminist *organizations* in America, see Ferree and Martin (1995); for a well-organized and usefully commented collection of American feminist *discourses* since the 1960s, see Schneir (1994). Other sources used in my analysis are specifically cited in the text.

chapel in Seneca Falls, New York, American feminists undertook a protracted struggle in defense of women's rights to education, work, and political power, culminating in the conquest of their right to vote in 1920. Then, afterwards, for almost half a century, feminism was kept in the backstage of the American scene. Not that women ceased to fight.[49] In one of the most noted expressions of women's struggles, the 1955 bus boycott in Montgomery, Alabama, that arguably ushered in the civil rights movement in the South, and changed American history for ever, was enacted predominantly by African-American women organizing their communities.[50] Yet, an explicitly feminist mass movement surged only in and from the 1960s social movements, both from their human rights component, and from their counter-cultural, revolutionary tendencies.[51] On the one hand, in the wake of the work of John F. Kennedy's Presidential Commission on the Status of Women, in 1963, and of the approval of Title VII of the 1964 Civil Rights Act concerning women's rights, a group of influential women, headed by writer Betty Friedan, created the National Organization of Women (NOW) on October 29, 1966. NOW would become the most comprehensive national organization in defense of women's rights, and over the following three decades it demonstrated extraordinary political skill and perdurability, in spite of recurrent ideological and organizational crises. It came to epitomize the so-called liberal feminism, focusing on equal rights for women in all spheres of social, economic, and institutional life.

Around the same time, women participating in various radical social movements, and particularly in SDS (Students for a Democratic Society), started to organize separately as a reaction against pervasive sexism and male domination in revolutionary organizations that led not only to the personal abuse of women, but to the ridiculing of feminist positions as bourgeois and counter-revolutionary. What started in December 1965 as a workshop on "Women in the Movement" in the SDS Convention, and became articulated as Women Liberation in a 1967 convention at Ann Arbor, Michigan, generated a flurry of autonomous women's groups, most of which split from male-dominated revolutionary politics, giving birth to radical feminism. In these founding moments it is fair to say that the feminist movement was ideologically split between its liberal and radical components. Whereas NOW's first statement of purpose started by saying "We, MEN AND WOMEN [capitals in the original] who hereby constitute ourselves as the National Organization for Women, believe that the

---

[49]   Rupp and Taylor (1987).
[50]   Barnett (1995).
[51]   Evans (1979).

time has come for a new movement toward a fully equal partnership
of the sexes, as part of the world-wide revolution of human rights now
taking place within and beyond our national borders,"[52] the 1969
Redstockings Manifesto, that propelled radical feminism in New York,
asserted: "We identify the agents of our oppression as men. Male
supremacy is the oldest, most basic form of domination. All other
forms of exploitation and oppression (racism, capitalism, imperialism
etc.) are extensions of male supremacy; men dominate women, a few
men dominate the rest."[53]

Liberal feminism centered its goals on obtaining equal rights for
women, including the adoption of a constitutional amendment, that,
after being approved by Congress, failed to obtain the required
ratification by two-thirds of the states, being finally defeated in 1982.
Yet, the significance of this amendment was more symbolic than
anything else, since the real battles for equality were won in federal
and state legislation, and in the courts, from the right to equal pay for
equal work to reproductive rights, including the right of access to all
occupations and institutions. These impressive achievements, in less
than two decades, were obtained by skillful political lobbying, media
campaigns, and support for women candidates or pro-women candidates in their bids for public office. Particularly important was the
presence in the media of women journalists who were either feminists
or supportive of feminist causes. A number of somewhat feminist
commercial publications, most notably *Ms Magazine* founded in 1972,
were also instrumental in reaching out to American women beyond
organized feminist circles.

Radical feminists, while participating actively in equal rights
campaigns, and particularly in the mobilizations to obtain and defend
reproductive rights, focused on *consciousness raising* (CR), through the
organization of women-only CR groups, and the building of institutions of a women's autonomous culture. Defense of women against
male violence (anti-rape campaigns, self-defense training, shelters for
battered women, psychological counseling for abused women)
provided a direct link between women's immediate concerns and the
ideological critique of patriarchalism in action. Within the radical
stream, lesbian feminists (one of whose first public political
demonstrations, the "Lavender Menace," appeared in the Second
Congress to Unite Women, in May 1970 in New York) quickly became
a source of dedicated activism, cultural creativity, and theoretical
innovation. The relentless growth and widespread influence of
lesbian feminism in the feminist movement was to become both a

---

[52]   Reproduced in Schneir (1994: 96).
[53]   Reproduced in Schneir (1994: 127).

major force and a major challenge for the women's movement, which had to face its own internal prejudice about forms of sexuality, and to confront the dilemma of where (or whether) to draw the line for women's liberation.

For a while, socialist feminists tried to associate the radical feminist challenge to broader issues of anti-capitalist movements, linking up when necessary with the political left, and engaging in an enriching debate with Marxist theory. Some of them worked in the labor unions. For instance, in 1972 a Coalition of Labor Union Women was formed. However, in the 1990s the fading away of socialist organizations, and of socialism as a historical point of reference, as well as the declining influence of Marxist theory, lessened the impact of socialist feminism, which remained by and large confined to academia.[54]

However, the distinction between liberal and radical feminism was blurred in the practice of the movement, and in the ideology of individual feminists from the mid-1970s onwards. Several factors contributed to the overcoming of ideological cleavages in a feminist movement that kept its diversity, and featured vibrant debates as well as internecine fights, but established bridges and coalitions among its components.[55] On the one hand, as Zillah Eisenstein pointed out,[56] the issues to be tackled by liberal feminism, namely equal rights and de-gendering of social categories, involved such a level of institutional transformation that patriarchalism would be ultimately called into question, even within the most restrained strategy of being practical about achieving gender equality. Secondly, the anti-feminist backlash of the 1980s, supported by the Republican administration that governed America in 1980–92, prompted an alliance between different strings of the movement, that, regardless of their lifestyles and political beliefs, found each other together in the mobilizations to defend women's reproductive rights or in the building of women's institutions to provide services and assert cultural autonomy. Thirdly, most radical feminist organizations had faded away by the late 1970s, with their founders personally exhausted, and their local utopias confronting daily battles with "really existing patriarchalism." Yet, since most radical feminists never gave up on their basic values, they found refuge in the established organizations of liberal feminism, and in the enclaves that feminism managed to build within mainstream institutions, particularly in academia (women's studies programs), in

[54] For an analysis of the rise and fall of one of the most dynamic and influential socialist feminist organizations, the Chicago Women's Liberation Union (CWLU), see Strobel (1995).
[55] Ferree and Hess (1994); Ferree and Martin (1995); Mansbridge (1995); Spalter-Roth and Schreiber (1995); Whittier (1995).
[56] Eisenstein (1981/1993).

non-profit foundations, and in women's caucuses of professional associations. These organizations and institutions were in need of militant support in their increasingly difficult task, when they began to move beyond the most obvious abuses of human rights into more controversial spheres, such as reproductive choice, sexual liberation, and advancement of women in men's various citadels. Indeed, it can be argued that the presence of liberal organizations helped radical feminism to survive as a movement, whereas most of men-based counter-cultural movements originated in the 1960s, with the major exception of ecologists, all but faded away, or were ideologically subdued during the 1980s. As a result of this multilayered process, liberalism and radicalism, in their different brands, became interwoven in their practice, and in the minds of most women supporting feminist causes and values. Even lesbianism became an accepted component of the movement, although still attached to some kind of tactical rejection within mainstream feminism (Betty Friedan opposed it), as exemplified by the tensions within NOW in the late 1980s after the "confession" of bisexuality by NOW's president Patricia Ireland.

Other distinctions became more relevant for the feminist movement, as it developed, diversified, and reached out, at least in their minds, to the majority of American women, between the mid-1970s and the mid-1990s. On the one hand, there were important distinctions in the kind of feminist *organizations*. On the other hand, there were substantial differences between what Nancy Whittier calls "political generations" within the feminist *movement*.[57]

In terms of organizations, Spalter-Roth and Schreiber[58] propose an empirically grounded, useful typology that differentiates between:

1 National membership organizations demanding equal rights, such as NOW or the Coalition of Labor Union Women, founded in 1972. They tried deliberately to avoid feminist language while advancing the cause of women in all domains of society, thus sacrificing principles for effectiveness in increasing women's participation in male-dominated institutions. Spalter-Roth and Schreiber conclude that "despite the hopes of organizations' leaders who wished to appeal to both liberals and radicals, the use of politically palatable language obscured relations of domination and subordination. Their efforts may have failed to raise the consciousness of the very women these organizations hoped to represent and empower."[59]

[57] Whittier (1995).
[58] Spalter-Roth and Schreiber (1995: 106–8).
[59] Spalter-Roth and Schreiber (1995: 119).

2 Direct service providers, such as the Displaced Homemakers Network, and the National Coalition against Domestic Violence. These are predominantly networks of local groups receiving support from government and corporations for their programs. Their main problem is the contradiction between assisting women and empowering them: usually, the urgency of the problem takes precedence over the long-term goals of consciousness raising and political self-organizing.

3 Staff-run and expert-based pro-women organizations, such as the Women's Legal Defense Fund, the Institute for Women Policy Research, the Center for Women Policy Studies, the Fund for Feminist Majority (supporting women in political institutions), the National Institute for Women of Color, or the National Committee for Pay Equity. The challenge for this type of organization is to broaden the range of their issues as more women are brought into the movement's sphere of influence, and as feminist themes become increasingly diversified, ethnically, socially, and culturally.

Beyond mainstream organizations, there are a myriad of local organizations of the women's community, many of them originally linked to radical feminism, then evolving along a great variety of trajectories. Alternative women's health clinics, credit unions, training centers, bookstores, restaurants, day-care centers, centers to prevent violence against women and to cope with its injuries, theater groups, music groups, writers' clubs, artists' studios, and a whole range of cultural expressions, went through ups and downs and, usually, when they survived they did so by downplaying their ideological character and becoming more integrated in society at large. They are, in the broader sense, feminist organizations that, in their diversity and with their flexibility, have provided the networks of support, the experience, and the discursive materials for a women's culture to emerge, thus undermining patriarchalism in its most powerful site: women's minds.

The other major distinction to be introduced in understanding the evolution of American feminism is Whittier's concept of political generations and micro-cohorts. In her insightful sociological study of the evolution of American radical feminism over three decades, she shows both the continuity of feminism, and the discontinuity of feminist styles between the early 1970s, the 1980s, and the 1990s:

Political generations are important to social movement continuity in three ways. First, the collective identity of a political generation remains consistent over time, as it has for women who participated in the feminist movement of the 1970s. Second, even when protest declines a social movement continues to have an impact if a generation of movement veterans carry its key elements into societal institutions and other social movements. Institutions and innovations established by activists within these other settings serve not only as agents of change themselves but also as resources for the resurgence of a future wave of mobilization. Third, a social movement changes as new participants enter the movement and redefine its collective identity. The continual entry of micro-cohorts at regular intervals produces gradual changes. Each micro-cohort constructs a collective identity that is shaped by its context, and therefore activists who enter during movement resurgence, growth, peak and decline differ from each other. Despite the gradual shifts that occur continually within social movements, there are clearly sharper changes at certain points. At these times, a series of micro-cohorts converge into one political generation, as their similarities to each other outweigh their differences from a distinct set of incoming micro-cohorts that make up a second political generation . . . The passing of social movements from one political generation to another thus becomes key to movement survival over the long haul.[60]

Whittier shows, on the basis of her case study of Columbus, Ohio, as well as by reviewing evidence from secondary sources, the persistence and renewal of feminist movement, including radical feminism, over three decades, from the 1960s to the 1990s. She is supported in her argument by a number of other sources.[61] It seems that the "post-feminist age" was an interested manipulation of some short-term trends, excessively highlighted in the media.[62] But Whittier also emphasizes, convincingly, the profound transformation of radical feminism, leading sometimes to considerable difficulty in the understanding between generations: "Newcomers to the women's movement are mobilizing for feminist goals in different ways from longtime activists, who sometimes see their successors' efforts as apolitical or misdirected . . . Newcomers constructed a different model of themselves as feminists."[63] As a result of these sharp differences,

it is painful for longtime feminists to see newer entrants to the movement dismissing their dearly held beliefs or changing

---

[60]   Whittier (1995: 254–6).
[61]   Buechler (1990); Staggenborg (1991); Ferree and Hess (1994); Ferree and Martin (1995).
[62]   Faludi (1991); Schneir (1994).
[63]   Whittier (1995: 243).

organizations they struggled to form. Recent debates within the feminist community exacerbate many women's feelings that they and their beliefs are vulnerable to attack. In the "sex wars" in particular, lesbian practitioners of sadomasochism, along with heterosexual women and others, argued that women should have the right to act freely on any sexual desires, and accused those who taught otherwise of being anti-sex, "vanilla", or puritanical.[64]

The main differences between feminist political generations do not seem to be related to the old divide between liberals and radicals, since Whittier concurs in her observation with the blurring of such an ideological definition in the collective action of the movement when confronted with a powerful patriarchal backlash. It seems that three different issues, somewhat interrelated, interfere with communication between veterans and newcomers in the radical feminist movement. The first concerns the growing importance of lesbianism in the feminist movement. Not that it was absent from radical feminism in earlier times, or that it is opposed by radical feminists. But the lifestyles of lesbians, and their emphasis on breaking the mold of heterosexual families, as well as the tactical problems in reaching out to mainstream women from the trenches of a movement with a lesbian heart, made the non-lesbian component of radical feminism increasingly uneasy about lesbian visibility. The second, and much sharper split, concerns the importance given to sexual expression in all its forms by the new generations of feminists. This includes, for instance, the breaking of the "classic" feminist dress code that used to avoid the traps of femininity, to emphasize sexiness and self-expression in women's self-presentation. It also extends to the acceptance of all manifestations of women's sexuality, including bisexuality, and experimentation. The third split is in fact the consequence of the two others. More assured of themselves, and more sharply separatist in their cultural and political values, younger radical feminists, and particularly lesbians, are more open than radical feminists were previously to cooperate with men's social movements, and to relate to men's organizations precisely because they feel less threatened by such alliances since they have already constructed their autonomy, often through separatism. The main point of alliance is between lesbians and gay men (for instance in Queer Nation), who share their oppression from homophobia, and meet in their defense of sexual liberation, and in their critique of the heterosexual/patriarchal family. However, Whittier also reports that old and new radical feminists share fundamental values and meet each other in the same struggles.

Other internal tensions in the feminist movement originate

---

[64]   Whittier (1995: 239).

precisely from its expansion into the whole range of classes and ethnic groups in America.[65] While the 1960s pioneers who rediscovered feminism were overwhelmingly white, middle class, and highly educated, in the next three decades feminist themes linked up with the struggles that African-American women, Latinas, and other ethnic minorities have traditionally carried out in their communities. Women workers, both through labor unions and through autonomous women workers' organizations, mobilized in defense of their demands, using to their advantage the new context of legitimacy for women's struggles. It followed an increasing diversification of the women's movement, and a certain vagueness in their feminist self-definition. Yet, according to opinion polls, from the mid-1980s most women related positively to feminist themes and causes, precisely because feminism did not become associated with any particular ideological stand.[66] Feminism became the common word (and banner) for the whole range of sources of women's oppression as women, to which each woman, or category of women, would attach her personal or collective claim, and label.

Thus, through a variety of practices and self-identifications, women from different origins and with different goals, but sharing a common source of oppression that defined women from outside themselves, constructed a new, collective identity: this is in fact what made possible the transition from women's struggles to a feminist movement. As Whittier writes: "I propose to define the women's movement in terms of the collective identity associated with it rather than in terms of its formal organizations . . . What makes these organizations, networks, and individuals part of a social movement is their shared allegiance to a set of beliefs, practices, and ways of identifying oneself that constitute feminist collective identity."[67]

Are these questions and answers, inspired by the American experience, relevant to feminism in other cultures and countries? Can women's issues, and women's struggles, be generally related to feminism? How collective is this collective identity when women are seen in a global perspective?

Is feminism global?

To advance a tentative answer to such a fundamental question, even superficially, we must distinguish various areas of the world. In the

[65]   Morgen (1988); Matthews (1989); Blum (1991); Barnett (1995); Pardo (1995).
[66]   Stacey (1990); Whittier (1995).
[67]   Whittier (1995: 23–4).

case of Western Europe, Canada, and Australia, it seems apparent that a widespread, diverse, multifaceted feminist movement is active, and growing in the 1990s, albeit with different intensities and characteristics. In Britain, for instance, after a decline in the early 1980s, largely motivated by the neo-conservative assault prompted by Thatcherism, feminist ideas, and the cause of women, permeated throughout the society.[68] As in the United States, on the one hand, women fought for equality, and engaged in self-empowerment in work, social services, legislation, and politics. On the other hand, cultural feminism and lesbianism emphasized women's specificity, and built alternative women organizations. The emphasis on singular identities gives the impression of fragmentation in the movement. Yet, as Gabriele Griffin writes:

> It is the case that many women's groups give themselves titles which specify certain identities . . . This identification provides the impetus for their activism. On one level, feminist activism based on identity politics leads to the fragmentation which many feminists regard as typical for the current political climate, and which is supposed to be in direct contrast to the homogeneity, common purpose and mass mobilization of the Women's (Liberation) Movement, all with capital letters. The latter seems to me to be a myth, a nostalgic retrospective view of some golden age feminism that probably never was. Single issue or single identity feminist organizations such as are common in the 1990s may have the drawback of overly localized politics but their very specificity can also be a guarantee for expertise and impact, for maximum, clearly defined effort within a specific arena.[69]

Thus, single-issue organizations may work on a multiplicity of women's issues, and women may participate in different organizations. It is this intertwining and networking of individuals, organizations, and campaigns that characterizes a vital, flexible, and diverse feminist movement.

Throughout Europe, in every single country, there is a pervasive presence of feminism, both in the institutions of society, and in a constellation of feminist groups, organizations, and initiatives, that feed each other, debate each other (sometimes sharply), and keep inducing a relentless flow of demands, pressures, and ideas on women's condition, women's issues, and women's culture. By and large, feminism, as in the United States, and in Britain, has fragmented, and no single organization or institution can pretend to

[68] Brown (1992); Campbell (1992); Griffin (1995); Hester et al. (1995).
[69] Griffin (1995: 4).

speak on women's behalf. Instead, there is a transversal line cutting across the entire society that emphasizes women's interests, and women's values, from professional caucuses to cultural expressions, and political parties, many of which have established a minimum percentage of women among their leadership (usually the norm, rarely fulfilled, is set at 25 percent of leaders and deputies, so that women are "only" 50 percent under-represented).

Ex-statist societies present a peculiar situation.[70] On the one hand, statist countries helped/forced the full incorporation of women into paid work, opened up educational opportunities, and set up a widespread network of social services and child care, although abortion was banned for a long time, and contraception was not available. Women's organizations were present in all spheres of society, albeit under the total control of the Communist party. On the other hand, sexism was pervasive, and patriarchalism paramount in society, institutions, and politics. As a result, a generation of very strong women grew up, feeling their potential, yet having to fight their way every day to accomplish some of this potential. After the disintegration of Soviet-style communism, feminism as an organized movement is weak, and, until now, limited to a few circles of Westernized intellectuals, while the old-style, patronizing organizations are fading away. Yet, women's presence in the public sphere is increasing dramatically in the 1990s. In Russia, for instance, the Women's Party, although rather conservative in its position and membership, received about 8 percent of the vote in the 1995 parliamentary elections, while a number of women were in the way of becoming key political figures. There is a widespread feeling in Russian society that women could play a decisive role in rejuvenating leadership in Russian politics. In 1996, for the first time in Russian history, a woman was elected Governor of Koryakiya Territory. Furthermore, the new generation of women, educated in the values of equality, and with room to express themselves personally and politically, seem to be ready to crystallize their individual autonomy in collective identity and collective action. It is easy to predict a major development of the women's movement in Eastern Europe, *under their own cultural and political forms of expression.*

In industrialized Asia, patriarchalism still reigns, barely challenged. This is particularly stunning in Japan, a society with a high rate of women's participation in the labor force, a highly educated female population, and a powerful string of social movements in the 1960s. Still, pressures from women groups, and from the Socialist party, led to legislation to limit work discrimination for women in 1986.[71] But,

[70] Funk and Mueller (1993).
[71] Gelb and Lief-Palley (1994).

overall, feminism is limited to academic circles, and professional women still suffer blatant discrimination. Structural features are fully present in Japan to unleash a powerful feminist critique, but the absence of such a critique on a scale large enough to impact society until now, clearly demonstrates that social specificity (in this case the strength of the Japanese patriarchal family, and men's fulfillment of their duties as patriarchs, in general) determines the actual development of a movement, regardless of structural sources of discontent. Korean women are even more subdued than Japanese women, although embryos of a feminist movement have appeared recently.[72] China is still on the edge of the contradictory statist model of supporting the rights of the "half of heaven," while keeping them under the control of the "half of hell." However, the development of a powerful feminist movement in Taiwan since the late 1980s belies the notion of the necessity of women's submission under the patriarchal tradition of Confucianism (see below).[73]

Throughout the so-called developing world, the situation is complex, indeed contradictory.[74] Feminism as an autonomous ideological or political expression is clearly the preserve of a small minority of intellectual and professional women, although their presence in the media amplifies their impact well beyond their numbers. Additionally, in a number of countries, particularly in Asia, women leaders have become towering figures in the politics of their countries (in India, Pakistan, Bangladesh, Philippines, Burma, maybe in Indonesia in a not too distant future), and they have come to represent the rallying symbols for democracy and development. While femaleness does not guarantee womanhood, and most women politicians operate within the framework of patriarchal politics, their impact as role models, particularly for young women, and for the breaking of society's taboos, cannot be neglected.

The most important development, however, from the 1980s onwards, is the extraordinary rise of grassroots organizations, overwhelmingly enacted and led by women, in the metropolitan areas of the developing world. They were spurred by the simultaneous processes of urban explosion, economic crisis, and austerity policies, that left people, and particularly women, with the simple dilemma of fight or perish. Together with the growing employment of women, both in the new industries and in the urban informal economy, it has indeed transformed the condition, organization, and consciousness

[72]   Po (1996).
[73]   Po (1996).
[74]   Kahne and Giele (1992); Massolo (1992); Caipora Women's Group (1993); Jaquette (1994); Kuppers (1994); Blumberg et al. (1995).

of women, as it has been shown, for instance, by the studies conducted by Ruth Cardoso de Leite, or Maria da Gloria Gohn in Brazil, Alejandra Massolo in Mexico, or Helena Useche in Colombia.[75] From these collective efforts not only grassroots organizations have developed, and have impacted on policies and institutions, but a new collective identity, as empowered women, has emerged. Thus, Alejandra Massolo, concluding her analysis of women-based urban social movements in Ciudad de Mexico, wrote:

> The women's subjectivity of experiences of struggle is a revealing dimension of the process of social construction of new collective identities through urban conflicts. Urban movements of the 1970s and 1980s made visible, and distinguishable, the unusual collective identity of segments of popular classes. Women were part of the social production of this new collective identity – from their daily territorial bases, transformed into bases for their collective action. They gave to the process of constructing collective identity the mark of plural motivations, meanings, and expectations from the feminine gender, a complex set of meanings found in the urban movements, even when gender issues are not explicit, and when their membership is mixed and men are in their leadership.[76]

It is this massive presence of women in the collective action of grassroots movements around the world, and their explicit self-identification as collective actors, that is transforming women's consciousness and social roles, even in the absence of an articulate feminist ideology.

However, while feminism is present in many countries, and women's struggles/organizations are exploding all over the world, *the feminist movement displays very different shapes and orientations, depending upon the cultural, institutional, and political contexts where it arises.* For instance, feminism in *Britain* was marked, from its inception in the late 1960s, by a close relationship with the trade unions, the Labour party, the socialist left, and, moreover, the welfare state.[77] It was more explicitly political – that is, geared toward the state – than American feminism, and more directly connected to the daily problems of working women. Yet, because of its proximity to left politics and to the labor movement, it suffered, during the 1970s, from debilitating internal fights with and between different brands of socialist and

---

[75] Cardoso de Leite (1983); Gohn (1991); Espinosa and Useche (1992); Massolo (1992).

[76] Massolo (1992: 338); my translation.

[77] Rowbotham (1989).

radical feminists. For instance, the popular "Wages for Housework" campaign of 1973 was criticized by some feminists because of its implicit acceptance of women's subordinate status at home, potentially inducing them to stay in their domestic enclosures. This contradictory linkage to labor and to socialist politics affected the movement itself. As Rowbotham wrote:

> There is probably some truth in the argument that the emphasis on trade-union support – much stronger in Britain than in many other women's liberation movements – influenced the terms in which the call for abortion was presented. Fusty trades council rooms are not the most commodious sites for learned perorations on the multiplicity of female desire. But . . . I think it is more likely to be partly because of an evasion within the women's liberation movement itself. The movement sought to avoid counterposing heterosexuality and lesbianism, but in the process the scope of sexual self-definition narrowed and any discussion of heterosexual pleasure went into defensive retreat.[78]

Partly as a result of this reluctance to face its diversity, and to drift away from the strategic rationality of traditional politics, British feminism was weakened by the 1980s' Thatcherite juggernaut. Yet, as soon as a new generation of feminists felt free of the old attachments of party politics and labor allegiance, feminism resurged in the 1990s, not only as cultural feminism, and lesbianism, but in a multiplicity of expressions that include, but not in an hegemonic position, socialist feminism, and institutionalized feminism.

Spanish feminism was even more obviously marked by the political context where it was born, the democratic movement against Franco's dictatorship in the mid-1970s.[79] Most women's organizations were linked to anti-Franquist, semi-clandestine opposition, such as the Communist party influenced *Asociacion de Mujeres Democratas* (a political association) and the *Asociaciones de Amas de Casa* (Housewives Associations, territorially organized). Every political tendency, particularly from the revolutionary left, had "its" women's "mass organization." In *Catalunya* and in the Basque Country, women's organizations, and feminists, also had their own organizations,

---

[78] Rowbotham (1989: 81).
[79] My understanding of Spanish feminism comes from direct, personal experience and observation, as well as from conversations with a number of women who played a significant role in the movement. I want to thank the women from whom I learned most, particularly Marina Subirats, Françoise Sabbah, Marisa Goñi, Matilde Fernandez, Carlota Bustelo, Carmen Martinez-Ten, Cristina Alberdi, and Carmen Romero. Naturally, responsibility for the analysis and information presented here is exclusively mine.

reflecting the national cleavages in Spanish politics. Toward the end of Franquism, in 1974–77, autonomous feminist collectives started to appear in the climate of cultural and political liberation that characterized Spain in the 1970s. One of the most innovative and influential was the Madrid-based *Frente de Liberacion de la Mujer*. Its membership was limited (less than one hundred women), but it focused its activity on impacting the media, using its network of women journalists, thus winning popularity for women's demands and discourses. It focused on abortion rights, divorce (both unlawful in Spain at that point), and free expression of women's sexuality, including lesbianism. It was mainly influenced by cultural feminism, and by the French/Italian ideas of *feminisme de la difference*, but it also participated in the political struggles pro-democracy, alongside communist and socialist women's organizations. However, with the establishment of democracy in Spain in 1977, and with the coming to power of the Socialist party in 1982, autonomous feminist movements all but disappeared, precisely because of their success at the institutional and political level. Divorce was legalized in 1981, and abortion, with restrictions, in 1984. The Socialist party promoted an *Instituto de la Mujer*, within the government, which acted as a lobby of feminists *vis à vis* the government itself. Many feminist activists, and particularly those from the *Frente de Liberacion de la Mujer*, joined the Socialist party, and occupied leadership positions in parliament, in the administration, and, to a lesser extent, in the cabinet. A leading socialist feminist, from the labor union movement, Matilde Fernandez, was appointed Minister of Social Affairs, and exercised her influence and strong will in strengthening women's causes in the second half of the Socialist regime. She was replaced as minister in 1993 by Cristina Alberdi, another veteran of the feminist movement, and a prestigious jurist. Carmen Romero, the country's first lady, and a socialist militant of long date, alongside her husband Felipe Gonzalez, was elected to parliament, and played a major role in modifying the party's traditional sexism. For instance, a rule was approved in the party's statutes reserving 25 percent of leadership positions to women (a promise that remained unfulfilled, although women's numbers did increase in the leadership of both party and government). Thus, on the one hand, feminism did have a major impact on improving Spanish women's legal, social, and economic condition, as well as in facilitating the entry of Spanish women to prominent positions in politics, business, and society at large. Attitudes of traditional machismo were dramatically eroded in the new generations.[80] On the other hand, the feminist movement practically disappeared as an

[80] Alonso Zaldivar and Castells (1992).

autonomous movement, emptied from its cadres and entirely focused on institutional reform. There was little room left for lesbian feminism, and for an emphasis on difference and sexuality. Yet, the new tolerance won in Spanish society helped the growth of a new, more culturally oriented feminism in the 1990s, closer to current feminist trends in Britain or France, and distant from traditional politics, except in the Basque Country where it kept self-damaging links with the radical Basque separatist movement. Thus, Spanish feminism exemplifies the potential of using politics and institutions to improve women's status, as well as the difficulty of remaining an autonomous social movement under conditions of successful institutionalization.

Our last exploration of variations of feminism, according to the broader social context in which the movement develops, takes us to *Italy*, the site of what was, arguably, the most potent and innovative mass feminist movement in the whole of Europe during the 1970s.[81]As Bianca Beccalli writes: "From the historical survey of Italian feminism, two themes emerge clearly: the close association between feminism and the Left, and the particular significance of the intertwining of equality and difference."[82] Indeed, contemporary Italian feminism emerged, like most other feminist movements in the West, from the powerful social movements that shook Italy in the late 1960s and early 1970s. But, unlike its counterparts, the Italian feminist movement included an influential current within the Italian trade unions, and was welcome in, and supported by, the Italian Communist party, the largest Communist party outside the Communist world, and Italy's largest membership party. Thus, Italian feminists succeeded in popularizing their themes, as feminists, among large sectors of women, including working-class women, during the 1970s. Economic demands and demands for equality were interwoven with women's liberation, the critique of patriarchalism, and the subversion of authority in the family as in society. However, relationships between feminists and the left, and particularly with the revolutionary left were not easy. Indeed, in December 1975, *the servizio d'ordine* (self-appointed marshals) of *Lotta Continua*, the largest and most radical extreme-left organization, insisted on protecting the demonstration of *Lotta Continua*'s women in Rome, and when women refused their protection, they beat them up, prompting the secession of women

---

[81] My understanding of the Italian feminist movement comes, to a large extent, from my friendship and conversations with Laura Balbo, as well as from personal observation of social movements in Milan, Turin, Venice, Rome, and Naples throughout the 1970s. For a more recent analysis, see the excellent overview of the movement by Bianca Beccalli (1994). On the formative stage of the movement, and its development during the 1970s, see Ergas (1985) and Birnbaum (1986).
[82] Beccalli (1994: 109).

from the organization, and the dissolution of *Lotta Continua* itself a few months later. The increasing autonomy of the Communist-inspired organization *Unione delle Donne Italiane* (UDI) *vis à vis* the party led ultimately to the self-dissolution of UDI in 1978. Yet, overall, there were many linkages between women organizing, labor unions, and left political parties (except socialists), and a great deal of receptivity among party and union leaders to women's issues, and even to feminist discourses. This close cooperation resulted in some of the most advanced legislation on working women in the whole of Europe, as well as in the legalization of divorce (by a 1974 Referendum), and of abortion. For a long period, in the 1970s, this political collaboration went hand in hand with the proliferation of women's collectives which raised issues of women's autonomy, women's cultural difference, sexuality, and lesbianism, as separate trends, yet interacting with the world of politics and class struggle. And yet

> by the end of the decade [1970s] feminism was in decline; and the beginning of the 1980s saw it virtually disappear as a movement. It lost its visibility in political struggles and grew ever more fragmented and out of touch, as feminist activists increasingly committed their energies to private projects and experiences, whether of an individual or communal nature. Thus it was that the "new" feminist movement, following the example of other "new social movements" of the 1970s, evolved into just another form of lifestyle politics.[83]

Why so? Here, I will not put Beccalli's words into my own interpretation, although I do not think I contradict her account. On the one hand, Italian women conquered substantial legal and economic reforms, entered massively the labor force and educational institutions, undermining sexism and, more importantly, the traditional power exercised by the Catholic Church over their lives. Thus, the open, clear battles in which the left, the unions, and women could easily converge, were won, although the victory was not always exploited to its utmost, as in the Law on Equality that, as Beccalli argues, stopped way short of its British model. At the same time, the close connection between the women's movement and the left prompted the crisis of political feminism together with the crisis of the left itself. The revolutionary left, living in a Marxist/Maoist fantasy (elaborated with remarkable intelligence and imagination, thus making artificial paradises even more artificial), disintegrated in the second half of the 1970s. The labor movement, while not having to confront a neo-conservative backlash as in Britain or the United

---

[83]   Beccalli (1994: 86).

States, was faced in the 1980s with the new realities of globalization and technological change, and had to accept the constraints of Italian capitalism's international interdependence. The networking economy, which actually took Emilia Romagna as its model, made Italian small firms dynamic and competitive, yet at the price of decisively undermining union bargaining power concentrated in large factories and the public sector. The Communist party was brushed aside from its power bid by an anti-Communist front led by the Socialist party. And the Socialist party used the levers of power to illegally finance itself to buy its dream of *sorpasso* (that is, overtaking the Communists in the popular vote): the justice system caught up with the Socialists before they could reach the Communists who, in the meantime, had ceased to be Communists, and had joined the Socialist International. It is hardly surprising that Italian feminists, as political as they were, went home. That is, not to their husbands'/fathers' homes, but to the House of Women, to a diverse and vital women's culture which, by the late 1980s, had reinvented feminism, emphasizing *differenzia* without forgetting *egalita*. Luce Irigaray and Adrienne Rich replaced Marx, Mao, and Alexandra Kollontai, as the intellectual points of reference. Yet, new feminist collectives continued in the 1990s to link up feminist discourse and women's demands, particularly in the local governments controlled by the left. One of the most innovative and active campaigns concerned the reorganization of time, from working time to the opening hours of stores and public services, to make flexible schedules adapted to women's multiple lives. In the 1990s, in spite of the political threat from Berlusconi and the neo-fascists, calling for the restoration of traditional family values, the coming to power of a center-left coalition, including the now Socialist, ex-Communist *Partito Democratico di Sinistra* in 1996, opened the way for a renewal of institutional innovation. This time, on the basis of a decentralized, autonomous feminist movement that had learned the lessons of "dancing with the wolves."

Thus, feminism, and women's struggles, go up and down throughout the whole landscape of human experience in this end of millennium, always resurfacing, under new forms, and increasingly linking up with other sources of resistance to domination, while maintaining the tension between political institutionalization and cultural autonomy. The contexts in which feminism develops shape the movement in an array of forms and discourses. And, yet, I contend that an essential (yes, I said essential) nucleus of values and goals constituting identitie(s) permeates across the cultural poliphony of feminism.

Feminism: an inducive polyphony[84]

The strength and vitality of the feminist movement lies in its diversity, in its adaptability to cultures and ages. Thus, trying to find the nucleus of fundamental opposition and essential transformation that is shared across movements, we must first acknowledge this diversity. To read meaningfully through this diversity, I propose a typology of feminist movements based, on the one hand, on observation, as referred to in the cited sources; and, on the other hand, on Touraine's categorization of social movements, as presented in chapter 2. The use of this typology is analytical, not descriptive. It cannot render the multi-faceted profile of feminism across countries and cultures in the 1990s. As all typologies, it is reductionist, a particularly unhappy circumstance concerning women's practices, since women have reacted, rightfully, against their constant cataloguing and labeling in their history as objects, rather than subjects. Furthermore, specific feminist movements, and individual women in the movements, often cut across these and other categories, mixing identities, adversaries, and goals in the self-definition of their experience and struggle. Besides, some of the categories may represent a very small segment of the feminist movement, although I consider them analytically relevant. Yet, overall, I believe it may be useful to consider the distinctions presented in Chart 4.1 as a way to begin with the diversity of feminist movements in a necessary step to investigate their commonality.

Under these types I have included, at the same time, collective actions and individual discourses which are debated in and around feminism. This is because, as stated above, feminism does not exhaust itself in militant struggles. It is also, and sometimes fundamentally, a discourse: a discourse subverting women's place in man's history, thus transforming the historically dominant relationship between space and time, as suggested by Irigaray:

> The gods, God, first create space . . . God would be time itself, exteriorizing itself in its action in space, in places . . . Which would be inverted in sexual difference? Where the feminine is experienced as space, but often with connotations of the abyss and

---

[84] In assessing the main themes of the feminist movement I do not pretend to give justice to the richness of the feminist debate, nor can I survey, even if I knew it, the full range of theories and positions that are now available for an in-depth understanding of women's sources of oppression and avenues of liberation. My analytical synthesis here is geared toward the theoretical purpose of this book: to interpret the interaction between social movements claiming the primacy of identity, and the network society, as the new structure of domination in the information age. If this disclaimer sounds defensive, it is.

Chart 4.1 Analytical typology of feminist movements

Type	Identity	Adversary	Goal
Women's rights (liberal, socialist)	Women as human beings	Patriarchal state and/or patriarchal capitalism	Equal rights (includes reproductive rights)
Cultural feminism	Women's commune	Patriarchal institutions and values	Cultural autonomy
Essentialist feminism (spiritualism, ecofeminism)	Female way of being	Male way of being	Matriarchal freedom
Lesbian feminism	Sexual/cultural sisterhood	Patriarchal heterosexuality	Abolition of gender through separatism
Women' specific identities (ethnic, national, self-defined: e.g. black lesbian feminist)	Self-constructed identity	Cultural domination	Degendered multi-culturalism
Practical feminism (workers, community self-defense, motherhood etc.)	Exploited/ abused women/ homemakers	Patriarchal capitalism	Survival/ dignity

night . . . while the masculine is experienced as time. The transition to a new age requires a change in our perception and conception of space-time, the inhabiting of places, and of containers, or envelopes of identity.[85]

This transition, and this change, are being operated through an array of women's insurgencies, some of which are presented in Chart 4.1, the content of which I will try to clarify by my commentary.

The *defense of women's rights* is the bottom line of feminism. Indeed, all other forms include this basic affirmation of women as human

[85] Irigaray (1984/1993: 7).

beings, not as dolls, objects, things, or animals, in the terms of classic feminist critique. In this sense, feminism is indeed an extension of the human rights movement. This movement comes in two versions, liberal and socialist, although this inclusion as variants of one type may be surprising given their sharp ideological opposition. Indeed, they are different, but in terms of identity they both assert women's rights as equal to men. They differ in their analysis of the roots of patriarchalism, and in their belief, or disbelief, in the possibility of reforming capitalism and operating within the rules of liberal democracy while fulfilling the ultimate goals of equality. Both include economic rights and reproductive rights in women's rights. And both consider the winning of these rights as the movement's goals, although they may diverge sharply in tactical emphases and language. Socialist feminists see the struggle against patriarchalism as necessarily linked to the supersession of capitalism, while liberal feminism approaches socio-economic transformation with a more skeptical view, focusing on advancing the cause of women independently from other goals.

Cultural feminism is based on the attempt to build alternative women's institutions, spaces of freedom, in the midst of patriarchal society, whose institutions and values are seen as the adversary. It is sometimes associated with the "feminism of difference," although it does not imply essentialism. It starts with the double affirmation that women are different, mainly because of their differential history, and that in any case they can only rebuild their identity, and find their own ways, by constructing their own commune. In many cases this implies the will of separation from men, or at least from men-dominated institutions. But it does not lead necessarily to lesbianism or to separatism from males. It aims at building cultural autonomy as a basis of resistance, thus inspiring women's demands on the basis of alternative values, such as non-competitiveness, non-violence, cooperation, and multidimensionality of the human experience, leading to a new women's identity, and women's culture, which could induce cultural transformation in society at large.

The "consciousness-raising" movement, at the origins of radical feminism, was linked to cultural feminism, and induced a whole network of women's organizations and institutions that became spaces of freedom, protection, support, and unfettered communication among women: women's bookstores, health clinics, women's cooperatives. While these organizations were providing services to women, and became organizing tools for a variety of women's rights mobilizations, they also generated and diffused an alternative culture, which established the specificity of women's values.

Essentialist feminism goes a step further, and proclaims, simultaneously, women's essential difference from men, rooted in biology and/or history, and the moral/cultural superiority of womanhood as a way of life. In Fuss's formulation, "essentialism can be located in appeals to a pure or original femininity, a female essence, outside the boundaries of the social and thereby untainted (though perhaps repressed) by a patriarchal order."[86] For instance, for Luce Irigaray, an articulate and influential voice of essentialist feminism, "by our lips we are women."[87]

> How can I say it? That we are women from the start. That we don't have to be turned into women by them, labeled by them, made holy and profaned by them. That that has always hap-pened, without their efforts. And that their history, their stories, constitute the locus of our displacement . . . Their properties are our exile. Their enclosures, the death of our love. Their words, the gag upon our lips . . . Let's hurry and invent our own phrases. So that everywhere and always we can continue to embrace . . . Our strength lies in the very weakness of our resistance. For a long time now they have appreciated what our suppleness is worth for their own embraces and impressions. Why not enjoy ourselves? Rather than letting ourselves be subjected to their branding. Rather than being fixed, stabilized, immobilized. Separated . . . We can do without models, standards, or exam-ples. Let's never give ourselves orders, commands or prohibitions. Let our imperatives be only appeals to move, to be moved, together. Let's never lay down the law to each other, or moralize, or make war.[88]

Liberation is "making each woman 'conscious' of the fact that what she has felt in her personal experience is a condition shared by all women, thus allowing that experience to be politicized."[89] By accepting the specificity of their bodies women are not captured in biology, but, on the contrary, escape from their definition by men that has ignored their true nature. In a masculine order, women will be permanently annihilated because they are characterized from outside their primordial, bodily experience: their bodies have been reinter-preted, and their experience reformulated by men,[90] Only by reconstructing their identity on the basis of their biological and cultural specificity can women become themselves.

[86] Fuss (1989: 2).
[87] Irigaray (1977/1985: 210).
[88] Irigaray (1977/1985: 215–17).
[89] Irigaray (1977/1985: 164).
[90] Fuss (1989).

For instance, the revival of Italian feminism in the early 1980s was somewhat marked by the affirmation of women's difference, and the primacy given to the reconstruction of women's identity on the basis of their biological/cultural specificity, as expressed in the highly popular *"Piu donne che uomini"* pamphlet published by the Women's Bookstore in Milan. It tried to address the inability of women to act in the public sphere by emphasizing the necessity of women working on their own personality, largely determined by their biological specificity. It found a wide echo among Italian women.[91]

Another stream of essentialism links womanhood to history and culture, and claims the myth of a matriarchal golden age when women's values, and the worshipping of the goddess, assured social harmony.[92] Spiritualism and ecofeminism are also among the most powerful manifestations of essentialism, bringing together biology and history, nature and culture, in the affirmation of a new age constructed around women's values and their merger with nature.[93]

Essentialism has come under spirited attack in the feminist movement, both on political grounds, and from opposing intellectual perspectives. Politically, it is argued,[94] that essentializing differences between men and women plays into the hands of traditional values of patriarchalism, and justifies keeping women in their private domain, necessarily in an inferior position. Intellectually, materialist feminists, such as Christine Delphy and Monique Wittig, consider anatomical sex as socially constructed.[95] For them, gender does not create oppression; rather, oppression creates gender. Womanhood is a man's category, and the only liberation consists in degendering society, cancelling the dichotomy man/woman.

Yet, the affirmation of women's irreducible specificity, and the proposal to rebuild society around women's values, does have an undeniable appeal among women, and feminists, while it provides the linkage to the powerful trends of spiritualism and radical ecologism characteristic of the information age.

Lesbian feminism has been the fastest growing, and most militant, component of the feminist movements in developed countries (and not only in the United States) in the past decade, organized in a number of collectives, as well as in caucuses and tendencies within broader feminist movements. It can certainly not be assimilated to a particular sexual orientation. Adrienne Rich proposes the notion of

---

[91]   Beccalli (1994).
[92]   Merchant (1980).
[93]   Spretnak (1982); Epstein (1991).
[94]   Beccalli (1994).
[95]   Delphy (1984); Wittig (1992).

a "lesbian continuum," to include a broad spectrum of women's experiences, marked by their oppression from, and resistance to, the inseparable institutions of patriarchy and compulsory heterosexuality.[96] Indeed, the 1970 Manifesto of American Radicalesbians, started with the following statement: "What is a lesbian? A lesbian is the rage of all women condensed to the point of explosion."[97] From this perspective, lesbianism, as women's radical, self-conscious separation from males as sources of their oppression, is the discourse/ practice of liberation. This explains the success of elective lesbianism for many women, as the way to express their autonomy *vis à vis* men's world in an uncompromising form. In Monique Wittig's words:

> The refusal to become (or to remain) heterosexual always meant to refuse to become a man or a woman, consciously or not. For a lesbian this goes further than the refusal of the role "woman". It is the refusal of the economic, ideological, and political power of a man . . . We are escapees of our class in the same way as the American runaway slaves were escaping slavery and becoming free. For us this is an absolute necessity; our survival demands that we contribute all our strength to the destruction of the class of women within which men appropriate women. *This can be accomplished only by the destruction of heterosexuality* as a social system which is based on the oppression of women by men and which produces the doctrine of the difference between sexes to justify this oppression.[98]

Because heterosexuality is the paramount adversary, lesbian feminism finds in the gay men's movement a potential, if ambivalent, ally (see below).

Increasingly, the feminist movement is being fragmented in a *multiplicity of feminist identities* that constitute the primary definition for many feminists. As I argued above, this is not a source of weakness but of strength in a society characterized by flexible networks and variable alliances in the dynamics of social conflicts and power struggles. These identities are self-constructed, even if they often use ethnicity, and sometimes nationality, as boundary making. Black feminism, Mexican American feminism, Japanese feminism, black lesbian feminism, but also sadomasochist lesbian feminism, or territorial/ethnic self-definitions, such as the Southall Black Sisters in England,[99] are but examples of endless possibilities of self-defined identities through

[96]   Rich (1980/1993).
[97]   Reproduced in Schneir (1994: 162).
[98]   Wittig (1992: 13–20); my italics.
[99]   Griffin (1995: 79).

which women see themselves in movement.[100] So doing, they oppose the standardization of feminism, which they see as a new form of cultural domination, not alien to the patriarchal logic of overimposing officialdom to actual diversity of women's experiences. In some instance, self-identity starts with a pseudonym, as in the case of black feminist writer bell hooks: "I chose the name bell hooks because it was a family name, because it had a strong sound. Throughout childhood, this name was used to speak to the memory of a strong woman, a woman who spoke her mind . . . Claiming this name was a way to link my voice to an ancestral legacy of women speaking – of woman power." [101] Thus, the self-construction of identity is not the expression of an essence, but a power stake through which women as they are mobilize for women as they want to be. Claiming identity is power-making.

I have deliberately chosen a controversial term, *practical feminists*, to refer to the widest and deepest stream of women's struggles in today's world, particularly in the developing world, but also among working-class women and community organizations in industrialized countries. Of course, all feminists are practical, in the sense that they all undermine everyday, in many different ways, the foundations of patriarchalism, be it by fighting for women's rights or by demystifying patriarchal discourses. But, it may also be that many women are feminist in practice, while not acknowledging the label or even having a clear consciousness of opposing patriarchalism. Thus, the question arises: *can feminism exist without feminist consciousness?* Aren't the struggles and organizations of women throughout the world, for their families (meaning, mainly, their children), their lives, their work, their shelter, their health, *their dignity*, feminism in practice? Frankly, I am hesitant on this point, and my work on Latin American grass-roots, and readings on other areas of the world, only deepens my ambivalence, so that the best I can do is to convey it.[102]

On the one hand, I stand by the classic norm of "no class without class consciousness," and by the fundamental methodological principle of defining social movements by the values and goals they express themselves. From this perspective, the overwhelming majority of women's struggles and organizations, in the developing world and beyond, do not express a feminist consciousness, and, more importantly, do not oppose explicitly patriarchalism and male domination, either in their discourse or in the goals of their move-

---

[100]   Whittier (1995); Jarrett-Macauley (1996).
[101]   hooks (1989: 161).
[102]   This issue has been discussed by some feminist historians. My category of "practical feminism" is close to what they call "social feminism"; see Offen (1988); Cott (1989).

ments. Issues of cultural feminism, of lesbian feminism, or of sexual liberation, are rarely present among common women's movements, although not absent, as the revealing experience of the Taiwanese lesbian movement shows (see below). Yet, overall, developing countries' explicit feminism is still, by and large, elitist. This would leave us with a rather fundamental split between feminism and women's struggles that would also have a North/South connotation. Indeed, the 1995 United Nations Women's Forum in Beijing showed some evidence of this split, amplified and highlighted by some interested parties, namely the "Crusade of the Half Moon" formed by the Vatican and Islamists, fighting hand in hand against feminism and women's reproductive rights.

On the other hand, through their collective action, women around the world are linking their struggle, and their oppression, to their everyday lives. They see the transformation of their condition in the family as connected to their intervention in the public sphere. Let us listen to the words of a woman in a Bogota shanty, as recorded by Helena Useche, in her women's stories reported from the trenches of activist social research:

> In recent years, women have made themselves noticed, and now men respect us. Just because of the fact that the compañero does not see the woman just at home, cooking, washing, ironing, but he also sees her as a compañera, contributing financially also. Because now it is very rare to see the husband telling the wife: I work and you stay home. Then, here there are the solutions we provide to our problems, such as building gardens, helping other women, making them aware of people's condition. Before, women were uninterested in all this. Now, we are concerned not only with being mothers, but with knowing how to be properly so.[103]

Is this feminism? Maybe the issue is one of cultural translation. Not between languages or continents, but between experiences. Maybe the parallel development of women's struggles and organizations, and feminist discourses and debates, is simply a stage in the historical development of a movement, whose fully fledged, global existence may result from the interaction and *reciprocal transformation* of both components.

If feminism is so diverse as to possibly include even women in movements who do not call themselves feminists, or even would object to the term, does it make sense to keep the word (after all invented by a man, Charles Fourier), or even to claim the existence of a feminist movement? I believe so, none the less, because of a major theoretical

---

[103]   Espinosa and Useche (1992: 48); my translation.

reason: in all types of feminism, as presented in Chart 4.1, *the funda-mental task of the movement, through struggles and discourses, is to de/re/construct woman's identity by degendering the institutions of society.* Women's rights are claimed on behalf of women as subjects autonomous from men, and from the roles they are assigned under patriarchalism. Cultural feminism builds the women's community to raise consciousness, and reconstruct personality. Essentialist feminism affirms woman's irreducible specificity, and proclaims her autonomous, superior values. Lesbian feminism, by rejecting hetero-sexuality, voids of meaning the sexual division of existence, underlying both manhood and womanhood. Women's multiple identities redefine ways of being on the basis of their actual experience, either lived or fantasized. And women's struggles for survival and dignity empower women, thus subverting the patriarchalized woman, precisely defined by her submission. Under different forms, and through different paths, feminism dilutes the patriarchal dichotomy man/woman as it manifests itself in social institutions and in social practice. So doing, feminism constructs not one but many identities, each one of which, by their autonomous existence, seizes micro-powers in the world wide web of life experiences.

The Power of Love: Lesbian and Gay Liberation Movements[104]

Any theory of cultural/political creation that treats lesbian existence as a marginal or less "natural" phenomenon, as mere "sexual preference" or as the mirror image of either heterosexual or male homosexual relations is profoundly weakened thereby . . . A feminist critique of compulsory hetero-sexual orientation for women is long overdue.
				Adrienne Rich, "Compulsory heterosexuality
				and lesbian existence", p. 229

Our movement may have begun as the struggle of a minority but what we should now be trying to "liberate" is an aspect of the personal lives of all people – sexual expression.
				John D'Emilio, "Capitalism and gay identity", p. 474

[104] The analysis presented here does not include the study of gay and lesbian *issues* and *values*, nor their relationship to social institutions. It is focused on lesbian and gay *movements*, and on their impact on patriarchalism through sexual liberation. In order to be specific, I will use two case studies, one for each movement. On the one hand, I will discuss the emergence of a powerful lesbian movement in Taipei, in the 1990s, in interaction with the feminist movement, and

Patriarchalism requires compulsory heterosexuality. Civilization, as historically known, is based on taboos and sexual repression. Sexuality, as Foucault argued, is socially constructed.[105] The regulation of desire underlies social institutions, thus channeling transgression and organizing domination. There is an endless spiral between desire, repression, sublimation, transgression, and punishment, accounting for much of human passion, accomplishment, and failure, when the epics of history are observed from the hidden side of experience. This coherent system of domination, which links the hallways of the state to the pulse of the libido through mothering, fathering, and the family, does have a weak link: the heterosexual assumption. If this assumption is challenged, the whole system crumbles down: the linkage between controlled sex and reproduction of the species is called into question; sisterhood, and then women's revolt, become possible, by undoing the gendered division of sexual labor that splits women; and male bonding threatens manhood, thus undermining the cultural coherence of men-dominated institutions. While historical accounts show permissiveness for male homosexuality in some cultures, particularly in classical Greece,[106] lesbianism was severely repressed throughout most of human experience, not in spite but because of resistance to heterosexuality. As Adrienne Rich writes:

> The fact is that women in every culture and throughout history have undertaken the task of independent, non-heterosexual, woman-connected existence, to the extent made possible by their context, often in the belief that they were the "only ones" ever to

---

with the gay movement. This is a deliberate effort to move away from North American and Western European scenes of lesbian liberation, and to emphasize the increasing influence of lesbianism on cultures as patriarchal as the Chinese culture. On the other hand, I will succinctly analyze the formation and development of the gay community in San Francisco, arguably one of the most powerful and visible gay communities/movements in the world. My presentation of the lesbian movement in Taipei primarily relies on an excellent study by my Berkeley doctoral student Lan-chih Po, who is also an active militant in the feminist movement in Taipei (Po, 1996). I have also used for my understanding of Taipei's scene, besides my personal knowledge, my Taiwan connection. For this, I am grateful to You-tien Hsing, and to Chu-joe Hsia. As for San Francisco, I have relied on the fieldwork study I conducted in the early 1980s, with the cooperation of Karen Murphy (Castells and Murphy, 1982; Castells, 1983: 138–72), adding some observations on recent developments. There is really no place here for a review of the abundant, relevant literature on gay and lesbian issues. For a scholarly overview of this bibliography in the English language, see the excellent *Lesbian and Gay Studies Reader*, edited by Abelove et al. (1993).

[105]   Foucault (1976, 1984a, b).
[106]   Halperin et al. (1990).

have done so. They have undertaken it even though few women have been in an economic position to resist marriage altogether, and even though the attacks against unmarried women have ranged from aspersion and mockery to deliberate gynocide, including the burning and torturing of millions of widows and spinsters during the witch persecutions of the fifteenth, sixteenth, and seventeenth centuries in Europe.[107]

Male homosexuality was generally confined in time and space by "knowingly ignoring" adolescent impulses or hidden expressions in specific contexts (for example, in the religious orders of the Catholic Church). Because men kept their gender, class, and race privileges, repression of homosexuality was/is highly socially selective. Yet, the norm, the fundamental norm of patriarchalism was, and is, life organized around the heterosexual family, occasionally allowing the private expression of same-sex desire for men, as long as it would be kept in the back alleys of society.

While resistance to compulsory heterosexuality has existed in all times and cultures, it is only in the past three decades that social movements in defense of lesbian and gay rights, and affirming sexual freedom, have spurred throughout the world, starting in the United States in 1969–70, then in Europe and, thereafter, over much of the planet. Why in this period? There seem to be some common factors, and some specific elements for each one of these two distinct movements, explaining the timing and circumstances of their development.

Lesbianism is, in fact, a component of the feminist movement, as I proposed above, albeit lesbians often seek alliances with gay men in fighting cultural domination from heterosexual women. Once the feminist critique of gendered institutions eroded patriarchal orthodoxy, the calling into question of sexual norms was the logical line of development for those sectors in the feminist movement who wanted to express their identity in all dimensions. Furthermore, the identification of men as the source of oppression of women made increasingly difficult for women their emotional and sexual partnership with their "class enemies," thus favoring the expression of the latent lesbianism existing in many women.

As for gay men, their coming into a movement seems to have been induced by three concurrent factors: the insurgent climate of the 1960s movements in which self-expression and the questioning of authority made it possible to think and act the unthinkable, thus "coming out of the closet"; the impact of feminism on patriarchalism,

[107]   Rich (1980/1993: 230).

calling into question the category of woman, and therefore, of man, since they can only exist in their dichotomy; and the ferocity of repression by a homophobic society that radicalized even those gay men who simply wanted an accommodation.[108]

In my view, there were three additional factors in inducing the extraordinary development of both gay and lesbian liberation movements in America and elsewhere. One is structural: the formation of an advanced informational economy in the largest metropolitan areas led to a diversified, innovative labor market and flexible business networks, and created new kinds of jobs, at all levels of skills, independent of the large-scale organizations where individual behavior could be more easily regulated. The second factor refers to the popularity of sexual liberation as a theme of the 1960s movements. For instance, having been a close witness of the 1968 May movement in Paris (I was assistant professor of sociology in the Nanterre campus where the movement started), I can say that sexual liberation and self-expression were *the* paramount goals of the radical student movement: in fact, the movement started as a joint protest by males and females to obtain free access to their university's dormitories. Around the banner of sexual liberation, which also sustained the daily morale of the movement, both in France and in the United States, the utopian wish of freeing desire was the driving force of the 1960s, the rallying cry around which a whole generation felt the possibility of a different life. But sexual liberation, if it is to be liberation, has no limits. Thus, the liberation of sexuality led to rejecting the diktat of heterosexuality and, in many cases, to the abolition of all limits to desire, opening up the exploration of transgression, for instance in the fast-growing, and ideologically articulate, sadomasochist movement.

The third factor that, in my view, induced, in parallel, lesbian and gay movements, is more controversial. It refers to the separation, physical and psychological, created among both men and women by the feminist challenge to patriarchalism. By this I do not mean that women became lesbians and men became gay because they were quarreling with their heterosexual partners. Indeed, homosexuality has its own existence and pattern of development independently from heterosexuality. Yet, the profound cleavage introduced by the joint effect of the feminist challenge and the inability of most men to cope with the ending of their privileges, reinforced the likelihood of same-sex support networks and friendships, creating a milieu where all kinds of desires could be more easily expressed.

Finally, while sexual liberation is at the heart of gay and lesbian

---

[108]   D'Emilio (1983).

movements, *gayness and lesbianism cannot be defined as sexual preferences. They are, fundamentally, identities,* and in fact two distinct identities: lesbian, and gay men. As such identities, they are not given; they do not originate from some form of biological determination. While biological predispositions do exist, most homosexual desire is mixed with other impulses and feelings (see figure 4.10), so that actual behavior, the boundaries of social interaction, and self-identity, are culturally, socially, and politically constructed. As for the specifics of this political process of constructing identity, I now turn to the case studies of the lesbian movement in Taipei, and of the gay community in San Francisco.

Feminism, lesbianism, and sexual liberation movements in Taipei[109]

In Taipei, as in most of the world, the lesbian movement emerged as a component of the feminist movement, and remained so, albeit in the 1990s it acted in close alliance with an equally powerful gay men's liberation movement. The fact that such a movement, with widespread influence among young women in Taipei, took place in a quasi-authoritarian political context, and amidst a deeply patriarchal culture, shows the breaking of traditional molds by global trends of identity politics.

Taiwan's feminist movement started in 1972, under the initiative of a pioneer intellectual woman, Hsiu-lien Lu who, returning to Taipei after completing her master's degree in the United States, created a women's group, set up "protection hot-lines," and founded the Pioneer Publishing Company to print women-related books. Lu's "new feminism" echoed closely the classic themes of liberal feminism, combined with the idea of modernization in the labor market, challenging sex discrimination, and the confinement of women in certain roles: "Women should first be human, and then women"; "women should walk out of the kitchen"; "sex discrimination against women should be removed and women's potential developed." At the same time, she emphasized the genuine Chinese character of her movement, and opposed some of the values of Western feminism, such as eliminating gender differences, or rejecting feminine dressing. For

---

[109] My analysis of Taipei's lesbian movement follows closely the study by Lan-chih Po (1996). In addition to her observations, she also relies partially on the papers (in Chinese) of a Conference on "New Maps of Desire: Literature, Culture, and Sexual Orientation" organized on April 20, 1996 at National Taiwan University, Taipei, and on the special issue of *Awakening* magazine (1995: no. 158–61) on relationships between feminism and lesbianism.

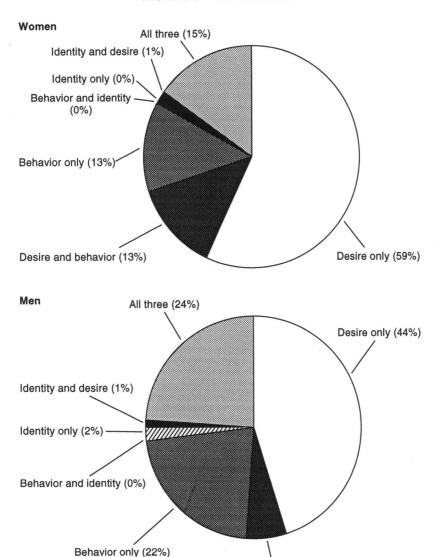

Figure 4.10 Interrelation of different aspects of same-gender sexuality: for 150 women (8.6% of the total 1,749) who report any adult same-gender sexuality; for 143 men (10.1% of the total 1,410) who report any adult same-gender sexuality
Source: Laumann et al. (1994)

Lu, "women should be like they are." In the late 1970s, feminists joined the political opposition movement, and after the 1979 Kaoshiung riot, they were repressed, and Lu was imprisoned. The organized movement could not survive repression, but women's networks did, so that a second wave of feminism developed in the early 1980s. In 1982, a small group of women created Awakening Magazine, a monthly, to voice women's opinions, and to press for women's rights. In January 1987 hundreds of women took to the streets of Taipei to protest against the sex industry in the city. In 1987, after the lifting of the martial law that had subdued Taiwan's opposition for decades, the Awakening Foundation was formally established: it went on to become the coordinating instance of Taiwan's women's struggles, mixing liberal themes, radical causes, and support for a whole array of women's initiatives. In a largely spontaneous movement, in the late 1980s, numerous women's groups were formed, such as associations of divorced women, housewives, groups to rescue youth from prostitution, and the like. The media started to report the activities of these groups, increasing their visibility, and attracting a growing number of women, particularly among the educated and professional groups in Taipei.

With the beginning of democratic political life in the 1990s (indeed, the democratic opposition conquered the municipality of Taipei in the local elections), a diversified culturally oriented social movement emerged in Taipei. The women's movement both grew in numbers and influence, and became internally differentiated between its struggle for women's rights, its defense of women workers, and the expression of new women's identities, including lesbianism. University campuses were literally taken by feminism. In May 1995, the chairwoman of the "women's studies group" in National Taiwan University (Taiwan's premier university) was elected as chairperson of the student body, displacing both the government's party candidate, and the political opposition students. The support found by the feminist movement, outside the University, among women, particularly married women, of the new Taiwanese society prompted a series of debates, particularly around the notion of family, on the occasion of the revision of the "family law" in the Taiwanese parliament.

It is in this context of cultural effervescence and rise of feminist ideas that a number of young radical feminists started to introduce the lesbian debate in Taipei. The "Axis Collective" diffused ideas from radical feminists and lesbian theorists, such as Audre Lorde, Adrienne Rich, Gayle Rubin, and Christine Delphy, and translated some of their texts into Chinese. Following Lorde's notion of the "erotic as power," a new field of identity politics, centered on women's body and sexuality, was created. Alongside the rise of women's groups on campuses, the first explicitly lesbian group was formed in Taiwan in 1990: "Between Us (*wo-men-chih-chien*)."

On May 22, 1994, an "anti-sexual harassment parade" was organized by feminists in the streets of Taipei, with about 800 women, mainly students, marching from their campuses to the center of the city. During the march, Ho, a feminist scholar who had advanced the discourse of sexual liberation, improvised a slogan: "I want sexual orgasm, I don't want sexual harassment!" which was enthusiastically repeated by participants in the march, and sounded loudly in the streets of a shocked patriarchal Taipei. It made the headlines of most newspapers. The publicity of this incident raised a fundamental debate within the feminist movement. When the movement was winning legitimacy and acceptance, improving women's condition and asserting gender equality, many feminists felt that it was embarrassing, and potentially destructive, to identify feminism with sexual liberation in public opinion. Moreover, some feminists also argued that sexual liberation in the West was a trap for women, and in fact worked to the advantage of men. They suggested, instead, to fight for the "right to autonomy of the body." Ho and other feminists, related to the lesbian movement, argued for the need for a feminist approach to sexual liberation, seeking at the same time the emancipation of women and that of women's sexuality. In their view, sexual liberation is the radical way of challenging patriarchal culture, manifested in the control over a woman's body. The sexual liberation women's movement, including, but not exclusively, a strong lesbian component, went into action. In 1995, the women's studies groups in Taiwan University, mobilizing to elect their candidate to the student government, began showing pornographic movies in the women's dormitories. Simultaneously, a "women's erotic pioneering festival" was organized in different campuses. The activities of these women, most of them very young, were highly publicized in the media, shocked Taipei's society, and created considerable concern among feminist leaders, inducing a sharp, sometimes acrimonious, debate within feminism.

It is in this context of both feminist awakening and sexual liberation that lesbian and gay men's groups proliferated, breaking a deep-seated taboo in Chinese culture. Furthermore, in the 1990s, the traditional marginality of homosexuals in Taiwan had been reinforced, and rationalized, by the stigma of AIDS. And yet, after the creation of the lesbian group "Between Us," there followed an explosion of both lesbian and gay collectives, most of them on university campuses: lesbian groups such as "Between Us," ALN, "Lambda" (Taiwan University), and "I Bao"; gay men's groups such as "Gay Chat"

(Taiwan University), "NCA," and "Speak Out." Other groups joined forces between lesbians and gays: "Queer Workshop," "We Can" (Chin-hua University), DV8 (She-shin College), "Quist" (Chong-yung University), and so on. These groups created a homosexual community. They "collectively came out," and linked sexuality, enjoyment, and politics, rediscovering that "the personal is political." Bars were critical for information, networking, education, and, ultimately, for the production of gay and lesbian culture. As Po writes: "Just like pubs for the making of British working class, gay bars play important roles for the formation of urban gay/lesbian communities in Taipei."[110]

Yet, in the Information Age, in which Taiwan is fully immersed, gays and lesbians are not limited to bars in their networking. They use extensively the Internet, and BBSs, as forms of contact, communication, and interaction. They have also created "alternative media," particularly through a number of gay/lesbian underground radio stations. In addition, in 1996 two gay/lesbian programs were broadcast on mainstream radio stations in Taipei.

Beyond communication, networking, and self-expression, the lesbian movement, in close political alliance with the gay movement, has been active in a number of campaigns, social protests, and political demands. Particularly significant was the mobilization around AIDS policy. On the one hand, feminists, lesbians and gay men took to the streets to protest the incrimination of gay men by government policies as responsible for the epidemic. On the other hand, since heterosexual women are the fastest growing group of HIV infected in Asia, the feminist group "Awakening" took up the issue as a woman's survival matter. Indeed, in Taiwan, the largest group of HIV-infected women are housewives, defenseless victims of their husbands' prostitution habits. Women's groups in Taiwan acted on the contradiction of policies to prevent the spread of AIDS: how could women escape infection from their husbands if they could not have control over their sexual lives? By bringing down to earth the issues of sexual liberation, and showing women that they were facing deadly sexual oppression, the anti-AIDS movement built by feminists, lesbians, and gay men together introduced a fundamental challenge to the patriarchal structure of sexual domination.

A second major line of action by lesbian and gay movements in an extremely patriarchal society was the fight against traditional stigma and invisibility in the public image. Gay men had to fight the stigma of abnormality. Lesbians had to fight invisibility. For both, coming out in the public sphere became a paramount goal to achieve social

[110]   Po (1996: 20).

existence. Cultural activities were essential to that end. A 1992 film festival of "queer cinema" was the starting point of public, collective self-affirmation. Lesbian and gay audiences packed several movie theaters, and the films were introduced with debates on "queer theory." Incidentally, Taiwanese and Hong Kong activists have creatively translated into Chinese the term "queer" by "*tong-chii,*" meaning "comrade," so that "comrade" does not refer any longer to communist fraternity but to "queer" identity. Starting with the film festival, a number of cultural activities, always communal and festive, substantially modified the perception of lesbian and gay culture in Taiwan to the point that in 1996, the movement felt strong enough to mark Valentine's Day by voting for the top ten "gay/lesbian idols" among prominent figures of entertainment, society, and politics (to be sure, not all of the chosen were enchanted with their popularity among gays and lesbians).

Thirdly, and not surprisingly, the lesbian and gay movements have been seeking control over public space, symbolized by their struggle around Taipei's New Park, which they vowed to "take back." The park, nearby the Presidential Hall, had become a "queer space," a major site for gathering and cruising for the gay community. In 1996, the new democratic municipal administration was planning the renewal of Taipei, including its parks. Fearful of being deprived of their "liberated space," lesbians and gays requested participation in the design project, as heavy users of the park, and organized themselves in the "Comrade Space Front Line" network, demanding free use of the park for their activities during daytime to escape their status as "the community in the darkness."

With the growing influence and militancy of lesbians, a series of conflicts emerged between them and the feminist movement at large. The major one concerned the revision of family law in the parliament. Lesbians criticized the proposal by women's groups because it assumed the norm of the heterosexual family, ignoring the rights of homosexuals. Thus, lesbians and gay men *mobilized actively for the legal sanction of same-sex marriage,* a fundamental issue, present in most lesbian/gay movements around the world, and on which I will elaborate below. The conflict stimulated thinking and debate in the feminist movement, particularly in the mainstream Awakening Foundation. Lesbians criticized the hypocrisy of feminist slogans, such as "women love women," as expressions of solidarity, while ignoring the sexual dimension of this love. Lesbians in 1996 were in the open within the feminist movement, and argued vehemently for their specific rights to be acknowledged, and defended, as a legitimate part of the women's movement.

Several elements deserve emphasis in this narrative of the lesbian movement in Taipei. It shattered the preconception of the solidity of patriarchalism, and heterosexuality, in cultures inspired by Confucianism. It was an extension of the feminist movement, while linking up at the same time with the gay liberation movement in a united front for the defense of rights to sexuality under all its forms. It joined the mobilization against AIDS, relating it to the consequences of housewives' sexual submission. It bridged the cutting-edge theoretical debates on feminism and lesbianism in the world with specific adaptations to Chinese culture and to Taiwan's social institutions in the 1990s. It used a whole range of cultural expressions to "come out collectively" in the midst of public attention. It made extensive use of the Internet, and of alternative means of communication, such as pirate broadcasting. It linked up with urban social movements and political struggles at the local level. And it deepened the critique of the patriarchal family, engaging in a legal and cultural battle to advance the notion of same-sex marriages, and non-heterosexual families. I will elaborate on these matters when summing up the relationship between lesbian and gay movements and their challenge to patriarchalism.

Spaces of freedom: the gay community in San Francisco[111]

The American gay liberation movement is generally considered to have as its starting point the Stonewall Revolt in New York's Greenwich Village on June 27, 1969, when hundreds of gays fought the police for three days in reaction to yet another brutal raid on The Stonewall, a gay bar. Thereafter, the movement grew with extraordinary speed, particularly in the major metropolitan areas, as gays came out of the closet, individually and collectively. In 1969 there were about 50 organizations nationwide; in 1973 the number had jumped to over 800. While New York and Los Angeles, because of their size, became home to the largest gay populations, San Francisco was the site of the formation of a visible, organized, and politicized gay community, which went on in the next two decades to transform the city in its space, its culture, and its politics. By my calculations (necessarily tentative, since, fortunately, there is no statistical recording of sexual preference), around 1980, the gay and lesbian population could account for about 17 percent of the city's adult residents (two-thirds of them gay men), and in important local elections, because of their high turn-out rate, they may have represented around 30

<hr>

[111] For sources and methods for my study of San Francisco's gay community, see Castells (1983), particularly the Methodological Appendix, pp. 355–62.

percent of voters. My guess is that in the 1990s, in spite of decimation by the AIDS epidemics in the mid-1980s, the gay and lesbian population in San Francisco has increased, mainly because of an increase in lesbians, continuing gay immigration, and the consolidation of stable same-sex partnerships. More significantly, gays settled predominantly in certain areas of the city, forming authentic communes, in which residences, businesses, real estate, bars, restaurants, movie theaters, cultural centers, community-based associations, street gatherings and celebrations weaved a fabric of social life and cultural autonomy: a space of freedom. On the basis of this space, gays and lesbians organized politically, and came to exercise considerable influence in the San Francisco local government, including the mandatory recruitment of gays and lesbians by the police department, to make up at least 10 percent of the force. This spatial concentration of gay populations is indeed a mark of the gay culture in most cities, albeit in the 1990s, with greater social tolerance and many more openly gay people, they have diffused into most of American metropolitan geography, to the great fear of homophobic conservatives. The reason for this geographic concentration in the formative stage of gay culture is twofold: visibility and protection. As Harry Britt, a political leader of San Francisco's gays, told me in an interview years ago: "When gays are spatially scattered, they are not gay, because they are invisible." The fundamental liberating act for gays was/is "to come out," to publicly express their identity and their sexuality, then to resocialize themselves. But how is it possible to be openly gay in the middle of a hostile and violent society increasingly insecure about its fundamental values of virility and patriarchalism? And how can one learn a new behavior, a new code, and a new culture, in a world where sexuality is implicit in everybody's presentation of self and where the general assumption is heterosexuality? In order to express themselves, gays have always met together – in modern times in night bars and coded places. When they became conscious enough and strong enough to "come out" collectively, they earmarked places where they could be safe together and could invent new lives. The territorial boundaries of their selected places became the basis for the building of autonomous institutions, and the creation of cultural autonomy. Levine has shown the systematic patterning of spatial concentrations of gays in American cities during the 1970s.[112] While he and others used the term "ghetto," gay militants speak of "liberated zones": and there is indeed a major difference between ghettos and gay areas since the latter are usually deliberately constructed by gay people to create their own city, in the framework of the broader urban society.

[112]   Levine (1979).

Why San Francisco? An instant city, a settlement for adventurers attracted by gold and freedom, San Francisco was always a place of tolerant moral standards. The Barbary Coast was a meeting point for sailors, travelers, transients, dreamers, crooks, entrepreneurs, rebels, and deviants – a milieu of casual encounters and few social rules where the borderline between the normal and the abnormal was blurred. Yet, in the 1920s, the city decided to become respectable, emerging as the cultural capital of the American West, and growing up gracefully under the authoritative shadow of the Catholic Church, relying on the support of its Irish and Italian working-class legions. With the reform movement reaching City Hall and the police in the 1930s, "deviants" were repressed and forced into hiding. Thus, the pioneer origins of San Francisco as a free city are not enough to explain its destiny as the setting for gay liberation. The major turning point was World War II. San Francisco was the main port for the Pacific front. About 1.6 million young men and women passed through the city: alone, uprooted, living on the edge of death and suffering, and sharing it most of the time with people from their own sex, many of them discovered, or elected, their homosexuality. And many were dishonorably discharged from the Navy, and disembarked in San Francisco. Rather than going home to Iowa bearing the stigma, they stayed in the city, joined by thousands of other gay people at the end of the war. They met in bars, and they built networks of support and sharing. A gay culture started to emerge from the late 1940s. The transition from the bars to the streets had to wait, however, for more than a decade, when alternative lifestyles flourished in San Francisco, with the beatnik generation, and around literary circles networked in the City Lights bookstore, with Ginsberg, Kerouac, and the Black Mountain poets, among others. This culture concentrated spatially in the old Italian North Beach area, near the red-light tourist zone of Broadway. Gays were fully accepted in this tolerant, experimental ambiance. When the media focused on the beatnik culture, they emphasized the widespread presence of homosexuality as a proof of its deviance. So doing, they publicized San Francisco as a gay Mecca, attracting thousands of gays from around America. City Hall responded with repression, leading to the formation, in 1964, of the Society of Individual Rights, that defended gays, in connection with the Tavern Guild, a business association of gay and bohemian bar owners fighting against police harassment. Then, in the late 1960s, the hippy culture, the social movements that took place in the San Francisco Bay Area, particularly in Berkeley/Oakland, and the emergence of the gay liberation movement throughout America, induced a qualitative change in the development of San Francisco's gay community, building on the strength of historically established networks. In 1971, for the first time, the California gay movement was strong enough to organize a march on the capital, Sacramento, in support of gay rights. In the 1970s, in San Francisco a gay community flourished in certain neighborhoods, particularly in the Castro area, buying or renting homes in a rundown, traditional working-class district, which came to be rehabilitated by gay households, gay realtors, and gay renovation companies. Gay-owned businesses also settled in the area. From scattered locations, following bars and counter-cultural areas, gays were able, by the 1970s, to concentrate on a neighborhood that they could call theirs. Figure 4.11 shows the expansion of gay residential areas in San Francisco between 1950 and 1980 on the basis of my fieldwork research.

Yet, the building of the gay community was not purely spontaneous. It was also the result of deliberate political action, particularly under the impulse of the historic leader of San Francisco's gay community, Harvey Milk. A graduate of the State University of New York at Albany,

██ 1950s ██ 1960s ██ Early 1970s ██ Mid 1970s ██ Late 1970s

Figure 4.11   Gay residential areas in San Francisco
Source: Castells (1983)

he was not able to teach after being discharged from the Navy because of homosexuality. Like thousands of gays, he migrated to San Francisco in 1969. After leaving a job as a financial analyst, he opened a photography business, Castro Camera, on Castro Street. He conceived a plan for gays to evolve from community, to business, to power. He called for "gays to buy gay," so that Castro would be more than a cruising place, but a space owned by gays, lived by gays, and enjoyed by gays. Then, if gays could buy gay, and live as gays, they could also vote gay. In 1973, he ran for supervisor (council member) of the city of San Francisco, explicitly as a gay candidate. He did well, but was not elected. He went back to work on building a political basis, strengthening gays' political clubs, linking up with the Democratic party, and broadening his program to address issues of local urban policies, such as the control of real estate speculation. A political event changed his destiny. In 1975, a liberal California Senator, George Moscone, was elected mayor of San Francisco by a narrow margin. To secure the support of the by then strong gay community, Moscone appointed Harvey Milk to an important post in the local adminis- tration. For the first time an openly gay leader became a city official. Around the same time, the powerful neighborhood movement in San Francisco obtained a reform of the electoral law, establishing elec- tions to the city council (Board of Supervisors) by local districts, instead of voting in the city at large. Then, on the basis of the terri- tory that the gay community had conquered in the Castro area, which became an electoral district, Harvey Milk was elected supervisor in 1977. From his new platform, he mobilized gay power around the city, and around the state. In 1978 a conservative proposition was put in the ballot to California voters to ban homosexuals from teaching in public schools. The voters rejected it by 58 percent of the vote in California, 75 percent in San Francisco. Harvey Milk, with skillful media performance, was the leader of the campaign. In April 1978, the Board of Supervisors approved a very liberal Gay Rights Ordinance. At the same time, two lesbian leaders, Del Martin and Phyllis Lyon, holding City Hall Posts, received from the city of San Francisco a certificate of honor for their civic services – including support for lesbians – and for their 25 years of living together. These, and other gay breakthroughs, were more than the homophobic culture could take. On November 27, 1978, a conservative city super- visor, Dan White, an ex-policeman who had campaigned against tolerance toward "sexual deviants," shot and killed mayor George Moscone and supervisor Harvey Milk in their offices at City Hall. He later surrendered to his former colleagues in the police department. The mourning of Moscone and Milk was one of the most impressive political demonstrations ever seen in San Francisco: 20,000 people marched with candles, in silence, after listening to speakers who called on the movement to pursue the struggle in the way shown by Harvey Milk. It did. The new mayor, Dianne Feinstein, appointed another gay leader, Harry Britt, a socialist, to replace Harvey Milk in his post, and he was subsequently elected supervisor. Over the next decade, gay and lesbian leaders increased their representation in the 11-member city Board of Supervisors, and although they lost one election, in 1992, to a conservative mayor, they became again a major component of the coalition that helped to elect Willie Brown, a veteran Black Democratic leader, mayor of San Francisco in 1996. An anecdote of the 1996 campaign reveals the state of mental confusion of the homophobic culture in San Francisco, lost in the uncertainty of long cherished values. The incumbent mayor, an ex-police chief, may have lost his re-election bid after a major political blunder. Trailing in the polls, and trying to find a way to ingratiate himself with the gay audience, he let himself be photographed naked, while giving an interview in his shower with radio journalists in the same attire. The backlash from both gay and straight offended voters doomed his chances. The new mayor renewed the by then two decades old commitment from the city to respect and enhance gay rights, and gay culture, celebrated in parades and festivities several times in the year.

However, the gay community of the 1990s is not the same as the one formed in the 1970s because in the early 1980s AIDS struck.[113] In the next 15 years, about 15,000 people died from AIDS in San Francisco, and several other thousands were diagnosed infected with the HIV virus. The reaction of the gay community was remarkable, as San Francisco became a model for the entire world in self-organization, prevention, and political action geared toward controlling the AIDS epidemics, a danger for humankind. I believe it is accurate to say that the most important gay movement of the 1980s/1990s is the gay component of the anti-AIDS movement, in its different manifestations, from health clinics to militant groups such as ACT UP! In San Francisco, the first effort was directed toward helping the ill, and preventing the spread of the disease. A large-scale effort for the education of the community was undertaken, with safe-sex procedures taught and diffused. After a few years, the results were spectacular. In the 1990s, in San Francisco, and in California, the incidence of new cases of AIDS is much greater in the heterosexual population, as a result of drug use, prostitution, and infection of women by careless

[113]   For a discussion of the relationship between the gay movement, the fight against AIDS, and society's reactions, see Coates et al. (1988); Mass (1990); Heller (1992); Price and Hsu (1992); Herek and Greene (1995); Lloyd and Kuselewickz (1995).

men, while the gay population, more educated and better organized, has seen a significant decline in new infections. The care of the ill was organized at all levels, with San Francisco General Hospital becoming the first hospital to establish a permanent AIDS section, and a whole network of volunteers providing help and comfort to people in the hospital and at home. Militant pressures to step up research efforts, and to obtain accelerated approval of experimental drugs as they became available, yielded significant results. The University of California at San Francisco Hospital became one of the leading centers in AIDS-related research. In a broader perspective, the 1996 worldwide AIDS Conference in Vancouver announced potential breakthroughs in controlling the disease and, maybe, in diminishing its lethality in the future.

But perhaps the most important effort by the gay community, in San Francisco and elsewhere, was the cultural battle to demystify AIDS, to remove the stigma, and to convince the world that it was not produced by homosexuality or, for that matter, by sexuality. Contact networks, including sexual contact, but comprising many other forms, were the lethal messengers, not homosexuality.[114] And the disconnection of these networks, thus controlling the epidemics, was not a matter of confinement but of education, organization, and responsibility, supported both by public health institutions and civic consciousness. That the gay community, starting in San Francisco, could win this uphill battle was a decisive contribution to humankind. Not only because a new crime against humanity was avoided, when the movement successfully fought back the calls for detection and confinement of HIV carriers. What was fundamentally at stake was the ability of the world to look AIDS directly into its horrifying eyes, and to face the epidemics in the terms of the virus(es) as it (they) is (are), not in terms of our prejudices and nightmares. We came very close, in the world at large, to considering AIDS as a deserved divine punishment against New Sodom, thus not taking the necessary measures to prevent an even greater spread of the disease until it may have been too late to control it at all. That we did not, that societies learned in time that AIDS was not a homosexual disease, and that the sources and vehicles of its spread had to be fought in society at large was, to a large extent, the work of the gay-community based, anti-AIDS movement, with its pioneers (many of them on their way to death) in the liberated city of San Francisco.

Not unrelated to the AIDS epidemic, another major trend took place in the 1990s in the San Francisco gay community. Patterns of sexual interaction became more stable, partly a sign of the aging and

---

[114]   Castells (1992c).

maturation of some segments of the community, partly as a way of channeling sexuality into safer patterns of love. The yearning for same-sex families became one of the most powerful cultural trends among gays and, even more so, among lesbians. The comfort of a durable, monogamous relationship became a predominant model among middle-aged gays and lesbians. Consequently, a new movement sprouted out from the gay community to obtain the institutional recognition of such stable relationships as families. Thus, certificates of partnership were sought from local and state governments, with this recognition carrying the entitlement to spousal benefits. Furthermore, the legalization of same-sex marriages became a major demand of the movement, taking conservatives at their word in promoting family values, and extending the value of the family to non-traditional, non-heterosexual forms of love, sharing, and child rearing. What started as a movement of sexual liberation came full circle to haunt the patriarchal family by attacking its heterosexual roots, and subverting its exclusive appropriation of family values.

Since any action brings a reaction, the relative taming of sexuality in new gay and lesbian families induced, in parallel, the development of sexual minority cultures (both heterosexual and homosexual), such as the sadomasochist movement, and voluntary sex-slave networks, a significant phenomenon in the San Francisco scene, particularly in the South of Market area, in the 1990s, although I identified the importance of this cultural/personal revolt in my fieldwork 15 years ago. Sadomasochists, whose culture includes some very articulate intellectuals, criticize mainstream gays for trying to define new norms of the "socially acceptable," thus reproducing the logic of domination that oppressed gays and lesbians throughout history. For sadomasochists the journey has no end. Thus, controlled violence, accepted humiliation, slave auctions, painful pleasure, leather dress, Nazi emblems, chains and whips, are more than sexual stimuli. They are cultural expressions of the need to destroy whatever moral values straight society has left them with since these values have traditionally been used to stigmatize and repress homosexuality, and sexuality. The considerable embarrassment that this cultural minority causes to most gays and lesbians is the symptom that they do address an important, if difficult, issue.

Left to itself, in its cultural ghetto, the gay community is unlikely to accomplish the sexual revolution and the subversion of patriarchalism that are, implicitly, the goals of the movement, even if they are not supported by the growing segment of male elites that consume rather than produce the gay movement. Strategic alliances with lesbians, and with the feminist movement at large seem to be a necessary condition for the fulfillment of gay liberation. Yet, gays are men, and their socialization as men, and the privileges they enjoy, particularly if they are white and middle class, limit their fully fledged incorporation into an anti-patriarchal alliance. This is why in San Francisco, in the 1990s, there is a growing split between a radically oriented gay and lesbian alliance, and a respectable gay elite that has established itself as an interest group to defend gay rights as a tolerated minority within the institutions of patriarchalism. Yet, if this diversity can be expressed within a broader movement that allows people freedom to chose whom they love, in contradiction with the heterosexual norm, it is because Harvey Milk, and other pioneers, built a free commune once upon a time in the West.

Summing up: sexual identity and the patriarchal family

Lesbian and gay movements are not simply movements in defense of basic human rights to choose whom and how to love. They are also powerful expressions of sexual identity, and therefore of sexual liberation. This is why they challenge some of the millennial foundations on which societies were built historically: sexual repression and compulsory heterosexuality.

When lesbians, in an institutional environment as repressive and patriarchal as the Chinese culture in Taipei, are able to openly express their sexuality, and to claim the inclusion of same-sex marriages in the family code, a fundamental breach has been opened in the institutional scaffolding constructed to control desire. If the gay community is able to overcome ignorant stigmatization, and to help prevent the plague of AIDS, it means that societies have become able to extract themselves from their darkness, and to look into the whole diversity of human experience, without prejudice and without violence. And if presidential electoral campaigns, in America for the moment, have unwillingly to reckon with the debate on gay rights, it means that the social movements' challenge to heterosexuality cannot be ignored or purely repressed any longer. Yet, the forces of transformation unleashed by sexual identity movements can hardly be confined within the limits of simple tolerance and respect for human rights. They bring into motion a corrosive critique of sexual normalization and of the patriarchal family. Their challenge is particularly frightening for patriarchalism because it comes at a historical time when biological research and medical technology allow the disassociation between heterosexuality, patriarchalism, and the reproduction of the species. Same-sex families, which will not give up rearing children, are the most open expression of this possibility.

On the other hand, the blurring of sexual boundaries, decoupling family, sexuality, love, gender, and power, introduces a fundamental

cultural critique to the world as we have known it. This is why the
future development of sexual liberation movements will not be easy.
By shifting from the defense of human rights to the reconstruction of
sexuality, family, and personality, they touch the nerve centers of
repression and civilization, and they will be responded to in kind.
There is a stormy horizon ahead for the gay and lesbian movements,
and AIDS will not be the only hideous face of anti-sexual backlash.
Yet, if the experience of the last quarter of the century has any indicative value, the power of identity seems to become magic when touched
by the power of love.

Family, Sexuality, and Personality in the Crisis of Patriarchalism[115]

*In the separating and divorcing society, the nuclear family generates a
diversity of new kin ties associated, for example, with the so-called recombinant families. However, the nature of these ties changes as they are
subject to greater negotiation than before. Kinship relations often used to
be taken for granted on the basis of trust; now trust has to be negotiated
and bargained for, and commitment is as much an issue as in sexual
relationships.*
> Anthony Giddens, *The Transformation of Intimacy*, p. 96.

The incredibly shrinking family

The crisis of patriarchalism, induced by the interaction between informational capitalism and feminist and sexual identity social
movements, manifests itself in the increasing diversity of partnership
arrangements among people to share life and raise children. I will
illustrate this point by using American data to simplify the argument.
I do not imply, however, that all countries and cultures will follow this
path. Yet, if the social, economic, and technological trends underlying
the crisis of patriarchalism are present around the world, it is plausible that most societies will have to reconstruct, or replace, their
patriarchal institutions under the specific conditions of their culture
and history. The following discussion, empirically based on American
trends, aims at identifying social mechanisms connecting the crisis of

---

[115]   Data reported in this section are from the US Bureau of the Census and from
The World Almanac and Book of Facts (1996), unless referred to otherwise. US
Bureau of the Census publications used to retrieve these data are: US Department
of Commerce, Economics and Statistics Administration, Bureau of the Census
(1989, 1991, 1992a–d).

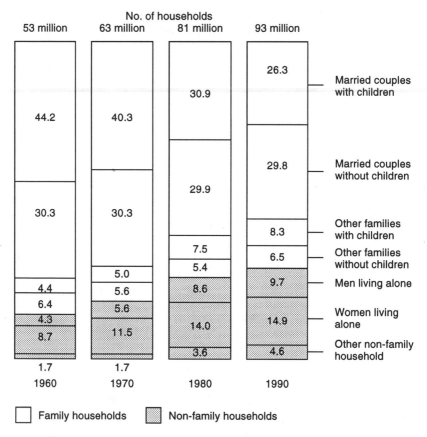

Figure 4.12a   Household composition in US, 1960–90 (%)
(children = own children under 18)
Source: US Bureau of the Census (1992a)

the patriarchal family, and the transformation of sexual identity, to the social redefinition of family life, thus of personality systems.

What is at issue is not the disappearance of the family but its profound diversification, and the change in its power system. Indeed, most people continue to marry: 90 percent of Americans do over their lifetime. When they divorce, 60 percent of women and 75 percent of men remarry, on average within three years. And gays and lesbians are fighting for their right to legal marriage. Yet, later marriages, frequence of cohabitation, and high rates of divorce (stabilized at about half of all marriages), and of separation, combine to produce an increasingly diverse profile of family and non-family life (figures 4.12a and 4.12b summarize its broad trends for 1960–90 and for 1970–95). The so-called "non-family households" doubled between

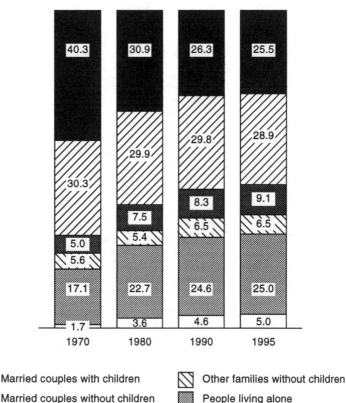

Married couples with children
Married couples without children
Other families with children

Other families without children
People living alone
Other (non-related persons)

Figure 4.12b Household composition in US, 1970–95 (%)
Source: US Bureau of the Census (1996)

1960 and 1995, increasing from 15 percent of all households to 29 percent of households, naturally including single elderly, and thus reflecting a demographic trend, as well as a cultural change. Women account for two-thirds of single-households. More significantly, the archetypical category "married couples with children" dropped from 44.2 percent of households in 1960 to 25.5 percent in 1995. Thus, the "model" of the patriarchal nuclear family is the reality for just over one-quarter of American households. Stacey quotes sources indicating that if we consider the most traditional version of patriarchalism, meaning the married couple with children in which the only breadwinner is the male, and the wife is a fulltime home-maker, the proportion drops to 7 percent of all households.[116]

[116] Stacey (1990: 28).

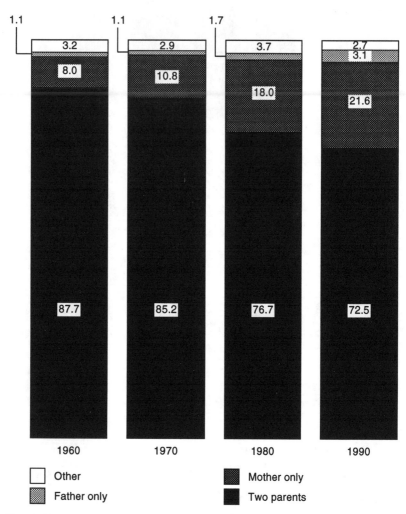

Figure 4.13   Living arrangements of children under the age of 18, by
presence of parent, in US, 1960–90 (% distribution)
Source: US Bureau of the Census (1992a)

The life of children has been transformed. As figure 4.13 shows,
over one-quarter of children did not live with two parents in 1990, in
contrast to less than 13 percent in 1960. Furthermore, according to a
US Bureau of the Census study, in 1991 the proportion of children
living with their two biological parents was only 50.8 percent[117]. Other

---

[117]   US Bureau of the Census (1994).

sources also estimate that "nearly 50 percent of all children do not live with both of their genetic parents."[118] Adoptions have substantially increased over the past two decades, and 20,000 babies have been born from *in vitro* fertilization.[119] The *trends*, all pointing in the same direction of the fading away of the patriarchal nuclear family, are what really matters: the proportion of children living with a lone parent doubled between 1970 and 1990, reaching 25 percent of all children. Among these children, the proportion who lived with a never-married mother increased from 7 percent in 1970 to 31 percent in 1990. One-parent female-headed households with children increased by 90.5 percent in the 1970s, and by an additional 21.2 percent in the 1980s. One-parent male-headed households with children, while accounting only for 3.1 percent of all households in 1990, are growing even faster: by 80.6 percent in 1970s, and by 87.2 percent in the 1980s. Female-headed families without a husband present grew from 11 percent of all families in 1970 to 18 percent in 1994. The percentage of children living only with their mother doubled between 1970 and 1994, from 11 to 22 percent, while the proportion of children living only with their father trebled in the same period, going from 1 to 3 percent.

New profiles of living arrangements multiply.[120] In 1980, there were 4 million recombinant families (including children from a previous marriage); in 1990, 5 million. In 1992, one-quarter of single women over 18 had children; in 1993, there were 3.5 million unmarried couples, of which 35 percent had children in the household; the number of unmarried fathers with children doubled from 1980 to 1992; 1 million children were living with their grandparents in 1990 (10 percent up from 1960), out of a total of 3.5 million children sharing their household with a grandparent. Marriages preceded by cohabitation increased from 8 percent in the late 1960s to 49 percent in the mid-1980s, and half of cohabiting couples have children.[121] Furthermore, with the massive entry of women into the paid labor force, and their indispensable role in providing for the family, few children can enjoy their mother's or father's full-time care. In 1990, both husband and wife worked outside the home in about 70 percent of married couple families, and 58 percent of mothers with young children worked outside the home. Child care is a major problem for families, and was performed in their home by relatives or neighbors for two-thirds of children,[122] to which we should add unregistered

[118]   Buss (1994: 168).
[119]   Reigot and Spina (1996: 238).
[120]   Reigot and Spina (1996).
[121]   Coleman and Ganong (1993: 113).
[122]   Farnsworth Riche (1996).

home helpers. Poor women, unable to pay for child care, are faced with the choice of separating from their children or giving up work, then falling into the welfare trap that may lead eventually to their children being taken away from them.[123]

There are few reliable estimates on same-sex households and families. One of the few is by Gonsioreck and Weinrich, according to whom an estimated 10 percent of the American male population is gay, and between 6 and 7 percent of the female population lesbian.[124] They estimate that about 20 percent of the gay male population were married once, and that between 20 and 50 percent of them had children. Lesbians are often mothers, many of them from previous heterosexual marriages. A very wide range evaluation puts the figure of children living with their lesbian mothers at between 1.5 and 3.3 million. The number of children living with either gay or lesbian parents is estimated at between 4 and 6 million.[125] Among non-family households, the fastest growth is in the category "other non-family households," which increased from 1.7 percent of total households in 1970 to 5 percent in 1995. In this group are, according to the US census, room-mates, friends, and unrelated individuals. In fact, this category would include both heterosexual and homosexual couples in cohabitation without children.

As for projections toward the near future, using Harvard University's estimates of household formation to the year 2000, as a percentage of total households, married couples with children are expected to decline further, from 31.5 percent in 1980 to 23.4 percent in 2000, while single-person households may increase from 22.6 percent to 26.6 percent in 2000, statistically overtaking the household type of married couples with children.[126] Lone parents would increase slightly from 7.7 to 8.7 percent. Married couples without children would become the most numerous, but not predominant, household type, remaining at about 29.5 percent of all households, an effect of the longer survival of both spouses, together with the replacement of these formerly married couples with children by a more diversified

---

[123]   Susser (1991).
[124]   Gonsioreck and Weinrich (1991).The 10 percent threshold of homosexuality for the population at large is a demographic myth inspired by a superficial reading of the half-century old Kinsey Report (in fact reporting on American white males). As Laumann et al. (1994) suggest, with a strong empirical basis, there is no clear boundary of homosexuality that can be traced back to some distinctive biological impulse. The extent of homosexual behavior, in its different manifestations, evolves according to cultural norms and social contexts. For a discussion of the matter, see Laumann et al. (1994: 283–320).
[125]   Reigot and Spina (1996: 116).
[126]   Masnick and Ardle (1994); Masnick and Kim (1995).

array of household forms. Indeed, what they call "other households," comprising miscellaneous living arrangements are projected to increase their share from 8.8 percent in 1980 to 11.8 percent in 2000. Overall, in the Harvard University estimates and projections, while in 1960 three-quarters of all US households were formed by married couples, and non-family households accounted for only 15 percent of households, in the year 2000, married couples will account for about 53 percent, and non-family households will increase their share to 38 percent. What emerges from this statistical overview is a picture of diversification, of moving boundaries in people's partnerships, with a large and increasing proportion of children being socialized under family forms that were marginal, or even unthinkable, only three decades ago, an instant by the standards of historical time.[127]

So, what are these new arrangements? How do people live now, in and outside the family, on the borderlines of patriarchalism? We know something about it, after pioneer research by Stacey, Reigot and Spina, Susser, and others.[128] As Stacey writes:

> women and men have been creatively remaking American family life during the past three decades of post-industrial upheaval. Out of the ashes and residue of the modern family they have drawn on a diverse, often incongruous array of cultural, political, economic, and ideological resources, fashioning these resources into new gender and kinship strategies to cope with post-industrial challenges, burdens and opportunities.[129]

Similar conclusions are reached in the qualitative study by Reigot and Spina on new forms of families.[130] There is no new prevailing type of family emerging, diversity is the rule. But some elements seem to be critical in the new arrangements: *networks of support, increasing female-centeredness, succession of partners and patterns throughout the life-cycle.* Networks of support, often between members of families of divorced couples are a new, important form of sociability and burden-sharing, particularly when children have to be shared and supported between the two parents after they both form new households. Thus, a study

---

[127] According to data cited by Ehrenreich (1983: 20), in 1957, 53 percent of Americans believed that unmarried people were "sick," "immoral," or "neurotic," and only 37 percent viewed them "neutrally." By 1976, only 33 percent had negative attitudes toward the unmarried, and 15 percent looked favorably upon people who remained single.

[128] Stacey (1990); Susser (1991, 1996); Reigot and Spina (1996); see also Bartholet (1990); Gonsiorek and Weinrich (1991); Brubaker (1993); Rubin and Riney (1994); Fitzpatrick and Vangelisti (1995).

[129] Stacey (1990: 16).

[130] Reigot and Spina (1996).

of middle-class divorced couples in the San Francisco suburbs found one-third of them sustaining kinship ties with former spouses and their relatives.[131] Women's support networks are critical for single mothers, as well as for full-time working mothers, according to the case studies reported by Reigot and Spina, and by Susser, as well as by Coleman and Ganong.[132] Indeed, as Stacey writes "if there is a family crisis, it is a male family crisis."[133] Furthermore, since most people keep trying to form families in spite of disappointments or misfits, step-parent families and a succession of partnerships become the norm. Because of both life experience and complexity of the households, arrangements within the family, with distribution of roles and responsibilities do not adjust to tradition any longer: they must be negotiated. Thus Coleman and Ganong, after observing widespread family disruption, conclude: "Does this mean the end of the family? No. It does mean, however, that many of us will be living in new, more complex families. In these new families, roles, rules and responsibilities may have to be negotiated rather than taken for granted as is typical in more traditional families."[134]

So, patriarchalism in the family is altogether eliminated in the case of the growing proportion of female-headed households, and seriously challenged in most other families, because of the negotiations and conditions requested by women and children in the household. Additionally, another growing proportion of households, maybe soon reaching almost 40 percent, relates to non-family households, thus voiding the meaning of the patriarchal family as an institution in much of the practice of society, in spite of its towering presence as a powerful myth.

Under such conditions, what happens to the socialization of children, underlying the reproduction of gender division in society, and thus the reproduction of patriarchalism itself?

The reproduction of mothering under the non-reproduction of patriarchalism

There is no place within the limits of this chapter to enter the detail of a complex, diversified, and controversial empirical record, most of which is hidden in the clinical files of child psychologists, on the transformation of family socialization in the new family environment. But, I think a number of hypotheses can be advanced, on the basis of the

---

[131]   Cited in Stacey (1990: 254).
[132]   Coleman and Ganong (1993); Reigot and Spina (1996); Susser (1996).
[133]   Stacey (1990: 269).
[134]   Coleman and Ganong (1993: 127).

classic work by feminist psychoanalyst Nancy Chodorow. In her *Reproduction of Mothering*, Chodorow proposed a simple, elegant, and powerful psychoanalytical model of the production/reproduction of gender, a model that she refined and complemented in her later writings.[135] Although her theory is controversial, and psychoanalysis is certainly not the only possible approach to understanding personality changes in the crisis of patriarchalism, it provides, in my view, a useful starting point to theorize these changes. Let me first summarize Chodorow's analytical model in her own words, then elaborate on the implications of this model for personality and gender under the conditions of the crisis of patriarchalism. Following Chodorow, the reproduction of mothering is central to the reproduction of gender. It happens through a social-structurally induced psychological process, which is not the product of either biology or institutional role-training. In her words:

> Women, as mothers, produce daughters with mothering capacities and the desire to mother. These capacities and needs are built into and grow out of the mother–daughter relationship itself. By contrast, women as mothers (and men as not-mothers) produce sons whose nurturant capacities and needs have been systematically curtailed and repressed. This prepares men for their affective later family role and for their primary participation in the impersonal, extra-familial world of work and public life. The sexual and familial division of labor in which women mother and are more involved in interpersonal, affective relationships than men, produces in daughters and sons a division of psychological capacities which leads them to reproduce this sexual and familial division of labor . . . Women have primary responsibility for child care in families and outside them; women by and large want to mother, and get gratification for their mothering; and with all the conflicts and contradictions, women have succeeded at mothering.[136]

This model of reproduction has an extraordinary impact on sexuality, and therefore on personality and family life: "Because women mother, the development of heterosexual object-choice differ for men and women."[137] Boys retain their mother as their primary love object in their boyhood, and, because of the fundamental taboo, they have to go through the classic process of separation, and resolution of their oedipus complex, by repressing their attachment to the

---

[135] Chodorow (1989, 1994).
[136] Chodorow (1978: 7).
[137] Chodorow (1978: 191).

mother. When becoming adults, men are ready to find a primary relationship with someone *like* their mother (Chodorow's italics). Things are different for girls:

> Because her first love object is a woman, a girl, in order to attain her *proper heterosexual orientation*,[138] must transfer her primary object-choice to her father and men . . . For girls, as for boys, mothers are primary love objects. As a result, the structural inner object setting of female heterosexuality differs from that of males. When a girl's father does become an important primary person, it is in the context of a bisexual relational triangle . . . For girls, then, there is no absolute change of object, nor exclusive attachment to their fathers . . . The implications of this are two-fold. First, the nature of the heterosexual relationship differs for boys and girls. Most women emerge from their oedipus complex oriented to their father and men as primary *erotic* objects, but it is clear that men tend to remain *emotionally* secondary, or at most emotionally equal, compared to the primacy and exclusivity of an oedipal boy's tie to his mother and women. Second . . . women, according to Deutsch, experience heterosexual relationships in a triangular context, in which men are not exclusive objects for them. The implication of her statement is confirmed by cross-cultural examination of family structure and relations between the sexes, which suggests that conjugal closeness is the exception and not the rule.[139]

Indeed, men tend to fall in love romantically, while women, because of their economic dependence and their women-oriented affective system, engage *vis à vis* men in a more complex calculation, in which access to resources is paramount,[140] according to the cross-cultural

---

[138] Adrienne Rich (1980) criticized Chodorow for not emphasizing the potential lesbian inclination of many women, in line with her theory. In my view, this criticism is unfair because Rich's "lesbian continuum" takes place within the context of institutionalized heterosexuality. What Chodorow explains is how the uninterrupted mother/daughter link is channeled toward the institutions of heterosexual marriage, from where it is also originates. It is essential for the psychoanalyst, and for the sociologist, to keep a distance between analysis and advocacy.

[139] Chodorow (1978: 192–3).

[140] Of course, the world's literature, as our personal experience, is full of examples of women abandoning everything in pursuit of romance. I would argue, however, that this is a manifestation of the ideological domination of the patriarchal model, and rarely resists the actual experience of the relationship. This is why it makes good material for novels!

study by Buss on strategies of human mating.[141] But let us pursue
Chodorow's logic:

[Women] while they are likely to become and remain erotically
heterosexual [Castells: albeit with more and more exceptions to
the rule], they are encouraged both by men's difficulties with
love and by their own relational history with their mothers to look
elsewhere for love and emotional gratification. One way that
women fulfill these needs is through the creation and maintenance of important personal relations with other
women . . . However, deep affective relationships to women are
hard to come by on a routine, daily, ongoing basis for many
women. Lesbian relationships do tend to recreate mother-
daughters, but most women are heterosexual . . . There is a
second alternative . . . Given the triangular situation and
emotional asymmetry of her own parenting, a woman's relation
to a man *requires* on the level of psychic structure a third person,
since it was originally established in a triangle . . . Then, a child
completes the relational triangle for a woman [142]

Indeed, "women come to want and need primary relationships to children."[143] For men, again, it is different, because of their primordial
attachment to their mother, and, later on, to their mother-like figure:
"For men, by contrast, the heterosexual relationship alone recreates
the early bond to their mother; *a child interrupts it* [my italics]. Men,
moreover do not define themselves in relationships, and have come
to suppress relational capacities and repress relational needs. This
prepares them to participate in the affect-denying world of alienated
work, but not to fulfill women's needs for intimacy and primary
relationships."[144] Thus, "men's lack of emotional availability and
women's less exclusive heterosexual commitment help ensure
women's mothering." Ultimately,

institutionalized features of family structure and the social
relations of reproduction reproduce themselves. A psychoanalytical investigation shows that women's mothering capacities
and commitments, and the general psychological capacities and
wants which are the basis of women's emotions work, are built
developmentally into feminine personality. Because women are
themselves mothered by women, they grow up with the relational

[141]   Buss (1994).
[142]   Chodorow (1978: 201).
[143]   Chodorow (1978: 203).
[144]   Chodorow (1978: 207).

capacities and needs, and psychological definition of self-in relationships, which commits them to mothering. Men, because they are mothered by women, do not. Women mother daughters who, when they become women, mother.[145]

Chodorow's model has been assailed, notably by lesbian theorists and materialist feminists, and unfairly accused of downplaying homosexuality, of fixing patriarchalism, and of predetermining individual behavior. In fact, it is not so. Chodorow herself has made clear her views: "I claim – against generalization – that men and women love in as many ways as there are men and women."[146] And she has refined her analysis by emphasizing that "differentiation is not distinctness and separateness, but a particular way of being connected to others."[147] The problem for women, she argues, and I concur, is not to claim their female identity, but their identification with an identity that has been socially devalued under patriarchalism. What Chodorow analyzes is not an eternal, biological process of male/female specificity, but a fundamental mechanism of reproduction of gender, and hence of identity, sexuality, and personality, *under the conditions of patriarchalism and heterosexuality*, as she has made clear repeatedly.

My question, then, is whether this institutional/psychoanalytical model can help us in understanding what happens when the patriarchal family disintegrates. Let me try to link up my observations on new forms of families and living arrangements with Chodorow's theory.[148] Under the classic, now fading, patriarchal/heterosexual condition, heterosexual women relate primarily to four kinds of objects: children as the object of their mothering; women's networks as their primary emotional support; men as erotic objects; and men as providers of the family. Under current conditions, for most families and women, the fourth object has been canceled as the exclusive provider. Women do pay a dear price, in working time, and in poverty, for their economic independence or for their indispensable role as family providers, but, by and large, the economic basis of family patriarchalism has been eroded, since most men also need women's income to reach decent living standards. As men were already secondary as assets of emotional

---

[145]   Chodorow (1978: 209).
[146]   Chodorow (1994: 71).
[147]   Chodorow (1989: 107).
[148]   I should remind the reader that Chodorow is primarily a psychoanalyst, focused on developing theory *on the basis of clinical evidence*. Therefore, this use of her cautious, psychoanalytical approach to construct my sweeping sociological generalizations goes far beyond her usual boundaries, and is undertaken, naturally, under my exclusive responsibility.

support, this leaves them, primarily, with their role as erotic objects, a dwindling source of interest for women in a time of widespread development of women's support networks (including expressions of affection in a "lesbian continuum"), and given women's focus on combining their mothering with their working lives.

Thus, the first living arrangement resulting from the crisis of patriarchalism, corresponding to the logic of Chodorow's model, is the formation of mother/children families, relying on the support of women's networks. These "women/children's communes" experience, from time to time, the visit of men, for heterosexual women, in a pattern of successive partnerships that leave behind additional children and further reasons for separatism. When mothers age, daughters mother, reproducing the system. Then, mothers become grandmothers, reinforcing the support networks, both *vis à vis* their daughters and grandchildren, and *vis à vis* the daughters and children of their networked households. This is not a separatist model, but a rather self-sufficient women-centered model, where men come and go. The main problem for the woman-centered model, as Barbara Ehrenreich pointed out years ago,[149] is its weak economic basis. Childcare, social services, and women's education and job opportunities are the missing links for this model to become a largely self-sufficient women's commune on a societal scale.

The situation for men, while being more socially privileged, is more complicated personally.[150] With the decline of their economic bargaining power, they usually cannot enforce discipline in the family any longer by withholding resources. Unless they engage in egalitarian parenting, they cannot alter the basic mechanisms by which their daughters are produced as mothers and they are produced as desirers of women/mothers *for themselves*. Thus, they continue to seek after *the* woman, as their object of love, not only erotic but emotional, as well as their safety blanket, and, not forgetting, their useful domestic worker. With fewer children, women working, men earning less and in less secure jobs, and with feminist ideas floating around, men face a number of options, none of which is the reproduction of the patriarchal family, if this analysis is correct.

The first is *separation*, "the flight from commitment,"[151] and, indeed, we observe such a trend in the statistics. Consumerist narcissism may help, particularly in the younger years. Yet, men do not do well in networking, solidarity, and relational skills, a feature that is also explained by Chodorow's theory. Male bonding is indeed a usual

---

[149]   Ehrenreich (1983).
[150]   Ehrenreich (1983); Astrachan (1986); Keen (1991).
[151]   Ehrenreich (1983).

practice in traditional patriarchal societies. But, as I remember from my Spanish experience (old and recent), "men only" social gatherings are based on the assumption of family/female support waiting at home. It is only on a stable structure of domination satisfying basic affective needs that men can then play together, generally talking about, boasting about, and parading for women. The men's *peñas* [152] become silent and depressing when women disappear, suddenly transformed into drinking mortuaries of male power. Indeed, in most societies, single men have poorer health, lower longevity, and higher suicide and depression rates than married men. The contrary is true for women who divorce or separate, in spite of frequent, but short post-divorce depressions.

A second alternative is *gayness*. Indeed, it seems that gayness is expanding among men whose biological predispositions allow both forms of sexual expression, but that, under circumstances of privileged patriarchalism, may have chosen to abstain from the homosexual stigma. Gayness increases the chances of support networks, of which men are usually deprived. It also makes easier egalitarian, or negotiated, partnerships, since social norms do not assign dominant roles in the couple. Thus, gay families may be the experimental milieux of everyday life's egalitarianism.

Yet, for most men, the most acceptable, stable, long-term solution is to *renegotiate the heterosexual family contract*. This includes domestic work sharing, economic partnership, sexual partnership, and, above everything else, *full sharing of parenting*. This latter condition is critical for men because only under such circumstances can the "Chodorow effect" be altered, and women could be produced not only as mothers, but as men-desiring women, and men could be raised not just as women-lovers, but as children's fathers. Indeed, unless this mechanism is reversed, the simple reform of economic and power arrangements in the family cannot last as a satisfactory condition for men because, as they are still yearning for *the* woman as *their* exclusive love-object, and they are decreasingly needed by women, their conditional surrender in the reformed nuclear family is structurally filled with resentment. Thus, beyond individual bargaining in the reformed family, the future possibility for reconstructing viable heterosexual

---

[152]   The *peña* is a medieval Spanish institution, originally for men only, and still male dominated, which brought/brings together the youth of the village or neighborhood around the preparation of the annual religious/folk festivity of the village. It serves as a socializing network for drinking and enjoying together the annual round, as in the most famous *peñas*, those of Pamplona's San Fermines. The word *peña* means solid rock. The *peñas* are the rocks of male bonding.

families lies in the subversion of gender through the revolution of parenting, as Chodorow suggested in the first place. Without going into another round of statistical detail, let me just say that, while considerable progress has been made in this direction,[153] egalitarian parenting has still a long way to go, and its growth is slower than the rise of separatism for both men and women.

The main victims of this cultural transition are children, as they have become increasingly neglected under current conditions of family crisis. Their situation may even worsen, either because women stay with their children under difficult material conditions, or because women, looking for autonomy and personal survival, begin to neglect their children the way men do. Since support from the welfare state is dwindling, men and women are left to themselves in handling their children's problems, while losing control over their lives. The dramatic increase in child abuse in many societies, particularly in the United States, could well be an expression of people's bewilderment concerning their family life. By saying so, I am certainly not espousing the neo-conservative argument that blames feminism, or sexual liberation, for the plight of children. I am pinpointing a fundamental issue in our society that must be addressed without ideological prejudice: children are being massively neglected, as documented by social scientists and journalists.[154] The solution is not an impossible return to an obsolete, and oppressive, patriarchal family. The reconstruction of the family under egalitarian relations, and the responsibility of public institutions in securing material and psychological support for children, are possible ways to alter the course toward mass destruction of the human psyche that is implicit in the currently unsettling life of millions of children.

Body identity: the (re)construction of sexuality

There is a sexual revolution in the making, but not the one announced, and sought, by the 1960s/1970s social movements, although they have been important factors in inducing the really existing sexual revolution. *It is characterized by the de-linking of marriage, family, heterosexuality, and sexual expression* (or desire, as I call it). These four factors, linked under modern patriarchalism for the past two centuries, are now in the process of autonomization, as a number of observations reported in this chapter seem to show. As Giddens writes:

---

[153]   Shapiro et al. (1995).
[154]   Susser (1996).

Heterosexual marriage superficially appears to retain its central position in the social order. In reality, it has been largely undermined by the rise of the pure relationship and plastic sexuality. If orthodox marriage is not yet widely seen as just one life-style among others, as in fact it has become, this is partly the result of the complicated mixture of attraction and repulsion which the psychic development of each sex creates with regard to the other . . . Some marriages may still be contracted, or sustained, mainly for the sake of producing, or bringing up, children. Yet . . . most heterosexual marriages (and many homosexual liaisons) which do not approximate to the pure relationship are likely to evolve in two directions if they do not lapse into co-dependence. One is a version of a companionate marriage. The level of sexual involvement of the spouses with each other is low, but some degree of equality and mutual sympathy is built into the relationship. . . . The other form is where marriage is used as a home base for both partners who have only a slight emotional investment in one another.[155]

In both cases, sexuality is de-linked from marriage. This was indeed the case for most women throughout history,[156] but the affirmation of women's sexuality, of homosexuality for both men and women, and of elective sexuality, are inducing an increasing distance between people's desire and their families. However, this does not translate into sexual liberation, but, for the majority of the population, scared by the consequences of infidelity (for which men now also have to pay), and, in the 1980s and 1990s, by the AIDS epidemic, the consequence is sexual poverty, if not misery. This is at least what can be inferred from the most comprehensive, recent empirical survey of sexual behavior in America, conducted in 1992 on a representative national sample.[157] Some 35.5 percent of men reported having sex a few times a month, and another 27.4 percent a few times a year or not at all. For women, respective percentages were 37.2 percent and 29.7 percent. Only 7.7 percent of men and 6.7 percent of women reported having sex four or more times per week, and even in the 18–24 age group (the most sexually active), the percentage of high frequency was 12.4 percent both for men and women. High activity rates (over four times a week) are slightly lower for married couples than for the population at large (7.3 percent for men, 6.6 percent for women). These data also confirm the gender gap in reported orgasms: 75 percent of sexual encounters for men, only 29 percent

[155]   Giddens (1992: 154–5).
[156]   Buss (1994).
[157]   Laumann et al. (1994).

for women, although the gap is narrower in reporting "pleasure."[158]
The number of sex partners in the last 12 months shows a limited
range of sexual partnerships for the overwhelming majority of the
population: 66.7 percent of men and 74.7 percent of women had
only one partner; and 9.9 percent and 13.6 percent respectively, had
none. So, no widespread sexual revolution in America in the early
1990s.

Yet, beneath the surface of sexual tranquility, the rich database of
this University of Chicago study reveals trends toward an increasing
autonomy of sexual expression, particularly among the younger age
groups. For instance, there has been a steady decrease over the past
four decades in the age of first intercourse: in spite of AIDS, teenagers
are more sexually active than ever. Secondly, cohabitation before
marriage has become the norm rather than the exception. Adults
increasingly tend to form sexual partnerships outside marriage.
About half of these cohabitations end within a year, 40 percent of
them being transformed into marriages, 50 percent of which will end
up in divorce, two-thirds of which will end up in remarriage, whose
likelihood of divorce is even greater than the average for all
marriages. It is this drying up of desire by successive efforts to link it
up to living arrangements that seems to characterize 1990s' America.

On the other hand, "consumerist sexuality" appears on the rise,
although the indications here are rather indirect. Laumann et al.
analyze their sample in terms of sexual normative orientations
following the classic distinction between traditional sexuality (pro-
creational), relational (companionship), and recreational (oriented
toward sexual enjoyment). They also isolate a "libertarian-
recreational" type that seems closer to the images of pop-sexual
liberation or, in Giddens' terms, "plastic sexuality." When analyzing
their sample by major regions in America, they found that 25.5
percent of their sample in New England, and 22.2 percent in the
Pacific region, could be included under such a "libertarian-recre-
ational" category: this is about one-quarter of the population in some
of the most culturally trend-setting areas of America.

A meaningful indicator of increasing sexual autonomy, as a
pleasure-oriented activity, is the practice of oral sex which, I remind
you, is catalogued as sodomy, and explicitly prohibited by law in 24
American states, albeit under conditions of doubtful enforcement.
Figure 4.14 displays the occurrence of oral sex by cohort, by which is
meant the percentages of women and men who have experienced
either cunnilingus or fellatio in their lifetime by birth cohort.
Laumann et al., commenting on these findings, assert that:

[158]   Laumann et al. (1994: 116).

Men

Women

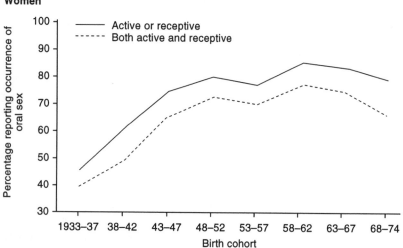

Figure 4.14 Lifetime occurrence of oral sex, by cohort: men and women
Source: Laumann et al. (1994)

The overall trend reveals what we might call a rapid change in sexual techniques if not a revolution. The difference in lifetime experience of oral sex between respondents born between 1933 and 1942 and those born after 1943 is dramatic. The proportion of men experiencing oral sex in their lifetime increases from 62 percent of those born between 1933–37 to 90 percent of those born between 1948–52 . . . The timing of sexual techniques appears to have been responsive to cultural changes in the late 1950s, changes that peaked in the mid to late 1960s, *when they approached saturation level of the population. The lower rates among the youngest groups in our survey are not necessarily evidence of decline in oral sex; these groups simply have not yet engaged in sexual relationships in which oral sex has become likely if not normative.*[159]

Incidentally, between 75 and 80 percent of women in the latest cohorts also experienced oral sex, and in the younger groups their occurrence is higher than for men. Laumann et al. also report widespread incidence of auto-eroticism (associated with high levels of partnered sexual activity), and of masturbation, hardly a novel technique, but that seems to involve two-thirds of men, and over 40 percent of women.

Thus, if instead of reading sexual behavior under the norm of heterosexual, repetitive partnership, we take a more "perverse" approach to it, the data reveal a different story, a story of consumerism, experimentation, and eroticism in the process of deserting conjugal bedrooms, and still searching for new modes of expression, while watching out for AIDS. Since these new patterns of behavior are more visible among younger groups, and in trend-setting cities, I feel safe to predict that, if, when, and where the AIDS epidemic comes under control, there will be one, two, three, many Sodoms, emerging from fantasies freed by the crisis of patriarchalism, and excited by the culture of narcissism. Under such conditions, as Giddens proposes, sexuality becomes the property of the individual.[160] Where Foucault saw the extension of apparatuses of power into the sexually constructed/construed subject, Giddens sees, and I concur, the fight between power and identity in the battleground of the body.[161] It is not necessarily a liberating struggle, because desire often emerges from transgression, so that a "sexually liberated society" becomes simply a supermarket of personal fantasies, in which individuals will consume each other rather than produce themselves. However, by assuming the body as identity principle, away from the institutions of patriarchalism, the multiplicity of sexual expressions empowers the individual in the arduous (re)construction of her/his personality.[162]

---

[159]   Laumann et al. (1994: 103–4); my italics.
[160]   Giddens (1992: 175).
[161]   Giddens (1992: 31).
[162]   Grosz (1995).

Flexible personalities in a post-patriarchal world

New generations are being socialized out of the traditional pattern of the patriarchal family, and are being exposed from an early age to the need to cope with different settings, and different adult roles. In sociological terms, the new process of socialization downplays to some extent the institutional norms of the patriarchal family and diversifies the roles within the family. In their insightful exploration of this matter, Hage and Powers propose that, as an outcome of such processes, new personalities emerge, more complex, less secure, yet more capable of adapting to changing roles in social contexts, as adaptive mechanisms are triggered by new experiences at an early age.[163] The increasing individualization of relationships within the family tends to emphasize the importance of personal demands beyond the rules of institutions. Thus, sexuality becomes, at the level of social values, a personal need that does not necessarily have to be channeled and institutionalized within the family. With the majority of the adult population, and one-third of children, living outside the boundaries of the traditional nuclear family, and with both proportions growing, the construction of desire increasingly operates on interpersonal relationships outside the lineage of traditional family context: it becomes an expression of the self. The socialization of teenagers under these new cultural patterns leads to a higher degree of sexual freedom than that of previous generations, including those in the liberated sixties, in spite of the menace of the AIDS epidemic.

Thus, the revolt of women against their condition, induced and allowed by their massive entry into the informational labor force, and the social movements of sexual identity have called into question the patriarchal nuclear family. This crisis has taken the form of a growing separation between the different dimensions that were previously held together in the same institution: interpersonal relationships between the two members of the couple; the working life of each member of the household; the economic association between members of the household; the performance of domestic work; the raising of children; sexuality; emotional support. The difficulty of coping with all these roles at the same time, once they are not fixed any longer in a formal, institutionalized structure, such as the patriarchal family, explains the difficulty of maintaining stable social relationships within the family-based household. For families to survive, new institutionalized forms of social relationships, in accordance with transformed relationships between genders, will have to emerge.

[163]   Hage and Powers (1992).

At the same time, technological change in biological reproduction has allowed the possibility of disassociating the reproduction of the species from the social and personal functions of the family. The possibilities of *in vitro* fertilization, of sperm banks, of surrogate mothers, of genetically engineered babies, open up a whole area of social experimentation that society will try to control and repress as much as possible because of its potential threat to our moral and legal foundations. Yet, the fact that women can have children on their own without having to even know the father, or that men, even after their death, can use surrogate mothers to have their children, severs the fundamental relationship between biology and society in the reproduction of human species, thus separating socialization from parenting. Under these historical conditions, families, and people's living arrangements, are being redefined in terms still unclear.

Because family and sexuality are fundamental determinants of personality systems, the calling into question of known family structures, and the coming into the open of personally projected sexuality, bring about the possibility of new types of personality that we are just beginning to perceive. Hage and Powers consider that the key ability to respond to current changes in society at the individual level is the ability to engage in "role redefinition," what they consider to be the "pivotal micro-process of postindustrial society."[164] While I concur with this most insightful analysis, I will add a complementary hypothesis to understand emerging personality systems. Daring to remain loyal to my psychoanalytical inclination, I would advance the idea that the open recognition of individual desire, as insinuated in the emerging culture of our society, would lead to such an aberration as the institutionalization of desire. Because desire is often associated with transgression, the recognition of sexuality outside the family would lead to extreme social strain. This is because as long as transgression consisted merely in expressing sexuality outside the family boundaries, society could easily cope with it, by channeling it through coded situations and organized contexts, such as prostitution, earmarked homosexuality, or condoned sexual harassment: this was Foucault's world of sexuality as normalization. Things are different now. If the patriarchal family is not there to be betrayed any longer, the transgression will have to be an individual act against society. The bumper function of the family is lost. This opens the way to the expression of desire in the form of non-instrumental violence. As welcome as it can be as a liberating development, the breakdown of the patriarchal family (the only one existing historically) is indeed giving way simultaneously to the normalization of sexuality (porno movies in

[164]   Hage and Powers (1992).

prime-time television), and to the spread of senseless violence in society through the back alleys of wild desire, that is, perversion. Liberation from the family confronts the self with its own inflicted oppression. The escape to freedom in the open, networked society will lead to individual anxiety and social violence, until new forms of coexistence and shared responsibility are found that bring together women, men, and children in a reconstructed, egalitarian family better suited to free women, informed children, and uncertain men.

The End of Patriarchalism?

The continuing struggles in and around patriarchalism do not allow a clear forecasting of the historical horizon. Let me again repeat that there is no predetermined directionality in history. We are not marching through the triumphant avenues of our liberation, and, when we feel so, we had better watch out to see where these shining paths ultimately lead. Life muddles through life and, as we know, is full of surprises. A fundamentalist restoration, bringing patriarchalism back under the protection of divine law, may well reverse the process of the undermining of the patriarchal family, unwillingly induced by informational capitalism, and willingly pursued by cultural social movements. The homophobic backlash may undo the recognition of homosexual rights, as shown by the overwhelming vote by the US Congress in July 1996 to declare heterosexuality a requisite for legal marriage. And, around the world, patriarchalism is still alive and well, in spite of the symptoms of crisis that I have tried to emphasize in this chapter. However, the very vehemence of the reactions in defense of patriarchalism, as in the religious fundamentalist movements thriving in many countries, is a sign of the intensity of the anti-patriarchal challenges. Values that were supposed to be eternal, natural, indeed divine, must now be asserted by force, thus retrenching in their last defensive bastion, and losing legitimacy in people's minds.

The ability or inability of feminist and sexual identity social movements to institutionalize their values will essentially depend on their relationship to the state, the last resort apparatus of patriarchalism throughout history. However, the extraordinary demands placed upon the state by social movements, attacking institutions of domination at their root, emerge at the very moment when the state seems to be itself in the midst of a structural crisis, brought about by the contradiction between the globalization of its future and the identification of its past.

━ 5 ━

A Powerless State?

"What is specific to the capitalist state," wrote Nicos Poulantzas in 1978, "is that it absorbs social time and space, sets up the matrices of time and space, and monopolizes the organization of time and space that become, by the action of the state, networks of domination and power. This is how the modern nation is the product of the state."[1] Not any longer. State control over space and time is increasingly bypassed by global flows of capital, goods, services, technology, communication, and information. The state's capture of historical time through its appropriation of tradition and the (re)construction of national identity is challenged by plural identities as defined by autonomous subjects. The state's attempt to reassert its power in the global arena by developing supranational institutions further undermines its sovereignty. And the state's effort to restore legitimacy by decentralizing administrative power to regional and local levels reinforces centrifugal tendencies by bringing citizens closer to government but increasing their aloofness toward the nation-state. Thus, while global capitalism thrives, and nationalist ideologies explode all over the world, the nation-state, as historically created in the Modern Age, seems to be losing its power, although, and this is essential, *not its influence*.[2] In this chapter I shall explain why, and elaborate on the potential consequences of this fundamental development. I shall use illustrations of nation-states in various countries to emphasize that we are observing a systemic, global phenomenon, albeit with a great variety of manifestations. Indeed, the growing challenge to states' sovereignty around the world seems to originate from the inability of the modern nation-state to navigate

---

[1] Poulantzas (1978: 109); my translation.
[2] Tilly (1975); Giddens (1985); Held (1991, 1993); Sklair (1991); Camilleri and Falk (1992); Guehenno (1993); Horsman and Marshall (1994); Touraine (1994); Calderon et al. (1996).

uncharted, stormy waters between the power of global networks and the challenge of singular identities.[3]

Globalization and the State

The instrumental capacity of the nation-state is decisively undermined by globalization of core economic activities, by globalization of media and electronic communication, and by globalization of crime.[4]

---

[3]   The analysis of the crisis of the nation-state presupposes a definition, and a theory, of the nation-state. But since my work in this matter builds on already developed sociological theories, from various sources, I will refer the reader to the definition of Anthony Giddens in *The Nation-state and Violence* (1985: 121): "The nation-state, which exists in a complex of other nation-states, is a set of institutional forms of governance, maintaining an administrative monopoly over a territory with demarcated boundaries (borders), its rule being sanctioned by law, and direct control of the means of internal and external violence." Yet, as Giddens writes, "only in modern nation-states can the state apparatus generally lay successful claim to the monopoly of the means of violence, and only in such states does the administrative scope of the state apparatus correspond directly with territorial boundaries about which that claim is made" (p. 18). Indeed, as he argues, "a nation-state is a bordered power-container, the pre-eminent power-container of the modern era" (p. 120). So, what happens, and how should we conceptualize that state, when borders break down, and when containers are becoming contained themselves? My investigation starts, in theoretical continuity, from where the nation-state, as conceptualized by Giddens, appears to be superseded by historical transformation.

[4]   For a definition and an analysis of globalization, as I understand it, see volume I, chapter 2. For a salutary critique of simplistic views on globalization, see Hirst and Thompson (1996). It has been often argued that globalization is not a new phenomenon, and has occurred in different historical periods, particularly with the expansion of capitalism at the end of the nineteenth century. It may be so, although I am not convinced that the new infrastructure based on information technology does not introduce a qualitative social and economic change, by enabling global processes to operate in real time. But I have really no quarrel with this argument: it does not concern my inquiry. I am trying to analyze, and explain, our society at the end of the twentieth century, in its variety of cultural, economic, and political contexts. So, my intellectual contribution should be discussed on its own ground, concerning contemporary processes as observed and theorized in the three volumes of this book. Undoubtedly, scholarly thinking would greatly benefit from comparative historical work contrasting current processes of interaction between technology, globalization of economy and communications, politics, and political institutions with past experience of a similar transformation. I am hopeful that such an effort will be undertaken by colleagues, primarily by historians, and I will be more than happy to rectify my general theoretical statements on the basis of implications from such research. For the time being, the few attempts I have seen in this direction pay insufficient attention, in my opinion,

The transnational core of national economies

The interdependence of financial markets and currency markets around the world, operating as a unit in real time, links up national currencies. The constant exchange between dollars, yens, and the European Union's currencies (euros in the future) forces systemic coordination between these currencies, as the only measure able to keep some degree of stability in the currency market, and thus in global investment and trade. All other currencies in the world have become linked, for all practical purposes, to this triangle of wealth. If the exchange rate is systemically interdependent, so are, or will be, monetary policies. And if monetary policies are somehow harmonized at a supranational level, so are, or will be, prime interest rates, and, ultimately, budgetary policies. It follows that individual nation-states are losing and will lose control over fundamental elements of their economic policies.[5] In fact, this was already the experience of developing countries in the 1980s, and of European countries during the early 1990s. Barbara Stallings has shown how economic policies in developing countries were shaped during the 1980s by international pressures, as international financial institutions and private banks moved to stabilize developing economies as a prerequisite to international investment and trade.[6] In the European Union, the Bundesbank is already the *de facto* European Central Bank. For instance, when, in order to control German inflation after the government's irresponsible decision to set the exchange rate of one Western mark per one Eastern mark to unify Germany, the Bundesbank tightened up interest rates, it forced a deflation throughout Europe, regardless of the performance of national economies. In 1992 the Bundesbank went so far as to leak to the media its criticism of British monetary policy in order to force the devaluation of the pound, as eventually happened.

Japanese economic policy is essentially determined by the relationship between trade balance and exchange rate with the United States. As for the United States, the most self-sufficient economy, it could only remain so in spite of a substantial trade deficit during the 1980s by financing increased government spending

---

to the radically new processes in technology, finance, production, communications, and politics, so that while they may be right on the historical record, it is unclear why the present is just a repetition of past experience, beyond the rather pedestrian view that there is nothing new under the sun.
[5] Moreau Deffarges (1993); *Business Week* (1995a); Orstrom Moller (1995); Cohen (1996).
[6] Stallings (1992).

through borrowing, to a large extent from foreign capital. So doing, the main issue in American economic policy in the 1990s became the reduction of a gigantic budget deficit which threatened to become the black hole of the economy. America's economic independence was an illusion, likely to dissipate in the future when living standards will reflect competitiveness in the global economy, once the cushion of massive government borrowing, which became out of control under the Reagan Administration, is lifted.[7] It can be argued that the degree of freedom of governments' economic policy has been drastically reduced in the 1990s, with their budget policy caught between automatic entitlements inherited from the past, and high capital mobility experienced in the present, and probably increasing in the future.[8]

This increasing difficulty of government control over the economy (that some economists eagerly welcome) is accentuated by the growing transnationalization of production, not just under the impact of multinational corporations, but mainly through the production and trade networks in which these corporations are integrated.[9] It follows a declining capacity of governments to ensure, in their territories, the productive basis for generating revenue. As companies and wealthy individuals alike find fiscal havens around the world, and as accounting of value added in an international production system becomes increasingly cumbersome, a new fiscal crisis of the state arises, as the expression of an increasing contradiction between the internationalization of investment, production, and consumption, on the one hand, and the national basis of taxation systems, on the other.[10] Is it an accident that the two wealthiest countries in the world, in *per capita* terms, are Luxembourg and Switzerland? It may well be that one of the last stands of the nation-state is being fought in cyber-accounting space, between dutiful tax inspectors and sophisticated transnational lawyers.

A statistical appraisal of the new fiscal crisis of the state in the global economy

At this point in the analysis, it may be helpful to look at the evolution of government finances in the period of stepped-up globalization of national economies between 1980 and the early 1990s. To limit the complexity of the analysis, I have selected six countries: the three

---

[7]   Thurow (1992); Cohen (1993).
[8]   Chesnais (1994); Nunnenkamp et al. (1994).
[9]   Buckley (1994).
[10]   Guehenno (1993).

largest market economies (US, Japan, Germany); the most open of
the large European economies (the UK); another European country,
Spain, which, while being the eighth largest market economy in the
world, is at a lower level of economic/technological development
than G-7 countries; and one major economy of the newly industrialized world, India. On the basis of statistics compiled and elaborated
by Sandra Moog, tables 5.1 and 5.2 have been constructed to provide
an overview of some indicators of government finance and economic
activity, related to the process of internationalization of economies. I
will not comment in detail. Rather, I will use these tables to expand
and specify the argument on globalization and the state as presented
in the preceding pages.

Let us first examine the group of four countries (US, UK, Germany,
and Spain) that seem to behave, in very broad terms, along similar
lines, albeit with differences that I shall emphasize. Government
expenditures have increased, and now represent between one-quarter
and over 40 percent of GDP. Government jobs have decreased everywhere. The share of government consumption has decreased in the
three major countries, while increasing in Spain. The share of government capital formation has increased in the US and declined in
Germany. Central government's tax revenue has decreased in the US,
while increasing in the other countries, substantially in Spain.
Government deficit has increased, and substantially so in the US and
Germany. Government debt has decreased in the UK, although it still
represents about 34 percent of GDP, and has dramatically increased
in Spain, Germany, and in the US, where in 1992 it represented 52.2
percent of GDP. The financing of government deficits has led the four
countries to increase, in some cases substantially, dependency on
foreign debt and foreign net lending. The ratios of government
foreign debt and government net borrowing on GDP, central banks'
currency reserves, government expenditures, and countries' exports
show, in general terms, *an increasing dependence of governments on global
capital markets*. Thus, for the United States, between 1980 and 1993,
government foreign debt as a percentage of GDP more than doubled;
as a percentage of currency reserves, it increased by 20 percent and,
in 1993, represented almost ten times the level of total currency
reserves; as a percentage of exports, it increased by 133 percent; and
as a percentage of government expenditures, it almost doubled, to
reach a level of 41.7 percent of total expenditures. As for the US
government's net foreign borrowing, it increased in these 14 years by
a staggering 456 percent, increasing by 203 percent its ratio to government expenditure, to reach a level equivalent to 6 percent of
government expenditure. Since US direct foreign investment abroad,
as a proportion of domestic investment, increased by 52.8 percent,

Table 5.1 Internationalization of the economy and public finance: rates of change, 1980–93 (and 1993 ratios, unless otherwise indicated)

	United States	United Kingdom	Germany	Japan	Spain	India
Gov. foreign debt/GDP %	104.2 (9.8)	31.8 (5.8/1992)	538.5 (p) (16.6) (p)	0.0 (0.3/1990)	1,066.7 (10.5)	-25.3 (5.9)
Gov. foreign debt/currency reserves %	20.1 (998.6)	44.7 (168.1/1992)	325.3 (p) (368.4) (p)	9.9 (12.2/1990)	674.5 (121.6)	-16.5 (149.4)
Gov. foreign debt/exports %	133.0 (134.0)	50.5 (32.2/1992)	590.8 (p) (75.3) (p)	9.5 (2.3/1990)	795.5 (79.7)	-55.6 (70.7)
Gov. foreign debt/gov. expenditures %	92.2 (41.7)	17.5 (13.5/1992)	423.5 (p) (44.5) (p)	—	586.8 (36.4)	-40.7 (35.4)
Gov. net foreign borrowing/gov. expenditures %	203.0 (6.12)	787.5 (14.2/1992)	223.4 (p) (15.2) (p)	—	—	10.3 (4.3)
Direct foreign investment abroad/domestic investment %	52.8 (5.5)	44.4 (17.9)	52.2 (3.5)	57.1 (1.1)	183.3 (2.8)	—
Inflow of direct foreign investment/domestic investment %	-35.5 (2.0)	-8.9 (10.2)	-50.0 (0.1)	—	236.7 (8.6)	—

(p) indicates preliminary data.

Note: For figures and details about sources and methods of calculation, please see the Methodological Appendix.

Sources: Compiled and elaborated by Sandra Moog from the following sources: *Government Finance Statistics Yearbook,* vol. 18 (Washington DC: IMF, 1994); *International Financial Statistics Yearbook,* vol. 48 (Washington DC: IMF, 1995); *The Europa World Yearbook* (London: Europa Publications, 1982, 1985, 1995); *National Accounts: Detailed Tables, 1980–1992,* vol. 2 (Paris: OECD, 1994); *OECD Economic Outlook,* vol. 58 (Paris: OECD, 1995); *World Tables, 1994* (The World Bank, Baltimore: The Johns Hopkins University Press, 1994)

Table 5.2 Government role in the economy and public finance: rates of change, 1980–92 (and 1992 ratios, unless otherwise indicated)

	United States	United Kingdom	Germany	Japan	Spain	India
Gov. expenditures/ GDP %	9.1 (24.0)	13.1 (43.2)	19.7 (34.6)	—	49.4 (25.1)	29.3 (p) (17.2) (p)
Budgetary central gov. tax revenue/GDP %	-15.6 (10.8)	8.0 (27.0)	11.6 (p) (13.5) (p)	18.2 (13.0/1990)	64.2 (17.4/1991)	17.3 (p) (11.2) (p)
Gov. budget deficit/GDP %	42.9 (4.8)	8.7 (5.0)	44.4 (2.6)	-78.6 (1.5/1990)	16.2 (4.3)	20.0 (p) (5.2) (p)
Gov. debt/GDP %	91.9 (52.2)	-26.0 (34.1)	78.1 (28.5)	30.1 (53.2/1990)	160.8 (39.9)	28.2 (p) (52.8) (p)
Gov. employment/ total employment %	-4.7 (16.2)	-3.1 (22.2)	-0.6 (16.4)	-20.9 (7.2)	—	—
Gov. capital formation/gross fixed capital formation %	21.2 (16.0)	—	-7.0 (27.9)	—	—	—
Gov. consumption/ private consumption %	-6.9 (27.2)	-2.7 (34.5)	-8.1 (32.7)	66.3 (16.3)	33.8 (26.9)	40.2 (p) (19.0) (p)

(p) indicates preliminary data.

Note: For figures and details about sources and methods of calculation, please see the Methodological Appendix.

Sources: Compiled and elaborated by Sandra Moog from the following sources: *Government Finance Statistics Yearbook,* vol. 18 (Washington DC: IMF, 1994); *International Financial Statistics Yearbook,* vol. 48 (Washington DC: IMF, 1995); *The Europa World Yearbook* (London: Europa Publications, 1982, 1985, 1995); *National Accounts: Detailed Tables, 1980–1992,* vol. 2 (Paris: OECD, 1994); *OECD Economic Outlook,* vol. 58 (Paris: OECD, 1995); *World Tables, 1994* (The World Bank, Baltimore: The Johns Hopkins University Press, 1994) while inflow of direct foreign investment, also as a proportion of US domestic investment, decreased by 35.5 percent, it can be argued that the US federal government has become largely dependent on global capital markets and foreign lending.

The story is somewhat different for the UK, Germany, and Spain, but trends are similar. It is important to notice that, while the UK seems to be less dependent, Germany is increasing its dependency on foreign capital much faster than the US, as shown by several indicators: government foreign debt over GDP (538.5 percent increase), over currency reserves (325.3 percent increase), and over exports (590.8 percent increase). The German government's net foreign borrowing in 1993 reached a level representing over 15 percent of government expenditure, and its foreign debt is the equivalent of 44.5 percent of government expenditure, in both cases a higher percentage than those for the US. Thus, in spite of a strong export performance in the 1980s, Germany, unlike Japan, has substantially increased the international dependence of its national state.

Interestingly enough, India, while increasing government expenditure, consumption, and indebtedness, seems to be much less dependent on foreign debt: indeed, all its indicators of financial dependency show negative growth for the period, with the exception of the ratio of government foreign borrowing on government expenditure, still kept at a modest level. A sizeable increase in the share of tax revenue in GDP is only part of the explanation, the main one being the substantial acceleration of economic growth in India in the past decade. I should emphasize, however, that while the rate of change of indicators of the government's financial dependency in India has been negative over the period, the level of dependency remains very high (government foreign debt represents over 70 percent of exports, and almost 150 percent of currency reserves).

As is often the case, Japan is different. The Japanese government was not affected by foreign borrowing during the 1980s. Its budget deficit over GDP is by far the lowest, and it substantially declined during the period 1980–93. On the other hand, government consumption increased, government debt also increased, and Japan is as high as America in the ratio of government debt to GDP (over 50 percent). These observations indicate that the Japanese government's finances rely, rather, on domestic borrowing. This also reflects the greater competitiveness of the Japanese economy, and the considerable trade and balance of payments surplus accumulated by the country. So, the Japanese state is much more autonomous than other states *vis à vis* the rest of the world but the Japanese economy is much more dependent on trade performance, since Japanese capital finances its government with the proceeds from its competitiveness.

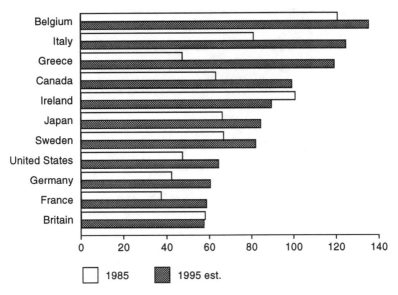

Figure 5.1 General government gross financial liabilities (% of GDP)
Source: OECD, elaborated by *The Economist* (January 20, 1996)

So, what appears to be an exception to the rule of government dependency, and increasing government deficit, is not. Japanese corporations take on the world economy, and their competitiveness finances the state, whose consumption has grown much faster than in any other of the countries studied. The Japanese state displays a second-order financial dependency on the movements of the international economy, via its borrowing from Japanese banks flourishing along with their *keiretsu*.

Three major trends can be underlined with regard to the arguments presented in this chapter:

1 In spite of a certain state's disengagement in the economy, particularly in terms of direct employment, and regulation, there is still a substantial economic role for the state that requires additional financing besides taxation, thus increasing the financial liability of the state, with the exception of the UK (see figure 5.1).

2 Governments' borrowing, with the major exception of Japan, is increasingly dependent on foreign lending, to an extent that already overwhelms central banks' currency reserves, and overshadows export performance. This reflects the broader phenomenon of an increasing gap between the faster growth of global financial markets in relation to the growth of global trade.

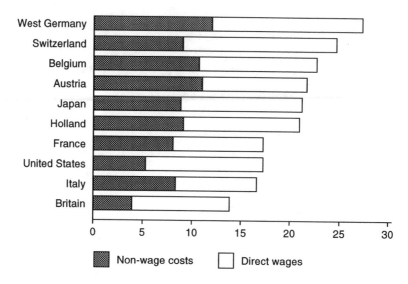

Figure 5.2   Labor costs in manufacturing, 1994 ($ per hour)
Source: Swedish Employers' Federation, elaborated by *The Economist*
(January 27, 1996)

3   The Japanese state has succeeded in establishing a measure of fiscal autonomy *vis à vis* foreign capital. However, it has done so on the basis of domestic borrowing, financed with Japanese corporations' earnings from protectionism and export performance; so that the Japanese economy, and the Japanese state, have become addicted to trade surpluses and recycling of profits in Japanese soil. This state of affairs led to the Japanese "bubble economy" of the late 1980s, and, subsequently, when the bubble burst, to the recession of the early 1990s.

Overall, the intertwining of national economies, and the dependency of government finance on global markets and foreign lending, have created the conditions for an international fiscal crisis of the nation-state, including the wealthiest and most powerful nation-states.

Globalization and the welfare state

The globalization of production and investment also threatens the *welfare state*, a key element in the policies of the nation-state in the past half-century, and probably the main building block of its legitimacy in industrialized countries.[11] This is because it becomes increasingly contradictory for firms to operate in globalized, integrated markets, while experiencing major cost differentials in social benefits, as well as distinct levels of regulation between countries. This happens not only between North and South, but between different OECD countries, as well: for example, social benefits-related labor costs are much lower in the US than in Germany (see figure 5.2). But what is a comparative advantage of US location *vis à vis* Germany becomes a disadvantage *vis à vis* Mexico, after the implementation of the NAFTA Treaty. Since firms, because of information technology, can locate in many different sites and still link up to global production networks and markets (see volume I, chapter 6), there follows a downward spiral of social costs competition. The limits to such "negative competitiveness" in the past have been twofold: on the one hand, the productivity and quality lag between countries protected workers from advanced economies *vis à vis* less-developed competitors; on the other hand, domestic pressure induced protectionism, so as to increase the price of imports, via tariffs, to a level where the comparative advantage of external sourcing would disappear. Both limits are withering away. The new World Trade Organization is setting up a watch dog system to detect and penalize barriers to free trade. While the politics of international trade condition the actual impact of such controls, it would seem that, unless there is a dramatic reversal in the process of global economic integration, blatant, large-scale protectionism will become increasingly subject to retaliation from other countries. As for the quality and productivity lag, Harley Shaiken's study of American automobile factories in Mexico has shown the rapid catch-up of Mexican workers' productivity which equalled that of American workers in about 18 months. Similar processes have been observed in Asia.[12] And (Europeans should be reminded) American labor productivity is still the highest in the world, so canceling a potential European competitiveness differential that could still allow for a generous welfare state. In an economy whose core markets for capital, goods, and services are increasingly integrated on a global scale, there is little room for vastly different welfare states, with relatively similar levels of labor productivity and production quality. Only a global social contract (reducing the gap, without necessarily equalizing social and working conditions), linked to international tariff agreements, could avoid the demise of the most generous welfare states. Yet, because in the new liberalized, networked, global economy such a far-reaching social contract is unlikely, welfare states are being

[11]   Wilensky (1975); Janowitz (1976); Navarro (1994, 1995); Castells (1996).
[12]   Shaiken (1990); Rodgers (1994).

downsized to the lowest common denominator that keeps spiraling downwards.[13] So doing, a fundamental component of the legitimacy and stability of the nation-state fades away, not only in Europe but throughout the world, from middle-class welfare states in Chile or Mexico to the remnants of statist welfare states in Russia, China, or India, or to the urban welfare state induced in the United States by the social struggles of the 1960s.

Therefore, the nation-state is increasingly powerless in controlling monetary policy, deciding its budget, organizing production and trade, collecting its corporate taxes, and fulfilling its commitments to provide social benefits. In sum, it has lost most of its economic power, albeit it still has some regulatory capacity and relative control over its subjects.

Global communication networks, local audiences, uncertain regulators

The prospects for national regulation and control are not much better in another decisive area of state power: media and communication. Control of information and entertainment, and, through them, of opinions and images has historically been the anchoring tool of state power, to be perfected in the age of mass media.[14] In this realm, the nation-state confronts three major, interrelated challenges: globalization and interlocking of ownership; flexibility and pervasiveness of technology; autonomy and diversity of the media (see volume I, chapter 5). In fact, it has already surrendered to them in most countries.[15] Until the early 1980s, with the major exception of the United States, most television in the world was government-controlled, and radios and newspapers were under the severe potential constraint of government good will, even in democratic countries. Even in the United States, the Federal Communications Commission exercised a close control of electronic media, not always exempt from special interest biases,[16] and the three major television networks monopolized 90 percent of the audience, framing, if not shaping, public opinion. Everything changed in a decade.[17] The change was technology-driven. The diversification of communication modes, the link-up of all media in a digital hypertext, opening the way

[13] Sengenberger and Campbell (1994); Navarro (1995); Castells (1996).
[14] Mattelart (1991).
[15] Blumenfield (1994); Brenner (1994); Chong (1994); Graf (1995).
[16] Cohen (1986).
[17] Doyle (1992); Irving et al. (1994); Negroponte (1995); Scott et al. (1995); Campo Vidal (1996).

for interactive multimedia, and the inability to control satellites beaming across borders or computer-mediated communication over the 'phone line, blew up the traditional lines of regulatory defense. The explosion of telecommunications, and the development of cable, provided the vehicles for unprecedented broadcasting power. Business saw the trend and seized the opportunity. Mega-mergers took place, and capital was mobilized around the world to take position in the media industry, an industry that could link up power in the economic, cultural, and political spheres.[18] Pressure was brought to bear on national governments during the 1980s under various forms:[19] public, or published, opinion, yearning for freedom and diversity in the media; buy-outs of national media in difficulty; syndication of columnists to write the apology of unfettered communication; promises of political complacency, if not support, to almost everyone in power or with the chance to be in the near future; and, not least, personal benefits for those officials who were consenting adults. Symbolic politics, assimilating liberalization of media to technological modernization, played a major role in tilting elite opinion in favor of the new media system.[20] There is hardly any country, outside China, Singapore, and the Islamic fundamentalist world, where the institutional and business structure of the media did not experience a dramatic turnaround between the mid-1980s and the mid-1990s.[21] Television and radio were privatized on a large scale, and those government networks that remained often became indistinguishable from private television since they were submitted to the discipline of audience ratings and/or advertising revenues.[22] Newspapers became concentrated in major consortiums, often with the backing of financial groups. And, most importantly, media business went global, with capital, talent, technology, and corporate ownership spinning all over the world, away from the reach of nation-states (see figure 5.3). It does not entirely follow that states have no stake in the media. Governments still control important media, own stock, and have means of influence in a vast array of the media world. And business is careful not to antagonize the gatekeepers of potential markets: when Murdoch's Star Channel was chastised by the Chinese government for its liberal views on Chinese politics, Star obliged with newly found restraint, canceling BBC's news service from the

[18]   MacDonald (1990).
[19]   Gerbner et al. (1993); Campo Vidal (1996).
[20]   Vedel and Dutton (1990).
[21]   MacDonald (1990); Doyle (1992); Perez-Tabernero et al. (1993); Dentsu Institute for Human Studies (1994); *The Economist* (1994, 1996).
[22]   Perez-Tabernero et al. (1993).

Figure 5.3 Size and location of activities of the 15 largest print and media multinationals (Germany, Canada, France, and Australia are major exporters; the US and UK are major importers)

Source: *Fortune* (April 23, 1990) and company annual reports, elaborated by MacDonald (1990) channel's Chinese programming, and investing in an on-line edition of *People's Daily*. But, if governments still have influence over the media, they have lost much of their power, except for those media under the direct control of authoritarian states. Moreover, the media need to build their independence as a key ingredient of their credibility – not only *vis à vis* public opinion, but with regard to the plurality of power-holders and advertisers, since the advertising industry is the economic foundation of the media business. If a given medium becomes predominantly attached to an explicit political option or systematically represses certain kinds of information, it will restrict its audience to a relatively small segment, will hardly be able to make a profit in the marketplace, and will not appeal to the interests of a plurality of constituencies. On the other hand, the more a medium is independent, broad, and credible, the more it attracts information, sellers and buyers from a wide spectrum. Independence and professionalism are not only rewarding ideologies for the media: they translate into good business, including, sometimes, the possibility of selling this independence at a higher price when the occasion arises. Once media are acknowledged in their independence, once the nation-state acquiesces to this quality as an essential proof of its democratic character, the circle is closed: any attempt to curtail the media's liberty will become politically costly, since the citizenry, not necessarily picky concerning the accuracy of news, defends jealously the privilege of receiving information from sources that are not submitted to the state. This is why even authoritarian states are losing the battle over media in the Information Age. The ability of information, and images, to diffuse via satellite, video-cassette, or the Internet has dramatically expanded, so that news black-outs are increasingly ineffective in the main urban centers of authoritarian countries, precisely those places where the educated, alternative elites live. Furthermore, since governments all over the world want also to "go global," and global media are their accessing tool, governments often enter into negotiating two-way communication systems that, even when proceeding slowly and cautiously, ultimately undermine their hold on communication.

In a parallel movement to globalization of the media, there has also been, in many countries, thanks to new communication technologies, such as cost-sharing satellite transmission, an extraordinary growth of local media, particularly for radio and cable television. Most of these local media, which often share programming, have established a strong connection to specific, popular audiences, bypassing the standardized views of mass media. So doing, they escape the traditional channels of control (be it direct or indirect) that nation-states had set up *vis à vis* television networks and major newspapers. The growing political autonomy of local and regional media, using flexible communication technologies, is as important a trend as the globalization of media in shaping public attitudes. Furthermore, the two trends converge in many instances, with global media corporations buying into niche markets, on the condition of accepting the specificity of audiences built around local media.[23]

Computer-mediated communication is also escaping the control of the nation-state, ushering in a new era of extra-territorial communication.[24] Most governments seem to be terrified at the prospect. In January 1996, the French Minister of Information Technology announced the intention of his government to propose to the European Union a series of measures to ban free access to the Internet. The event that prompted this scheme of technological censorship from the country that spurred revolutionary ideals of liberty in Europe, as well as Minitel, was Mitterrand's last battle. After his death, a book was published by his doctor revealing that Mitterrand had had prostate cancer for all the 14 years of his presidency. The book was banned in France, at the request of Mitterrand's family, but everybody could read it on the Net. The fury of the French government went far beyond this particular issue. There was a clear understanding that government's or court's decisions over information could no longer be implemented. And the control of information has been, long before the Information Age, the foundation of state power.[25] Similar initiatives came, around the same time, from the Chinese, German, and American governments, on a variety of issues ranging from financial and political information in China to child pornography in the United States.[26] At the heart of the matter was the question of trans-border information flows that make it difficult to prosecute the source of information even if it were detected. It is still under debate what are the real technical possibilities of cutting access to the Internet without shutting off a whole country from the network. It would seem that *ex post facto* censorship and penalties, and self-operated screening devices, are easier than the jamming of communication. But even if external screening measures become effective, they will shrink the network, thus undermining access to much useful information and diminishing the extent and scope of interactivity. Furthermore, to be able to shrink the Net selectively, all countries connected to it will have to agree on

---

[23] Levin (1987); Abramson et al. (1988); Scheer (1994); Spragen (1995); Fallows (1996).

[24] Kahn (1994); *Financial Technology International Bulletin* (1995); Kuttner (1995); Ubois (1995).

[25] Couch (1990).

[26] Berman and Weitzner (1995); Faison (1996); Lewis (1996a).

the topics they want to see banned, and then set up a joint monitoring system that will certainly be challenged as unconstitutional in democratic countries. Indeed, in the United States, in June 1996, a federal judicial panel in Pennsylvania declared unconstitutional most of the new federal law intended to regulate pornographic material diffused over the Net. In a forceful decision, the three judges wrote: "Just as the strength of the Internet is chaos, so the strength of our liberty depends upon the chaos and cacophony of the unfettered speech the First Amendment protects."[27] Thus, for the years to come, nation-states will be struggling to control information circulating in globally interconnected telecommunication networks. I bet it is a lost battle. And with this eventual defeat will come the loss of a cornerstone of state power.

Altogether, the globalization/localization of media and electronic communication is tantamount to the de-nationalization and de-statization of information, the two trends being inseparable for the time being.

A lawless world?

The globalization of crime further subverts the nation-state, profoundly transforming processes of governance, and actually paralyzing the state in many instances. This is a crucial trend which is as easily acknowledged as promptly ignored in its consequences.[28] A whole chapter (in volume III, chapter 3) analyzes what is one of the most relevant trends of our world, and a distinctive one in respect of other periods, but it is necessary, at this point in the argument, to include such a critical trend in our understanding of the current crisis of the nation-state. What is new is not the pervasiveness of crime and its impact on politics. What is new is the global linkage of organized crime, its conditioning of international relations, both economic and political, because of the scale and dynamism of the criminal economy. What is new is the deep penetration, and eventual destabilization, of national states in a variety of contexts under the influence of trans-national crime. While drug traffic is the most significant industrial sector in the new criminal economy, all kinds of illicit traffics come together in this shadow system that extends its reach and power over the world: weapons, technology, radioactive materials, art treasures, human beings, human organs, killers for hire, and smuggling of every

---

[27] Cited by Lewis (1996b).
[28] Arrieta et al. (1991); Roth and Frey (1992); Smith (1993); Lodato (1994); Sterling (1994); Golden (1995); Handelman (1995); Johnson (1995); WuDunn (1996).

profitable item from anywhere to anywhere are connected through the mother of all crimes – money laundering. Without it, the criminal economy would neither be global nor very profitable. And, through money laundering, the criminal economy is connected to the global financial markets, of which it is a sizeable component, and a relentless source of speculation. According to the United Nations Conference on the Global Criminal Economy held in Naples in October 1994,[29] a reasonable estimate would put the figure of capital from illegal sources being laundered in the global financial system at about US $ 750 billion a year. These capital flows need to be processed with greater mobility and flexibility than those originating from any other industry, since it is their constant swirling that makes them avoid tracking by law enforcement agencies.

The impact of these trends on national states occurs along three main lines:

1 In many instances, the entire structure of the state, often including the highest levels of power, is penetrated by criminal linkages, either through corruption, threats, or illegal political financing, thus creating havoc in the conduct of public affairs.
2 International relations between nation-states, in many countries, come to be dependent, in various degrees, on the handling or mishandling of cooperation in the fight against the criminal economy. The typical case until now has been that of relationships between the United States and some Latin American countries (Colombia, Bolivia, Mexico, Paraguay, Panama), but it is becoming a broader phenomenon, as the criminal economy diversifies (for instance, Germany's concern with Russian Mafia-originated traffic of radioactive materials; or the Russian government's worries about the increasing involvement of the Sicilian Mafia and of Colombian cartels with the Russian *Mafiya*).
3 The growing importance of financial flows from criminal origin are key elements in stimulating or destabilizing entire national economies, so that economic policy cannot be properly conducted in many countries and areas without including into the picture this highly unpredictable factor.

It used to be that national governments deeply affected by the wheelings and dealings of the criminal economy were a handful of usual suspects, such as Italy or Colombia. Not any more. The importance of the phenomenon, its global reach, the size of its wealth and influence, and its entrenched connection with international finance, make criminal linkages to political corruption a frequent feature in

29   United Nations, Economic and Social Council (1994).

major countries. For instance, the Japanese *Yakuza* has recently internationalized its connections. And the open, and less open, linkages
of the *Yakuza* with Japanese government leaders are well known, to
the point that the Ministry of Construction was considered, over a
long period, as the way to exchange government contracts in public
works for generous contributions from *Yakuza*-sponsored businesses
to the Liberal Democratic party – a system not too dissimilar to that
of Italian Christian Democracy's *Mezzogiorno* development programs
in relation to the Mafia. Or, when in 1996 a series of bank crises
rocked Japan, resulting in unpaid loans for hundreds of billions of
dollars, serious suspicions arose on the role of *Yakuza* in forcing bank
managers to grant these loans, including the killing of two bankers.[30]
In another context, the suspected penetration of internationally connected Russian criminal organizations in various spheres of
government of one of the world's most powerful states, including
the armed forces, is a worrisome development. And the chain of
political scandals that have shaken governments all over the world in
the 1990s (a topic that I shall analyze in chapter 6) is not unrelated,
in many instances, to the continuing power struggle between the
structures of global crime and the structures of nation-states.
Furthermore, even major governments, which think they are relatively immune to penetration by crime in their higher levels, do
suffer the aftershocks of criminal political maneuvering. For
instance, when in 1994–95 the Mexican economy crumbled, in spite
of massive US lending, because of a political crisis partly prompted,
as I will argue below, by the penetration of drug traffickers in the
highest levels of the Mexican ruling party, the dollar went sharply
down, and the German mark skyrocketed in the currency markets,
destabilizing the European monetary system, because of investors'
fears that the US government deficit would balloon in the effort to
lift Mexico out of its potential crash. In this entangled whirlwind of
crime, capital, and power, there is no safe place. Or, for that matter,
no safe national institutions.

Thus, globalization, in its different dimensions, undermines the
autonomy and decision-making power of the nation-state. And this
happens at the very moment when the exercise of state power in the
international area is also subject to the constraints of multilateralism
in defense, foreign policy, and global public policies, such as environmental policy.

[30] WuDunn (1996).

The Nation-state in the Age of Multilateralism

The post-Cold War period is characterized by increasing multilateral interdependence between nation-states.[31] This is due, primarily, to three factors: the dissolution or loosening of the military blocs built around the two superpowers; the dramatic impact of new technologies on warfare; and the social perception of the global character of major challenges to humankind because of increased knowledge and information, as in the case of environmental security.

With the disappearance of the Soviet Union, and regardless of possible future tensions between Russia, China, and NATO, the major mechanism for the stabilization of strategic links for most nation-states around the two superpowers disappeared as well.[32] While NATO continues to be organized around a US-led Western alliance, its functions are being redefined in the second half of the 1990s toward the fulfillment of security tasks on behalf of a broad consortium of nations, in association, whenever possible, with the United Nations. The new notion of global, collective security,[33] which emerged for the first time with the Gulf War to face the common threat to the oil supply from the Middle East, involves a symbiotic relationship between the most capable military forces (US and UK professional armies), the financiers of operations (Japan, Germany, the Arab princes, in the first place), and the rhetorical statements on behalf of the civilized world (often enacted by French leaders). The deliberate attempt by this NATO-based alliance to involve Russia in joint operations, as in Bosnia, is indicative of the transformation of military alliances from superpower domination to joint policing of a shaky world order, against potential unpredictable threats to the system. The new security system is being built, primarily, against outer barbarians without a name as yet.[34] So doing, nation-states, including the most powerful, are enmeshed in a web of interests and negotiations that reshapes itself into a different format for each issue to be tackled. Without the need for dramatic decisiveness in life and death situations, as was the case in the potential confrontation of superpowers and their allies in the Cold War nuclear age, the muddling through of a foreign policy with variable geometry translates into the growing inability of any state to act on its own in the international arena. Foreign policy is, by essence, multilateral in this end of millennium.[35]

[31] Baylis and Rengger (1992); McGrew et al. (1992); Falk (1995); Orstrom Moller (1995); Alonso Zaldivar (1996).
[32] Alonso Zaldivar (1996); McGrew (1992b).
[33] McGrew (1992a); Mokhtari (1994).
[34] Rosenau (1990); Berdal (1993); Guehenno (1993).
[35] Frankel (1988); McGrew et al. (1992).

Two major reservations concern the degree of integration into this system of collective security of Russia, still a nuclear superpower, and of China, superpower in the making.[36] Yet, since it is unlikely that any of them will organize a set of permanent allies around their interests (in spite of China's links to Pakistan), their relative isolation, and deep-seated distrust between them, does not contradict the multilateral character of the new security system, but simply adds complexity to it.

Fast changes in military technology are also undermining the capability of the nation-state to stand alone.[37] Warfare is now essentially dependent upon electronics and communications technology, as demonstrated by the Gulf War. The massive devastation that can be inflicted from a distance, through missile launchings and air strikes, can cripple in a few hours a sizeable army, particularly if its defenses are made blind by electronic counter-measures, and if targets have been identified by satellite and processed by computers thousands of kilometers away to direct actual fire in this invisible war. Conventional warfare is, as it always was, technologically dependent. The difference in the current period is, on the one hand, the speed of technological change, which makes weapons obsolete in a short time span.[38] This forces the continuous upgrading of weapons systems if armies are supposed to really fight other armies, instead of controlling their own people, as is still the case for much of humankind. Low-tech armies are not armies at all, but disguised police forces. On the other hand, the character of new military technology makes necessary a professional army in which personnel is equipped with advanced knowledge to manipulate semi-automated weaponry, and communication systems. This gives an advantage to countries with an advanced technological level, regardless of the size of their armed forces, as the cases of Israel and Singapore illustrate. Because of the essential role of technology, nation-states still wanting to assert their capacity to exercise violence become permanently dependent on technological suppliers, not just on hardware, but on human resources. This dependency, however, has to be placed in the context of a growing diversification of conventional war weapons, as countries industrialize and technology diffuses.[39] Thus, Brazil or Israel can be efficient suppliers of advanced warfare equipment. France, the UK, Germany, Italy, and China have increased their role, together with the United States and Russia, as suppliers of the world's armies. An increasingly

---

[36]   Boardmann (1994); Alonso Zaldivar (1996).
[37]   McInnes (1992).
[38]   McInnes and Sheffield (1988); Grier (1995).
[39]   McGrew (1992b).

complex pattern of cooperation and competition emerges, with China buying advanced fighters from Russia and communications technology from the United States, and France selling missiles to whoever wants to buy them, with after-sale services for training and maintenance included. Furthermore, illegal global markets for weapons, for any kind of weapons, have proliferated, making possible widespread diffusion of whichever technology becomes available, from "Stingers" to "Patriots," from nerve gas to electronic jamming devices. It follows that, unlike in other historical periods, no single state is self-sufficient in the production of warfare equipment, with the essential exception of the United States (since Russia is now technologically dependent on microelectronics and communications). But this does not imply that all nation-states are doomed to become an American colony. It is, rather, the opposite. The lack of a clear adversary has relaxed technology controls from the US Defense Department, so that most essential technologies and conventional weapons are widely available. Because nation-states cannot control sources for the supply of state-of-the-art equipment, they are permanently dependent, in the potential exercise of their war-making power, not on the US, but on diverse, global supplier networks. The fact that the United States is technologically self-sufficient (and only because of the Pentagon's effort to fight off dependency on Japanese semiconductor manufacturing equipment) gives to the United States the title of being the only true superpower. Yet, even this fact does not translate into full sovereignty in its foreign policy because of the weak financial and political position of the US toward committing its forces abroad.[40] Furthermore, as McInnes argues, "the character of modern warfare has led military thinkers to question whether a high intensity conflict could ever be worth the costs involved (regardless of whether nuclear weapons are used), and even if such a war did occur, whether it could be sustained by any length of time [given how expensive high-tech weapons are and how fast they can be destroyed]."[41]

Technological evolution adds a new twist to international relations toward multilateralism. Industrialization of new areas of the world, diffusion of scientific and technological knowledge, and illegal trade in everything have pushed, and are pushing, toward proliferation of nuclear, chemical, and biological warfare capabilities.[42] Thus, while nation-states are increasingly dependent on cutting-edge technology in conventional warfare, they may nevertheless have access to what I

[40] Savigear (1992).
[41] McInnes (1992: 156).
[42] McGrew (1992b).

would call "veto technologies," that is, weapons of mass destruction that by their existence can deter a more powerful state from winning. The global "terror equilibrium" is in the process of being decentralized to many local "terror equilibria." This trend forces, on the one hand, major powers to undertake concerted, multilateral action to prevent the control of these weapons by new countries, political forces, or terrorist groups. On the other hand, once some countries come, anyway, into the possession of these weapons, the global security system is compelled to intervene and assist in balancing powers of destruction in each area of the world to prevent dangerous local confrontations.[43] It follows a complex, entangled web of different levels of destructive power, controlling each other with *ad hoc* agreements, and negotiated processes of disarmament and disengagement. In such a web no nation-state, not even the United States, is free any longer, since a miscalculation, or an excess in exercising superior power, could trigger a nuclear, or bacteriological, local holocaust. Humankind will live for a long time with the monsters of destruction we have created, either for mass, standardized annihilation, or miniaturized for customized carnage. Under such circumstances, the most fundamental task of nation-states (and not just for the superpowers as in the Cold War period) has become to limit the actual exercise of their own military power, thus weakening their original *raison d'être*.

Nation-states also confront the limits of their legitimacy, and thus ultimately of their power, regarding the global management of the planet's environment.[44] Science and technology are producing, because of increased computing capacity, unprecedented new knowledge on the degradation of nature, and on its consequences for our species. In a related development, as shown in chapter 3, the environmental movement has raised ecological consciousness in societies around the world, putting increasing pressure on the responsibility of governments to halt the path toward catastrophe. Yet, individual nation-states are powerless, on their own, to act on issues such as global warming, the ozone layer, the deforestation of the planet, the pollution of water reserves, the depletion of life in the oceans, and the like. Efforts for states to come together take, more often than not, the form of international shows and solemn rhetoric, rather than actual implementation of joint action programs. Lipschutz and Coca write, in concluding their global survey on concerted environmental policies:

[43] Daniel and Hayes (1995).
[44] Rowlands (1992); Vogler (1992); Morin and Kern (1993); Wapner (1995); Hempel (1996).

The possibility of an hegemonic direction or the emergence of a central coordinating authority seem remote with respect to environmental matters. And the likelihood of effective multilateral coordination seems small, as well, because of major uncertainties about the costs and benefits of environmental protection and management. To these barriers and conditions we would add a number of factors that stem from the nature of the state itself: the fundamental incapacity of governments to control the destructive processes involved, the scarcity of effective policy levers, and the importance of key resource-extraction (and hence environmental destruction) for key state-society alliances.[45]

This is not necessarily because of ignorance or ill-faith on the part of governments, but because each nation-state continues to act on behalf of its own interests, or of the interests of constituencies it values most.[46] So doing, multilateralism becomes a forum of debate and a negotiating arena, rather than a tool for exercising collective responsibility. Following a Habermasian logic of "crisis displacement," "the fundamental and global environmental-economic contradiction," as Hay puts it, "becomes displaced to the level of the nation-state."[47] This structurally induced stubbornness of nation-states paradoxically leads to their weakening as viable political institutions, as citizens around the world realize the incapacity of these rather expensive and cumbersome apparatuses in dealing with the major issues challenging humankind. Thus, to overcome their growing irrelevance, nation-states increasingly band together, shifting gears toward a new supranational order of governance.

Global Governance and the Super Nation-state

"If one wants a shorthand explanation for the renewed momentum of European integration in the mid-1980s," as Streeck and Schmitter wrote, "one would probably account for it as the result of an alignment between two broad interests – that of large European firms struggling to overcome perceived competitive advantages in relation to Japanese and US capital and that of state elites seeking to restore at least part of the political sovereignty they had gradually lost at the national level as a result of growing international interdependence."[48]

---

[45]   Lipschutz and Coca (1993: 332).
[46]   Castells (forthcoming).
[47]   Hay (1994: 87).
[48]   Streeck and Schmitter (1991: 148).

On both counts, for business interests and political interests, what was sought for was not supranationality, but the reconstruction of nation-based state power at a higher level, at a level where some degree of control of global flows of wealth, information, and power could be exercised. *The formation of the European Union (as I will argue in volume III) was not a process of building the European federal state of the future, but the construction of a political cartel, the Brussels cartel, in which European nation-states can still carve out, collectively, some level of sovereignty from the new global disorder, and then distribute the benefits among its members, under endlessly negotiated rules.* This is why, rather than ushering in the era of supranationality and global governance, we are witnessing the emergence of the super nation-state, that is of a state expressing, in a variable geometry, the aggregate interests of its constituent members.[49]

A similar argument can be extrapolated to the plurality of international institutions that share the management of the economy, of security, of development, of the environment, in this world *fin de millénium.*[50] The World Trade Organization has been set up to make compatible free trade with trade restrictions in a non-disruptive mechanism of control and negotiation. The United Nations is vying to establish its new, double role as a legitimate police force on behalf of peace and human rights, and as a world media center, staging global conferences every six months on the headlines of humankind: environment, population, social exclusion, women, cities, and the like. The G-7 countries club has appointed itself as the supervisor of the global economy, letting Russia watch through the window, just in case, and instructing the International Monetary Fund and the World Bank to keep financial markets and currencies under discipline, both globally and locally. Post-Cold War NATO has emerged as the nucleus of a credible military force to police the new world disorder. NAFTA is tightening up the economic integration of the Western hemisphere, with the potential incorporation of Chile belying its Northern label. MERCOSUR, on the other hand, is asserting South America's independence by increasingly trading with Europe rather than with the United States. Various Pacific cooperation international institutions are trying to build the commonality of economic interests, bridging over the historical mistrust between major players in the Asian Pacific (Japan, China, Korea, Russia). Countries around the world are using old institutions, such as ASEAN or the Organization

---

[49] Orstrom Moller (1995).
[50] Berdal (1993); Rochester (1993); Bachr and Gordenker (1994); Dunaher (1994); Falk (1995); Kraus and Knight (1995); Oversight of IMF/World Bank (1995).

of African Unity, or even post-colonial institutions, such as the British Commonwealth, or the French cooperation system, as platforms for joint ventures toward a diversity of goals that could hardly be reached by individual nation-states. Most assessments of this growing process of internationalization of state policies seem to doubt the feasibility of global governance as fully shared sovereignty, in spite of this notion's powerful rationale. Rather, global governance is usually considered as the negotiated convergence of national governments' interests and policies.[51] Nation-states, and their elites, are too jealous of their privileges to surrender sovereignty, except under the promise of tangible returns. In addition, according to opinion polls, it is highly unlikely, in the foreseeable future, that the majority of citizens in any country would accept full integration in a supranational, federal state.[52] The US experience of federal nation building is so historically specific that, in spite of its forceful appeal, it can hardly be a model for late millennium federalists in other areas of the world.

Furthermore, the growing incapacity of states to tackle the global problems that make an impact on public opinion (from the fate of whales to torture of dissidents around the world) leads civil societies to increasingly take into their own hands the responsibilities of global citizenship. Thus, Amnesty International, Greenpeace, *Medecins sans frontières*, Oxfam, and so many other humanitarian non-governmental organizations have become a major force in the international arena in the 1990s, often attracting more funding, performing more effectively, and receiving greater legitimacy than government-sponsored international efforts. The "privatization" of global humanitarianism is gradually undermining one of the last rationales for the necessity of the nation-state.[53]

In sum, what we are witnessing is, at the same time, the irreversible sharing of sovereignty in the management of major economic, environmental, and security issues, and, on the other hand, the entrenchment of nation-states as the basic components of this entangled web of political institutions. However, the outcome of such a process is not the reinforcement of nation-states, but the systemic erosion of their power in exchange for their durability. This is, first of all, because the processes of relentless conflict, alliance, and negotiation make international institutions rather ineffective, so that most of their political energy is spent in the process, rather than in the product. This seriously slows down the intervening capacity of states, unable to act by themselves, yet paralyzed when trying to act collec-

[51] United Nations Commission on Global Governance (1995).
[52] Orstrom Moller (1995).
[53] Guehenno (1993); Rubert de Ventos (1994); Falk (1995).

tively. Moreover, international institutions, partly to escape from such a paralysis, partly because of the inherent logic of any large bureaucracy, tend to take on a life on their own. So doing, they define their mandate in ways that tend to supersede the power of their constituent states, instituting a *de facto* global bureaucracy. For instance, it is essentially wrong, as leftist critics often argue, that the International Monetary Fund is an agent of American imperalism or, for that matter, of any imperialism. It is an agent of itself, fundamentally moved by the ideology of neoclassical economic orthodoxy, and by the conviction of being the bulwark of measure and rationality in a dangerous world built on irrational expectations. The cold-bloodedness I have personally witnessed of IMF technocrats' behavior in helping to destroy Russian society in the critical moments of transition in 1992–95 had nothing to do with capitalist domination. It was, as in Africa, as in Latin America, a deep-seated, honest, ideological commitment to teach financial rationality to the people of the world, as the only serious ground to build a new society. Claiming victory in the Cold War for free-wheeling capitalism (a historical affront to the harsh combats of social democracy against Soviet communism), IMF experts do not act under the guidance of governments who appoint them, or of citizens who pay them, but as self-righteous surgeons skillfully removing the remnants of political controls over market forces. So doing, they may trigger a deep resentment among citizens all over the world, who feel the full impact of these global institutions on their lives, bypassing their obsolete nation-states.

Thus, the growing role played by international institutions and supranational consortia in world policies, cannot be equated to the demise of the nation-state. But the price paid by nation-states for their precarious survival as segments of states' networks, is that of their decreasing relevance, thus undermining their legitimacy, and ultimately furthering their powerlessness.

Identities, Local Governments, and the Deconstruction of the Nation-state

On December 25, 1632, the Count-Duke of Olivares wrote to his king, Philip IV:

> The most important business in your Monarchy is for Your Majesty to make yourself King of Spain; I mean, Sir, that Your Majesty should not be content with being King of Portugal, Aragon, Valencia, and Count of Barcelona, but should work and secretly scheme to reduce these kingdoms of which Spain is

composed to the style and laws of Castile, with no differentiation in the form of frontiers, custom posts, the power to convoke the Cortes of Castile, Aragon and Portugal wherever it seems desirable, and the unrestricted appointment of ministers of different nations both here and there ... And if Your Majesty achieves this, you will be the most powerful prince in the world.[54]

The king acted on this advice, thus inducing a process that ultimately led to the Revolt of the Reapers in Catalonia, the revolt against the salt tax in the Basque Country, and the rebellion and eventual independence of Portugal. At the same time, he also built, in the process, the foundations of the modern, centralized, Spanish nation-state, albeit in such a precarious condition that prompted almost three centuries of uprisings, repressions, civil wars, terrorism, and institutional instability.[55] Although the Spanish state, until 1977, represented an extreme situation of imposed homogeneity, most modern nation-states, and particularly the French revolutionary state, have been built on the denial of the historical/cultural identities of its constituents to the benefit of that identity that better suited the interests of the dominant social groups at the origins of the state. As argued in chapter 1, the state, not the nation (defined either culturally or territorially, or both), created the nation-state *in the Modern Age*.[56] Once a nation became established, under the territorial control of a given state, the sharing of history did induce social and cultural bonds, as well as economic and political interests, among its members. Yet, the uneven representation of social interests, cultures, and territories in the nation-state skewed national institutions toward the interests of originating elites and their geometry of alliances, thus opening the way for institutional crises when subdued identities, historically rooted or ideologically revived, were able to mobilize for a renegotiation of the historical national contract.[57]

The structure of the nation-state is territorially differentiated, and this territorial differentiation, with its sharing, and not sharing, of powers, expresses alliances and oppositions between social interests, cultures, regions, and nationalities that compose the state. As I elaborated elsewhere,[58] the territorial differentiation of state institutions explains to a large extent the apparent mystery of why states are often ruled on behalf of the interests of a minority while not necessarily

[54]   Cited by Elliott and de la Pena (1978: 95); translation by Elliott.
[55]   Alonso Zaldivar and Castells (1992).
[56]   Norman (1940); Halperin Donghi (1969); Tilly (1975); Gellner (1983); Giddens (1985); Rubert de Ventos (1994).
[57]   Hobsbawm (1990): Blas Guerrero (1994).
[58]   Castells (1981).

relying on repression. Subordinate social groups, and cultural, national, regional minorities, do have access to power at lower levels of the state, in the territories where they live. Thus, a complex geometry emerges in the relationship between the state, social classes, social groups, and identities present in civil society. In each community and in each region, the social alliances and their political expression are specific, corresponding to the existing local/regional power relationships, the history of the territory, and its specific economic structure. This differentiation of power alliances according to various regions and communities is an essential mechanism for keeping in balance, overall, the interests of various elites which jointly benefit from the policies of the state, albeit in different proportions, in different dimensions, and in different territories.[59] Local and regional notables trade power in their territory for their allegiance to structures of dominance at the national level, where interests of national or global elites are more powerful. Local notables are intermediaries between local societies and the national state: they are, at the same time, political brokers and local bosses. Since agreements reached between social actors at the level of local government do not often correspond to the political alliances established between various social interests at the national level, the local system of power does not develop easily along strict party lines, even in the European situation of party-dominated democracies. Local and regional social alliances are frequently *ad hoc* arrangements, organized around local leadership. Thus, local and regional governments are, at the same time, the manifestation of decentralized state power, the closest point of contact between the state and civil society, and the expression of cultural identities which, while hegemonic in a given territory, are sparsely included in the ruling elites of the nation-state.[60]

I have argued, in chapter 1, that the increasing diversification and fragmentation of social interests in the network society result in their aggregation under the form of (re)constructed identities. Thus, a plurality of identities forwards to the nation-state the claims, demands, and challenges of the civil society. The growing inability of the nation-state to respond *simultaneously* to this vast array of demands induces what Habermas called a "legitimation crisis,"[61] or, in Richard Sennett's analysis, the "fall of public man,"[62] the figure that is the foundation of democratic citizenship. To overcome such a

[59] Dulong (1978); Tarrow (1978).
[60] Gremion (1976); Ferraresi and Kemeny (1977); Rokkan and Urwin (1982); Borja (1988); Ziccardi (1995); Borja and Castells (1996).
[61] Habermas (1973).
[62] Sennett (1978).

legitimation crisis, states decentralize some of their power to local and regional political institutions. This movement results from two convergent trends. On the one hand, because of the territorial differentiation of state institutions, regional and national minority identities find their easiest expression at local and regional levels. On the other hand, national governments tend to focus on managing the strategic challenges posed by the globalization of wealth, communication, and power, hence letting lower levels of governance take responsibility for linking up with society by managing everyday life's issues, so to rebuild legitimacy through decentralization. However, once this decentralization of power occurs, local and regional governments may seize the initiative on behalf of their populations, and may engage in developmental strategies *vis à vis* the global system, eventually coming into competition with their own parent states.

This trend is apparent all over the world in the 1990s. In the United States, the growing distrust of federal government goes hand in hand with a revival of local and state governments as sites of public attention. Indeed, according to opinion polls in the mid-1990s,[63] this re-localization of government offers the most immediate avenue for the re-legitimation of politics, be it in the form of ultra-conservative populism, as in the "county rights" movement or the born-again Republican party, building its hegemony on attacking the federal government.[64] In the European Union, while substantial areas of sovereignty have been transferred to Brussels, responsibility for many everyday life matters has been shifted to regional and local governments, including, in most countries, education, social policy, culture, housing, environment, and urban amenities.[65] Furthermore, cities and regions across Europe have gathered together in institutional networks that bypass national states, and constitute one of the most formidable lobbies, acting simultaneously on European institutions and on their respective national governments. In addition, cities and regions actively engage in direct negotiations with multinational corporations, and have become the most important agents of economic development policies, since national governments are limited in their actions by EU regulations.[66] In Latin America, the restructuring of public policy to overcome the crisis of the 1980s gave new impetus to municipal and state governments, whose role had been traditionally overshadowed by dependency on the national government, with the important exception of Brazil. Local, provin-

[63] Roper Center of Public Opinion and Polling (1995).
[64] Balz and Brownstein (1996).
[65] Orstrom Moller (1995).
[66] Borja et al. (1992); Goldsmith (1993); Graham (1995).

cial, and state governments in Mexico, in Brazil, in Bolivia, in Ecuador, in Argentina, in Chile, benefitted, in the 1980s and 1990s, from decentralization of power and resources, and undertook a number of social and economic reforms which are transforming Latin America's institutional geography. So doing, not only did they share power with the nation-state, but, most importantly, they created the basis for a new political legitimacy in favor of the local state.[67]

China is experiencing a similar fundamental transformation, with Shanghai and Guandong controlling the main avenues of access to the global economy, and many cities and provinces around the country organizing their own linkages to the new market system. While Beijing seems to be keeping political control with an iron hand, in fact the power of the Chinese Communist party relies on a delicate balance of power-sharing and wealth distribution between national, provincial, and local elites. This central/provincial/local arrangement of the Chinese state in the process of primitive accumulation may well be the key mechanism in ensuring an orderly transition from statism to capitalism.[68] A similar situation can be observed in post-Communist Russia. The balance of power between Moscow and local and regional elites has been critical for the relative stability of the Russian state in the midst of a chaotic economy, as in the sharing of power and profits between the federal government and the "oil generals" in Western Siberia; or between Moscow elites and local elites in both European Russia and in the Far East.[69] On the other hand, when demands of national identity were not duly acknowledged, and eventually mishandled, as in Chech'nya, the ensuing war was largely responsible for derailing the course of the Russian transition.[70] Thus, from the glory of Barcelona to the agony of Grozny, territorial identity and local/regional governments have become decisive forces in the fate of citizens, in the relationships between state and society, and in the reshaping of nation-states. A survey of comparative evidence on political decentralization seems to support the popular saying according to which national governments in the Information Age are too small to handle global forces, yet too big to manage people's lives.[71]

---

[67] Ziccardi (1991, 1995); Laserna (1992).
[68] Cheung (1994); Li (1995); Hsing (1996).
[69] Kiselyova and Castells (1997).
[70] Khazanov (1995).
[71] Borja and Castells (1996).

The Identification of the State

The selective institutionalization of identity in the state has a very important, indirect effect on the overall dynamics of state and society. Namely, not all identities are able to find refuge in the institutions of local and regional governments. In fact, one of the functions of territorial differentiation of the state is to keep the principle of universal equality, while organizing its application as segregated inequality. Separate and unequal from the norm that underlies, for instance, the strong local autonomy of American local government.[72] The concentration of poor people and ethnic minorities in America's central cities or in French *banlieues* tends to confine social problems spatially, while decreasing the level of available public resources precisely by keeping local autonomy. Local/regional autonomy reinforces territorially dominant elites and identities, while depriving those social groups who are either not represented in these autonomous government institutions or, else, are ghettoized and isolated.[73] Under such conditions, two different processes may take place. On the one hand, identities that tend to be inclusive use their control of regional institutions to broaden the social and demographic basis of their identity. On the other hand, local societies retrenched in a defensive position build their autonomous institutions as mechanisms of exclusion. An example of the first process is democratic Catalonia: it is run by Catalans and in Catalan, although in the 1990s the majority of the adult population was not born in Catalonia, since genuine Catalan women have been traditionally giving birth below the replacement rate. Yet, the process of cultural integration and social assimilation for immigrants from Southern Spain is relatively smooth, so that their children will be culturally Catalan (see above chapter 1). What is important in this example is to observe how a given cultural/national identity, to be Catalan, uses the control of the local/regional state to survive as an identity, both by reinforcing its bargaining position *vis à vis* the Spanish nation-state, and by using its hold on the regional/local institutions to integrate non-Catalans, thus producing them as Catalans, and reproducing Catalonia through surrogate families.

A totally different situation arises when identities and interests dominating in local institutions reject the notion of integration, as in ethnically divided communities. More often than not, the rejection of official culture is answered by the excluded building pride in their excluded identity, as in many Latino communities in American cities,

---

[72]   Blakely and Goldsmith (1993).
[73]   Smith (1991).

or with the young *beurs* of French North African ghettos.[74] These excluded ethnic minorities do not aim at the local state but call upon the national state in order to see their rights acknowledged, and their interests defended, above and against local/state governments, as in the case of American minorities requesting "affirmative action" programs to make up for centuries of institutional and social discrimination. However, the nation-state, in order to survive its legitimation crisis *vis à vis* the "majority," increasingly shifts power and resources to local and regional governments. So doing, it becomes less and less able to equalize the interests of various identities and social groups represented in the nation-state at large. Thus, mounting social pressures threaten the equilibrium of the whole nation. The nation-state's growing inability to respond to such pressures, because of the decentralization of its power, further de-legitimizes its protective and representative role *vis à vis* discriminated minorities. Subsequently, these minorities seek refuge in their local communities, in non-governmental structures of self-reliance.[75] Thus, what started as a process of re-legitimizing the state by shifting power from national to local level, may end up deepening the legitimation crisis of the nation-state, and the tribalization of society in communities built around primary identities, as shown in chapter 1.

In the limit, when the nation-state does not represent a powerful identity, or does not provide room for a coalition of social interests that empower themselves under a (re)constructed identity, a social/political force defined by a particular identity (ethnic, territorial, religious) may take over the state, to make it the exclusive expression of such an identity. This is the process of formation of fundamentalist states, such as the Islamic Republic of Iran, or the institutions of American governance proposed by the Christian Coalition in the 1990s. At first glance, it would seem that fundamentalism gives a new, and powerful, breadth to the nation-state, in an updated historical version. Yet, it is in fact the deepest manifestation of the demise of the nation-state. As explained in chapter 1, the expression of Islam is not, and cannot be, the nation-state (a secular institution), but the *umma*, the community of believers. The *umma* is, by definition, transnational, and should reach out to the entire universe. This is also the case with the Catholic Church, a transnational, fundamentalist movement seeking to convert the entire planet to the only true God, using when possible the support of any state. Under this perspective, a fundamentalist state is not a nation-state, both in its relationship to the world and in its relationship to the

---

[74] Sanchez Jankowski (1991); Wieviorka (1993).
[75] Wacquant (1994); Trend (1996).

society living in the national territory. *Vis à vis* the world, the fundamentalist state has to maneuver, in alliance with other believers' apparatuses, states or not, toward the expansion of the faith, toward the molding of institutions, national, international, and local, around the principles of the faith: the fundamentalist project is a global theocracy, not a national, religious state. *Vis à vis* a territorially defined society, the fundamentalist state does not aim at representing the interests of all citizens, and of all identities present in the territory, but aims at helping those citizens, in their various identities, to find the truth of God, the only truth. Therefore, the fundamentalist state, while unleashing the last wave of states' absolute power, does so, in fact, by negating the legitimacy and durability of the nation-state.

Thus, the current death dance between identities, nations, and states, leaves, on the one hand, historically emptied nation-states, drifting on the high seas of global flows of power; on the other hand, fundamental identities, retrenched in their communities or mobilized toward the uncompromising capture of an embattled nation-state; in between, the local state strives to rebuild legitimacy and instrumentality by navigating transnational networks and integrating local civil societies.

Let me illustrate the full meaning of this proposition by focusing on contemporary developments in two major nation-states undergoing (as many others in the world) a structural crisis in the 1990s: Mexico and the United States.

Contemporary Crises of Nation-states: Mexico's PRI State and the US Federal Government in the 1990s

The analysis of the crisis of nation-states, as presented in this chapter, may be clarified by illustrating it with a summary account of specific crises. The reader should be aware, however, that observations and interpretation presented below are not intended to be fully fledged studies of state crises, given the limits of this chapter, even if they are grounded on empirical knowledge of the matter. From a wide range of possibilities around the world, I have selected, partly for reasons of personal acquaintance, two important cases. First, the Mexican PRI state because, *after having been one of the most stable political regimes in the world for about six decades, it disintegrated in a few years under the combined impact, I will argue, of globalization, identity, and a transformed civil society.* Secondly, I consider it meaningful to explore the actual effects of the processes described above on the US federal government, even if the US is an exceptional case because of the size of its economy, the flexibility of its politics, and the the high degree of decentralization in the structure of the state. Yet, it is precisely this exceptionalism[76] that makes the observation of the American nation-state analytically relevant. This is because *if even a state with a global reach, rooted in flexible federalism, becomes embattled by current trends as presented in this chapter, the proposed analysis might be considered to carry general value.*

NAFTA, Chiapas, Tijuana, and the agony of the PRI state[77]

After two decades of post-revolutionary instability, Mexico went on to build one of the most effective, if not most democratic, states in the world. It was organized around what came to be known as *Partido Revolucionario Institucional* (PRI), literally emphasizing the political project of institutionalizing the 1910–17 revolution in the diversity of its ideals and actors. The PRI state was able to subdue the competing power centers that haunted Latin American politics in most other countries of the region: the Army and the Catholic Church. It skillfully survived its unescapable, intimate connection with the United States, keeping alive Mexican nationalism and asserting political autonomy while enjoying generally good relations with its powerful neighbor. It managed to build a strong national, indigenous identity, bridging to the memories of pre-Colombian civilizations, while keeping in obscured marginality its 10 percent Indian population. It succeeded, also, in fostering substantial economic growth between 1940 and 1974, to create the world's twelfth largest economy by the 1990s. And, with the exception of targeted killings by landowners and local *caciques*, occasional political massacres (for example, Tlatelolco in 1968), and some limited action by leftist guerrillas, violence was rare in Mexican politics. Indeed, transmission of power from president to president was orderly, predictable, and unchallenged. Each president would designate his successor, and step out of the open political arena for ever. And each president would betray his predecessor, but never criticize him, and never investigate his actions. Systemic, widespread corruption was orderly, played by the rules, and,

---

[76] Lipset (1996).
[77] The analysis of Mexico presented here is based on three sets of sources: (a) newspapers and magazines from Mexico and other countries, as well as *Revista Mexicana de Sociologia*; (b) a number of published sources, including Mejia Barquera et al. (1985); Berins Collier (1992); Gil et al. (1993); Cook et al. (1994); *Partido Revolucionario Institucional* (1994); Trejo Delarbre (1994a,b); Aguirre et al. (1995); *Business Week* (1995c); Golden (1995); Marquez (1995); Perez Fernandez del Castillo et al. (1995); Summers (1995); *The Economist* (1995b, c); Tirado and Luna (1995); Woldenberg (1995); Ziccardi (1995); Moreno Toscano (1996); and (c) my personal knowledge of Mexico after 25 years of regularly studying that country.

in fact, was a major stabilizing factor in Mexican politics: each president renewed the distribution of political appointments in the entire
structure of the state, leading to tens of thousands of new appointments every six years. During their tenure appointees would have the
chance of benefitting personally from their position, under different
forms. This collective rotation of political elites in a very rewarding
system, ensured collective discipline, everybody waiting for his opportunity (it was usually *his*) which would likely come on the condition of
respecting the rules of the game. The penalty for breaking the rules
of discipline, silence, patience, and, above all, hierarchy was eternal
exile from any relevant position of power and wealth in the country,
including media presence and meaningful academic appointments.
Inside the PRI, different political factions (*camarillas*) competed for
power, but never breaking the collective discipline of the party, and
never challenging the authority of the president, decider of last resort
in any dispute. Yet, the key to social and political stability in the
Mexican state was the elaborate system of connections between the
PRI and the civil society. It relied on the organic incorporation of
popular sectors, mainly through the trade unions (*Confederacion de
Trabajadores Mexicanos*, CTM), which controlled the working class; the
Confederacion Nacional Campesina (CNC), which controlled peasants
and farmers, most of them in a system of communal use of the land
on state property (*ejidos*), established by the agrarian revolution; and
the *Confederacion Nacional de Organizaciones Populares* (CNOP), which
tried to organize miscellaneous urban popular sectors, although with
notably less success. This system of political clientelism was, for the
most part, not based on manipulation and repression, but on actual
delivery of jobs, wages, social benefits, goods (including land), and
services (including urban amenities) in a comprehensive populist
scheme. The Mexican bourgeoisie, and foreign capital, were essentially excluded from the power system, although their interests were
frequently represented by the PRI, certainly a pro-capitalist party,
albeit in a national populist version. Indeed, most business groups,
with the exception of the autonomous Monterrey group, were
outgrowths of the Mexican state. Last, and least, elections were systematically rigged by fraud and intimidation when necessary. But, in most
cases, PRI would have won (although not in all cases, in all elections,
as it came to be) because of the effectiveness of a populist system,
socially engineered through networks, familism, and personal loyalties in a vertical chain of reciprocities covering the whole country. In
this sense, the PRI system was not simply a political regime, but the
very structure of the Mexican state, as it existed in the twentieth
century.

Then, it all went down in less than a decade, between the mid-

1980s and the mid-1990s. Even in the unlikely event that the first Mexican president of the twenty-first century will again be a PRI candidate, he would preside over a very different state, since the political system above described has already collapsed. In 1994, the first year of the legal existence of NAFTA, the institutional expression of full-scale globalization of the Mexican economy, the following events took place: the *Zapatistas* insurged in Chiapas, on the first day of the year; the PRI presidential candidate, Luis Donaldo Colosio, was assassinated (the first time that such an event had occurred in half a century); the Mexican peso collapsed, and Mexico almost defaulted, in spite of unprecedented US and IMF support, sending shock waves throughout the world economy; the General Secretary of PRI, Jose Francisco Ruiz Massieu (whose first wife was President Salinas' sister) was assassinated, and his brother, Mexico's Deputy Attorney General was suspected of a cover-up in the assassination, and fled the country; Raul Salinas, brother of the then president Carlos Salinas, and a close business associate of the president, was accused of masterminding the assassination of Ruiz Massieu, and jailed; Raul Salinas' connections to the drug cartels, and to the laundering of hundreds of millions of dollars were exposed; President Carlos Salinas, a few days after stepping down in December 1994, rejected any wrong-doings, staged a 24-hour hunger strike, and, after receiving polite comfort from his successor, President Zedillo, left the country; his departure opened, for the first time ever, a flurry of public denunciations and reciprocal accusations by Mexican politicians from all factions, including former presidents, who decided that now it was all for all. Although the August 1994 presidential election was won by the PRI, in a relatively clean electoral process, widespread fear of instability and violence if the PRI were defeated was critical for such a victory. Electoral results in state, municipal, and congressional elections held afterwards indicated a clear upward trend of votes toward the conservative opposition, the *Partido de Accion Nacional* (PAN), and, to a lesser extent, toward the left-wing critics organized around the *Partido de la Revolucion Democratica* (PRD). President Zedillo relinquished considerable control over the electoral machine, appointed independents and members of PAN to high levels in his administration, and seemed to be prepared to be the president of the transition toward a different kind of regime, and, maybe, state. But the PRI seemed to think otherwise. In November 1996, it rejected the agreement with other parties on the law on political reform.

The political future of Mexico is unclear at the time of writing (1996) with political forces, and political leaders of various origins and ideologies, positioning themselves for the new political era. The only certainty is that the PRI state has ended its historical course.[78] And *the question is why, and how this major political event relates to the overall argument presented here on the crisis of the nation-state as a result of conflicts induced by the contradiction between globalization and identity.*

The current transformation of Mexico, and the demise of its nation-state, started in 1982, when Mexico became unable to pay interest on its foreign debt, in spite of the fact that Mexico's oil production picked up exactly at the time when the two oil supply crises of 1974 and 1979 substantially increased oil prices in the world. After Lopez Portillo's administration (1976–82) ended with the sudden nationalization of Mexico's banks, in a desperate attempt to reassert state control over a rapidly internationalizing economy, Mexico's political and business elites, the US, and international corporate interests decided somehow (I do not know exactly how) that Mexico was too important a country to be left to traditional populists to run it. A new generation of *tecnicos*, rather than *politicos*, came to power, substituting US-trained economists, financiers, and political scientists, for *licenciados* from the Universidad Nacional Autonoma de Mexico's Law School, as was the tradition. None the less, new elites still had to be *licenciados* of the UNAM as well, and they still had to be in the lineage of one of the traditional PRI political families. In the case of Carlos Salinas, it was the former president Miguel Aleman's network, via Salinas' father, Secretary of Commerce 1958–64, and Salinas' uncle, Ortiz Mena, Mexico's Treasury Secretary between 1958 and 1982. Miguel de la Madrid, a technocrat linked to Catholic integrist circles, was the transition president, in 1982–88, in charge of putting Mexico's finances in order, and grooming the new team of young, technically competent, politically daring leaders who would create a new country, and a new state, from within the PRI: Harvard's Carlos Salinas, Secretary of the Budget, and Princeton's Manuel Camacho, Secretary of Urban Development, were the leading figures. But the austerity program implemented by de la Madrid in the 1980s plunged Mexico into a recession, and for all practical purposes broke the social pact with labor and the urban popular sectors. Union leaders were careful not to jeopardize their privileges, but industrial workers, public sector employees, and popular neighborhoods felt the pain of restructuring. Then, in 1985, an earthquake struck Ciudad de Mexico, wrecking homes and businesses, and triggering social protests. An alternative political coalition, the FDN, organized by Cuauthemoc Cardenas (the

---

[78] In November 1996, local elections in the states of Mexico and Hidalgo were overwhelmingly won by opposition parties. The local elections sheduled for July 1997 in Mexico City and Monterrey are expected to inflict another major defeat on PRI.

son of General Cardenas, the 1930s' historic, populist leader of PRI) picked up steam, attracting the left of the PRI, from where Cuauthemoc Cardenas originated. The PRI barely survived the 1988 presidential election: Mexico City, Guadalajara, and Ciudad Juarez voted against the PRI. Carlos Salinas, the designated PRI candidate was elected because of fraud, this time the difference in votes being small enough that fraud became the decisive factor. Salinas, an intelligent, well-educated man, got the message. He appointed his old-time friend Manuel Camacho as *Regente* (Mayor) of Mexico City, and let him give free rein to his instincts: social programs, negotiation with civil society, democratization. The new president (with the influential help of the "Mexican Rasputin," French-born-of-Spanish-ancestry, international consultant Jose Cordoba) focused on ensuring the full integration of Mexico into the global economy. Salinas' views were straightforward: "We see an intense economic globalization of markets, and the revolution in knowledge and technology makes all of us live, more than ever, a single universal history."[79] Indeed, his career goal (and semi-official candidacy) for his after-presidency life, was to become the first Secretary General of the newly instituted World Trade Organization. Accordingly, he tightened Mexico's belt, sharply reduced public spending, modernized communications and telecommunications infrastructure, privatized most public enterprises, internationalized banking, liberalized trade, and set the country wide open for foreign investment. While standards of living plummeted for the majority of people, inflation was sharply reduced, the Mexican economy grew substantially, exports boomed, investment poured in, so that in 1993 Mexico became the country with the highest amount of foreign direct investment in the developing world. Currency reserves accumulated quickly. Foreign debt payments were under control. It was successful globalization at work. Salinas also launched an unprecedented attack on corrupt labor leaders (actually a warning to all organized labor), and vowed to fight corruption and drug traffic, although on these matters history, maybe soon, will judge his actual record. In the process, he dramatically reduced the real wages of Mexican workers and impoverished large sectors of the population. He did launch a charity program, *Pronasol*, led by one of his closest collaborators, Luis Donaldo Colosio, while charging Camacho with helping out restless Mexico City dwellers, and Ernesto Zedillo with modernizing the educational system. Against the background of much human suffering, the Mexican economy was indeed transformed in a few years, to the point that the US, and international investors, decided that it was time to graduate Mexico, welcoming this

---

[79]   Cited by Berins Collier (1992: 134).

nation of over 90 million people into the First World Club (the OECD), even if over 50 percent of its citizens were living below the poverty line, and about 30 percent in absolute poverty. The signing of NAFTA, in 1993, was the high point of this strategy of integration of Mexico into the global economy. It was the moment of Salinas' triumph. It was also time to designate the next president-to-be. Instead of selecting Camacho, the strongest and most popular of his inner circle, he went for Colosio, another young *tecnico*, who, although not from the old guard of the PRI, was president of the party, and was considered more open to compromise by the party apparatus. Ironically, Camacho's best friend in the PRI, Ruiz Massieu, was the party's General Secretary. But, he was there precisely to fight off the "dinosaurs," the old guard. Camacho was disgruntled by his demotion, both for personal and political reasons, and, for the first time in Mexican politics, he made clear his thoughts, to the president, and in public. But he had no option. By the end of 1993, everything seemed under control, and Salinas appeared to have succeeded in his *perestroyka* precisely by avoiding the mistake that, in his opinion, Gorbachev had committed: to reform politics before reforming the economy.

Then, on January 1, 1994, the first day of the NAFTA era, the *Zapatistas* attacked. I have already analyzed the causes, circumstances, and meaning of the *Zapatista* movement (chapter 2), so that I am simply considering here the movement's impact on the crisis of the Mexican state. It was devastating. Not because it really endangered state power from the military standpoint. But because it quickly became the rallying cry of a civil society that, in its large majority, was economically hurting and politically alienated. Furthermore, a genuinely Indian and peasant rebellion struck a major blow to PRI's mythology. The poor, the peasant, the Indian, were not the subdued, thankful, beneficiaries of the revolution, but the excluded, and they were fighting back. The veil of hypocrisy behind which Mexico had been living for decades was irreversibly torn. The king was naked, and so was the PRI.

Second act. Salinas, nervous with Camacho's reaction, decided to request his services again (with purposes and intentions unknown to me) to repair the damage in Chiapas. Camacho was appointed President's Commissioner for Peace. His skillful, conciliatory negotiation, and the popularity of the *Zapatistas*, triggered a new round of intrigue in the PRI in early 1994. With the Colosio campaign slow in taking off, the possibility of a reversal of the president's decision, nominating Camacho instead of Colosio, became the talk of the town. Colosio, the presidential candidate, a very capable and well-intentioned technocrat (a University of Pennsylvania-trained regional planner) was not a member of the old guard. The party apparatus was already tense about his appointment. But Camacho was too much: he was politically savvy, had his own party connections, grassroots support, good opinion polls, and an uncompromising attitude. Both Colosio and Camacho spelled future trouble for the party if they were to become presidents. But even worse than one or the other was the uncertainty about whom, and even the possibility of an alliance between them. As negotiations in Chiapas went on, and as Colosio's campaign seemed to be in a holding pattern, tensions in the party apparatus intensified, particularly in some sectors with very specific interests, and much to lose.

Having reached this point in the analysis, I have to introduce a new element that, in my informed opinion, is absolutely decisive, even if I have no hard evidence: *Mexico's new role in global organized crime*. Since the 1960s, Mexico cultivated, and exported, marihuana, but not more (actually less) than some areas in the US, such as northern California and Kentucky. Heroin production started on a limited scale in the 1970s. But the big change came in the 1980s when the formation of global drug networks, and stepped-up pressure on the Caribbean and Central American routes in the US, led the Colombian cartels to share part of the US-bound commerce with Mexican cartels, by giving them an amount of cocaine equivalent to what they were able to smuggle into the US at the service of the Colombians. Traffic skyrocketed, and powerful Mexican cartels were organized: in Tamaulipas and the Gulf around Garcia Abrego; in Ciudad Juarez around Amado Carrillo; in Tijuana around the Arellano Felix brothers, among others. They added profitable heroine cultivation, and traffic. Then, amphetamines. Then, everything. In the tens of billions of dollars. To work quietly, and professionally, they followed the Cali model, rather than Medellin's. Avoid unnecessary killing, be discreet. Just be cool, efficient, buy whomever you need: police, drug investigators, judges, prosecutors, local and state officials, and PRI bosses, as high as possible. Every dollar invested in corruption is profitable because it creates a network that, by extending itself, multiplies support, and ensures silence. Thus, while the new techno-political elite of Mexico was busy linking up with the global economy, important sectors of the traditional PRI apparatus, together with state and local officials of various political affiliations, established their own connection to the "other global economy." By 1994, the new "mafiocracy" was strong enough to defend its interests, but not established enough to cash out, and disappear into the financial avenues of money laundering. They needed more time, predictable time. And both Colosio and Camacho were unpredictable and dangerous to their interests. They decided to kill them both: Colosio, with a bullet; Camacho with a well-organized opinion campaign that blamed him, morally, for Colosio's fate. They succeeded. Not accidentally, Colosio was killed in Tijuana. Zedillo, Colosio's campaign manager, and one of the four of Salinas' inner circle (the other was Pedro Aspe, the Finance Minister), took his place. He is a competent, Yale-educated economist. Yet, his political connections were tenuous and his political skills untested. Not that the criminal connection had its way fully. But at least they changed the rules of the game. Whoever trespassed into their territory would do it at their peril.

Next in line was the Secretary General of the PRI, who appeared to go too far in investigating Colosio's death, still unsolved at the time of writing. This time, the assassin of Secretary General Jose Francisco Ruiz Massieu was traced back to a prominent PRI parliamentarian, to the Tamaulipas cartel, and, ultimately, to Raul Salinas, the brother, and close associate, of the president. Oddly enough, Ruiz Massieu's brother, who was the government's Special Prosecutor against Drug Traffic, has been formally accused of being on the cartels' payroll. It is too early to assert beyond doubt who was doing what, and certainly beyond my knowledge and competence. Yet, what is analytically relevant is that in the 1994 decisive political crisis, the drug traffickers–PRI connection played a major role in the assassinations, intimidations, and cover-ups that destroyed traditional rules of the political game, and opened the way for the demise of the PRI state. It must be emphasized that this was not a typical case of political infiltration by the mob. *It was the global reach of these criminal networks, their implication for US–Mexican relations, and the involvement of the higher levels of the state that make the crisis significant as an illustration of how the globalization of crime overwhelms powerful, stable nation-states.*

The political killings, the obvious infiltration of criminal elements in the state, the challenge from the *Zapatistas*, supported by a majority of public opinion, and the internal conflicts in the PRI, shook foreign investors' confidence in the stability of Mexico's emergent market. Capital outflow started in March 1994, after Colosio's assassination on March 23. In spite of this, Salinas, and his minister, Aspe, decided to keep the fixed exchange rate, using Mexico's abundant reserves to make up for loss of foreign capital. They were counting on reversing the trend. It did not happen. When Zedillo took control, on December 1, 1994, he panicked at the real situation, as reflected in secret book-keeping. He rushed a devaluation that made things worse. Ensuing capital flight left Mexico on the edge of defaulting, and shook up markets in Buenos Aires and Sao Paulo. The US president came to the rescue, NAFTA obliging, going as far as to bypass Congress, and to bring in $20 billion as collateral guarantee, pulled from the federal pockets. IMF also pitched in with an $8 billion loan (its largest ever), and arranged a few deals, so that by mid-1995 Mexico found itself somewhat cushioned by $50 billion, in exchange for which it lost its economic independence for ever.

Beyond economic restructuring, with its high social cost, and the new linkages with global crime, another essential element in the demise of the PRI state was the mobilization of Mexico's civil society, particularly in major urban centers. This mobilization was ambiguous because it was made up of very different social interests, cultures, and political projects. It brought together important sectors of the professional middle class, benefitting from the prospects of a dynamic economy, but yearning for democratization, clean government, and limits to bureaucracy. But it also threw into the battle against the PRI state, public sector employees threatened in their security; disaffected urban popular neighborhoods, fearful of the breakdown of mechanisms of redistribution of land and services; students, mobilizing around the renewed symbols of social change; and poor people, millions of them, in cities and the countryside, fighting to survive by any means. And although political skepticism is on the rise, and not many Mexicans truly believe that their fate depends on alternative political parties, there is consensus on the inability of the PRI state to deliver. The breakdown of populist legitimacy is tantamount to the end of populist, organic alliances at the heart of the system.

The democratizing effort during the Salinas administration took the form of devolution of power and resources to local and state governments, along with the tolerance of electoral victories for the opposition in a number of important states and cities, particularly in the North. The series of monographs on municipal governments in the 1990s, coordinated by Alicia Ziccardi,[80] show important improvements in local administration, particularly in Leon, Durango, Torreon, and in Mexico DF, among others. Yet, the political impact of these relative successes was to further undermine the PRI state, since in all these cases a stronger connection was established between the municipal administrations, in many instances in the hands of opposition parties, and local civil societies. Even in Mexico DF the municipal administration of presidential appointee, *Regente* Manuel Camacho, ended up establishing his own electoral basis among the population, bypassing the traditional PRI apparatus. Thus, overall, the effort at democratizing and decentralizing power to the lower levels of the state, while the president and his technocrats were riding the global economy, created greater distance between all segments of the population and the presidential quarters. Since the essence of the Mexican state was the godly status of the president while being

---

[80]   Ziccardi (1991, 1995).

president, the widespread lack of reverence, even in the moments of Salinas' triumph, rang the bell for one of the most durable political regimes in this century.

The Mexican nation-state will go on, in a new historical course, because the roots of nationalism are solidly planted in the hearts of Mexicans. However, it will not be the same nation-state created by the PRI, and, while still influential and resourceful, I dare to say, it will be increasingly powerless.

Economically, Mexico, and the world, have entered a new era, of which Mexico is probably a pioneer. Larry Summers, one of the most distinguished international finance experts, and a key player in the Mexican bail-out, wrote at the end of 1995, with the hindsight of time: "The form of Mexico's crisis [in 1994] was shaped by the financial innovations of recent years: and advances in information and communications technology caused it to be propagated in a way that is without precedent. It is little wonder, then, that the International Monetary Fund's Michel Camdessus, has labeled it as the first crisis of the 21st century."[81] This translated into the fact that Mexico's economic policy in the future, any kind of policy, will have to be closely coordinated with US economic policy, and with international financial markets.

Politically, Mexico has to reckon, from now on, with the penetration of its state apparatus, at any level, by global crime networks. It is doubtful that its own police and judicial system are immune from such penetration, so making extremely difficult the recovery of the state's full autonomy *vis à vis* crime. Indeed, it appears that most of the revelations about drug connections with the political system, including those referring to Raul Salinas, came from investigative work by US intelligence – which makes Mexican leaders dependent on American intelligence.

In domestic politics, a more educated and mobilized civil society is experimenting with new ways of expression and organization, all in direct contradiction to the PRI state, and often more developed at the local level. Increasing globalization and segmentation of the media are relaxing the grip that the Televisa group, a private multimedia empire traditionally allied with the PRI state, had on "infotainment."

And symbolically, the power of identity, as claimed by Marcos and the *Zapatistas*, has done more than to unveil Mexico's ideological self-complacency: it has built bridges between the real Indians, the real poor, and the educated urban sectors in search of new mobilizing utopias. In the process, the Mexican nation was reunited, this time against the PRI state.

[81]   Summers (1995: 46).

The people versus the state: the fading legitimacy of US federal government [82]

The crisis of the American state in the 1990s is a crisis of legitimacy that, I contend, goes far beyond the traditional libertarian strain in US politics. It starts from the depths of civil society, expressing its griefs on several, distinct issues that converge into questioning the role, function, and power of the federal government, as asserted by the Supreme Court since its landmark decisions of 1810 and 1819. The immediate political impact of this renewed distrust of government is the growing ascendance of a rebuilt Republican party, clearly skewed to the right, as resoundingly expressed in the 1994 congressional and gubernatorial elections and to some extent confirmed in the 1996 congressional elections that kept the GOP in control of both the House and the Senate. Yet, the influence of anti-state feelings goes far beyond the Republican electorate to embrace independent voters, such as those represented by Ross Perot, who reject altogether the current party system. Anti-state standing also includes a growing number of democratic constituencies, so that President Clinton in his 1996 State of the Nation address went into announcing "the end of big government."

Indeed, Clinton's re-election in 1996 was largely due to his embracing of many of the Republican themes against the welfare state, and against government spending, together with a tough stand on law and order, and the promise to preserve entitlements for the middle class, thus skillfully occupying the center-right of the political spectrum. As Theda Skocpol stated, commenting on the 1996 presidential election results, "Regardless of the partisan balance, something about the shift in the debate that was registered in 1994 is going to stay with us. There is just a sense that you can't use the Federal Government for big initiatives even if the national problems are big."[83]

[82] One of the best accounts of political developments in the US in the first half of the 1990s is Balz and Brownstein (1996). I refer to this book for additional sources. To place American anti-government culture in a historical perspective, see Lipset (1996) and Kazin (1995). For additional, useful information and analyses underlying the matters covered in this section, see: Stanley and Niemi (1992); Davidson (1993); Bennett (1994); Black and Black (1994); Murray and Herrnstein (1994); Woodward (1994); Barone and Ujifusa (1995); Campbell and Rockman (1995); Greenberg (1995); Himmelfarb (1995); Pagano and Bowman (1995); Roper Center of Public Opinion and Polling (1995); Dionne (1996); Fallows (1996). For a rigorous, sociological critique of Murray's theses, see Fischer et al. (1995).
[83] Cited by Toner (1996).

Furthermore, the 1996 election registered increasing disaffection from the electorate toward all political candidates: only 49 percent of eligible voters bothered to vote, and Clinton obtained only 49 percent of this 49 percent. Keeping the executive and legislative powers in different political hands seemed to be the result of an implicit collective will to reinforce the system of checks and balances so to deny excessive power to any kind of government.

This powerful anti-state trend, for the time being, deeply affects politics but not the structure of the state. Yet, it seems to be on its way to transforming the institutional basis and political purpose of governance in America. If the proposals approved by the Republican Congress in 1995, or a modified version of these policies, become enacted, as is possible, the federal government would transfer to state governments by 2002 the responsibility and funds to manage dozens of major programs, including welfare, Medicaid, job training, and environmental protection, for a total estimated amount of $200 billion in annual spending.[84] Furthermore, funds would be provided as block grants, so that final decision for their use would be in the hands of the states, although with some provisions, whose content is the object of ferocious infighting in Congress. The Clinton administration was also planning to shift increasing responsibility to the states in several major areas, including transportation policy and welfare. In addition, efforts to cut the budget deficit in seven years, both by Republicans and by President Clinton, will lead to a substantial reduction in spending both at the federal and state levels. Medicaid spending may be reduced by 30 percent (that is, $270 billion) between 1995 and 2002. Federal agencies playing a major role in government regulation, such as the Environmental Protection Agency and the Federal Communications Commission, would most likely see their power and funding sharply curtailed. Indeed, reducing the budget deficit, while based on a strong economic rationale, has become the most powerful tool in shrinking the federal government, posting a $203 billion dollar annual deficit in 1995. The combined movement toward devolution of power to the states and counties, deregulation, disentitlement of welfare rights, drastic reduction of spending and borrowing, and tax cuts (including the possibility, in the future, of a true fiscal revolution, as illustrated by the recurrent debate on a flat income tax) are operating a fundamental redefinition of the power and aims of federal government, and thus of the American state.

The forces driving this transformation of the role of government in the United States emerge from a profound, explicit rejection of the federal government by a large majority of Americans in the 1990s (see

[84]　*Business Week* (1995e).

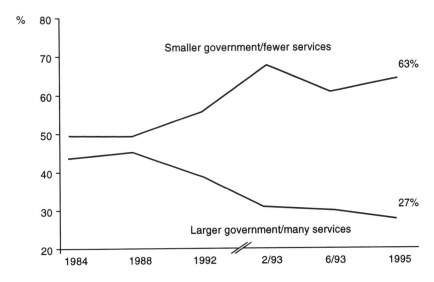

Figure 5.4 Public opinion attitudes toward size of government and service delivery, in US, 1984–95 (results of the survey question: "Would you say you favor smaller government with fewer services or larger government with many services?")
Source: Surveys by ABC News/*The Washington Post*, 1984, 1988, 1992, and February 1993; and *The Los Angeles Times*, June 1993 and January 1995

figure 5.4). Balz and Brownstein summarize data from opinion polls and political studies on the matter in the following way:

Discontent about government now runs down two powerful streams. On the one hand, the vast majority of Americans subscribe to a populist critique that assails Washington as wasteful, ineffective, in thrall to special interests, and crowded with duplicitous self-serving politicians who will say anything to be elected. (This populist alienation from government is strongest among working-class white voters – the same group that has faced the most economic pressure over the past two decades.) From a second front, a smaller, but still substantial number of Americans indict government on ideological grounds – as an overreaching behemoth that is eroding individual liberty and self-reliance, discouraging religion, and favoring minorities and the poor. The distrust of Washington has proven a huge hurdle for Democratic efforts to assemble support behind new government initiatives –

even those aimed at combating economic insecurity through expanded job training or guaranteed health care. Hostility toward Washington is now as much a part of American culture as reverence for the flag.[85]

It is precisely this divide between strengthened allegiance to the nation's symbol (the flag), and growing disobedience to the state's institutions (Washington) that characterizes a legitimacy crisis.

In chapter 2, while discussing social movements, I briefly analyzed the insurgency against the new global order in the United States, putting forward a number of ideas on the roots and characteristics of movements such as the American militia, the "county rights," "wise use" movement, and miscellaneous "patriot" anti-government mobilizations. In this chapter, my focus is on the impact of such movements, and of broader trends in public opinion on politics and the state. Anti-state feelings in 1990s' American society cannot be reduced to their most extreme manifestation, although the Patriot movement does epitomize the values and the anger expressed in large sectors of the society, as echoed in the diatribes of Rush Limbaugh's radio talk shows. Anti-federal government feelings and politics are the converging point of a vast array of ideological, economic, and social trends so deeply rooted in the relationship between globalization, construction of identity, and politics that it is safe to predict that whichever party wins in 2000, be it the GOP, or a renewed Democratic party, it may well be pushed into an overhaul of American political institutions in the twenty-first century. A review of the main components of this 1990s' conservative populism will help to understand the complexity of the process, and the extent of the crisis looming on the horizon, beyond variations of the political cycle.

A first, powerful, trend is a new brand of economic populism, reacting to the disfranchisement of a substantial proportion of American workers under the impact of global economic restructuring. Corporate profits and the stock market were at an all-time high in 1996, although the Dow Jones index was falling sharply each time substantial job creation was announced. Technology is, slowly but surely, inducing growth in productivity. Most women are now earning income. Jobs are being created in record numbers (10 million new jobs during the Clinton administration). Yet, deep-seated dissatisfaction and insecurity are a reflection of stagnant or declining living standards for the majority of the population, together with the structural instability introduced in the labor market by flexible work, networking of firms, and increasing dependence on transnational

---

[85]   Balz and Brownstein (1996: 13).

patterns of investment, production, and trade (see volume I). To be sure, this is an anti-corporate, rather than an anti-state feeling, and in fact implicitly calls for more active government intervention, as in the drive toward protectionism. Yet, it fuels anger against federal government because Washington is seen, correctly, as the manager of globalization, particularly after the signing of the NAFTA treaty, which came to symbolize increasing American economic interdependence. Policy issues involved in this movement lead, potentially, to economic protectionism, restriction of immigration, and discrimination against immigrants. Its implications lead to a frontal opposition to corporate interests, for whom free trade and free movement of capital, and of highly skilled labor, are essential, thus introducing an explosive contradiction within the Republican party, as demonstrated in the 1996 presidential primaries, with the alarm of GOP's leadership confronted with the initial success of Buchanan's populist candidacy. A similar contradiction exists also in the Democratic party, with most labor unions, and many minority groups, opposing NAFTA, and the full mobility of capital and jobs in an open, global economy, an agenda generally supported by Democratic leaders, and certainly fostered by Clinton.

Another current of public opinion, partly coincidental with economic protectionism, is the one proposing political isolationism, manifested by widespread popular opposition to committing American troops abroad in the absence of a clearly perceived threat to national security at home, a condition to which Somalia or Bosnia did not qualify. With the fading away of the Soviet Union, the rationale for national mobilization was lost in the minds and hearts of people, and the regular exercise of military superpower status, so appealing to economic, intellectual, and political elites, does not seem to justify cost or suffering. Rejection of American troops serving under the United Nations flag became the rallying point against multilateralism, and against the blurring of US sovereignty in the complex web of international institutions characterizing the post-Cold War era, such as the World Trade Organization.

A third current of opinion refers to a widespread rejection of what is considered to be government interference in private lives, family, and local communities. This is the case of the "home school movement," often associated with Christian fundamentalism, in which parents refuse to send their children to school, and reject the need for certification. Or of the "county rights" and "wise use" movements against environmental regulation, mixing defense of local autonomy, particularly in the West, with the interests of logging and mining companies. Or the growing, widespread concern about threats to privacy from the computerized state, fueling libertarianism of different brands, depending on levels of education and social context.

Family values, anti-abortion movements, anti-gay campaigns, and religious fundamentalism (most often from white evangelicals) form the basis of a wide, diversified social current, of which, as mentioned in chapters 1 and 2, the Christian Coalition is the most potent, and organized political expression, with 1.5 million members, and 1,200 chapters in 50 states. Indeed, the Christian Coalition has become, by the mid-1990s, the most important single bloc of voters in the Republican party, and a deciding force in many elections, at the local, state, and federal level, credited as being the functional equivalent of what organized labor used to be in the Democratic party. Christian fundamentalists are not, in principle, an anti-state movement. Indeed, their dream would be a theocracy, a God-abiding nation, with government enforcing the rules of God, as they have done in some school boards which they came to control in California, or in the vote of the Tennessee Senate in February 1996 to post the Ten Commandments in public offices and schools, requiring their observance. Yet, under the current constitutional regime of religious freedom, and separation between Church and state, the rebuilding of the Christian nation demands first of all the dismantlement of the secularized state, as it is today. The extraordinary development of Christian fundamentalism in the past decade in the United States, and its conversion into a well-organized political force, can be related to the reconstruction of identity, and to resistance to the disintegration of the traditional family. It is a rejection of feminism, gay liberation, and the end of patriarchalism. And of government efforts to implement laws supporting women's choice, gender equality, and cultural tolerance. But beyond this reaction, rooted in personal insecurity, there is an attempt at reconstructing identity and meaning on the basis of an idealized past, the past of family and community in a homogeneous society now being rebuilt in the new suburbia, and in the small towns of a vanishing rural life. This reaction is particularly dramatic against the background of the current collapse of the patriarchal family in America (see chapter 4). The insurgency against the crisis of patriarchalism is as powerful as the opposition to the new global economic order in challenging liberal values and the political establishment, thus delegitimizing their perceived enforcer, the federal government.

The critique of federal laws and institutions becomes even more vitriolic when it links up with class and racial hostility toward the poor and racial minorities. This is why the selective delegitimation of the welfare state, already embattled by economic trends, crystallizes popular sentiment, political votes, and anti-government hostility. I say selective because Social Security and Medicare (which account for

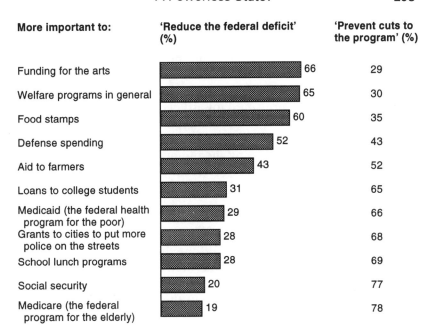

More important to:	'Reduce the federal deficit' (%)	'Prevent cuts to the program' (%)
Funding for the arts	66	29
Welfare programs in general	65	30
Food stamps	60	35
Defense spending	52	43
Aid to farmers	43	52
Loans to college students	31	65
Medicaid (the federal health program for the poor)	29	66
Grants to cities to put more police on the streets	28	68
School lunch programs	28	69
Social security	20	77
Medicare (the federal program for the elderly)	19	78

Figure 5.5 Attitudes toward federal government programs and reduction of federal budget deficit, in US, 1995 (results of the survey question: "For each of the following programs, do you think it is more important to reduce the federal budget or more important to prevent that program from being significantly cut?")
Source: Survey by the Gallup Organization for CNN/*USA Today*, February 24–26, 1995

about two-thirds of the budget of the US welfare state) continue to receive the support of a large majority of the population, so as to make the system very difficult to reform (see figure 5.5). On the other hand, welfare programs, social benefits for the poor, training programs, and affirmative action for minorities are under attack by a majority that refuses to pay taxes to sustain "the others," and stigmatizes the poor, blaming them for their behavior, for example attributing to welfare payments the exponential growth in the number of "babies born to babies." In the "theories" presented by the academic advisors of the anti-welfare movement, Victorian England and its rigorous morality becomes the model, and the poor and minorities are sentenced to a permanent lesser status by their biologically determined IQ.[86] A further manifestation of the break up of social solidarity is the special

[86] Murray and Herrnstein (1994); Himmelfarb (1995).

rage developed by "angry white males," extending the rejection of affirmative action to women, thus inducing an additional potential split among disaffected citizens. The mobilization of a substantial proportion of civil society against the welfare state in America leads, at the same time, to segmentation of society and to the weakening of the state, increasingly pressured toward becoming, predominantly, a repressive apparatus against the rising "dangerous classes." The emphasis on community volunteerism and charity as substitutes for the welfare state, while stressing the importance of a concerned civil society, is essentially an ideological screen not to face the cynical abandonment of collective responsibility under the pretext of exercising individual responsibility.

All these dimensions of citizens' revolt are sometimes coincident with the unfettered interests of corporate capitalism (as in the critique of welfarism or environmentalism), sometimes sharply in opposition to them (as in the critique of globalization and work flexibility). But, while being very different, and stemming from different sources, they all converge into frontal opposition to the extensive role of federal government, characterizing the American nation-state as constituted in the past half-century.

But let me be clear on this point. As a whole, 1990s' conservative populism in America is not a libertarian movement, and does not echo the tradition of anti-government republicanism. Some of its most important components, as described above, demand, in fact, very statist policies, imposing values of some organized segments of society over individuals and families by the state. This is clearly the case of Christian fundamentalists, whose growing influence in local and state governments is seen as a means of imposing godly behavior over the whole society under their jurisdiction. This is also the case of protectionist economic policies, whose full implementation would require a decisive effort by federal government to control and gear the entire American economy. Therefore, *the crisis of the nation-state does not come, only, from the cultural hegemony of anti-state values, but from the convergence of challenges from various ideologies and interests into the calling into question of the US federal government, as it is historically constituted* – either to sharply reduce its role (traditional libertarianism), or to capture it on behalf of a new mission to rebuild the American nation under the guidance of God, and/or in isolation of the new global order. This is why this crisis of legitimacy, although underlying the "Republican revolution" of 1994, cannot be equated with it. It cuts across parties, and constituencies, and it affects industrial workers as much as farmers, angry males as much as angry tax-payers.

These very diverse, powerful currents often organize around two issues that become a shared banner for many of them: refuse taxes, bear arms. By depriving government, and particularly the federal government, of fiscal revenues, state action becomes gradually subdued. In a society and economy of rising demands *vis à vis* public policies, a dwindling tax base forces the state to concentrate on its core, strategic functions, essentially to keep law and order, and to provide the infrastructure for the new informational, global economy, while paying the interests of a debt inherited from Reagan's Cold War. Therefore, it becomes unable to perform other functions, and so is actually forced "off people's backs."

On the other hand, in the minds of a substantial proportion of the population, the right to bear arms is the ultimate foundation of citizens' freedom, under the invocation of the American constitution. Although many Americans do not agree with this state of affairs, the fact of the matter is that there are 300 million handguns in US households, and war weaponry is available on the open market.

Powerful organizations and lobbies, such as Americans for Tax Reform, the National Federation of Independent Business, and the legendary National Rifle Association, fight, with success, to undermine state control over money and guns. My God, my family, my community, my money, my gun, seem to be the set of values that shape the consciousness and behavior of an increasingly important proportion of American people, in direct opposition to the rules, programs, and personnel of the federal government, and with increasing hostility toward global corporatism and institutional multilateralism.

The diffusion of these themes and attitudes in American society has been helped by the increasing localization, segmentation, and differentiation of the media, and by the spread of interactive, electronic communication. The key development in this sense is the growing influence of local radio, broadcasting syndicated programs, and the explosion of talk shows and call-in talk radio. Between 1988 and 1995, the number of stations specializing in talk radio doubled, reaching 1,200. New satellite technology, and the loosening of regulations on distorted allegations, helped their development and influence. Rush Limbaugh, the star of talk shows, enjoyed a weekly audience of 20 million over 600 stations in the whole country, thus becoming a potent political force by himself. The new GOP, in 1994, paid homage, in a public dinner, to Limbaugh, the man who, more than anyone else, had popularized the cause of ultra-conservatism and anti-government stands throughout the country. Besides radio, the new populist, grassroots movement, as indicated in chapter 2, used all the potential of new communication technologies, including the Internet, but also Fax machines, to coordinate their action and ideas, and to diffuse them among targeted receivers and elected officials.

The de-massification of the media bypassed the traditional channels of indirect control between the political establishment and the audience, unleashing the diffusion of all kinds of information and ideas, including the most outrageous, distorted, and unfair, among millions of people. The borderline between publishing the fit and the unacceptable, carefully established over decades by a generally responsible freedom of the press, became irreversibly blurred.

However distorted are the expressions of anger, these social trends are not temporary moods of public opinion. Available opinion polls in the 1990s show their persistence, and their depth (see chapter 6). They are rooted in major structural transformations, as presented in this book, and processed under the specific culture and institutions of American society. As Balz and Brownstein write:

> Behind all these swirling, swelling movements on the Right is the fear of a world spinning out of control . . . As the economy restructures under the pressures of globalization and advancing technology, and society's cultural framework strains under the breakdown of the two-parent family, this is one of those times [when large numbers of Americans feel themselves uprooted by developments that they cannot understand or control]. "People feel they don't have control over their own lives," said Republican pollster Frank Luntz. "That they can no longer shape their future."[87]

And they blame for it the state they have built over the past half-century, yearning to retake control over their lives in their communities and with their families, and moving away from government. They are helped in this process by a Republican party that had been out of parliamentary power for three decades, and then saw the opportunity to assert its power for decades to come. But the GOP is doing so by riding the wave of anti-government, and anti-establishment feelings, thus playing with fire. As Balz and Brownstein conclude: "All the intellectual energy in the Republican party is now focused in finding new ways to reduce the scope and reach of the federal government."[88] However, since the GOP also represents powerful corporate interests, embedded in a global economy and in international institutions, by becoming the instrument of anti-state populism it builds an explosive internal contradiction between its anti-government and fundamentalist popular base, and its traditional role of representing corporate capitalism and the defense establishment. The coming into the open of such a contradiction, and the

---

[87] Balz and Brownstein (1996: 173).
[88] Balz and Brownstein (1996: 295).

ensuing probable disaffection of a powerful populist trend, that cuts across party lines, may induce a fundamental crisis in the American political system. It may well destabilize the careful balance that the founding fathers and the Supreme Court had historically established between the local and the federal, between government and society, thus potentially triggering the crisis of the American nation-state.

Structure and process in the crisis of the state

Let me emphasize the relevant analytical elements derived from these succinct case studies of state crisis. In both, Mexico and the United States, we observe the direct impact of globalization and capitalist restructuring on the legitimacy of the state, through the partial dismantlement of the welfare state, the disruption of traditional productive structures, increasing job instability, extreme social inequality, and the link up of valuable segments of economy and society in global networks, while large sectors of the population and territory are switched off from the dynamic, globalized system: all processes that I have analyzed in volume I, and which are shown to take their toll on the state's ability to respond to social demands, and, ultimately, on the state's legitimacy. Furthermore, the close connection of the Mexican economy with the US economy, institutionalized by NAFTA, and the electronic linkage of its financial markets with global markets in real time, made the collapse of the peso in 1994–95 very different from any previous economic crisis, actually exemplifying, as reported above, "the first financial crisis of the twenty-first century." Additionally, in the case of Mexico, the penetration of the state by the global criminal economy adds a powerful twist to the disorganization of political institutions and to their crisis of legitimacy.

In the case of the United States (not in Mexico, as yet), the crisis of patriarchalism, with its roots in the informational economy and in the challenge from social movements, deepened insecurity and fear among large sectors of people, prompting a withdrawal from the legal and political institutions that were receptive to women's rights, and from the secular state. For a significant segment of the population, it led to retrenchment in the affirmation of God, family, and community, as eternal values beyond contest from social challenges.

In both cases, the structural crises that undermined the state's legitimacy interacted with the development of social movements which, under forms specific to each society, affirmed alternative identities, and explicitly rejected the legitimacy of the federal government. Although these identity-based movements involved only a minority of activists, their demands and claims were indeed processed by the political system, and found an echo, admittedly distorted, in the population at large. There is an undeniable connection between the symbolic impact of the *Zapatistas* and the widespread rejection of the PRI state in Mexican society, ending what was one of the most perdurable political systems in the world. As for the United States, while the Patriots are more a symptom than a cause, the crisis of legitimacy manifests itself in the broad distrust of government, particularly of the federal government, and of politicians and parties, particularly of those linked to mainstream politics. The rise of popularity of conservative Republicans in the mid-1990s is, to a large extent, linked to their politically suicidal campaigning against the very government institutions which they want to control.

In both cases, Mexico and the United States, new electronic communication systems have been decisive in amplifying the impact of relatively small movements on public opinion at large by their feeding of the media and by their horizontal, unfettered networking.

Thus, there is an empirically observable, analytically meaningful connection between globalization, informationalization, capitalist restructuring, identity-based social movements, and the crisis of political legitimacy in both Mexican and American states, albeit with different forms, specific to each society. What is first in inducing causality is, methodologically, a wrong question because structure and process interact inseparably in the sequence leading to the crisis of the state. It would be difficult to imagine the impact of the *Zapatistas* on Mexico without the profound impact of globalization in economy and society. But the *Zapatistas* were not the result of economic crisis: they existed before, in the struggles of Indians and peasants supported by Catholic priests, and in the revolutionary will of refugees from the 1970s radical left movements. Libertarianism in America has a long tradition, and isolationism is a perennial temptation of a continental-sized, powerful country, as is the opposite temptation toward imperialism. That one or the other prevail in a particular historical period is not pre-scripted, since the precise outcome of interaction between the elements I have identified, constituting, at the same time, structure and process, is largely undetermined. So, in spite of the Republican revolution of 1994, Clinton still won the 1996 presidential election, to a large extent precisely because of the internal contradictions of the Republican electorate in being mobilized, at the same time, on behalf of corporate interests and by the themes of right-wing populism. Yet, Clinton himself, in order to win, had to depart sharply from the traditional Democratic platform, thus furthering the distance between the hopes of many Democrats and the realities of politics.

Why the social and political response to the new global disorder came from "the left" in Mexico and from "the right" in the United

States is due, partly, to specific political agencies, and, partly, to the characteristics of the crisis to be dealt with. Namely, since the state, in both cases, was unable to deliver its promised protection, and became, instead, the active manager of the globalization/restructuring process, the challenge against the state was mounted from outside the traditional basis of support for government-led reforms: the pro-federal government Democrats in the United States; the PRI populist system in Mexico. This does not preclude that a pro-welfare state, pro-government, left-wing movement could develop in the future in both countries, but it would have to grow away from the halls of the political establishment, precisely because of the crisis of its legitimacy.

This openness of political processes does not invalidate the interest of an in-depth, analytical understanding because the materials we have uncovered, and their linkages, are indeed the stuff of which political institutions and political processes are made in our time. As for analyzing the relationship between the sources of state crisis and the new forms of political struggle and competition, I need to consider, first, the specific dynamic of political actors in the new, informational paradigm – an exercise that I will attempt in chapter 6.

The State, Violence, and Surveillance: from Big Brother to Little Sisters

Is the state really powerless in the network society? Aren't we witnessing, instead, a surge of violence and repression throughout the world? Isn't privacy facing the greatest dangers in human history, because of the pervasiveness of new information technologies? Didn't Big Brother arrive, as Orwell predicted, around 1984? And how could the state be powerless when mastering a formidable technological capacity, and controlling an unprecedented stock of information?[89]

These essential, and usual, questions mix contradictory evidence with confused theory. Yet, their treatment is central in the understanding of the crisis of the state. First of all, the Big Brother imagery must be empirically dismissed, as it refers to the connection between our societies and the Orwellian prophecy. Indeed, George Orwell could well have been right, *vis à vis* the object of his prophecy, Stalinism, not the liberal, capitalist state, if political history and technology had followed a different trajectory in the past half-century, something that was certainly within the realm of possibility. But statism disintegrated in contact with new information technologies,

---

[89] Burnham (1983); Lyon (1994).

instead of being capable of mastering them (see volume III); and new information technologies unleashed the power of networking and decentralization, actually undermining the centralizing logic of one-way instructions and vertical, bureaucratic surveillance (see volume I). Our societies are not orderly prisons, but disorderly jungles.

However, new, powerful information technologies might indeed be put to the service of surveillance, control, and repression by state apparatuses (police, tax collection, censorship, suppression of political dissidence, and the like). But so might they be used for citizens to enhance their control over the state, by rightfully accessing information in public data banks, by interacting with their political representatives on-line, by watching live political sessions, and eventually commenting live on them.[90] Also, new technologies may enable citizens to videotape events, so providing visual evidence of abuses, as in the case of global environmental organizations that distribute video power to local groups around the world to report on environmental crimes, thus putting pressure on the ecological culprits. What the power of technology does is to extraordinarily amplify the trends rooted in social structure and institutions: oppressive societies may be more so with the new surveillance tools, while democratic, participatory societies may enhance their openness and representativeness by further distributing political power with the power of technology. Thus, the direct impact of new information technologies on power and the state is an empirical matter, on which the record is mixed. But, a deeper, more fundamental trend is at work, actually undermining the nation-state's power: the increasing diffusion of both surveillance capacity and the potential for violence outside the institutions of the state and beyond the borders of the nation.

Reports of the growing threat to privacy concern less the state as such than business organizations and private information networks, or public bureaucracies following their own logic as apparatuses, rather than acting on behalf of government. States, throughout history, have collected information on their subjects, very often by rudimentary but effective brutal means. Certainly, computers qualitatively changed the ability to cross-refer information, combining social security, health, ID cards, residence, and employment information. But with the limited exception of Anglo-Saxon countries, rooted in a libertarian tradition, people around the world, from democratic Switzerland to Communist China, have spent their lives dependent on files of information of residence, work, and on every domain of their relationship to government. On the other hand, if it is true that police work has been facilitated by new technologies, it has

---

[90]	Anthes (1993); Betts (1995); Gleason (1995).

also become extraordinarily complicated by the similar, and sometimes superior, sophistication of organized crime in using new technologies (for instance, interfering with police communications, linking up electronically, accessing computing records and so on). *The real issue is somewhere else: it is in the gathering of information on individuals by business firms, and organizations of all kinds, and in the creation of a market for this information.* The credit card, more than the ID card, is giving away privacy. This is the instrument through which peoples' lives can be profiled, analyzed, and targeted for marketing (or blackmailing) purposes. And the notion of the credit card as life in the public record must be extended to a variety of business offerings, from frequent flyer programs to consumer services of every possible item, and to membership of miscellaneous associations. *Rather than an oppressive "Big Brother," it is a myriad of well-wishing "little sisters," relating to each one of us on a personal basis because they know who we are, who have invaded all realms of life.* What computers do, indeed, is to make possible the gathering, processing, and using for specific purposes of a mass of individualized information, so that our name can be printed, and the offering personalized, or an offer mailed out, or beamed in, to millions of individuals. Or, in a telling illustration of new technological logic, the V-chip, to be implanted in American TV sets in 1997, allows households to program censorship according to a system of codes that will also be implanted in the television signals emitted from the stations. So doing, it decentralizes surveillance rather than centralizing control.

David Lyon, in his insightful book on the matter, has insisted on the critical development of this extension of surveillance way beyond the boundaries of the state.[91] What he calls "the electronic eye" is indeed a surveillance "society," rather than a "surveillance state." This is, after all, the heart of Foucault's theory of micro-powers, although he confused many of his superficial readers by calling "state" what, in his own view, is in fact "the system;" that is, the network of sources of power in various domains of social life, including the power in the family. If, in the Weberian tradition, we restrict the concept of state to the set of institutions holding the legitimate monopoly of means of violence, and by nation-state the territorial delimitation of such a power,[92] it would seem that we are witnessing in fact the diffusion of the power of surveillance and of violence (symbolic or physical) into society at large.

This trend is even more apparent in the new relationship between state and media. Given the growing financial and legal independence

[91] Lyon (1994).
[92] Giddens (1985).

of the media, increased technological capacity puts into the hands of the media the ability to spy on the state, and to do so on behalf of society and/or of specific interest groups (see chapter 6). When, in 1991, a Spanish radio station recorded the conversation over cellular 'phones of two socialist officials, the broadcasting of their very critical remarks about the socialist Prime Minister triggered a political crisis. Or when Prince Charles and his friend indulged over the 'phone in postmodern elaborations on Tampax and related matters, the tabloid printing of these conversations shook the British Crown. To be sure, media revelations, or gossip, have always been a threat to the state, and a defense of citizens. But new technologies, and the new media system, have exponentially increased the vulnerability of the state to the media, thus to business, and to society at large. In historically relative terms, today's state is more surveilled than surveillant.

Furthermore, while the nation-state keeps the capacity for violence,[93] it is losing its monopoly because its main challengers are taking the form of, either, transnational networks of terrorism, or, communal groups resorting to suicidal violence. In the first case, the global character of terrorism (political, criminal, or both), and of their supplier networks in information, weapons, and finance, requires a systemic cooperation between nation-states' police, so that the operating unit is an increasingly transnational police force.[94] In the second case, when communal groups, or local gangs, renounce their membership of the nation-state, the state becomes increasingly vulnerable to violence rooted in the social structure of its society, as if states were to be permanently engaged in fighting a guerrilla war.[95] Thus the contradiction the state faces: if it does not use violence, it fades away as a state; if it uses it, on a quasi-permanent basis, there will go a substantial part of its resources and legitimacy, because it would imply an endless state of emergency. So, the state can only proceed with such a durable violence when and if the survival of the nation, or of the nation-state, is at stake. Because of the increasing reluctance of societies to support a lasting use of violence, except in extreme situations, the difficulty of the state to actually resort to violence on a scale large enough to be effective leads to its diminishing ability to do so frequently, and thus to the gradual loss of its privilege as holding the means of violence.

Thus, the capacity of surveillance is diffused in society, the monopoly of violence is challenged by transnational, non-state

---

[93]   Tilly (1995).
[94]   Fooner (1989).
[95]   Wieviorka (1988).

networks, and the ability to repress rebellion is eroded by endemic communalism and tribalism. While the nation-state still looks imposing in its shiny uniform, and people's bodies and souls still are routinely tortured around the world, information flows bypass, and sometimes overwhelm, the state; terrorist wars criss-cross national boundaries; and communal turfs exhaust the law and order patrol. The state still relies on violence and surveillance, but it does not hold their monopoly any longer, nor can it exercise them from its national enclosure.

The Crisis of the Nation-state and the Theory of the State

In his seminal article on democracy, the nation-state, and the global system, David Held summarizes his analysis by writing that

> the international order today is characterized by both the persistence of the sovereign state system and the development of plural authority structures. The objections to such a hybrid system are severe. It is open to question whether it offers any solutions to the fundamental problems of modern political thought which have been preoccupied by, among other things, the rationale and basis of order and toleration, of democracy and accountability, and of legitimate rule.[96]

Although he goes on to offer his own optimistic proposal for re-legitimizing the state in its postnational reincarnation, the powerful arguments against continuing state sovereignty that he puts forward in the preceding pages explain his hesitant concluding line: "There are good reasons for being optimistic about the results – and pessimistic."[97] In this context, I am not sure what "optimistic" and "pessimistic" mean. I have no particular sympathy for modern nation-states that have eagerly mobilized their people for reciprocal mass slaughter in the bloodiest century of human history – the twentieth century.[98] But this is a matter of opinion. *What really matters is that the new power system is characterized*, and I agree with David Held on this, *by the plurality of sources of authority (and, I would add, of power), the nation-state being just one of these sources.* This, in fact, seems to have been the historical rule, rather than the exception. As Spruyt argues, the modern nation-state had a number of "competitors" (city-states,

---

[96] Held (1991: 161).
[97] Held (1991: 167).
[98] Tilly (1995).

trading pacts, empires),[99] as well, I would add, as military and diplomatic alliances, which did not disappear, but coexisted with the nation-state throughout its development in the Modern Age. However, what seems to be emerging now, for the reasons presented in this chapter, is the de-centering of the nation-state within the realm of shared sovereignty that characterizes the current world's political scene. Hirst and Thompson, whose vigorous critique of simplistic views on globalization emphasizes the continuing relevance of nation-states, acknowledge, none the less, the state's new role:

> The emerging forms of governance of international markets and other economic processes involve the major national governments but in a new role: states come to function less as "sovereign" entities and more as components of an international "polity". The central functions of the nation-state will become those of providing legitimacy for and ensuring the accountability of supra-national and subnational governance mechanisms.[100]

Furthermore, in addition to its complex relationship to miscellaneous expressions of political power/representation, the nation-state is increasingly submitted to a more subtle, and more troubling, competition from sources of power that are undefined, and, sometimes, undefinable. These are networks of capital, production, communication, crime, international institutions, supranational military apparatuses, non-governmental organizations, transnational religions, and public opinion movements. And below the state, there are communities, tribes, localities, cults, and gangs. So, while nation-states do continue to exist, and they will continue to do so in the foreseeable future, they are, and they will increasingly be, *nodes of a broader network of power*. They will often be confronted by other flows of power in the network, which directly contradict the exercise of their authority, as it happens nowadays to central banks whenever they have the illusion of countering global markets' runs against a given currency. Or, for that matter, when nation-states, alone or together, decide to eradicate drug production, traffic, or consumption, a battle repeatedly lost over the past two decades everywhere – except in Singapore (with all the implications of this remark). Nation-states have lost their sovereignty because the very concept of sovereignty, since Bodin, implies that it is not possible to lose sovereignty "a little bit": this was precisely the traditional *casus belli*. Nation-states may retain decision-making capacity, but, having become part of a network

---

[99]   Spruyt (1994).
[100]   Hirst and Thompson (1996: 171).

of powers and counterpowers, they are powerless by themselves: they are dependent on a broader system of enacting authority and influence from multiple sources. This statement, which I believe to be consistent with the observations and elaborations presented in this chapter, has serious consequences for the theory and practice of the state.

The theory of the state has been dominated, for decades, by the debate between institutionalism, pluralism and instrumentalism in their different versions.[101] Institutionalists, in the Weberian tradition, have emphasized the autonomy of state institutions, following the inner logic of a historically given state once the winds of history planted its seeds in a territory that became its national basis. Pluralists explain the structure and evolution of the state, as the outcome of a variety of influences in the endless (re)formation of the state, according to the dynamics of a plural civil society, in a constant enacting of the constitutional process.

Instrumentalists, Marxists or historicists, see the state as the expression of social actors pursuing their interests and achieving domination, be it without challenge within the state ("the executive committee of the bourgeoisie"), or as the unstable result of struggles, alliances, and compromise. But, as Giddens, Guehenno, and Held argue, in all schools of thought, *the relationship between state and society, and thus the theory of the state, is considered in the context of the nation, and has the nation-state as its frame of reference.* What happens when, in Held's formulation, the "national community" is not any more the "relevant community" as such a frame of reference?[102] How can we think of non-national, diversified social interests represented in, or fighting for, the state? The whole world? But the unit relevant for capital flows is not the same as that for labor, for social movements, or for cultural identities. How to link up interests and values expressed, globally and locally, in a variable geometry, in the structure and policies of the nation-state? Thus, *from the point of view of theory* we must reconstruct the categories to understand power relationships without presupposing the necessary intersection between nation and the state, that is, separating identity from instrumentality. New power relationships, beyond the powerless nation-state, must be understood as the capacity to control global instrumental networks on the basis of specific identities, or, seen from the perspective of global networks, to subdue any identity in the fulfillment of transnational instrumental goals. The control of the nation-state, one way or the other, becomes just one means among others to assert power; that is the capacity to impose a

[101]   Carnoy (1984).
[102]   Held (1991: 142-3).

given will/interest/value, regardless of consensus. The theory of power, in this context, supersedes the theory of the state, as I shall elaborate in the Conclusion to this volume.

However, it does not follow that nation-states have become irrelevant, or that they will disappear. They will not, in most cases, at least for a long time. This is for paradoxical reasons that have to do more with communalism than with the state. Indeed, in a world of a-cultural, transnational global networks, societies tend, as proposed in the preceding chapters, to retrench themselves on the basis of identities, and to construct/reconstruct institutions as expressions of these identities. This is why we witness, at the same time, the crisis of the nation-state and the explosion of nationalisms.[103] The explicit goal of most, but not all, of these nationalisms is to build or rebuild a new nation-state, one based on identity, not just on historical heritage of territorial control. So doing, in many instances, nationalisms challenge, and ultimately bring into crisis, existing nation-states that were built on historic alliances, or on the total or partial negation of some of the identities that form their constituencies. Thus, contemporary nationalisms are, in fact, a major factor in prompting the crisis of nation-states as historically constituted, as illustrated by recent experiences in the Soviet Union, in Yugoslavia, and in Africa, and as may be the case in the future in Asia (India, Sri Lanka, Burma, Malaysia, Indonesia), and even (who knows?) in Europe (Spain, UK, Italy, Belgium). If and when these new, identity-based nationalisms reach the stage of statehood they will find the same limits of current nation-states *vis à vis* global flows of power. However, their construction will not be aimed at asserting sovereignty, but at resisting other states' sovereignty, while navigating the global system in an endless process of bargaining and adjustment. Some authors use the concept of "neo-medieval form of universal political order."[104] As with any "neo" characterization, I suspect it belies history. It is, however, an interesting image to convey the notion of autonomous, powerless states that remain none the less instruments of political initiative and sources of conditional authority.

Nation-states that remain strong in the middle of historical turbulence, such as Japan or South Korea, also do so on the basis of social homogeneity and cultural identity. Although even in such cases a growing contradiction is emerging between the interests of Japanese or Korean multinational corporations, now becoming truly global in order to survive cut-throat competition, and the territorial domain and political interests of Japanese or Korean states, thus undermining

---

[103]   Cohen (1996).
[104]   Bull (1977: 254), cited by Held (1991).

what constituted the historical basis of the successful, developmental state. [105]

Thus, communalism indeed constructs/maintains states in the newly globalized society, but, in the process, it weakens decisively the nation-state as constituted in the Modern Age, and maybe questions the very notion of the nation-state by capturing it into specific identities.[106]

Conclusion: the King of the Universe, Sun Tzu, and the Crisis of Democracy

So, whither the nation-state as far as historical practice is concerned? Answering this question, Martin Carnoy issues a resounding no.[107] He argues, and I concur with him, that national competitiveness is still a function of national policies, and the attractiveness of economies to foreign multinationals is a function of local economic conditions; that multinationals depend heavily on their home states for direct or indirect protection; and that national human–capital policies are essential for the productivity of economic units located in a national territory. Supporting this argument, Hirst and Thompson show that, if in addition to the relationship between multinational corporations and the state, we include the wide range of policies through which nation-states can use their regulatory powers to ease or block movements of capital, labor, information, and commodities, it is clear that, at this point in history, the fading away of the nation-state is a fallacy.[108]

However, in the 1990s, nation-states have been transformed from sovereign subjects into strategic actors, playing their interests, and the interests they are supposed to represent, in a global system of interaction, in a condition of systemically shared sovereignty. They marshall considerable influence, but they barely hold power by themselves, in isolation from supranational macro-forces and subnational micro-processes. Furthermore, when acting strategically in the international arena, they are submitted to tremendous internal stress. On the one hand, to foster productivity and competitiveness of their economies they must ally themselves closely with global economic interests, and abide by global rules favorable to capital flows, while their societies are being asked to wait patiently for the trickled down

---

[105] Johnson (1982); Castells (1992a).
[106] Guehenno (1993).
[107] Carnoy (1993: 88).
[108] Hirst and Thompson (1996).

benefits of corporate ingenuity. Also, to be good citizens of a multilateral world order, nation-states have to cooperate with each other,
accept the pecking order of geopolitics, and contribute dutifully to
subdue renegade nations and agents of potential disorder, regardless
of the actual feelings of their usually parochial citizens. Yet, on the
other hand, nation-states survive beyond historical inertia because of
the defensive communalism of nations and people in their territories,
hanging onto their last refuge not to be pulled away by the whirlwind
of global flows. Thus, the more states emphasize communalism, the
less effective they become as co-agents of a global system of shared
power. The more they triumph in the planetary scene, in close partnership with the agents of globalization, the less they represent their
national constituencies. End of millennium politics, almost everywhere in the world, is dominated by this fundamental contradiction.

Thus, it may well be that nation-states are reaching the status of
Saint-Exupery's King of the Universe, fully in control of ordering the
sun to rise every day. From the East. But, at the same time, while losing
sovereignty, they emerge as major intervening players, in a purely
strategic world, such as the one informing Sun Tzu's war treatise 2,500
years ago:

> It is the business of a general to be quiet and thus ensure secrecy;
> upright and just, and thus maintain order. He must be able to
> mystify his officers and men by false reports and appearances,
> and thus keep them in total ignorance. By altering his arrange-
> ments and changing his plans he keeps the enemy without
> definite knowledge. By shifting his camp and taking circuitous
> routes, he prevents the enemy from anticipating his purpose. At
> the critical moment the leader of an army acts like one who has
> climbed up a height and then kicks away the ladder behind
> him.[109]

This is how powerless states can still be victorious, and so increase
their influence, on the condition of "kicking away" the ladder of their
nations, thus ushering in the crisis of democracy.

---

[109] Sun Tzu (c.505–496 BC, 1988: 131–3).

— 6 —

Informational Politics and the Crisis of Democracy

Introduction: the Politics of Society

Power used to be in the hands of princes, oligarchies, and ruling elites; it was defined as the capacity to impose one's will on others, modifying their behavior. This image of power does not fit with our reality any longer. Power is everywhere and nowhere: it is in mass production, in financial flows, in lifestyles, in the hospital, in the school, in television, in images, in messages, in technologies . . . Since the world of objects escapes to our will, our identity is no longer defined by what we do but by what we are, thus making our societies somewhat closer to the experience of so-called traditional societies, searching for balance rather than for progress. Such is the central question to which political thought and action must respond: how to restore a link between the excessively open space of the economy, and the excessively closed, and fragmented world of cultures? . . . The fundamental matter is not seizing power, but to recreate society, to invent politics anew, to avoid the blind conflict between open markets and closed communities, to overcome the breaking down of societies where the distance increases between the included and the excluded, those in and those out.
Alain Touraine, *Lettre à Lionel*,
pp. 36–8, 42; my translation

The blurring of boundaries of the nation-state confuses the definition of citizenship. The absence of a clear situs of power dilutes social control and diffuses political challenges. The rise of communalism, in its different forms, weakens the principle of political sharing on which democratic politics is based. The growing inability of the state to control capital flows and ensure social security diminishes its relevance for the average citizen. The emphasis on local institutions of governance increases the distance between mechanisms of political control and management of global problems. The voiding of the social contract between capital, labor, and the state, sends everybody home to fight for their individual interests, counting exclusively on their own forces. As Guehenno writes:

Liberal democracy was based on two postulates, currently called into question: the existence of a political sphere, site of social consensus and general interest; and the existence of actors provided with their own energy, who exercised their rights, and manifested their powers, even before society constituted them as autonomous subjects. Nowadays, instead of autonomous subjects, there are only ephemeral situations, which serve as support to provisional alliances supported by capacities mobilized for each occasion. Instead of a political space, site of collective solidarity, they are just dominant perceptions, as ephemeral as the interests that manipulate them. There is simultaneous atomization and homogenization. A society that is endlessly fragmented, without memory and without solidarity, a society that recovers its unity only in the succession of images that the media return to it every week. It is a society without citizens, and ultimately, a non-society. This crisis is not – as Europeans would like in the hope of escaping from it – the crisis of a particular model, the American model. The United States certainly pushes to the extreme the logic of confrontation of interests that dissolves the idea of a common interest; and the management of collective perceptions reaches in America a degree of sophistication without parallel in Europe. Yet, cases at the limit help us to understand average situations, and the American crisis reveals our future.[1]

The transformation of politics, and of democratic processes, in the network society is even deeper than presented in these analyses. Because, to the processes cited above, I shall add, as a major factor inducing this transformation, the direct consequences of new information technologies on the political debate and power-seeking strategies. This technological dimension interacts with the broader trends characteristic of the network society, and with the communal reactions to the dominant processes emerging from this social structure. But it adds a powerful twist to this transformation, inducing what I call *informational politics*. Thus, while Bobbio is correct in pinpointing the persistent differences between political right and political left throughout the world (basically because of their sharply divergent concern with social equality),[2] right, left, and center must process

[1]   Guehenno (1993: 46); my translation.
[2]   Bobbio (1994).

their projects and strategies through a similar technological medium if they wish to reach society, so securing the support of enough citizens to win access to the state. I contend that this technological sharing induces new rules of the game that, in the context of the social, cultural, and political transformations presented in this book, dramatically affect the substance of politics. The key point is that electronic media (including not only television and radio, but all forms of communication, such as newspapers and the Internet) have become the privileged space of politics. Not that all politics can be reduced to images, sounds, or symbolic manipulation. But, without it, there is no chance of winning or exercising power. Thus, everybody ends up playing the same game, although not in the same way or with the same purpose.

For the sake of clarity, let me warn the reader, from the outset of this analysis, against two simplistic, erroneous versions of the thesis according to which electronic media dominate politics. On the one hand, it is sometimes argued that the media impose their political choices on public opinion. This is not so, because, as I will elaborate below, the media are extremely diverse. Their linkages to politics and ideology are highly complex, and indirect, albeit with obvious exceptions, whose frequency depends on countries, periods, and specific media. In fact, in many cases, media campaigns may support the public against the political establishment, as was the case in America during the Watergate crisis, or in 1990s Italy, when most of the media supported the judicial anti-corruption drive against both traditional political parties, and against Berlusconi, in spite of Berlusconi's ownership of the three private national television channels. On the other hand, public opinion is often considered to be a passive recipient of messages, easily open to manipulation. Again, this is belied by the empirical record. As I argued in volume I, chapter 5, there is a two-way process of interaction between the media and their audience concerning the actual impact of messages, which are twisted, appropriated, and occasionally subverted by the audience. In the American context, the analysis by Page and Shapiro of citizens' attitudes toward policy issues in a long-term perspective shows the independence and commonsense of collective public opinion in most circumstances.[3] Overall, the media are rooted in society, and their interaction with the political process is highly undetermined, depending on context, strategies of political actors, and specific interaction between an array of social, cultural, and political features.

By pinpointing the critical role of electronic media in contemporary politics I am saying something different. I am saying that, because

[3] Page and Shapiro (1992).

of the convergent effects of the crisis of traditional political systems and of the dramatically increased pervasiveness of the new media, political communication and information are essentially captured in the space of the media. Outside the media sphere there is only political marginality. What happens in this media-dominated political space is not determined by the media: it is an open social and political process. But the logic, and organization, of electronic media frame and structure politics. I shall argue, on the basis of some evidence, and with the help of a number of cross-cultural examples, that this framing of politics by their capture in the space of the media (a trend characteristic of the Information Age) impacts not only elections, but political organization, decision-making, and governance, ultimately modifying the nature of the relationship between state and society. And because current political systems are still based in organizational forms and political strategies of the industrial era, they have become politically obsolete, and their autonomy is being denied by the flows of information on which they depend. This is a fundamental source of the crisis of democracy in the Information Age.

To explore its contours, I will use data and examples from various countries. The United States is the democracy that first reached this technological stage, in a very open, unstructured political system, and thus it better manifests the broader trend. However, I certainly reject the idea that the "American model" will have to be followed by other countries in the world. Nothing is more specifically rooted in history than political institutions and political actors. Yet, in the same way that democratic habits and procedures, originated in England, America, and France, diffused around the world in the past two centuries, I would argue that informational politics, as it is practiced in the United States (for example, the dominance of television, computerized political marketing, instant polling as an instrument of political navigation, character assassination as political strategy and so on) is a good indicator of the times to come, with all due cultural/institutional translations. To broaden the scope of analysis, I will be discussing, as well, examples of recent political processes in the UK, Russia, Spain, Italy, Japan, and, in an effort to reach out to new democracies in less-developed countries, I shall focus on the case of Bolivia. On the basis of these observations, I shall try to link up processes of social, institutional and technological transformation at the roots of the crisis of democracy in the network society. In conclusion, I shall explore the potential for new forms of "informational democracy."

Media as the Space of Politics in the Information Age

Politics and the media: the citizens' connection

I shall state my argument before elaborating it empirically. In the context of democratic politics, access to state institutions depends on the ability to mobilize a majority of votes from citizens. In contemporary societies people receive their information, and form their political opinion, essentially through the media, and fundamentally from television (tables 6.1 and 6.2). Furthermore, at least in the United States, television is the most credible source of news, and its credibility has increased over time (figure 6.1). Thus, to act on people's minds, and wills, conflicting political options, embodied in parties and candidates, use the media as their fundamental vehicle of communication, influence, and persuasion. So doing, as long as the

Table 6.1   Sources of news in the US, 1959–92 (%)

Date	Tele-vision	News-papers	Radio	Magazines	People
December 1959	51	57	34	8	4
November 1961	52	57	34	9	5
November 1963	55	53	29	6	4
November 1964	58	56	26	8	5
January 1967	64	55	28	7	4
November 1968	59	49	25	7	5
January 1971	60	48	23	5	4
November 1972	64	50	21	6	4
November 1974	65	47	21	4	4
November 1976	64	49	19	7	5
December 1978	67	49	20	5	5
November 1980	64	44	18	5	4
December 1982	65	44	18	6	4
December 1984	64	40	14	4	4
December 1986	66	36	14	4	4
November 1988	65	42	14	4	5
December 1990	69	43	15	3	7
February 1991	81	35	14	4	6
November 1992	69	43	16	4	6

Note: The question asked was: "Where do you usually get most of your news about what's going on in the world today – from the newspapers, or radio, or television, or magazines, or talking to people or where?" (multiple responses permitted).
Source: Roper Organization Surveys for the Television Information Service (various years)

Table 6.2   Sources of political information of residents of
Cochabamba, Bolivia, 1996

Source of information	% declaring main source of information	% expressing preference for source
Newspapers	32.0	8.7
Radio	43.3	15.7
Television	51.7	46.0
Other	4.7	–

Source: Survey of Information Sources of Cochabamba Residents, Centro de
Estudios de la Realidad Economica y Social, Cochabamba, 1996

media are relatively autonomous from political power, political actors
have to abide by the rules, technology, and interests of the media. The
media frame politics. And because governance is dependent on re-
election, or election to a higher office, governance itself becomes
dependent on the daily assessment of the potential impact of government decisions on public opinion, as measured by opinion polls, focus
groups, and image analyses. Furthermore, in a world increasingly saturated by information, the most effective messages are the most simple,
and the most ambivalent, so that they leave room for people's own
projections. Images fit best into this characterization. Audiovisual
media are the primary feeders of people's minds, as they relate to
public affairs.

But who are the media? What is the source of their political
autonomy? And how do they frame politics? In democratic societies,
mainstream media are, essentially, business groups, increasingly
concentrated and globally interconnected, although they are, at the
same time, highly diversified and geared toward segmented markets
(see chapter 5, and volume I, chapter 5). Government-owned television and radio have come close to the behavior of private media
groups in the past decade, in order to be able to survive global competition, so becoming equally dependent on audience ratings.[4]
Audience ratings are essential because the main source of income in
the media business is advertising.[5] Performance in audience ratings
requires an appealing medium, and, in the case of news, credibility.
Without credibility, news is worthless, either in terms of money or
power. Credibility requires relative distance *vis à vis* specific political
options, within the parameters of mainstream political and moral

[4]   Perez-Tabernero et al. (1993).
[5]   MacDonald (1990).

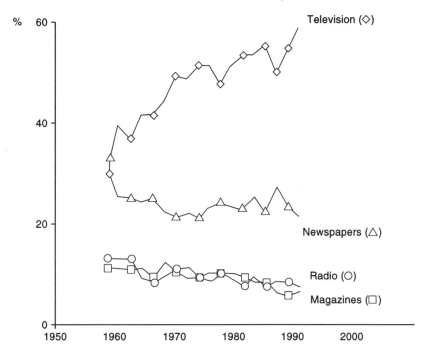

Figure 6.1   Credibility of news source in US, 1959–91
Source: Roper Organization, *America's Watching: Public Attitudes toward Television* (New York, 1991)

values. Furthermore, only from a credible position of independence can this independence be parlayed occasionally into an open, opportunistic political endorsement, or into a hidden financial deal in exchange for support by diffusing or suppressing information. This autonomy of the media, rooted in their business interests, also fits well with the ideology of the profession, and with the legitimacy and self-respect of journalists. They report, do not take sides. Information is paramount, news analysis must be documented, opinion must be regulated, and detachment is the rule. This double bind of independence, from corporations and from professionals, is reinforced by the fact that the media world is submitted to relentless competition, even if it is increasingly oligopolistic competition. Any breach in credibility for a given TV network or newspaper, and the competition will take audience (market) share away. Thus, on the one hand, the media must be close to politics and government, close enough to access information, to benefit from regulation, and, in many countries, to receive considerable subsidies. On the other hand, they must be neutral enough and distant enough to maintain their credibility, so being the intermediaries between citizens and parties in the production and consumption of information flows and images, at the roots of public opinion formation, voting, and political decision-making.

Once politics is captured in the space of the media, political actors themselves close the field of media politics by organizing political action primarily around the media: for instance, by leaking information to advance a given personal or political agenda. This leads, inevitably, to counter-leaks, so making the media the battleground in which political forces and personalities, as well as pressure groups, try to undermine each other, to collect the benefits in opinion polls, in the polling booths, in parliamentary votes, and in government decisions.

Naturally, media politics does not preclude other forms of political activity. Grassroots campaigns have proved their vitality in recent years, as shown by the Christian Coalition in the United States, the Green party in Germany, or the Communist party in Russia. Mass gatherings and street demonstrations are still essential rituals in Spanish, French, Italian, or Brazilian political campaigns. And candidates must still travel, appear, shake hands, go to meetings, kiss children (but carefully), address students, policemen, and every possible ethnic group (but not in France). Yet, with the exception of fundraising activities, the main target of these various forms of person-to-person politics is to stage the persona, or the message, in the media, be it prime-time TV news, a radio talk show, or a featured article in an influential newspaper. In Spanish political campaigns (and I suppose in other countries as well), leading candidates speaking at a public meeting are warned by a red light in their micro when there is live TV coverage (for one or two minutes), so that he/she switches automatically to a pre-programmed sound bite on a topic of choice, regardless of what he/she was saying to the live audience. In American elections, town meetings, school children's gatherings, stops along a candidate's bus, train, or plane route, are arranged in accordance with times and sites of potential media coverage. Cheerers and jeerers are on stage to provide the chance for interesting footage.

However, let me repeat again: to say that the media are the space of politics does not mean that television dictates what people decide, or that the ability to spend money in TV advertising or to manipulate images is, by itself, an overwhelming factor. All countries, and particularly the United States, are full of examples in which a television advertising barrage was not enough to elect a candidate, or a mediocre media performance did not preclude a candidate from winning (although examples also abound of the enhancing impact of TV presence in launching, and sustaining, a politician; for example, Ronald Reagan or Ross Perot in the United States, Felipe Gonzalez in Spain, Berlusconi in Italy, Jirinovsky in Russia in 1993, Aoshima in Tokyo in 1995). In 1990s' Brazil, Collor de Mello was elected president out of nowhere because of his masterful television performance, but people took to the streets to force his resignation once it became clear that he was a crook pillaging the state. Three years later, Fernando Henrique Cardoso, not unskillful on TV, but obviously disliking media gimmicks, was overwhelmingly elected president because, as Finance Minister, he was able to subdue hyperinflation for the first time in decades, although the support of *O Globo Televisao* for his candidacy did help. Neither television nor other media determine political outcomes by themselves, precisely because media politics is a contradictory realm, where different actors and strategies are played out, with diverse skills, and with various outcomes, sometimes resulting in unexpected consequences. *Mediacracy* is not contradictory to democracy because it is as plural and competitive as the political system is. That is, not much. Furthermore, if we consider the previous system, of a party-dominated democracy, where party organizations, largely insulated from the majority of citizens, entirely decided political programs and candidates, it is arguable which system provides for broader citizen input, at least once we passed the mythical times of communal town meetings.

Yet, *the critical matter is that, without an active presence in the media, political proposals or candidates do not stand a chance of gathering broad support.* Media politics is not all politics, but all politics must go through the media to affect decision-making. So doing, *politics is fundamentally framed, in its substance, organization, process, and leadership, by the inherent logic of the media system, particularly by the new electronic media.* As for how exactly this framing occurs it will help to refer to the actual evolution of media politics, starting with the American experience of the past three decades.

Show politics and political marketing: the American model

The transformation of American politics in the last decades of the twentieth century resulted from three interconnected processes: (a) the decline of political parties, and of their role in selecting candidates; (b) the emergence of a complex media system, anchored in television, but with an increasing diversity of flexible media, electronically interconnected; and (c) the development of political marketing, with constant opinion polling, feedback systems between polling and politicking, media spinning, computerized direct mailing and 'phone banks, and real time adjustments of candidates and issues to the format that can win.[6]

Although the transformation of the American political system has deep roots in social and cultural trends, the most direct manifestation of these transformations were the electoral reforms by the McGovern–Frazer Committee in response to the 1968 Democratic National Convention where the party apparatus chose Humphrey as a presidential candidate over the more popular Eugene McCarthy. Under the new system delegates to the convention were elected, in their vast majority, through direct primaries among presidential contenders.[7] Thus, while in the 1950s 40 percent of the delegates were chosen by this method, in the 1990s the proportion reached 80 percent.[8] In addition, a series of campaign finance reforms have forced candidates to rely more on their fundraising skills, and direct contacts with society, and much less on party support. Interest groups and citizens at large have pushed party organizations to the backstage of American politics.[9] Both trends have extraordinarily reinforced the role of the media: they have become the privileged intermediaries between candidates and the public, decisively influencing presidential primaries, as well as congressional and gubernatorial elections. And, because media advertising and media-oriented campaigning are very expensive, candidates have to rely on the support of private donors and political action committees external to the party system.[10]

The political role of the media has evolved considerably in the last three decades, both technologically and organizationally. Experts consider that the turning point in the relationship between media, polls, and politics was John Kennedy's campaign in 1960.[11] Not only did Kennedy base for the first time his campaign on polling and television strategy, but his victory was largely credited to his televised debate with Nixon (the first of the genre), which he dominated, while the radio audience of the same debate selected Nixon as the winner.[12] Subsequently, television became the agenda-setting device of American politics. While influential newspapers, such as *The New York Times* or *The Washington Post* are critical sources of investigative reporting, and of opinion trends, only events that are played out in

[6]   Abramson et al. (1988); Patterson (1993); Roberts and McCombs (1994); Balz and Brownstein (1996).
[7]   Patterson (1993: 30-3).
[8]   Ansolabehere et al. (1993: 75).
[9]   Magleby and Nelson (1990).
[10] Garber (1984, 1996); Gunlicks (1993).
[11] Jacobs and Shapiro (1995).
[12] Ansolabehere et al. (1993: 73).

television reach an audience large enough to set, or reverse, a trend
in public opinion. Thus, television, newspapers, and radio work as a
system, with newspapers often reporting an event, and elaborating on
it, television digesting it and diffusing it to a broad audience, and
radio talk shows providing the opportunity for citizen interaction, and
for customized, partisan debate on the issues raised by television.[13]
This increasingly central political role of television has induced two
major features. On the one hand, political spending on television has
skyrocketed: in the early 1960s, about 9 percent of the budgets of
national political campaigns were spent on TV advertising, while in
the 1990s, the proportion was about 25 percent of much larger
budgets; in 1990, an estimated $203 million went on airtime political
advertising;[14] and in 1994, $350 million were spent on television polit-
ical advertising.[15] The figure for the 1996 elections may have been
over $800 million. On the other hand, political spinning by advisors
to political candidates has become an essential factor in political
campaigning, as well as in obtaining support, or opposition, for
government decisions. What really matters is not so much the event
that is originally reported but the debate around it, how it is debated,
by whom it is debated, and for how long it is debated. Victory, not
explanation or clarification, becomes the critical matter. For instance,
in 1993–94, after months of acrimonious debate on Clinton's health
plan reform proposal, which occupied extensive media attention,
polls indicated that the large majority of Americans were confused
and unsure about the content of the proposal, and about the
substance of criticisms aimed at the plan. Never mind. What the
barrage of media controversy, fed by insurance companies, medical
associations, and the pharmaceutical industry, succeeded in doing
was to kill the proposal even before it came before Congress for a vote,
let alone was discussed by the citizenry.[16] Media have become the main
political arena.

Technology has transformed the political role of the media, not
only by its effects on the media themselves, but by linking up the
media system in real time with political marketing.[17] Starting in
the late 1960s, the introduction of computers in the tabulation of
polls led to the emergence of "strategic polling," testing different
political strategies on targeted groups of potential voters, so as to
modify the strategy, the form, and even the substance of the message

[13] Friedland (1996).
[14] Ansolabehere et al. (1993: 89).
[15] Freeman (1994).
[16] Fallows (1996).
[17] D. West (1993).

as the campaign develops.[18] In the next two decades pollsters such as Patrick Caddell, Peter Hart, and Robert Teeter, decisively influenced campaign strategy, and became key intermediaries between candidates, citizens, and the media. Together with image makers and political advertisers, they built campaigns, platforms, issues and personas by feeding back opinion trends into media reports and vice versa.[19] As technology accelerated media reporting, and increased the speed and flexibility of information systems, feedback effects, and spins, became daily activities, so that in most high political offices, starting with the White House, communication strategists meet every day early in the morning to monitor the pulse of the nation, being ready to intervene in real time, even changing messages and schedules between morning and afternoon, depending on reporting in the main sources (CNN, TV networks, leading morning newspapers).[20] The fact that the media themselves are able to break the news any time, through uninterrupted reporting, means that communication warriors must be constantly on the alert, actually codifying and translating any political decision into the language of media politics, and measuring effects by polls and focus groups. Pollsters and image makers have become decisive political actors, able to make, and unmake, presidents, senators, congressmen, and governors, by blending information technology, mediology, political savvy, and cocky wizardry. And when they are mistaken, in their polls for instance, they still are influential, because their mistakes change political trends, as in the 1996 New Hampshire Republican primary, in which polls' errors undermined Forbes' performance by measuring his votes against mistaken upward predictions of polls in previous days.[21]

As the media diversified and decentralized their scope in the 1990s, their grasp on political attitudes and behavior became ever more comprehensive.[22] Local cable television and radio talk shows customized audiences and allowed politicians to better target their message, while interest groups and ideological constituencies were more able to forward their arguments without the cautious filter of mainstream media. VCRs became essential tools in distributing packaged video messages in town meetings and private homes through direct mailing. Around the clock coverage by C-Span and CNN allowed for instant delivery of politically packaged news and information. In one instance, Republican leader Newt Gingrich was able

[18] Moore (1992: 128–9).
[19] Mayer (1994).
[20] Fallows (1996).
[21] Mundy (1996).
[22] Garber (1996); Hacker (1996).

to televise (by C-Span) a passionate, anti-liberal speech on the Congress floor, with no fear of stirring hostile reactions since, beyond the cameras' reach, the room was empty. Narrowcasting of messages to certain areas or social groups, through local stations, are fragmenting national politics, and undermining the influence of TV networks, yet embracing an even greater share of political expressions in the universe of electronic media. Additionally, the Internet has become in the mid-1990s the vehicle for campaign propaganda, controlled debate forums, and linking up with supporters.[23] Often, television programs, or ads, refer to an Internet address where information or development of arguments can be found, while computer-mediated communication picks up on media events, or on televised political advertising, to set up an electronic hook for concerned citizens.

By incorporating politics into their electronic space, the media decisively frame process, messages, and outcomes, regardless of the actual purpose or effectiveness of specific messages. Not that the medium is the message, because political options do differ, and the differences matter. But by entering the media space, political projects, and politicians, are shaped in particular ways.[24] In which ways?

To understand the framing of politics by the logic of the media, we must refer to *the overarching principles governing news media: the race for audience ratings, in competition with entertainment; the necessary detachment from politics, to induce credibility.* These translate into traditional assumptions in news coverage, as identified by Gitlin: "News concern the event, not the underlying condition; the person, not the group; conflict, not consensus; the fact that 'advances the story', not the one that explains it."[25] Only "bad news," relating to conflict, drama, unlawful deals, or objectionable behavior, is interesting news. Since news is increasingly framed to parallel (and compete with) entertainment shows, or sports events, so is its logic. It requires drama, suspense, conflict, rivalries, greed, deception, winners and losers, and, if possible, sex and violence. Following the pace, and language, of sports casting, "horse race politics" is reported as an endless game of ambitions, maneuvers, strategies and counter-strategies, with the help of insider confidences and constant opinion polling from the media themselves. The media provide decreasing attention to what politicians have to say: the average soundbite shrank from 42 seconds in 1968 to less than 10 in 1992.[26] The media's detached attitude turns

---

[23]   Klinenberg and Perrin (1996).
[24]   Patterson (1993); Balz and Brownstein (1996); Fallows (1996).
[25]   Gitlin (1980: 28).
[26]   Patterson (1993: 74).

into cynicism when literally everything is interpreted as a pure strategic game. News reporting provide the basis for these analyses, but they are considerably reinforced by pundit shows (such as CNN's *Crossfire*), which are built around sharply opposing, impolite, vociferous commentators, who of course, smile and shake hands at the end, thus underscoring that everything is a show. On the other hand, as James Fallows argues, the fast-paced, punchy, summary assessments of politics by increasingly popular television pundits directly impact the coverage of events in the TV news, and in newspapers.[27] In other words, media statements about politics become political events by themselves, with weekly announcements of winners and losers in the political race. As Sandra Moog writes:

> News stories are tending to devolve into mere discussions of public reactions to recent news coverage. Who are the winners and the losers, whose popularity ratings have crept up and whose have dropped, as a result of political events of the last month, last week, or last day. Frequent public opinion polling by news agencies makes this kind of hyper-reflexivity possible, by providing supposedly objective grounding for journalists' speculations about the impacts of political actions and the journalistic reactions to those actions, on the public's assessment of different politicians.[28]

An additional, and powerful, framing of political news reporting is the personalization of events.[29] Politicians, not politics, are the actors of the drama. And because they may change their programmatic proposals, while navigating the political waters, what remains in the minds of most people is personal motivation, and personal images, as the source of politics. Thus, questions of character come to the forefront of the political agenda, as the messenger becomes the message.

The framing of political news expands into the framing of politics itself, as strategists play in and with the media to influence voters. Thus, because only bad news is news, political advertising concentrates on negative messages, aimed at destroying the opponent's proposals, while advancing one's own program in very general terms. Indeed, experiments show that negative messages are much more likely to be retained, and to influence political opinion.[30] Furthermore, because politics is personalized in a world of image

[27] Fallows (1996).
[28] Moog (1996: 20).
[29] Ansolabehere et al. (1993); Fallows (1996).
[30] Ansolabehere and Iyengar (1995).

making and soap operas, character assassination becomes the most potent weapon.[31] Political projects, government proposals, and political careers can be undermined or even destroyed with the revelation of improper behavior (Nixon's Watergate inaugurated the new era); with the exposure of private life departing from strict moral standards, and of the cover-up of the information (Gary Hart); or with the accumulation of various accusations, rumors, insinuations, relayed one after another in the media, as soon as the impact of one allegation starts fading away (Bill and Hillary Clinton?). In some cases, unproven allegations lead to dramatic personal consequences, such as the suicide of the targeted politician (for example, French Socialist Minister of Finance Pierre Beregovoy in 1993). Therefore, the monitoring of personal attacks on a daily basis, and counter-attacking, or threatening to, with similar allegations, becomes a fundamental part of political life. Indeed, in the 1992 presidential campaign Clinton's advisers forced Republicans to downplay their focus on Clinton's extramarital affair by threatening to elaborate on Bush's alleged involvement with a former assistant at the White House: they had found another Jennifer.[32] Communication strategists and spokepersons are at the center of informational politics.

The increasing restriction of media exposure to the content of political proposals (except in segmented media away from a mass audience; for example, public television or newspapers' lengthy special reports) leads to an extreme simplification of political messages. Complex political platforms are scrutinized to select a few key issues that will be highlighted, for a broad audience, in dichotomous terms: pro-life or pro-choice; gay rights or gay-bashing; social security and budget deficit versus balanced budget and dismantling of Medicaid. Referendum politics mimics television game shows, with the electoral buzzer announcing winners and losers, and pre-electoral bells (polls) sounding warnings. Images, coded messages, and horse-race politics between heroes and villains (they switch roles periodically), in a world of faked passions, hidden ambitions, and back-stabbing: such is American politics as framed in and by the electronic media, thus transformed into political real virtuality, determining access to the state. Could this "American model" be the forebear of a broader political trend, characterizing the Information Age?

---

[31]   Garramone et al. (1990); Fallows (1996).
[32]   Swan (1992).

Is European politics being "Americanized"?

No and yes. No, because European political systems rely much more extensively on political parties, with a long, established tradition, and considerable roots in their specific history, culture, and society. No, because national cultures matter, and what is admissible in America would be inadmissible in most of Europe, and would actually backfire on the would-be aggressor: for instance, it was a known fact in French political circles that late President Mitterrand had a long-lasting, extramarital relationship, from which he had a daughter. It was never used against him, in spite of his many enemies, and, if it had been used, most citizens would have found it disgraceful to interfere with the privacy of the president. (UK media occupy an intermediate position between America and most of Europe concerning respect for political leaders' private lives.) Also, until the late 1980s, most of European television was controlled by government, so that political access to television was regulated, and paid advertising is still forbidden. Even with the liberalization and privatization of television, private networks (for example Britain's ITV, or Spain's Antena-3 TV) follow a self-regulating pattern of political balance to preserve their credibility. Thus, there are indeed substantial differences both in the media and in their relationship to political systems in America and in Europe.[33]

On the other hand, while candidates and programs are selected and decided by parties, the media have become as important in Europe as in America in deciding the outcome of political bids.[34] The media (and particularly television) are the fundamental source of political information and opinion for people, and the main attributes of informational politics, as identified in America, characterize European politics as well: simplification of messages, professional advertising and polling as political tools, personalization of options, negativism as a predominant strategy, leaking of damaging information as a political weapon, image-making and spin control as essential mechanisms in seizing power, and in keeping it. Let us briefly review some comparative evidence.

In the UK, television was the main source of political news for 58 percent of people in the 1980s: it increased to 80 percent in the 1990s,[35] with newspapers being the main source for the other 20 percent. However, paid TV advertising is illegal in Britain, and parties are given free broadcasts both during campaign times, and out of them. Yet, deregulation, privatization, and multiplication of sources

[33]   Siune and Truetzschler (1992); Kaid and Holtz-Bacha (1995).
[34]   Guehenno (1993); Kaid and Holz-Bacha (1995).
[35]   Moog (1996).

of televised information have driven audiences away from formal political advertising, and toward political reporting.[36] Commentary on parties' advertising in regular programs becomes more influential than advertising itself. For instance, in 1992, the Labour party broadcast a spot about Jennifer, a young girl who had to wait a year for an ear operation because of the crisis in the health system. When her identity (to be kept anonymous) was revealed, the real issue became the inability of Labour to keep confidential information, thus undermining its ability to be trusted in government.[37] Negative advertising, particularly from the Tories, became a focus of the 1992 campaign, and played a role in the Conservative victory.[38] Reliance on instant polling, targeted mailing, use of professional advertising and public relation firms, events and speeches oriented toward image-making and soundbites, slick professional advertisements using actors and photo montages, focus on image rather than on policy, are in the 1990s the staple of British politics, as much as they are in America.[39] Personalization of politics has a long tradition in Britain, with leaders as forceful as Winston Churchill, Harold Wilson, or Margaret Thatcher. However, the new wave of personalization does not relate to historic, charismatic leaders, but to anyone applying for the Prime Minister's job. Thus, in 1987, Labour focused its campaign on a "young and glamorous" couple, Neil and Glenys Kinnock, and ran as its main Party Election Broadcast (PEB), a televised biography titled *Kinnock*, produced by Hugh Hudson, the director of *Chariots of Fire*.[40] In 1992, two out of five Conservative PEBs focused on John Major (*Major – The Journey*, produced by Schlesinger, the director of *Midnight Cowboy*, depicting Major's rise from working-class Brixton).[41] Personalization leads to character assassination as political strategy, and such was the case as well in recent British politics: in the 1992 campaign, Kinnock was attacked in the Tory tabloid press (with the stories then being picked up by television news), with attacks ranging from alleged Mafia connections to his private life (the so-called "Boyo affair"). Paddy Ashdown, the Liberal Democrat leader, was publicly attacked with regard to his sex life. And while Axford et al. suggest that after the 1992 election, British media appeared ready to restrain themselves in the use of "dirty tricks," this new-found discipline does not seem to have spared the Royal Family.[42] Indeed, I feel safe in

[36] Berry (1992).
[37] Scammell and Semetko (1995).
[38] Berry (1992); Scammel and Semetko (1995).
[39] Axford et al. (1992); Philo (1993); Franklin (1994).
[40] Philo (1993: 411).
[41] Scammell and Semetko (1995: 35).
[42] Axford et al. (1992).

forecasting, writing in 1996, that the next British general election, marked by the likelihood of a Labour victory, will be characterized by an explosion of "character assassination" attempts aimed at Tony Blair's emergent leadership.

The advent of Russian democracy meant also the introduction of American-style, television-oriented political campaigns since the parliamentary elections of December 1993.[43] In the decisive 1996 Russian presidential elections, Yeltsin was able to regain control of the electorate, in danger of turning to Zyuganov out of desperation, in the last weeks of the campaign, by launching a media barrage, and by using, for the first time in Russia, computerized direct mailing, targeted polling, and segmented propaganda. Yeltsin's campaign combined old and new strategies of media use, but, in both approaches, television was the focus. On the one hand, government and private television channels aligned themselves with Yeltsin, and used news and programming as vehicles of anti-Communist propaganda, including the broadcasting of several films on the horrors of Stalinism in the week before the vote. On the other hand, Yeltsin's political advertising was carefully designed. A political consulting company, "Niccolò M" (M for Machiavelli) played a major role in designing a media strategy in which Yeltsin would appear on regular television news while TV political advertising would focus on real people (I know one of them) who would explain their support for Yeltsin. The spots ended with the words "I believe, I love, I hope," followed by Yeltsin's signature, his only presence in the advertisement. Yekaterina Yegorova, director of "Niccolò M," understood that, in her own words: "The idea behind his absence is that Yeltsin, as president, appears so often on the screen [in the regular news] that if he were on commercials as well, people would get sick of him."[44] Thus, "absent personalization," by combining different forms of media messages, becomes a new, subtle strategy in a world saturated by audiovisual propaganda. Some California Republican consultants also played an advisory role on political technology in the Yeltsin campaign (albeit to a much lesser extent than they claimed), as well as a variety of media and political advisors, propelling Russia into informational politics even before it had time to become an information society. It worked: outfinanced, outpowered, and outsmarted, the Communists relied on large-scale grassroots organizing, too primitive a medium to counter the alliance of television, radio, and major newspapers that rallied around Yeltsin. Although other factors played a role in the Russian election (rejection of Communism, fear of disorder, electoral dema-

[43]   Hughes (1994).
[44]   *Moscow Times* (1996: 1).

goguery, skillful last-minute presidential decisions, particularly about Chech'nya, the incorporation of Lebed in the Yeltsin administration before the second round of the election), the old and new system of politics measured it up, and the result was a one-sided Yeltsin victory, after badly trailing in the polls four months earlier.

Spain's young democracy also learned quickly the new trades of informational politics.[45] In the 1982 general election, the skillful use of media and personalization, around the figure of an extraordinary leader, Felipe Gonzalez, led the socialists (PSOE) to an unprecedented electoral landslide. Subsequently, in 1986 and 1989, Gonzalez's Socialists were twice re-elected with an absolute majority, and even won in 1985 a national referendum to join NATO, in the most difficult conditions. In addition to Socialist policy's own merits, three major factors contributed to overwhelming political domination by the Socialist party in the 1980s: the charismatic personality of Felipe Gonzalez, and his powerful presence in the media, particularly in television, whether in face-to-face debates, journalists' interviews, or televised political events; the technological sophistication of Socialist political strategists, which, for the first time in Spain, used focused groups, constant polling, image analysis/design, and targeting of issues in time and space, in a coherent, sustained strategy of political propaganda that did not stop after election day; and the government monopoly on television, giving a clear edge to the government, until relentless criticism by the opposition on television coverage, as well as Gonzalez's democratic convictions, led to the liberalization and partial privatization of television in the 1990s. On the other hand, it was the losing of the battle in the media in the 1990s that first eroded the Socialist government in Spain in 1993, and later brought a center-right government into power in 1996. I will elaborate, in the following section, on scandal politics and the politics of corruption as an essential strategy of informational politics, again using, among other cases, this most revealing contemporary Spanish example. But it is important to underline, while discussing the possible extrapolation of American-style politics to Europe, that contemporary Spain had nothing to learn from America concerning techniques of media politicking, character assassination, and feedback loops between polling, broadcasting, and play acting.

Although in a less dramatic manner (after all, Spain is a high-drama country), politics in most European democracies has come to be dominated by similar processes. Thus, observers in France rebelled against "*telecratie*,"[46] while others emphasize the coming of "virtual

---

[45]   Alonso Zaldivar and Castells (1992).
[46]   *Esprit* (1994: 3—4).

democracy."[47] The sudden rise to power of Berlusconi in Italy was directly linked to the new role played by the media in Italian politics.[48] Comparative analysis of other European countries in the 1990s[49] describes a complex, transitional situation, of media dominating the diffusion of information, while parties are unequipped, under-financed, and strictly regulated, thus finding it hard to adapt to the new technological environment. The outcome seems to be that, on the one hand, political parties keep, by and large, their autonomy *vis à vis* the media, with the support of the state. On the other hand, because of restricted access of parties to the media, people increasingly form their political opinions from sources external to the political system, thus accentuating the distance between parties and citizens.[50] Thus, while institutions, culture, and history make European politics highly specific, technology, globalization, and the network society incite political actors and institutions to engage in technology driven, informational politics. I contend that this is a new, historical trend, affecting, by successive waves, the entire world, albeit under specific historical conditions that introduce substantial variations in political competition, and in the conduct of politics. Bolivia provides an exceptional opportunity to test this hypothesis.

Bolivia's electronic populism: *compadre* Palenque and the coming of *Jach'a Uru* [51]

If we had to select the most likely country in the world to resist globalization of culture, and to assert grassroots politics, Bolivia would be an obvious candidate. Its Indian identity is extremely present in the collective memory of its population (even if 67 percent consider themselves *mestizos*), and Aymara and Quechua are widely spoken. Nationalism is the paramount ideology of all political parties. Since the 1952 revolution, Bolivian miners and peasant unions have been among the most conscious, organized, and militant social actors in Latin America. The main nationalist-populist party, the *Movimiento*

---

47   Scheer (1994).
48   Di Marco (1994); Santoni Rugiu (1994); Walter (1994).
49   Kaid and Holz-Bacha (1995).
50   Di Marco (1993).
51   I am indebted, for their help in the elaboration of this section on Bolivian media politics, to Fernando Calderon in La Paz, and to Roberto Laserna in Cochabamba. The analysis is based on the following studies by Bolivian researchers: Mesa (1986); Archondo (1991); Contreras Basnipeiro (1991); Saravia and Sandoval (1991); Laserna (1992); Albo (1993); Mayorga (1993); Perez Iribarne (1993a, b); Ardaya and Verdesoto (1994); Calderon and Laserna (1994); Bilbao La Vieja Diaz et al. (1996); Szmukler (1996).

Nacionalista Revolucionario, has been in and out of power for the past four decades, still holding the presidency in 1996, with the support of left nationalists of the *Movimiento Bolivia Libre,* and of the Katarist (indigenist) movement. Social tensions and political militancy in the country prompted frequent military coups, not always disliked by the US Embassy, until the open participation of the high ranks of the army in drug traffic in the late 1970s, and the change of policy under Carter, modified the US attitude, facilitating the restoration of stable democracy in 1982, with a left coalition coming to power. Since then, while social tensions did heighten, because of the structural adjustment policies introduced by the MNR in 1985 (later to be followed by other governments), democracy seems solidly established. A most lively political struggle developed, with parties being formed, split, and reformed, and the most unlikely political alliances being forged to reach state power. Thus, social mobilization and democratic politics were, and are, alive and well in Bolivia, apparently leaving little room for the transformation of the political scene by an Andean brand of informational politics. And yet, since 1989, the politics of La Paz–El Alto (the Bolivian capital and its periphery of popular settlements) has been dominated by a political movement built around Carlos Palenque, a former folk musician from humble origin, who became a radio and television show host, then the owner of a media network (RTP, *Radio Television Popular*), and finally leader of *Conciencia de Patria* (Condepa), founded on September 21, 1988, in Tihuanaco, the ancient capital of the Aymara world. Although the story may sound familiar to those aware of the old tradition of Latin American populism, it is in fact unusual, complex, and revealing.

Palenque's saga started in 1968 when, around his folk group, *Los Caminantes,* he created a radio program that gradually incorporated direct contact with the audience, using popular language, including a mixture of Spanish and Aymara, which made it easier for people from poor urban strata to communicate without being intimidated by the formalism of the medium. In 1978, he started a television show, where he offered a platform for people to voice their complaints. He introduced himself as the compadre of his audience, and he also referred to his interlocutors as *compadres* and *comadres,* thus leveling the field of communication, and introducing a reference to a fundamental communality, rooted in the Aymara and Catholic traditions.[52] In 1980, he succeeded in buying Radio Metropolitana,

---

[52] *Compadre* and *comadre* are terms signifying membership in the community. They bring together elements of Aymara tradition and of Catholic celebration (e.g godfathers and godmothers for christened children). As such, *compadres* and *comadres* are expected to understand, to contribute, to share, and to assume reciprocity.

and later on Canal 4, a television station in La Paz. They soon became the most listened-to media in the La Paz area, and they remain so: indeed, 25 percent of the radio audience declared that they listen exclusively to Metropolitana.

Five elements are critical in Palenque's communication strategy. The first is the personalization of the shows, with forceful *compadres* and *comadres* representing various constituencies, such as *comadre* Remedios Loza, a common woman (*mujer de pollera*), a human type never before seen on television, in spite of being the very image of La Paz's popular families; or *compadre* Paco, closer to the middle class; or his own wife, Monica Medina de Palenque, a former flamenco ballet dancer, assuming the role of the bottom-line, wise woman. The personalization of interaction with the audience does not stop with live shows, but extends to much of the programming. For instance, while Canal 4 broadcasts the same Latin American soap operas that capture attention throughout the entire Spanish-speaking world, *compadre* Palenque and his team personally comment on the events and drama of various episodes, and engage with their audience in relating the soap opera's story to the daily lives of *paceños*. Secondly, is the targeting of women, particularly of lower-class women, and the prominent presence of women in the programs. Thirdly, there is a direct connection to people's concerns, and joys, with programs such as *People's Saturdays* broadcast live with the participation of hundreds of people from urban locations; or *The People's Tribune*, in which people denounce live the abuses to which they are submitted by whoever. Fourthly, there is a willingness to listen to people's complaints, providing an ear open to the laments arising from the painful integration of rural and Indian life in the sprawling urban periphery of La Paz. And, fifthly, is the religious reference, legitimizing hope as God's will, with the promise of the coming of *Jach'a Uru*, the day when, according to the Aymara tradition, all suffering will come to an end.

However, Palenque's path to prominence was not a smooth one. Because of his criticism of authorities, under the pretext of a radio interview with a leading drug trafficker, RTP media network was twice closed by the government, in June and November 1988. But mass protests, and a decision by the Supreme Court, reopened it months later. Palenque answered by creating a party (Condepa), and running for president. In the first election in which it participated, in May 1989, Condepa became the fourth largest national party, and the first party in the capital. In the municipal elections, it won the Mayoralty of El Alto (fourth largest urban area of Bolivia), and entered in the municipal council of La Paz. In the next municipal election, Monica Medina de Palenque became the Mayor of La Paz, a post she kept until

1996. Condepa is also present in the National Congress: among other deputies, *comadre* Remedios played a leading role in pushing legislation for Bolivian women. In spite of its populism, Condepa did not develop a confrontational attitude toward various governments. In 1989 its votes helped to elect in the Congress President Jaime Paz Zamora, in spite of his third place in the popular vote. And when a new MNR President, Sanchez de Losada, was elected in 1993, Condepa, while not participating in the government, cooperated with the government in several legislative initiatives.

The success of *compadre* Palenque did not take place in a social vacuum. He had a pointed message, not just a medium, which seemed to fit well with the actual experience of the urban masses in La Paz. He appealed to the cultural identity of La Paz's recent immigrants, by the use of language, by the emphasis on Aymara traditions, by the reference to folk and religion. Against policies of economic adjustment, and integration in the global economy, he exposed the daily suffering of displaced workers and urban poor, the abuses imposed upon them under the pretext of economic rationality. *Compadre* Palenque became the voice of the voiceless. Using the media as platform, but linking up with local institutions where Condepa was present, Palenque ran a number of social programs, one of the most successful geared toward helping industrial workers displaced by economic restructuring and privatization. Refusing the categorical imperative of globalization, *compadre* Palenque proposed (albeit in rather vague terms) a model of "endogenous development," based on Bolivia's own resources, and counting on the communal spirit of its people. Thus, Condepa's influence is not just a media manipulation: its themes refer to the actual suffering of people in La Paz, and its language directly communicates to the cultural and local identity of popular strata in La Paz and El Alto (to the point that the movement remains by and large local, authorizing some analysts to speak of a "metropolitan ayllu").[53] However, without the power of the media, and without a perceptive communication strategy mixing entertainment radio and television with a space for public complaints, and with the building of charismatic trust between the leaders and the audience, Condepa would have been reduced to a minor role, as happened to other populist movements in Bolivia, such as Max Fernandez's *Unidad Cívica Solidaridad.* Indeed, in 1996, Bolivians trust the media more than they trust their political representatives (table 6.3).

So, media politics does not have to be the monopoly of influential

---

[53]   *Ayllu* is the traditional form of a territorial/cultural community in the Aymara tradition.

Table 6.3 Opinion of Bolivian citizens on which institutions represent their interests

Institution	% of favorable opinion
Congress of Deputies	3.5
Any political party	3.4
President	3.3
Mayor	6.9
Neighborhood committee	11.3
Labor union	12.6
Mass media	23.4

Note: Answers to the question: "Do you feel that the following institutions represent your interests?" (percentage over total of polled citizens; national representative sample).
Source: Collective Author (1996)

interest groups, or of established political parties using the power of technology to perfect the technology of power. As *compadre* Palenque's ascendance seems to indicate, identity-based communalism, and poor people's movements, sometimes under the form of religious millennialism, can access the political mainstream by using the media. By so doing, they force other political actors to play a similar game (as is the case in Bolivia in the 1990s), thus contributing to the gradual enclosing of politics in the media space, albeit with specific characteristics fitting the Bolivian cultural tradition, economic condition, and political dynamics. Furthermore, in spite of the communal orientation of Condepa, we find in the experience of *compadre* Palenque a series of features not dissimilar to the broader trends of informational politics, as described above: the extreme personalization of leadership; the simplification of messages in dichotomous terms: good and evil; the pre-eminence of moral and religious judgments in framing public and personal life; the decisive importance of electronically broadcast language, images, and symbols in mobilizing consciousness and deciding politics; the volatility of public mood, lost in the feeling of a world spinning out of control; the difficulty of fitting these new political expressions into traditional political categories (to the point that some Bolivian analysts refer to the emergence of "informal politics," parallel to the "informal economy");[54] and, ultimately, we also find, among these *compadres* and *comadres*, a dependence on their financial ability to support media politics, thus creating a feedback loop (or a vicious circle) between power, media, and money. While the "resurrection of a metropolitan

[54]   Ardaya and Verdesoto (1994).

ayllu"[55] shows the limits to globalization, it is by inhabiting the space of media flows that traditional cultures and popular interests assert their power. So doing, they survive, but they transform themselves at the same time, entering a new world of sounds and images, of electronically modulated *charangos*, environmentally preserved condors, and television scripted *Jach'a Uru*.

Informational Politics in Action: the Politics of Scandal[56]

In the past decade, political systems have been shaken all over the world, and political leaders have been destroyed, in a relentless succession of scandals. In some cases, political parties solidly entrenched in power for about half a century have collapsed, taking along in their demise the political regime they had shaped in their interest. Among important examples of this evolution are: the Italian Christian Democrats, which literally disintegrated in the 1990s; Japan's Liberal Democratic Party which was split and lost the government, for the first time, in 1993, although the party as such survived, and still governs in coalition or in minority; or India's Congress Party, which, after governing the largest democracy in the world for 44 years of the more than 48 years since Independence, suffered a humiliating defeat, to the benefit of Hindu nationalists in the 1996 elections, after a major scandal involving Congress leader Narasimha Rao, seemingly putting an end to a political system built around uncontested domination of Nehru's successors. With the exception of Scandinavian

---

[55] Archondo (1991).

[56] This section is partly based on a reading of mainstream newspapers and magazines from different countries, as well as on personal knowledge of some events. I consider it unnecessary to provide detailed references for facts that are public knowledge. An international overview of political scandals is Longman (1990) *Political Scandals and Causes Célèbres since 1945*. A major scholarly, comparative volume on the topic is Heidenheimer et al. (1989). Historical accounts of American scandal politics can be found in Fackler and Lin (1995), and Ross (1988). A recent account of congressional scandals in America is in Balz and Brownstein (1996: 27ff). An annotated bibliography on American political corruption is Johansen (1990). Additional sources used in this section are: King (1984); Markovits and Silverstein (1988a); Bellers (1989); Ebbinghausen and Neckel (1989); Bouissou (1991); Morris (1991); Sabato (1991); Barker (1992); *CQ Researcher* (1992); Meny (1992); Phillips (1992); Swan (1992); Tranfaglia (1992); Barber (1993); Buckler (1993); DeLeon (1993); Grubbe (1993); Roman (1993); *Esprit* (1994); Gumbel (1994); Walter (1994); Arlachi (1995); Fackler and Lin (1995); Garcia Cotarelo (1995); Johnson (1995); Sechi (1995); Thompson (1995).

democracies, and a few other small countries, I cannot think of any country in North America, Latin America, Western and Eastern Europe, Asia, or Africa, where major political scandals, with significant, and sometimes dramatic, consequences, have not exploded in recent years.[57]

In a few instances, scandals referred to the personal morality of a leader (usually a man improperly driven by sexuality or drunkenness). But, in most cases, the matter was political corruption, that is, in Carl Friedrich's definition: "Whenever a powerholder who is charged with doing certain things, i.e., who is a responsible functionary or office-holder, is by monetary or other rewards not legally provided for, induced to take actions which favor whoever provides the rewards and thereby does damage to the public and its interests."[58] In some cases, government officials simply took the money, without even needing to run with it. Or so they believed. From South Korea's President Roh to Brazil's President Collor de Mello, and from some members of Russia's military, or of the United States' Congress, to some high-ranking members of Spanish and French Socialist administrations, wave after wave of corruption-related political scandals have become the main staple of public life throughout the world in the 1990s. Why so? Are our political systems the most corrupt in history? I doubt it. Use and abuse of power for personal benefit is one of these features that would qualify as "human nature," if such an entity were to exist.[59] This is precisely one of the reasons why democracy was invented, and became the most sought after, if not ideal, form of governance. Behind the scenes, in situations of the control of information by the state, political elites, in ancient times as in recent years, went happily into establishing their personalized tax system on subjects and interest groups, the main differences being in the degree of arbitrariness in bribing, and in the variable disfunctionality of hidden contributions for the conduct of public affairs. Thus, a first observation points to the fact that denunciation of corruption could precisely be a good indicator of a democratic society, and of freedom of the press.[60] For instance, Spain under the dictatorship of Franco suffered from direct pillage of the country by the dictator's entourage, starting with Mrs Franco's notorious visits to jewelry stores whose owners never dared to send the bill to his excellency. No serious observer would assert that

[57]   Heidenheimer et al. (1989); Longman (1990); Garment (1991); *CQ Researcher* (1992); Meny (1992); Grubbe (1993); Roman (1993); Gumbel (1994); Walter (1994); Thompson (1995).
[58]   Friedrich (1966: 74).
[59]   Leys (1989).
[60]   Markovits and Silverstein (1988).

political corruption in Spain was more pervasive during the 1980s' Socialist governments than under Franco.[61] And yet, while, during the dictatorship, corruption was mainly a matter of gossip among reliable friends, political life in 1990s' Spanish democracy was entirely shaped by revelations, and allegations, of government corruption and unlawful behavior. Furthermore, in long-established democracies, with freedom of the press, such as the United States, the occurrence of political corruption, as reported in the press, goes up and down, with no clear long-term trend, as can be observed in figure 6.2, elaborated by Fackler and Lin for the past hundred years.[62] There is, however, a most spectacular surge of reporting on political corruption around the time of Nixon's Watergate, precisely the event that struck the imagination of both journalists and politicians with the possibility of bringing down the most powerful political office on earth, by obtaining and diffusing damaging information. The historical study by King on political corruption in nineteenth-century Britain[63] shows the pervasiveness of the phenomenon, prompting the 1867 Reform Act to curtail such practices, as democracy made progress. And Bouissou reports that in 1890 the Japanese press denounced widespread electoral fraud, with the newspaper *Asahi* writing that "whoever buys his election will be for sale once elected."[64] Moreover, in a most insightful analysis, Barker has shown that when unlawful actions by politicians do not provide enough ammunition to discredit them, other types of behavior (for example, improper sex) become the raw material for political scandal.[65] Thus, using the Longman international series of political scandals,[66] he calculated that the proportion of unlawful and not unlawful political scandals for all countries (73 : 27) was relatively close to the proportion in the US or France, but very different in the UK (41 : 59), so that sex and espionage became in Britain the functional equivalent of graft and bribery in other countries. Corruption *per se* seems to be less significant than scandals (that is, corruption or wrong doing revealed) and their political impact.[67]

So, why now? If it is unlikely that corruption is at a historical highpoint, why does it explode all over the media, and why does it so devastatingly affect political systems and political actors in the 1990s? There are a number of structural factors, and macro-political trends,

[61]   Alonso Zaldivar and Castells (1992).
[62]   Fackler and Lin (1995).
[63]   King (1989).
[64]   Bouissou (1991: 84).
[65]   Barker (1992).
[66]   Longman (1990).
[67]   Lowi (1988).

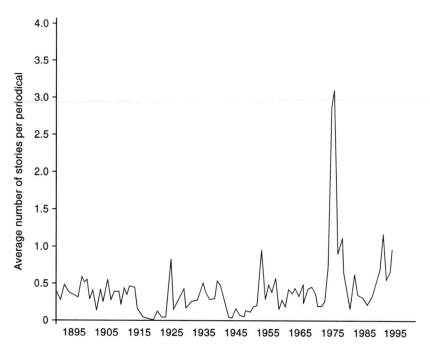

Figure 6.2   Average number of corruption stories per periodical in
US, 1890–1992
Source: Fackler and Lin (1995)

which have weakened political systems, making them more vulnerable
to turmoil created in public opinion. Political competition, and the
struggle to influence the center of the electorate's political spectrum,
have downplayed ideological contrasts, as parties/coalitions, having
secured their hard-core supporters, strive to steal adversaries' themes
and positions as much as possible. It follows a blurring of political
positions, and the tendency by citizens to be more sensitive to the
reliability of parties and candidates than to their professed positions
on issues. Personalization of politics also focuses attention on leaders,
and on their character, thus opening the way for attacks on precisely
those qualities as a form of winning votes. The rise of a potent global
criminal economy has penetrated state institutions in many countries,
often at the highest levels of government, thus providing ammunition
for scandal-making, and also using information to blackmail politicians into submission. Geopolitical factors also play a role: thus, the
Italian and Japanese political systems, organized around the Christian
Democratic and the Liberal Democratic parties respectively, were set
up in the aftermath of World War II, with considerable help and

influence from the US, to establish a bulwark against communism in two democracies that were critical in the Cold War context, and where communist and socialist parties were strong.[68] The long-standing, well-known connections of some leading Christian Democrats with the Mafia,[69] and of some Liberal Democrat leaders with the *Yakuza*,[70] were not an obstacle to the unrelenting support of international and domestic forces for these parties, as long as their replacement was an excessively risky operation. In the post-Cold War environment, each party is left to itself, to the movements of each country's political market; discipline inside the parties becomes less strict, because fierce competition can be better afforded in the absence of an external enemy. Guehenno has also suggested that, in a world of fading nation-states and uncertain ideological commitments, the rewards for being in office are no longer distinct from those offered in society at large, that is, ultimately, money, as the key to personal or organizational projects, from enjoying life to providing for the family, or helping humanitarian causes.[71]

All these factors seem to contribute to making political systems vulnerable to corruption. But there is something else, something that, in my view, changes the nature of political systems in contemporary societies. *I contend that scandal politics is the weapon of choice for struggle and competition in informational politics.* The argument goes like this. Politics has been, by and large, enclosed in the space of the media. The media have become more powerful than ever, technologically, financially, and politically. Their global reach, and networking, allow them to escape from strict political controls. Their capacity for investigative reporting, and their relative autonomy *vis à vis* political power, makes them the main source of information and opinion for society at large. Parties and candidates must act in and through the media to reach society. Not that the media are the Fourth Power: they are, instead, the ground for power struggles. Media politics is an increasingly expensive operation, made even more expensive by the whole paraphernalia of informational politics: polling, advertising, marketing, analyzing, image-making, and information processing. Current institutional systems of political financing are not up to the task. Political actors are chronically underfinanced, and the gap between necessary expenses and legal revenues has grown exponentially, and continues to grow.[72] Thus, after exhausting all legal sources,

[68]   Johnson (1995).
[69]   Tranfaglia (1992).
[70]   Bouissou (1991); Johnson (1995).
[71]   Guehenno (1993).
[72]   Weinberg (1991); Freeman (1994); Pattie et al. (1995).

personal contributions, and business deals, parties and politicians often resort to the only real source of money: under the table contributions from business and interest groups, obviously in exchange for government decisions in favor of these interests.[73] *This is the matrix of systemic political corruption, from which develops a shadow network of front businesses and intermediaries.* Once corruption becomes widespread, and after a few people add their personal take to the channels of political funding, everybody in politics, and in the media, knows (or thinks he/she knows) that, if looking closely, and long enough, damaging information can be found on almost anyone. Thus, the hunt starts, by political advisors to prepare ammunition to attack or to defend; by journalists to fulfill their job as investigative reporters, finding material to boost their audience and their sales; by freelancers, and crooks, to find information that can be used in potential blackmail, or for sale to interested parties. In fact, most of the damaging material published by the media is leaked by political actors themselves, or by associated business interests. Finally, once the market of damaging political information is created, if there is not enough clear-cut material, then allegations, insinuations, and even fabrications, may come in, depending, of course, on the individual ethics of politicians, journalists, and the media. Indeed, the strategy in scandal politics does not necessarily aim at an instant blow on the basis of one scandal. It is the relentless flow of various scandals of different kinds, and with different levels of likelihood, from solid information on a minor incident to shaky allegations on a major issue, that weave the thread where political ambitions are finally strangled, and political dreams subdued – unless a deal is made, thus feeding back into the system. What counts is the final impact on public opinion, by the accumulation of many different touches.[74] As in the old Russian saying: "I cannot remember if she stole a coat, or if a coat was stolen from her."

The superior stage of scandal politics is the judicial or parliamentary investigation, leading to indictments, and, with increasing frequency, to imprisonment of political leaders.[75] Judges, prosecutors, and investigative committee members enter into a symbiotic relationship with the media. They protect the media (ensuring their independence), and often feed them with calculated leaks. In exchange, they are protected by the media, they become media heroes, and, sometimes successful politicians with the support of the media. Together, they fight for democracy and clean government, they control the excesses of politicians, and, ultimately, they seize

[73]   Meny (1992).
[74]   Barker (1992); *CQ Researcher* (1992).
[75]   Garment (1991); Garcia Cotarelo (1995); Thompson (1995).

power away from the political process, diffusing it into the society. While doing so, they may also delegitimize parties, politicians, politics, and, ultimately, democracy in its current incarnation.[76] The politics of scandal, as practiced in the 1990s against the governing Spanish Socialist party, offers an interesting illustration of this analysis. After the 1989 Socialist victory in the Spanish general election (the third in a row), a behind-the-scenes coalition of interest groups (*probably without the participation of the leaders of political opposition parties*) decided it was time to check the uncontested domination of the Socialists in Spain's political life, a domination that could be foreseen going into the twenty-first century.[77] Explosive political files were leaked, discovered, manipulated, or invented, and published in the press. Because of self-restraint by the main Spanish newspapers (*El Pais, El Periodico, La Vanguardia*) most of the potential anti-Socialist "scandals" were first published in *El Mundo*, a professionally sophisticated newspaper created in 1990. From there, weekly tabloids and radio talk show pundits (mainly from the Catholic Church-owned radio network) would hammer the audience until the rest of the media, including television, echoed the news. Scandals started to be revealed in January 1990 with information on the brother of the then vice-president of the government selling his assumed political influence to various businessmen. Although the wrongdoings of this little crook were not of great significance, and the courts cleared the vice-president of any impropriety, the "affair" occupied the political headlines of the Spanish media for almost two years, actually prompting the resignation of the vice-president, the influential number two of the Socialist party, who refused to condemn his brother publicly. As soon as this scandal started to fizzle out, a new media campaign started, focusing on illegal financing of the Socialist party, after a party accountant defected and gave information to the media, apparently out of a personal vendetta. A judicial investigation was opened, leading to the indictment of some Socialist leaders. When, in spite of all these accusations, the Socialist party still retained enough seats to form a government in the 1993 elections, scandal politics accelerated its tempo in the Spanish media and judicial scene: the Governor of the Bank of Spain was suspected of insider trading, and confessed to tax fraud; the first civilian director of the legendary Guardia Civil was caught requesting bribes, fled the country, was arrested in Bangkok, and returned to a Spanish prison, in a sequence that fell between the thriller and the burlesque; more seriously, a resentful officer of the Spanish military intelligence leaked papers

---

[76]   Bellers (1989); Arlachi (1995); Garcia Cotarelo (1995); Fallows (1996).
[77]   Cacho (1994); Garcia Cotarelo (1995); *Temas* (1995).

showing unlawful eavesdropping on Spanish leaders, including the king; and, to complete the disintegration of public morale, former special agents of the Spanish police, incarcerated for organizing assassinations in the "dirty war" carried on in the 1980s against Basque terrorists (emulating Thatcher's tactics against the IRA), turned their coats against the government, and involved the Minister of the Interior, and several high-ranking officials in the conspiracy. Of paramount importance in this political process was the attitude of the Spanish judges, who pursued earnestly the slightest possibility of embarrassing the Socialist party. Felipe Gonzalez executed what was considered a brilliant maneuver by recruiting the most famous of these zealous judges as an independent deputy in the Socialist ticket in the 1993 election, and appointing him to a high post in the Ministry of Justice. It was a disaster: whether because the post was not high enough (Socialist version), or that the judge was disappointed by what he saw (his version), he quit the government, and engaged in a most militant prosecution against any potential wrongdoing from the highest levels of the Socialist government. After parliamentary and judicial investigations were opened, some leading to indictments, others fizzling out because of lack of substance, political scandals became the daily headlines of the Spanish media for about five years, literally paralyzing the action of government, destroying a number of political and business figures, and shaking up the most potent political force in Spain. The Socialists were eventually defeated in 1996, although still surviving the onslaught thanks to the personal credibility of their charismatic leader.

Why and how this judicial/media anti-Socialist barrage happened in Spain is a complex matter that has not been brought to public light as yet. There was, in any case, a combination of several factors reinforcing each other: the illegal financing of the Socialist party, which involved several members of its leadership in setting up a network of shadow businesses; the actual corruption, and unlawful actions, of several high-ranking members of the Socialist administration, and of many local Socialist bosses; the exasperation of some groups against the government (some fringe businessmen, including a financial tycoon expropriated by the Socialists; some ultra-conservative forces; probably some elements of the integrist wing of the Catholic Church; some special interests; disaffected journalists who felt marginalized by Socialist power); the internal in-fighting in the Socialist party, with several leaders leaking information against each other to undermine the credibility of their rivals in the eyes of Felipe Gonzalez, the undisputed leader above the fray; the fight between two major financial groups, one of them representing traditional Spanish finance, close to the economic team of the Socialist government, the other organized around an outsider trying to make inroads into the system, and attempting alliances with some Socialist factions against others; a battle between media groups, jockeying for control of the new media system in Spain; personal vendettas, as the one by the editor of the most militantly anti-Socialist newspaper, convinced that he had lost his job as a result of government pressures; and a more complex, diffused opinion in the media world, and in other circles of Spanish life, according to which Socialist dominance was excessive, and the arrogance of some Socialist leaders intolerable, so that informed social elites should react and expose the true face of the Socialists to a seduced electorate which, in its majority, kept voting Socialist in four consecutive elections. Thus, ultimately, and regardless of personal motivation or specific business interests, the media asserted their power collectively, and, in alliance with the judiciary, made sure that the Spanish political class, including the conservatives (*Partido Popular*), learned the lesson for the future. While it is indisputable that there was unlawful behavior and a significant level of corruption in the Socialist administration and in the Socialist party, what really matters for our analytical purpose is the use of scandal politics in and by the media as the fundamental weapon utilized by political actors, business interests, and social groups to fight one another. So doing, they transformed for ever Spanish politics by making it dependent upon the media.

What is characteristic of scandal politics is that all political actors practicing it become entrapped by the system, often reversing roles: today's hunter is tomorrow's game. A case in point is the political adventure of Berlusconi in Italy. The facts are known: he parlayed his control of all three private TV networks into mounting a devastating campaign against the Italian corrupt political system.[78] Then, he created, in three months, an *ad hoc* "party" (*Forza Italia*, named after the fans' rallying cry for the Italian national football team), and, in alliance with the neo-Fascist party and the Northern League, won the 1994 general election and became Prime Minister. Control of government gave him, theoretically, authority over the three other, government-owned, TV networks. Yet, the autonomy of the media, and of journalists, was strongly asserted. In spite of his overwhelming presence in the media business (in newspapers and magazines, as well as in television), as soon as Berlusconi became Prime Minister, the judiciary and the media, again together, launched an all-out assault on Berlusconi's financial frauds and bribery schemes, undermining his business, bringing some of his associates to justice, indicting Berlusconi himself, and ultimately damaging his image in such a way

[78] Walter (1994).

that parliament censored his government. Then, in 1996 the electorate rejected Berlusconi, electing instead *Il Ulivo*'s center-left coalition, whose main component, the ex-Communist, now Socialist, *Partito Democratico di Sinistra*, had not yet been in the national government, and thus had salvaged its reputation.

The extremely important lesson of this development in Italian politics is that overwhelming business influence in the media is not tantamount to political control in informational politics. The media system, with its symbiotic linkages to the judiciary and prosecutorial institutions of democracy, sets its own pace, and receives signals from the whole spectrum of the political system, to transform them into sales and influence, regardless of the origin and destination of political impacts. The golden rule is that what is more valuable is what makes the greater impact on any given situation. Once a politician, or party, becomes irrelevant – they are no longer news matter. The political system becomes engulfed in the endless turbulence of media reporting, leaking, counter-leaking, and scandal-making. To be sure, some daring political strategists try to ride the tiger, by positioning themselves in the media business, by making alliances, by targeting and timing informational strikes. This is exactly what Berlusconi tried. His fate ended up being similar to the fate of those financial speculators who pretended to know the course of navigation in unpredictable, global financial markets. In scandal politics, as in other domains of the network society, the power of flows overwhelms the flows of power.

The Crisis of Democracy

Let us bring together the various threads we have identified concerning the transformation of the nation-state, and of the political process in contemporary societies. When weaved into a historical framework, they reveal the crisis of democracy as we have known it in the past century [79]

The nation-state, defining the domain, procedures, and object of citizenship, has lost much of its sovereignty, undermined by the dynamics of global flows and trans-organizational networks of wealth, information, and power. Particularly critical for its legitimacy crisis is the state's inability to fulfill its commitments as a welfare state, because of the integration of production and consumption in a globally interdependent system, and the related process of capitalist restructuring.

[79]   Minc (1993); Guehenno (1993); Patterson (1993); Ginsborg (1994); Touraine (1995b); Katznelson (1996); Weisberg (1996).

Indeed, the welfare state, in its different manifestations, depending on the history of each society, was a critical source of political legitimacy in the reconstitution of government institutions after the Great Depression of 1930s, and World War II.[80] The rejection of Keynesianism, and the decline of the labor movement, may accentuate the demise of the sovereign nation-state because of the weakening of its legitimacy.

The (re)construction of political meaning on the basis of specific identities fundamentally challenges the very concept of citizenship. The state could only shift the source of its legitimacy from representing people's will and providing for their well-being, to asserting collective identity, by identifying itself with communalism to the exclusion of other values and of minorities' identities. This is indeed the source of fundamentalist nationalist, ethnic, territorial, or religious states, which seem to emerge from current political crises of legitimacy. I contend that they cannot, and will not, sustain democracy (that is, liberal democracy) because the very principles of representation between the two systems (national citizenship, singular identity) are contradictory.

To the crisis of legitimacy of the nation-state we must add the crisis of credibility of the political system, based on open competition between political parties. Captured into the media arena, reduced to personalized leadership, dependent on technologically sophisticated manipulation, pushed into unlawful financing, driven by and toward scandal politics, the party system has lost its appeal and trustworthiness, and, for all practical purposes, is a bureaucratic remainder deprived of public confidence.[81]

As a result of these three convergent and interacting processes, public opinion, and citizens' individual and collective expressions, display a growing and fundamental disaffection *vis à vis* parties, politicians, and professional politics. Thus, in the United States, according to a Times Mirror Center survey in September 1994: "Thousands of interviews with American voters this summer find no clear direction in the public's political thinking other than frustration with the current system and an eager responsiveness to alternative political solutions and appeals."[82] In 1994, 82 percent of respondents to a national Harris Poll did not think that the government represented their interests (against 72 percent in 1980), and 72 percent considered that in fact the government represented interest groups

---

[80] Navarro (1995).
[81] West (1993); Anderson and Comiller (1994). Mouffe (1995); Navarro (1995); Salvati (1995); Balz and Brownstein (1996).
[82] Quoted by Balz and Brownstein (1996: 28).

Question: Do you approve or disapprove of the way Bill Clinton is handling his job as president?

United States

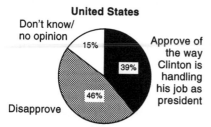

Don't know/ no opinion 15%

Approve of the way Clinton is handling his job as president 39%

Disapprove 46%

Note: In a CBS News/*New York Times* survey conducted just before the November 1992 election, 37% of respondents said they approved of the way Bush was handling his job as president, 56% disapproved.
Source: Survey by CBS News/*New York Times*, June 21–24, 1993

Question: Are you satisfied or dissatisfied with Mr Major as prime minister?

Great Britain

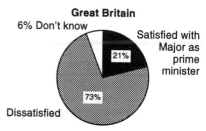

6% Don't know

Satisfied with Major as prime minister 21%

Dissatisfied 73%

Note: The percentage saying they are satisfied is the lowest ever for any British prime minister for which polling data is available.
Source: Survey by Social Surveys (Gallup Poll) Ltd, May 26–31, 1993

Question: Are you satisfied or dissatisfied with Mr François Mitterrand as president of the Republic?

France

No opinion 11%

Satisfied with Mitterrand as president of the Republic 39%

Dissatisfied 50%

Source: Survey by the Institut Français d'Opinion Publique et d'Étude de Marchés (IFOP) for *Le Journal du Dimanche*, May 6–13, 1993

Question: Do you approve or disapprove of the way Brian Mulroney is handling his job as prime minister?

Canada

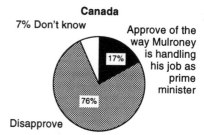

7% Don't know

Approve of the way Mulroney is handling his job as prime minister 17%

Disapprove 76%

Note: Brian Mulroney was succeeded as Prime Minister by Kim Campbell, June 25, 1993.
Source: Survey by Gallup Canada, January 13–18, 1993

Question: Do you support the Miyazawa cabinet?

Japan

No answer/ other 14%

Yes, support the Miyazawa cabinet 26%

Do not 59%

Source: Survey by the *Yomiuri Shimbun*, May 1993

Question: Are you happy or unhappy with the job done, in the last month, by Guiliano Amato as president of the cabinet?

Italy

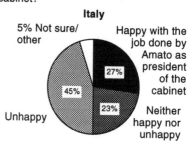

5% Not sure/ other

Happy with the job done by Amato as president of the cabinet 27%

Neither happy nor unhappy 23%

Unhappy 45%

Source: Survey by DOXA, January 19, 1993

Figure 6.3 (opposite)   Approval ratings for various governments,
c. 1993
Source: Compiled and elaborated by Roper Center of Public Opinion
and Polling (1995)

(with 68 percent indentifying these groups as business interests);
along the same lines, a 1995 Roper Poll found that 68 percent of
respondents thought that there were not many differences between
Republicans and Democrats, and 82 percent wished that a new party
could be created.[83] Figure 6.3 displays widespread dissatisfaction with
governments of all political affiliations in six of seven countries,
members of the G-7 club, as reflected in public opinion polls.

However, this skepticism toward mainstream parties and politics
does not necessarily mean that people do not vote any longer, or that
they do not care about democracy. For that matter, in much of the
world, democracy has been attained only recently after a tremendous
effort, conquered with blood, sweat, and tears, so that people are not
easily ready to give up hope. Indeed, when people perceive the chance
of meaningful political action, they mobilize enthusiastically, as they
did around the election of Fernando Henrique Cardoso to the presidency of Brazil in 1994. Even in veteran democracies, where the rituals
of free elections have been practiced for two hundred years (except
for half of the people, that is women), political participation goes up
and down. People do not vote much in the United States (49 percent
in the 1996 presidential election, 54 percent in 1992, 51 percent in
1984, down from 68 percent in 1968), but participation rates are
consistently high (between 65 percent and 80 percent) in France,
Italy, Spain, Germany and most European countries (see table 6.4).
Yet, Europeans do not trust their politicians more than Americans
do.[84] It would seem than individualism, rather than political disaffection, accounts for American exceptionalism.[85]

There are, nevertheless, powerful expressions of growing political
alienation worldwide, as people observe the state's incapacity to solve
their problems, and experience cynical instrumentalism from professional politicians. One of these expressions is the increasing support
for a variety of "third party" forces, and for regional parties, since, in
most political systems, the final showdown to seize national executive
power takes place between two candidates, representing two broad
coalitions. Thus, voting for someone else becomes a protest vote

[83]   Cited by Navarro (1995: 55).
[84]   *Eurobarometer* (various years).
[85]   Lipset (1996).

Table 6.4   Turnout in elections to lower house of parliament: recent figures compared to rates for the 1970s and 1980s (%)

| | 1970s–1980s | | 1990s |
	Average turnout	*Turnout range*	*(one election)*
France (1st ballot)	76.0	66.2–83.2	68.9 (1993)
Germany	88.6	84.3–91.1	79.1 (1994)
Italy	91.4	89.0–93.2	86.4 (1992)
Japan	71.2	67.9–74.6	67.3 (1993)
Spain	73.9	70.6–77.0	77.3 (1993)
United Kingdom	74.8	72.2–78.9	75.8 (1992)
United States	42.6	33.4–50.9	50.8 (1992)
			36.0 (1994)

Sources: 1970s and 1980s: *The International Almanac of Electoral History* (rev. 3rd edn, Thomas T. Mackie and Richard Rose, Washington, DC: Macmillan Press, 1991); recent elections: *The Statesman's Yearbook, 1994–1995 and 1995–1996* (Brian Hunter, ed., New York: St Martin's Press, 1994, 1995); United States: *Vital Statistics on American Politics,* 4th edn, Harold W. Stanley and Richard G. Niemi, Washington DC: CQ Press, 1994) Compiled by Sandra Moog

against the overall political system, and maybe the attempt to help build a different alternative, often on a local or regional basis. Sandra Moog and I have built an index of voting for mainstream parties for some major democracies in different continents, measuring its evolution at several points in time in the 1980s and 1990s.[86] As shown in figure 6.4, the overall trend seems to confirm the declining proportion of the vote for mainstream parties over time. There are, however, some inflexions of the tendency, when one party succeeds in mobilizing its electorate, as did the Conservative party in Spain in the 1996 election. Specific political rhythms introduce variations in the overall trend. Yet, at the macro-level, the predicted trend seems to appear distinctly. While the majority of voters are still geared toward instrumental voting – that is, supporting candidates with a real chance of being elected – the erosion of this support affects the very predictability of electoral chances, so reinforcing the crisis of credibility of major coalitions, and eventually precipitating their demise, as happened in Italian politics (Christian Democrats, Socialists), and in American politics (Democratic Congress) in 1994. However, Zaller and Hunt, in their excellent analysis of Ross Perot's 1992 presidential campaign, warn of the limits of "third party" politics: As they write:

[86]   For sources, definitions and methods of calculation, see the Methodological Appendix.

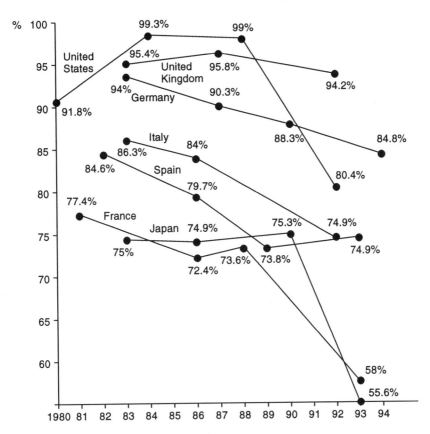

Figure 6.4 Level of support for mainstream parties in national
elections, 1980–94 (US figures are for presidential elections; all
others are returns for lower house of parliament)
Source: see Methodological Appendix for figures and sources; compiled
and elaborated by Sandra Moog

Even in a mass democracy such as the United States, great skill as
a communicator is insufficient to win the nation's highest office.
One must still pass muster with the powers that be. The American
system of choosing presidents, despite the inherent volatility of a
nomination process that gives final authority to masses of volatile
and often politically inattentive voters, remains a powerful institutional force capable of forcing candidates to run through it
rather than around it.[87]

---

[87]   Zaller and Hunt (1994: 386).

The question is: until when? How much distance, and for how long, can be kept between the yearning of the electorate for alternative political options and their framing by the institutions of mainstream politics, in a situation where media politics can launch (and extinguish) new stars in a matter of hours?

Nevertheless, for the time being, most people in most countries are still constrained in their choices by the weight of institutions, political machines, and political traditions. Under these circumstances, an additional indicator of political disaffection with the traditional party system is the volatility of the electorate worldwide, bringing down governing parties, and accelerating the tempo of political alternation. In 1992–96, voters switched from Republicans to Democrats in the American presidency in 1992, from Democrats to Republicans in the congressional elections in 1994, and back to Clinton (after he emphasized his "new Democrat" look) in 1996 (but not back to Democrats in Congress); from Socialists to Gaullists in the French presidency; from center to right, then to center-left in Italy; from Socialists+ Nationalists to Conservatives+Nationalists in Spain; from Conservatives to a multiple coalition, then to Conservatives in minority government in Japan; from Socialists to Conservatives, then back to Socialists in Greece; from nowhere to Fernando H. Cardoso in Brazil; from democrats to Communists in the Russian parliamentary elections, then back to Yeltsin in the presidential elections; and, most likely, from Tories to Labour in the UK in 1997. Thus, people, discontented and disheartened, switch from one option to another at increasing speed, experiencing, in most cases, successive disappointments. With each new one, morale deteriorates, cynicism sets in, and hope fades away.

As a result of the trends presented above, another major feature is taking place: the growing fragmentation of the political system. Thus, if the 1996 Indian elections probably marked the end of an era of Congress Party dominance, Hindu nationalists, the winners of the election, could not hold onto government, having only one-third of the seats. A miscellaneous "united front" was constituted in May 1996 to bring into government an uncertain alliance of left parties, regional parties, and lower-caste parties, whose emergence in the election was the main reason for the crisis of the political regime. India, whose democratic political stability was the envy of the developing world, may have entered a condition of structural political fragmentation, and of regionalization of politics.

Among major democracies, only Germany seemed to keep political stability in the 1990s, but this was before Kohl undertook in 1996, under the pressures of global competition, the retrenchment of the German welfare state, and the reform of industrial co-determination, at the heart of the German political consensus.

As a consequence of these developments, we do not witness, in general terms, people's withdrawal from the political scene, but the penetration of the political system by symbolic politics, single-issue mobilizations, localism, referendum politics, and, above all, *ad hoc* support for personalized leadership. With political parties fading away, it is the time of saviors. This introduces systemic unpredictability. It could turn out to be the regeneration of politics, as with Fernando Henrique Cardoso, or maybe with Colin Powell (it would be ironic, but historically stimulating, to see a Republican African-American, the son of a Jamaican immigrant, re-legitimizing American politics). Or, else, it could end up in a demagogic flare up, disintegrating political institutions, jeopardizing world stability, or launching a new assault on reason.

Whatever the future, what the observation of the present seems to indicate is that, under different forms, and through the variety of processes I have outlined in this and previous chapters, we are witnessing the fragmentation of the state, the unpredictability of the political system, and the singularization of politics. Political freedom may still exist, as people will continue to fight for it. But political democracy, as conceived by the liberal revolutions of the eighteenth century, and as diffused throughout the world in the twentieth century, has become an empty shell. Not that it was just "formal democracy": democracy lives out of these very "forms," such as secret, universal suffrage, and respect of civil liberties.[88] But the new institutional, cultural, and technological conditions of democratic exercise have made obsolete the existing party system, and the current regime of competitive politics, as adequate mechanisms of political representation in the network society. People know it, and feel it, but they also know, in their collective memory, how important it is to prevent tyrants from occupying the vanishing space of democratic politics. Citizens are still citizens but they are uncertain of which city, and of whose city.

Conclusion: Reconstructing Democracy?

These are alarming words, indeed. It would be tempting at this point to seize the opportunity to lecture you on my personal model of informational democracy. Do not worry. For reasons that I will present in the general conclusion to this book (in volume III), I have forbidden myself normative prescriptions, and political admonition.

---

[88] Katznelson (1996).

However, in strict fairness to political hope, I will conclude by commenting on potential paths of democratic reconstruction, *as they manifest themselves in the observed practice of societies in the mid-1990s*, regardless of my personal views on their goodness. Since, fortunately, embryos of new democratic politics are numerous, and diverse around the world, I will restrain my commentary to three trends that I consider particularly relevant for the future of informational politics.

The first one is the re-creation of the local state. In many societies around the world, local democracy, for reasons exposed in chapter 5, appears to be flourishing, at least in terms relative to national political democracy. This is particularly true when regional and local governments cooperate with each other, and when they extend their reach to neighborhood decentralization, and citizen participation. When electronic means (computer-mediated communication, or local radio and television stations) are added to expand participation and consultation by citizens (for example, in Amsterdam, or in Fukuoka Prefecture), new technologies contribute to enhanced participation in local government. Experiences of local self-management, such as the one developed by the municipality of Cuiaba, in the Brazilian Mato Grosso, show the possibility of reconstructing links of political representation to *share* (if not control) the challenges of economic globalization and political unpredictability. There are obvious limits to this localism since it accentuates the fragmentation of the nation-state. But, strictly in terms of observation, the most powerful trends legitimizing democracy in the mid-1990s are taking place, worldwide, at the local level.[89]

A second perspective often discussed in the literature,[90] and in the media,[91] is the opportunity offered by electronic communication to enhance political participation and horizontal communication among citizens. Indeed, on-line information access, and computer-mediated communication facilitate the diffusion and retrieval of information, and offer possibilities for interaction and debate in an autonomous, electronic forum, bypassing the control of the media. Indicative referendums on a variety of issues may provide a useful tool, when used carefully without yielding to the oversimplified frame of referendum politics. More importantly, citizens could form, and are forming, their own political and ideological constellations, circumventing established political structures, thus creating a flexible,

---

[89]   Cooke (1994); Graham (1995); Ziccardi (1995); Borja and Castells (1996).
[90]   Ganley (1991).
[91]   *The Economist* (1995a).

adaptable political field. However, serious criticism may be addressed, and has indeed been addressed to the prospects of electronic democracy.[92] On the one hand, should this form of democratic politics emerge as an important instrument of debate, representation, and decision, it would certainly institutionalize a form of "Athenian democracy," both nationally, and internationally. That is, while a relatively small, educated, and affluent elite in a few countries and cities would have access to an extraordinary tool of information and political participation, actually enhancing citizenship, the uneducated, switched off masses of the world, and of the country, would remain excluded from the new democratic core, as were slaves and barbarians at the onset of democracy in classical Greece. On the other hand, the volatility of the medium could induce an accentuation of "show politics," with the flaring up of fashions, and myths, once the rationalizing power of parties and institutions was bypassed by the flows of suddenly convergent and divergent political moods. In other words, on-line politics could push the individualization of politics, and of society, to a point where integration, consensus, and institution building would become dangerously difficult to reach.

To explore the matter, my students in the graduate seminar on Sociology of the Information Society at Berkeley proceeded with some on-line observation of the Internet in the spring of 1996. The results of their analysis reveal some interesting trends. Thus, Klinenberg and Perrin observed that, in the 1996 American presidential Republican primaries, Internet usage played an important role in diffusing information about the candidates (Dole), as well as in reaching out for support (Buchanan), and contributions (all candidates).[93] Yet, the channels of communication were monitored and tightly controlled, thus becoming, in fact, one-way communication systems, more powerful and flexible than television, but not more open to citizen participation. This could change in the future, but it seems that the logic of informational politics restrains openness of the system, since candidates must control the messages in their networks, not to be made responsible for positions or statements that are prejudicial, or out of touch with the electorate. Tight political control and electronic openness seem to be mutually exclusive in the present system. Thus, as long as political parties and organized campaigns control the political procedure, electronic citizen participation will take a back seat in informational politics, as it refers to formal elections and decision-making.

---

[92]   High Level Experts Group (1996).
[93]   Klinenberg and Perrin (1996).

Yet, on the other hand, Steve Bartz on the environmental movement, and Matthew Zook on the American militia movement, found a process of empowerment for grassroots groups using the Internet as an instrument of information, communication, and organization.[94] It appears that it is in the realm of symbolic politics, and in the development of issue-oriented mobilizations by groups and individuals outside the mainstream political system that new electronic communication may have the most dramatic effects. The impact of such developments on democracy is unclear. On the one hand, allowing issue mobilization to bypass formal politics may undermine even further the institutions of democracy. On the other hand, if political representation and decision-making could find a linkage with these new sources of inputs from concerned citizens, without yielding to a technologically savvy elite, a new kind of civil society could be reconstructed, thus allowing for electronic grassrooting of democracy.

The development of symbolic politics, and of political mobilization around "non-political" causes, electronically or otherwise, is the third trend that could be in the process of reconstructing democracy in the network society. Humanitarian causes, such as the ones supported by Amnesty International, *Medecins sans frontières*, Greenpeace, Oxfam, Food First, and thousands and thousands of both local and global, activist groups and non-governmental organizations around the world, are the most powerful proactive, mobilizing factor in informational politics.[95] These mobilizations develop around issues that receive a wide consensus, and that are not necessarily aligned with one or another political party. Indeed, in terms of official position, most political parties apparently support most of these causes. And most humanitarian organizations abstain from supporting a given political party, except on specific issues at specific times. Most of these mobilizations are in between social movements and political actions, since they address themselves to citizens, asking people to put pressure on public institutions or private firms that can make a difference on the particular matter targeted by the mobilization. In other instances, they do appeal to people's solidarity directly. Ultimately, their horizon is to act on the political process; that is, to influence the management of society by the representatives of society. But they do not necessarily, and in fact not frequently, use the channels of political representation and decision-making, for instance by electing their candidates to office. These forms of political mobilization, which could be defined as issue-oriented, non-

---

[94] Bartz (1996); Zook (1996).
[95] Guehenno (1993).

partisan politics, seem to win increasing legitimacy in all societies, and to condition the rules and outcomes of formal political competition. They re-legitimize the concern with public affairs in people's minds and lives. They do so by introducing new political processes, and new political issues, thus furthering the crisis of classic liberal democracy while fostering the emergence of the yet to be discovered, informational democracy.

Conclusion: Social Change in the Network Society

At the dawn of the Information Age, a crisis of legitimacy is voiding of meaning and function the institutions of the industrial era. Bypassed by global networks of wealth, power, and information, the modern nation-state has lost much of its sovereignty. By trying to intervene strategically in this global scene the state loses capacity to represent its territorially rooted constituencies. In a world where multilateralism is the rule, the separation between nations and states, between the politics of representation and the politics of intervention disorganizes the political accounting unit on which liberal democracy was built and came to be exercised in the past two centuries. The privatization of public agencies and the demise of the welfare state, while alleviating societies from some bureaucratic burden, worsen living conditions for the majority of citizens, break the historic social contract between capital, labor, and the state, and remove much of the social safety net, the nuts and bolts of legitimate government for common people. Torn by internationalization of finance and production, unable to adapt to networking of firms and individualization of work, and challenged by the degendering of employment, the labor movement fades away as a major source of social cohesion and workers' representation. It does not disappear, but it becomes, primarily, a political agent integrated into the realm of public institutions. Mainstream churches, practicing a form of secularized religion dependent either on the state or on the market, lose much of their capacity to enforce behavior in exchange for providing solace, and selling heavenly real estate. The challenge to patriarchalism, and the crisis of the patriarchal family, disturb the orderly sequence of transmitting cultural codes from generation to generation, and shake the foundations of personal security, thus forcing men, women, and children to find new ways of living. Political ideologies that emanate from industrial institutions and organizations, from nation-state-based democratic liberalism to labor-based socialism, find themselves deprived of actual meaning in the new social context. Therefore, they lose their appeal, and, trying to survive, they engage in a series of endless adaptations, running behind the new society, as dusty flags of forgotten wars.

As a result of these convergent processes, the *sources* of what I call in chapter 1 *legitimizing identities* are drained away. The institutions and organizations of civil society that were constructed around the democratic state, and around the social contract between capital and labor, have become, by and large, empty shells, decreasingly able to relate to people's lives and values in most societies. It is indeed a tragic irony that when most countries in the world finally fought their way to access the institutions of liberal democracy (in my view, the foundation of all political democracy), these institutions are so distant from the structure and processes that really matter that they appear to most people as a sarcastic grimace in the new face of history. In this end of millennium, the king and the queen, the state and the civil society, are both naked, and their children-citizens are wandering around a variety of foster homes.

The dissolution of shared identities, which is tantamount to the dissolution of society as a meaningful social system, may well be the state of affairs in our time. Nothing says that new identities have to emerge, new social movements have to re-create society, and new institutions will be rebuilt toward the *lendemains qui chantent*. At first sight, we are witnessing the emergence of a world exclusively made of markets, networks, individuals, and strategic organizations, apparently governed by patterns of "rational expectations" (the new, influential economic theory), except when these "rational individuals" suddenly shoot their neighbor, rape a little girl, or spread nerve gas in the subway. No need for identities in this new world: basic instincts, power drives, self-centered strategic calculations, and, at the macro-social level, "the clear features of a barbarian nomadic dynamic, of a Dionysian element threatening to inundate all borders and rendering international political-legal and civilizational norms problematic."[1] A world whose counterpoint could be, as we are seeing already in a number of countries, a nationalist reassertion by the remnants of state structures, abandoning any pretension to legitimacy, and clawing back from history to the principle of power for the sake of power, sometimes wrapping it in nationalist rhetoric. In the landscapes we have crossed in the first two volumes of this book, we have perceived the seeds of a society whose *Weltanschauung* would split between the old logic of *Macht* and a new logic of *Selbstanschauung*. [2]

[1]   Panarin (1994: 37).
[2]   *Macht* = strong power; *Weltanschauung* = culture-centered view of the world; *Selbstanschauung* (proposed neologism) = self-centered view of the world.

However, we have also observed the emergence of powerful resistance identities, which retrench in communal heavens, and refuse to be flushed away by global flows and radical individualism. They build their communes around the traditional values of God, nation, and the family, and they secure the enclosures of their encampments with ethnic emblems and territorial defenses. Resistance identities are not limited to traditional values. They can also be built by, and around, proactive social movements, which choose to establish their autonomy in their communal resistance as long as they are not powerful enough to mount an assault on the oppressive institutions they oppose. This is, by and large, the case of the women's movement, building women's spaces where a new anti-patriarchal consciousness may rise; and it is certainly the case of the sexual liberation movements, whose spaces of freedom, from bars to neighborhoods, are essential devices of self-recognition. Even the environmental movement, whose ultimate horizon is cosmological, more often than not starts in the backyards and communities around the world, protecting spaces before engaging in the conquest of time.

Thus, resistance identities are as pervasive in the network society as are the individualistic projects resulting from the dissolution of former legitimizing identities that used to constitute the civil society of the industrial era. However, these identities resist, they barely communicate. They do not communicate with the state, except to struggle and negotiate on behalf of their specific interests/values. They rarely communicate with each other because they are built around sharply distinct principles, defining an "in" and an "out." And because the communal logic is the key to their survival, individual self-definitions are not welcome. Thus, on the one hand, the dominant, global elites inhabiting the space of flows tend to consist of identity-less individuals ("citizens of the world"); while, on the other hand, people resisting economic, cultural, and political disfranchisement tend to be attracted to communal identity.

We should, then, add another layer to the social dynamics of the network society. Together with state apparatuses, global networks, and self-centered individuals, there are also communes formed around *resistance identity*. However, all these elements do not glue together, their logic excludes each other, and their coexistence is unlikely to be peaceful.

The key issue becomes then the emergence of *project identities* (see chapter 1), potentially able to reconstruct a new civil society of sorts, and, eventually, a new state. On this matter, I will not be prescriptive or prophetic, but, rather, I will elaborate on the provisional results of my observation of social movements and political processes. My analysis does not preclude the possibility that social movements quite

different from those considered here may have a major role in constituting future society. But, as of 1996, I have not detected their
signals.

New *project identities* do not seem to emerge from former identities
of the industrial era's civil society, but from a development of current
resistance identities. There are, I believe, theoretical reasons, as well as
empirical arguments, for such a trajectory in the formation of new historical subjects. But, before proposing some ideas on the matter, let
me clarify how project identities may emerge from the resistance
identities we have observed.

The fact that a commune is built around a resistance identity does
not mean that it will likely evolve toward building a project identity. It
may well remain as a defensive commune. Or else, it may become an
interest group, and join the logic of generalized bargaining, the dominant logic of the network society. Yet, in other cases, resistance
identities may generate project identities, aiming at the transformation of society as a whole, in continuity with the values of communal
resistance to dominant interests enacted by global flows of capital,
power, and information.

Religious communes may develop into religious fundamentalist
movements aimed at re-moralizing society, re-establishing godly, eternal values, and embracing the whole world, or at least the nearby
neighborhood, in a community of believers, thus founding a new
society.

The trajectory of nationalism in the Information Age is more undetermined, according to observation of recent experience. On the one
hand, it can lead to retrenchment into a reconstructed nation-state,
re-legitimizing it on behalf of the nation, rather than of the state. On
the other hand, it may supersede the modern nation-state, by affirming nations beyond the state, and building multilateral networks of
political institutions in a variable geometry of shared sovereignty.

Ethnicity, while being an essential ingredient of both oppression
and liberation, seems to be usually framed in support of other communal identities (religious, national, territorial), rather than
inducing either resistance or new projects by itself.

Territorial identity is at the root of the worldwide surge of local and
regional governments as significant actors in both representation and
intervention, better suited to adapt to the endless variation of global
flows. The reinvention of the city-state is a salient characteristic of this
new age of globalization, as it was related to the rise of a trading,
international economy at the origin of the Modern Age.

Women's communes, and the spaces of sexual identity's freedom,
project themselves into society at large by undermining patriarchalism, and by reconstructing the family on a new, egalitarian basis that

implies the degendering of social institutions, in opposition to patriarchal capitalism and to the patriarchal state.

Environmentalism shifts from the defense of one's environment, health, and well-being, to the ecological project of integrating humankind and nature, on the basis of the socio-biological identity of the species, assuming humankind's cosmological meaning.

These identity projects emerge from communal resistance rather than from the reconstruction of institutions of civil society, because the crisis of these institutions, and the emergence of resistance identities, originate precisely from the new characteristics of the network society that undermine the former and induce the latter. Namely, globalization, capitalist restructuring, organizational networking, the culture of real virtuality, and the primacy of technology for the sake of technology, the key features of social structure in the Information Age, are the very sources of crisis of state and civil society as constituted in the industrial era. They are also the forces against which communal resistance is organized, with new identity projects potentially emerging around these resistances. Resistance and projects contradict the dominant logic of the network society by engaging defensive and offensive struggles around three foundational realms of this new social structure: space, time, and technology.

The communes of resistance defend their space, their places, against the placeless logic of the space of flows characterizing social domination in the Information Age (volume I, chapter 6). They claim their historic memory, and/or affirm the permanence of their values, against the dissolution of history in timeless time, and the celebration of the ephemeral in the culture of real virtuality (volume I, chapter 7). They use information technology for people's horizontal communication, and communal prayer, while rejecting the new idolatry of technology, and preserving transcendent values against the deconstructing logic of self-regulating computer networks.

Ecologists affirm the control of uses of space on behalf of both people and nature against the a-natural, abstract logic of the space of flows. They advance the cosmological vision of glacial time, integrating the human species into its evolving environment, and reject the annihilation of time by de-sequencing, a logic embedded in timeless time (volume I, chapter 7). And they support the use of science and technology for life, while opposing the domination of life by science and technology.

Feminists and sexual identity movements affirm the control of their most immediate spaces, their bodies, over their disembodiment in the space of flows, influenced by patriarchalism, where reconstructed images of the woman, and fetishes of sexuality, dissolve their humanity and deny their identity. They also fight for the control of their time, as the timeless logic of the network society piles up roles and functions over women without adapting their new lives to new timing; so that alienated timing becomes the most concrete expression of the chores of being a liberated woman in a non-liberated social organization. Women and sexual identity movements also aim at using technology to enhance their rights (for instance, their reproductive rights, and the right to control their bodies), against the patriarchal uses of science and technology, as expressed in the submission of women to arbitrary medical rituals and prejudices; or in the temporary lack of will of some scientific institutions in fighting AIDS so long as it was considered to be a homosexual disease. At the moment when humankind reaches the technological frontier of the social control over the biological reproduction of the species, a fundamental battle is being fought between bodies as autonomous identities, and bodies as social artifacts. This is why identity politics start with our bodies.

Thus, the dominant logic of the network society triggers its own challenges, in the form of communal resistance identities, and of project identities potentially emerging from these spaces, *under conditions and through processes that are specific to each institutional and cultural context.* The resulting contradictory dynamics is at the heart of the historical process through which a new social structure, and the flesh and blood of our societies, are being constituted. Where is power in this social structure? And what is power under these historical conditions?

Power, as argued, and to some extent shown, in this and in volume I of this book, is no longer concentrated in institutions (the state), organizations (capitalist firms), or symbolic controllers (corporate media, churches). It is diffused in global networks of wealth, power, information, and images, which circulate and transmute in a system of variable geometry and dematerialized geography. Yet, it does not disappear. *Power still rules society; it still shapes, and dominates, us.* Not only because apparatuses of different kinds can still discipline bodies and silence minds. This form of power is, at the same time, eternal, and fading away. It is eternal because humans are, and will be, predators. But, in its current form of existence, it is fading away: the exercise of this kind of power is increasingly ineffective for the interests that it is supposed to serve. States can shoot, but because the profile of their enemies, and the whereabouts of their challengers, are increasingly unclear, they tend to shoot randomly, with the probability that they may shoot themselves in the process.

The new power lies in the codes of information and in the images of representation around which societies organize their institutions, and people build their lives, and decide their behavior. The sites of this power are people's minds. This is why power in the Information Age is at the same time identifiable and diffused. We know what it is, yet we cannot seize it because power is a function of an endless battle around the cultural codes of society. Whoever, or whatever, wins the battle of people's minds will rule, because mighty, rigid apparatuses will not be a match, in any reasonable timespan, for the minds mobilized around the power of flexible, alternative networks. But victories may be ephemeral, since the turbulence of information flows will keep codes in a constant swirl. This is why identities are so important, and ultimately, so powerful in this ever-changing power structure – because they build interests, values, and projects, around experience, and refuse to dissolve by establishing a specific connection between nature, history, geography, and culture. Identities anchor power in some areas of the social structure, and build from there their resistance or their offensives in the informational struggle about the cultural codes constructing behavior and, thus, new institutions.

Under these conditions, who are the subjects of the Information Age? We already know, or at least I suggest we know, the sources from which they are likely to emerge. I would also add that I think we know from where they are not likely to develop. For instance, the labor movement seems to be historically superseded. Not that it will entirely disappear (although it is dwindling down in much of the world), or that it has lost all relevance. In fact, labor unions are influential political actors in many countries. And in many instances they are the main, or the only, tools for workers to defend themselves against abuses from capital and from the state. Yet, because of the structural features and historical processes that I have tried to convey in the first two volumes of this book, the labor movement does not seem fit to generate by itself and from itself a project identity able to reconstruct social control and to rebuild social institutions in the Information Age. Labor militants will undoubtedly be a part of new, transformative social dynamics. I am less sure that labor unions will.

Political parties have also exhausted their potential as autonomous agents of social change, caught into the logic of informational politics, and with their main platform, the institutions of the nation-state, having lost much of its relevance. They are still, however, essential instruments in processing the demands of society, spearheaded by social movements, into the realms of national, international, and supranational polities. Indeed, while social movements will have to provide the new codes under which societies may be re-thought, and re-established, political parties of some kind (maybe under new, informational incarnations) are still crucial agencies in institutionalizing social transformation. They are influential brokers rather than powerful innovators.

Thus, social movements emerging from communal resistance to

globalization, capitalist restructuring, organizational networking, uncontrolled informationalism, and patriarchalism – that is, for the time being, ecologists, feminists, religious fundamentalists, nationalists, and localists – are the potential subjects of the Information Age. In what forms will they express themselves? My analysis here is necessarily more speculative, although I feel obliged to suggest some hypotheses, as grounded as possible on the observations reported in this volume.

The agencies voicing identity projects aimed at changing cultural codes must be symbol mobilizers. They ought to act on the culture of real virtuality that frames communication in the network society, subverting it on behalf of alternative values, and introducing codes emerging from autonomous identity projects. I have observed two main sorts of such potential agencies. The first I will call *the Prophets*. They are symbolic personalities whose role is not that of charismatic leaders, or of shrewd strategists, but to give a face (or a mask) to a symbolic insurgency, so that they speak on behalf of the insurgents. Thus, voiceless insurgents have a voice, and their identity may enter the realm of symbolic struggles, and stand a chance of seizing power – in people's minds. This is, of course, the case of Subcomandante Marcos, Mexico's *Zapatistas* leader. But also of *compadre* Palenque in La Paz–El Alto. Or of Asahara, the guru of the murderous Japanese cult. Or, to emphasize the diversity of expression of such potential oracles, the case of the Catalan nationalist leader, Jordi Pujol, whose moderation, rationality, and strategic wit often hide his patient determination to insert *Catalunya* as a nation among other European nations, speaking on its behalf, and reconstructing a Carolingian identity for *Catalunya*. He may be the voice of a new, original, state-less brand of nationalism in informational Europe. In another, different example, ecological consciousness is often represented by popular rock singers, such as Sting in his campaign to save Amazonia; or by movie stars, such as Brigitte Bardot, engaging in a crusade on behalf of animal rights. A different kind of prophet could be the neo-luddite Unabomber in America, linking up the anarchist tradition to violent defense of essential nature against the evils of technology. In the Islamic or Christian fundamentalist movements, a number of religious leaders (I will not name names) assume a similar leading role by interpreting the holy texts, thus restating God's truth in the hope it will reach, and touch, the minds and souls of would-be believers. Human rights movements are also often dependent on the agency of symbolic, uncompromising personalities, as is the case in the tradition of Russian dissidents, historically represented by Sakharov, and exemplified in the 1990s by Sergei Kovalov. I deliberately chose to mix the genres in my examples to indicate that there are "good" and "bad" prophets, depending on individual preferences, including my own. But they are all prophets in the sense that they declare the path, affirm the values, and act as symbol senders, becoming a symbol in themselves, so that the message is inseparable from the messenger. Historical transitions, often operated in the midst of crumbling institutions and exhausted political forms, have always been a time for prophets. And it should be even more so in the transition to the Information Age, that is, a social structure organized around information flows and symbol manipulation.

However, the second and *main agency* detected in our journey across the lands inhabited by social movements, is a *networking, decentered form of organization and intervention, characteristic of the new social movements*, mirroring, and counteracting, the networking logic of domination in the informational society. This is clearly the case in the environmentalist movement, built around national and international networks of decentralized activity. But I have also shown this to be the case among women's movements, insurgents against the global oruer, and religious fundamentalist movements. These networks do more than organizing activity and sharing information. *They are the actual producers, and distributors, of cultural codes.* Not only over the Net, but in their multiple forms of exchange and interaction. Their impact on society rarely stems from a concerted strategy, masterminded by a center. Their most successful campaigns, their most striking initiatives, often result from "turbulences" in the interactive network of multilayered communication – as in the production of a "green culture" by a universal forum of putting together experiences of preserving nature and surviving capitalism at the same time. Or in the demise of patriarchalism resulting from the exchange of women's experiences in women's groups, women's magazines, women's bookstores, women's films, women's clinics, and women's networks of support in raising children. It is this decentered, subtle character of *networks of social change* that makes it so difficult to perceive, and identify, new identity projects coming into being. Because our historical vision has become so used to orderly battalions, colorful banners, and scripted proclamations of social change, we are at a loss when confronted with the subtle pervasiveness of incremental changes of symbols processed through multiform networks, away from the halls of power. It is in these back alleys of society, whether in alternative electronic networks or in grassrooted networks of communal resistance, that I have sensed the embryos of a new society, labored in the fields of history by the power of identity.

To be continued.

Methodological Appendix

Appendix for Tables 5.1 and 5.2

The ratios and rates of change in tables 5.1 and 5.2 were calculated using data from a number of different statistical sources. The tables below have been organized in order to show the actual figures used in the calculations, as well as the ratios and rates of change that were calculated using these data. In those rows in which the original data are presented, sources have been indicated in the far right-hand column, using the following abbreviations:

GFSY	=	*Government Finance Statistics Yearbook*, vol. 18 (Washington DC: IMF, 1994)
IFSY	=	*International Financial Statistics Yearbook*, vol. 48 (Washington, DC: IMF, 1995)
EWY	=	*The Europa World Yearbook* (London: Europa Publications, 1982, 1985, 1995)
OECDNA	=	*National Accounts: Detailed Tables, 1980–1992*, vol. 2 (Paris: OECD, 1994)
WT	=	*World Tables, 1994* (The World Bank, Baltimore: The Johns Hopkins University Press, 1994)

The tables are arranged alphabetically by country. For each country, table 5.1A provides data, calculations and sources for table 5.1, and table 5.2A provides information for table 5.2.

Listed below are a few definitions and explanations of our calculations. Full definitions of all categories included in these tables, and descriptions of the original sources of data and methods of calculation, can be found in the appendices of the source materials.

Exchange rates	=	period averages of market exchange rates and official exchange rates.
Currency reserves	=	reserves, other than gold, at national valuation.
Exports	=	merchandise exports, f.o.b.
Foreign debt	=	distinguished from domestic debt according to the residence of the lender, where possible, and otherwise, according to the currency in which the debt instruments are denominated.
Domestic investment	=	calculated by multiplying each country's figures in the IFSY's "Investment as Percent of GDP" world table by that country's GDP. Investment comprises Gross Fixed Capital Formation and Increase in Stocks.

A (p) following a figure indicates that it is a preliminary figure.

An (f) indicates a final figure.

An * indicates that there is a change in methods of calculation in relation to previous years' figures.

Tables 5.1 and 5.2 and these appendices have been compiled and elaborated by Sandra Moog.

Germany: Table 5.1A Internationalization of the economy and public finance
(in billions of deutschmarks, unless otherwise indicated)

	1980	1991	1992	1993	1994	Rate of change 1980–93%	Source
Average exchange rate (DM per US $)	1.8177	1.6595	1.5617	1.6533	1.6228		IFSY'95
GDP (DM) (1990 DM)	1,470.0 (1,942.4)	2,647.6 (2,548.6)	2,813.0 (2,593.5)	2,853.7 (2,549.5)	2,977.7 (2,608.3)		IFSY'95 IFSY'95
Gov. foreign debt	38.05	243.21	311.73*	472.87(p)		538.5	IFSY'95
Gov. foreign debt/GDP (%)	2.6	9.2	28.5	16.6			
Gov. net foreign borrowing	20.84	45.05	68.52*	161.14(p)			IFSY'95
Total currency reserves minus gold (in millions of US $)	48,592	63,001	90,967	77,640	77,363		
Total currency reserves minus gold (in billions of DM)	88.33	104.55	121.25	128.36	125.54		
Gov. foreign debt/currency reserves (%)	43.1	232.6	257.1	368.4		325.3(p)	
Exports	350.33	665.81	658.47	628.39	677.81		IFSY'95
Gov. foreign debt/ exports (%)	10.9	36.5	47.3	75.3		590.8	
Gov. expenditures	447.54	860.74	1,022.95*	1,062.38(p)			IFSY'95

Gov. foreign debt/ gov. expenditures (%)	8.5	28.3	30.5	44.5		423.5(p)	IFSY'95
Gov. net foreign borrowing/ expenditures (%)	4.7	5.2	6.7	15.2		223.4	IFSY'95
Domestic investment (gr. fixed cap. form. + increases in stocks)	367.73	680.43	706.06	684.89	738.47		
Direct foreign investment abroad (in billions of US $)	4.7	23.72	19.67	14.48	14.65		
Direct foreign investment abroad (in billions of DM)	8.54	39.36	30.72	23.94	23.77		
Direct foreign investment abroad/ domestic investment (%)	2.3	5.8	4.4	3.5	3.2	52.2	
Inflow foreign direct investment (in billions of US $)	0.33	4.07	2.44	0.32	-3.02		IFSY'95
Inflow foreign direct investment (in billions of DM)	0.60	6.75	3.81	0.53	-4.90		
Inflow foreign direct investment/ domestic investment (%)	0.2	1.0	0.5	0.1	-0.7	-50.0	

Germany: Table 5.2A Government role in the economy and public finance
(in billions of deutschmarks, unless otherwise indicated)

	1980	1991	1992	1993	1994	Rate of change 1980–92(%)	Source
GDP	1,470.9	2,647.6	2,813.0	2,853.7	2,977.7		IFSY'95
Gov. expenditures	447.54	860.74	1,022.95*	1,062.38(p)			IFSY'95
Gov. expenditure/GDP (%)	30.4	32.5	36.4	37.2(p)		19.7	
Tax revenue (budgetary central gov.)	177.54	351.74	378.82(p)*				GFSY'90,'94
Tax revenue/GDP (%)	12.1	13.3	13.5(p)			11.6(p)	
Gov. budget deficit	–26.91	–62.29	–73.10*	–75.56(p)			IFSY'95
Gov. budget deficit/GDP (%)	1.8	2.3	2.6	2.6		44.4	
Gov. debt	235.77	680.81	801.57	902.52(p)			IFSY'95
Gov. debt/GDP (%)	16.0	25.7	28.5	31.6		78.1	
Gov. employment (employees in thousands)	3,929	4,307	4,340				OECDNA'92

Total employment	23,818	26,183	26,432				OECDNA'92
Gov. employment/ total employment (%)	16.5	16.5	16.4			-0.6	
Gov. consump.	298.0	466.5	502.9	508.5	520.2		IFSY'95
Private consump.	837.0	1,448.8	1,536.3	1,588.9	1,644.5		IFSY'95
Gov. consump./ private consump. (%)	35.6	32.2	32.7	32.0	31.6	-8.1	
Gov. capital expenditures	101.52	175.92	197.72	199.51			EWY'84,'95
Gross fixed capital formation	337.98	652.07	709.22	705.71			EWY'85,'95
Gov. capital expenditures/ gross fixed capital formation (%)	30.0	27.0	27.9	28.3		-7.0	

India: Table 5.1A Internationalization of the economy and public finance (in billions of rupees, unless otherwise indicated)

	1980	1991	1992	1993	1994	Rate of change 1980–93(%)	Source
Average exchange rate (rupees per US $)	8.659	22.724	25.918	30.493	31.374		IFSY'95
GDP (rupees) (1990 rupees)	1,360.1 (3,031.6)	6,160.6 (5,381.3)	7,028.3 (5,629.1)	7,863.6 (5,824.6)			IFSY'95
Gov. foreign debt	107.6	369.5	412.2(p)	464.5(f)			IFSY'95
Gov. foreign debt/GDP (%)	7.9	6.0	5.3(p)	5.9(f)		−25.3	
Gov. net foreign borrowing	7.0	54.2	46.8	55.8			
Total currency reserves minus gold (in milllions of US $)	6,944	3,627	5,757	10,199	19,698		IFSY'95
Total currency reserves minus gold (in billions of rupees)	60.13	82.42	149.21	311.00	618.01		

Gov. foreign debt/currency reserves (%)	178.9	448.3	276.3(p)	149.4(f)		-16.5	IFSY'95
Exports	67.52	401.23	508.71	656.89	785.94		IFSY'95
Gov. foreign debt/exports (%)	159.4	92.1	81.0(p)	70.7(f)		-55.6	IFSY'95
Gov. expenditures	180.3	1,050.5	1,209.6(p)	1,310.7(f)			
Gov. foreign debt/gov. expenditures (%)	59.7	35.2	34.1(p)	35.4(f)		-40.7	
Gov. net foreign borrowing/ expenditures (%)	3.9	5.2	3.9	4.3		10.3	
Domestic Investment (gr. fixed cap. form. + increases in stocks)	284.26	1,410.78	1,637.59	1,674.95			IFSY'95

India: Table 5.2A Government role in the economy and public finance
(in billions of rupees, unless otherwise indicated)

	1980	1991	1992	1993	1994	Rate of change 1980–92(%)	Source
GDP	1,360.1	6,160.6	7,028.3	7,863.6			IFSY'95
Gov. expenditures	180.3	1,050.5	1,209.6(p)	1,310.7(f)			IFSY'95
Gov. expenditures/ GDP (%)	13.3	17.1	17.2(p)	16.7(f)		29.3(p)	
Tax revenue (consolidated central gov.)	132.7	673.6	787.8(p)	848.7(f)			GFSY'90,'94
Tax revenue/ GDP (%)	9.8	10.9	11.2	10.8(f)		17.3(p)	
Gov. budget deficit	–88.6	–358.2	–366.5(p)	–372.0			IFSY'95
Gov. budget deficit/GDP (%)	6.5	5.8	5.2	4.7		–20.0(p)	
Gov. debt	561.0	3,312.0	3,714.0(p)	4,136.6(f)			IFSY'95
Gov. debt/GDP (%)	41.2	53.8	52.8(p)	52.6		28.2	
Gov. consump.	130.8	694.6	785.9	910.5			IFSY'95
Private consump.	992.9	3,848.0	4,245.6	4,795.9			IFSY'95

	13.2	18.1	18.5	19.0	40.2
Gov. consump./ private consump. (%)					
Gross fixed capital formation	262.8	1,367.8	1,511.8	1,643.8	EWY'85,'95

Japan: Table 5.1A Internationalization of the economy and public finance
(in billions of yen, unless otherwise indicated)

	1980	1991	1992	1993	1994	Rate of change 1980–93(%)	Source
Average exchange rate (yen per US $)	226.74	134.71	126.65	111.20	102.21		IFSY'95
GDP (yen) (1990 yen)	240,176 (271,500)	451,297 (422,720)	463,145 (428,210)	465,972	469,240		IFSY'95 (WT'94)
Gov. foreign debt	621	1,186 ('90)					IFSY'95
Gov. foreign debt/ GDP (%)	0.3	0.3				0.0('90)	
Total currency reserves minus gold (in millions of US $)	24,636	72,059	71,623	98,524	125,860		IFSY'95
Total currency reserves minus gold (in billions of yen)	5,586	9,707.1	9,071.1	10,956	12,864		
Gov. foreign debt/ currency reserves (%)	11.1	12.2				9.9('90)	
Exports	29,382	42,359	43,011	40,200	40,470		IFSY'95
Gov. foreign debt/ exports (%)	2.1	2.3('90)				9.5('90)	

Gov. expenditures	44,137						IFSY'95
Gov. foreign debt/gov. expenditures	1.4						
Domestic investment (gr. fixed cap. form. + increases in stocks)	77,337	146,672	144,038	139,326	135,610		IFSY'95
Direct foreign investment abroad (in billions of US $)	2.39	30.74	17.24	13.74	17.97		IFSY'95
Direct foreign investment abroad (in billions of yen)	541.91	4,140.99	2,183.45	1,527.89	1,836.71		
Direct foreign investment abroad/domestic investment (%)	0.7	2.8	1.5	1.1	1.4	57.1	
Inflow foreign direct investment (in billions of US $)	0.28	1.37	2.72	0.10	0.89		IFSY'95
Inflow foreign direct investment (in billions of yen)	63.49	184.55	344.49	11.12	90.97		
Inflow foreign direct investment/domestic investment (%)	0.08	0.13	0.23	0.01	0.07		(erratic)

Japan: Table 5.2A: Government role in the economy and public finance
(in billions of yen, unless otherwise indicated)

	1980	1991	1992	1993	1994	Rate of change 1980–92(%)	Source
GDP	240,176	451,297	463,145	465,972	469,240		IFSY'95
Gov. expenditures	44,137						IFSY'95
Gov. expenditures/ GDP (%)	0.18						
Tax revenue (budgetary central gov.)	26,392	58,730('90)					GFSY'90,'94
Tax revenue/GDP (%)	11.0	13.0('90)				18.2('90)	
Gov. budget deficit	16,872	6,781('90)					IFSY'95
Gov. budget deficit/GDP (%)	7.0	1.5				−78.6('90)	
Gov. debt	98,149	239,932('90)					IFSY'95
Gov. debt/GDP (%)	40.9	53.2('90)				30.1('90)	
Gov. employment (employees in thousands)	43,070	54,185	55,381				OECDNA'92
Total employment	3,911	3,960	3,975				OECDNA'92

Gov. employment/total employment (%)	9.1	7.3	7.2			−20.9	IFSY'95
Gov. consump.	23,568	41,232	43,258	44,666	46,108		IFSY'95
Private consump.	240,176	255,084	264,824	270,919	277,677		IFSY'95
Gov. consump./private consump. (%)	9.8	16.2	16.3	16.5	16.6	66.3	EWY'85,'95
Gross fixed capital formation	75,420	143,429	142,999	141,322			EWY'85,'95

Spain: Table 5.1A Internationalization of the economy and public finance
(in billions of pesetas, unless otherwise indicated)

	1980	1991	1992	1993	1994	Rate of change 1980–93(%)	Source
Average exchange rate (pesetas per US $)	71.70	103.91	102.38	127.26	133.96		IFSY'95
GDP (psts) (1990 psts)	15,168 (37,305)	54,901 (51,269)	59,002 (51,625)	60,904 (51,054)	64,673 (52,064)		IFSY'95
Gov. foreign debt	133.6	2,968.8	3,259.9	6,364.6	5,893.0		IFSY'95
Gov. foreign debt/GDP (%)	0.9	5.4	5.5	10.5	9.1	1,066.7	
Gov. net foreign borrowing		1,775.0	124.2	2,712.9	462.4		
Total currency reserves minus gold (in millions of US $)	11,863	65,822	45,504	41,045	41,569		IFSY'95
Total currency reserves minus gold (in billions of pesetas)	850.60	6,839.56	4,658.70	5,233.39	5,568.58		
Gov. foreign debt/currency reserves (%)	15.7	43.4	70.0	121.6	105.8	674.5	
Exports	1,493.2	6,225.7	6,605.7	7,982.3	9,795.2		IFSY'95
Gov. foreign debt/exports (%)	8.9	47.7	49.3	79.7	60.2	795.5	
Gov. expenditures	2,522.7	13,102.1	14,835.5	17,503.0	17,034.0		IFSY'95

							Source
Gov. foreign debt/ gov. expenditures (%)	5.3	22.7	22.0	36.4	34.6	586.8	IFSY'95
Gov. net foreign borrowing/ gov. expenditures (%)		13.5	0.9	15.5	2.7		IFSY'95
Domestic investment (gr. fixed cap. form. + increases in stocks)	3,518.98	13,505.65	13,393.45	12,119.90	12,740.85		
Direct foreign investment abroad (in millions of US $)	311	4,442	2,192	2,652	4,170		
Direct foreign investment abroad (in billions of pesetas)	22.30	461.57	224.42	337.49	558.61		
Direct foreign investment abroad/ domestic investment (%)	0.6	3.4	1.7	2.8	4.4	183.3	
Inflow foreign direct investment (in millions of US $)	1,493	12,493	13,276	8,144	9,700		IFSY'95
Inflow foreign direct investment (in billions of pesetas)	107.05	1,298.15	1,359.20	1,306.41	1,299.41		
Inflow foreign direct investment/ domestic investment (%)	3.0	9.6	10.1	8.6	10.2	236.7	

Spain: Table 5.2A Government role in the economy and public finance
(in billions of pesetas, unless otherwise indicated)

	1980	1991	1992	1993	1994	Rate of change 1980–92(%)	Source
GDP	15,168	54,901	59,002	60,904	64,673		IFSY'95
Gov. expenditures	2,552.7	13,102.1	14,835.5	17,503.0	17,034.0		IFSY'95
Gov. expenditures/ GDP (%)	16.8	23.9	25.1	28.7	26.3	49.4	
Tax revenue (budgetary central gov.)	1,602.4	9,530.6					GFSY'90,'94
Tax revenue/ GDP (%)	10.6	17.4				64.2('91)	
Gov. budget deficit	−555.8	−1,758.0	−2,523.5	−4,221.4	−4,943.9		IFSY'95
Gov. budget deficit/GDP (%)	3.7	3.2	4.3	6.9	7.6	16.2	
Gov. debt	2,316.7	20,837.3	23,552.7	28,708.9	34,448.0		IFSY'95
Gov. debt/GDP (%)	15.3	38.0	39.9	47.1	53.3	160.8	
Gov. employment (employees, in thousands)		2,041	2,084				OECDNA'92

							OECDNA'92
Total employment		9,789	9,616				
Gov. employment/ total employment (%)		20.8	21.7				
Private consump.	9,992	34,244	37,220	38,511	40,854		IFSY'95
Gov. consump.	2,008	8,882	10,027	10,669	10,992		IFSY'95
Gov. consump./ private consump. (%)	20.1	25.9	26.9	27.7	26.9	33.8	
Gross fixed capital formation	3,368	13,041	12,859	12,040	12,709		IFSY'95

United Kingdom: Table 5.1A Internationalization of the economy and public finance
(in billions of pounds sterling, unless otherwise indicated)

	1980	1991	1992	1993	1994	Rate of change 1980–93(%)	Source
Average exchange rate (pounds per US $)	0.4299	0.5652	0.5664	0.6658	0.6529		IFSY'95
GDP (pounds) (1990 pounds)	231.7 (423.49)	575.32 (540.31)	597.24 (537.45)	630.71 (549.59)	668.87 (570.72)		IFSY'95
Gov. foreign debt	10.14	28.45	34.89				IFSY'95
Gov. foreign debt/ GDP (%)	4.4	4.9	5.8			31.8('92)	
Gov. net foreign borrowing	1.43	5.50	4.71				
Total currency reserves minus gold (in billions of US $)	20.65	41.89	36.64	36.78	41.01		IFSY'95
Total currency reserves minus gold (in billions of pounds)	8.73	23.68	20.75	24.49	26.78		
Gov. foreign debt/ currency reserves (%)	116.2	120.1	168.1			44.7('92)	
Exports	47.36	104.88	108.51	120.94	133.03		IFSY'95
Gov. foreign debt/ exports (%)	21.4	27.1	32.2			50.5('92)	
Gov. expenditures	88.48	229.15	257.89				GSFY'90,'94

						('92)	Source
Gov. foreign debt/gov. expenditures (%)	11.5	12.4	13.5			17.4('92)	IFSY'95
Gov. net foreign borrowing/expenditures (%)	1.6	18.3	14.2			787.5('92)	
Domestic investment (gr. fixed cap. form. + increases in stocks)	38.94	92.63	91.97	95.24	103.67		IFSY'95
Direct foreign investment abroad (in millions of US $)	11.23	16.40	19.35	25.64	29.95		
Direct foreign investment abroad (in millions of pounds)	4.83	9.27	10.96	17.07	19.55		
Direct foreign investment abroad/domestic investment (%)	12.4	10.0	11.9	17.9	18.9	44.4	
Inflow foreign direct investment (in millions of US $)	10.12	16.06	16.49	14.56	10.94		IFSY'95
Inflow foreign direct investment (in millions of pounds)	4.35	9.08	9.34	9.69	7.14		
Inflow foreign direct investment/domestic investment (%)	11.2	9.8	10.2	10.2	6.9	-8.9	

United Kingdom: Table 5.2A   Government role in the economy and public finance
(in billions of pounds sterling, unless otherwise indicated)

	1980	1991	1992	1993	1994	Rate of change 1980–92(%)	Source
GDP (pounds) (1990 pounds)	231.7 (423.49)	575.32 (540.31)	597.24 (537.45)	630.71 (549.59)	668.87 (570.72)		IFSY'95
Gov. expenditures	88.48	229.15	257.89				GSFY'90,'94
Gov. expenditures/ GDP (%)	38.2	39.8	43.2			13.1	
Tax revenue (budgetary central gov.)	58.04	159.87	161.21			8.0	GSFY'90,'94
Tax revenue/ GDP (%)	25.0	27.8	27.0				
Gov. budget deficit	–10.73	–5.69	–30.0				IFSY'95
Gov. budget deficit/ GDP (%)	4.6	1.0	5.0			8.7	
Gov. debt	106.75	189.65	203.51				IFSY'95
Gov. debt/GDP (%)	46.1	33.0	34.1			–26.0	
Gov. employment (employees in thousands)	5,349	5,129	4,915				OECDNA'92

							OECDNA'92
Total employment	23,314	22,559	22,138				OECDNA'92
Gov. employment/total employment (%)	22.9	22.7	22.2			-3.1	
Gov. consump.	49.98	124.11	131.88	137.97	144.08		IFSY'95
Private consump.	138.56	364.97	381.72	405.46	428.08		IFSY'95
Gov. consump./private consump. (%)	36.1	34.0	34.5	34.0		-2.7	
Gov. capital expenditures		20.23	20.08	19.64			EWY'95
Gov. fixed capital formation		41.79	45.99	49.56			EWY'95
Gov. capital expenditures/gross fixed capital formation (%)	48.4	43.7	39.6				EWY'95

United States: Table 5.1A Internationalization of the economy and public finance
(in billions of dollars, unless otherwise indicated)

	1980	1991	1992	1993	1994	Rate of change 1980–93(%)	Source
GDP ($) (1990 $)	2,708.1 (4,275.6)	5,722.9 (5,458.3)	6,020.2 (5,673.5)	6,343.3 (5,813.2)	6,738.4 (6,050.4)		IFSY'95
Gov. foreign debt	129.7	491.7	549.7	622.6			IFSY'95
Gov. foreign debt/ GDP (%)	4.8	8.6	9.1	9.8		104.2	
Gov. net foreign borrowing	0.2	68.8	57.6	91.4			IFSY'95
Total currency reserves minus gold	15.60	66.66	60.27	62.35	63.28		IFSY'95
Gov. foreign debt/ currency reserves (%)	831.4	737.6	912.1	998.6		20.1	
Exports	225.57	421.73	448.16	464.77	512.52		IFSY'95
Gov. foreign debt/ exports (%)	57.5	116.6	122.7	134.0		133.0	
Gov. expenditures	596.6	1,429.1	1,445.1	1,492.4			IFSY'95
Gov. foreign debt/ gov. expenditures (%)	21.7	34.4	38.0	41.7		92.2	

Gov. net foreign borrowing/gov. expenditures	0.03	4.8	4.0	6.12		203.0	IFSY'95
Domestic investment (gr. fixed cap. form. + increases in stocks)	541.62	875.60	939.15	1,052.99	1,246.60		IFSY'95
Direct foreign investment abroad	19.23	31.30	41.01	57.87	58.44		IFSY'95
Direct foreign investment abroad/ domestic investment (%)	3.6	3.6	4.4	5.5	4.7	52.8	
Inflow foreign direct investment	16.93	26.09	9.89	21.37	60.07		IFSY'95
Inflow foreign direct investment/ domestic investment (%)	3.1	3.0	1.1	2.0	4.8	−35.5	

United States: Table 5.2A Government role in the economy and public finance
(in billions of dollars, unless otherwise indicated)

	1980	1991	1992	1993	1994	Rate of change 1980–92(%)	Source
GDP	2,708.1	5,722.9	6,020.2	6,343.3	6,738.4		IFSY'95
Gov. expenditures	596.6	1,429.1	1,445.1	1,492.4			IFSY'95
Gov. expenditures/ GDP (%)	22.0	25.0	24.0	23.5		9.1	
Tax revenue (budgetary central gov.)	346.83	635.54	651.00	706.79			GFSY'88,'94
Tax revenue / GDP (%)	12.8	11.1	10.8	11.1		−15.6	
Gov. budget deficit	−76.2	−272.5	−289.3	−254.1			IFSY'95
Gov. budget deficit/GDP (%)	2.8	4.8	4.0			42.9	
Gov. debt	737.7	2,845.0	3,142.4	3,391.9			IFSY'95
Gov. debt/GDP (%)	27.2	49.7	52.2	53.5		91.9	
Gov. employment (employees in thousands)	14,890	16,893	16,799				OECDNA'95

							OECDNA'92
Total employment	87,401	103,499	103,637				OECDNA'92
Gov. employment/total employment (%)	17.0	16.3	16.2			−4.7	
Gov. consump. & investment	507.1	1,099.3	1,125.3	1,148.4	1,175.3		IFSY'95
Private consump.	1,748.1	3,906.4	4,136.9	4,378.2	4,628.4		IFSY'95
Gov. consump./private consump. (%)	29.0	28.1	27.2	26.2	25.4	−6.9	
Gov. capital formation	72.7	139.6	150.6	155.1	160.8		IFSY'95
Gross fixed capital formation	549.8	876.5	938.9	1,037.1	1,193.7		IFSY'95
Gov. capital formation/gross fixed capital formation (%)	13.2	15.9	16.0	15.0	13.5	21.2	

Appendix for Figure 6.4: Level of Support for Mainstream Parties in National Elections, 1980–1994

The percentages in figure 6.4 have been calculated using the electoral returns for elections to the lower house of parliament, except in the case of the United States, in which returns for presidential elections were used. Parties were considered to be mainstream if they had served in government, with the exceptions of the French Communist Party and the Italian Communist Party.

For sources, see the last row of the table for each country below. All data come from one of the following sources:

EWY = *Europa World Yearbook* (London: Europa Publications, 1982–1995)

SY = *Statesman's Yearbook* (ed. Brian Hunter, New York: St Martin's Press, 1994–1995, 1995–1996)

MDI = *Ministerio del Interior* (cited in *Espana, fin del siglo,* by Carlos Alonso Zaldivar and Manuel Castells, Madrid: Alianza Editorial, 1992)

Valles = "The Spanish general election of 1993," by Joseph M. Valles, *Electoral Studies*, 1994, 13 (1): 89

All figures in tables are percentages.

France   First round votes for National Assembly

	1981 (1st ballot)	1986 (1st ballot)	1988 (1st ballot)	1993 (1st ballot)
Mainstream parties				
RPR	20.8	11.2	19.2	20.4
UDF	19.2	8.3	18.5	19.1
RPR + UDF		21.5		
Socialists (PS)		31.0	34.8	17.6
MR de G		0.4	1.1	0.9
PS + MR de G	37.4			
Other parties				
Communists (PCF)	16.1	9.8	11.3	9.2
Other left wing	0.8	1.0	1.7	3.6
Extreme gauche	1.4	1.5		3.6
Other right wing	2.8	3.9	2.9	5.0
Extreme droit	0.4	0.2		
Front National		9.7	9.7	12.4
Ecologists		1.2		0.1
Les Vert				4.0
Regionalists		0.1		
Others			0.9	4.2
Total vote for mainstream parties	**77.4**	**72.4**	**73.6**	**58**
Source	EWY-82	EWY-88	EWY-90	EWY-95

Germany: Votes for Bundestag

	1983	1987	1990	1994
Mainstream parties				
CDU/CSU	48.8	44.2	43.8	41.5
Social Democratic Party (SPD)	38.2	37.0	33.5	36.4
Free Democrats (FDP)	7.0	9.1	11.0	6.9
Other parties				
Communists (DKP)	0.2			
Dem. Socialists (former Com.)				
Party of Dem. Soc. (PDS) (former Com. Party of GDR)			2.4	4.4
Republican Party			1.2	1.9
Nat. Dem. Party (NDP)	0.2	0.6		
Greens (+ Alliance '90 in 1990 & 1994)	5.6	8.3	5.0	7.3
Ecological Dem. Party (ODP)		0.3		
Women's Party		0.2		
Others		0.3	2.1	1.7
Total vote for mainstream parties	**94.0**	**90.3**	**88.3**	**84.8**
Source	EWY-84	EWY-88	EWY-92	EWY-95

Italy Votes for Chamber of Deputies

	1983	1987	1992
Mainstream parties			
Republicans (PRI)	5.1	3.7	4.4
Liberals (PLI)	2.9	2.1	2.8
Christian Democrats (DC)	32.9	34.3	29.7
Social Democrats (PSDI)	4.1	3.0	2.7
Socialists (PSI)	11.4	14.3	13.6
Communist Party (PCI)	29.9	26.6	
Dem. Party of the Left			16.1
(formerly communists)			
Refounded communists			5.6
(formerly communists)			
Other parties			
Italian Social Movement (MSI)	6.8	5.9	5.4
New United Left			
(Proletarian Democrats			
+ Lotta Continua)			
Proletarian Dem.	1.5	1.7	
Radicals (PR)	2.2	2.6	
Regional parties			
Northern League			8.7
Sudtiroler Volkpartei	0.5		
La Rete			1.9
Greens		2.5	2.8
Others	2.7	3.3	6.3
Total vote for			
mainstream parties	**86.3**	**84.0**	**79.9**
Source	EWY-84	EWY-88	SY-94-5

Japan   Votes for House of Representatives

	1983	1986	1990	1993
Mainstream parties				
Liberal Dem. (LDP)	45.8	49.4	46.1	36.62
New Lib. Club (NLC)	2.4	1.8		
(rejoins LDP in '86)				
Dem. Soc. Party (DSP)	7.3	6.5	4.8	3.51
Socialists (JSP)	19.5	17.2	24.4	15.43
(becomes Soc. Dem. Party				
of Japan in 1992)				
Other parties				
Progressive Party			0.4	
Komeito	10.1	9.4	8.0	8.14
Japan New Party (JNP)				8.05
Japan Renewal Party				10.10
Soc. Dem. Fed. (SDF)	0.7	0.8	0.9	0.73
(+Un. Soc. Dem. P. in '93)				
Communists (JCP)	9.3	8.8	8.0	7.70
Independent	4.9	5.8	7.3	6.85
Sakigake				2.00
Others	0.1	0.2	0.1	0.23
Total vote for				
mainstream parties	**75.0**	**74.9**	**75.3**	**55.56**
Source	EWY-86	EWY-88	EWY-90	EWY-95

Spain   Votes for Congress of Deputies

	1982	1986	1989	1993
Mainstream parties				
ADP + PDP (+ PL in '88 = CP)	26.4	26.1		
Popular Party (AP -->PP in 1989)			26.0	34.6
Union de Centro Dem. (UCD)	9.8			
Social and Democratic		9.2	8.0	1.8
Center (CDS)				
Spanish Workers' Socialist	48.4	44.4	39.8	38.5
Party (PSOE)				
Other parties				
Span. Communist Party (PCE)	3.9			
United Left (IU)		4.7	9.1	9.5
Basque Nationalist Party (PNV)	1.9	1.5	1.2	1.2
Convergence and Union (CiU)	3.7	5.1	5.1	4.9
Others	5.9	9.1	10.8	9.4
Total vote for				
mainstream parties	**84.6**	**79.7**	**73.8**	**74.9**
Source	MDI	MDI	MDI	Valles

United Kingdom   Votes for House of Commons

	1983	1987	1992
Mainstream parties			
Conservatives	42.4	42.3	41.9
Liberals (+ Soc. Dem.)	25.4	22.6	17.9
Labour Party	27.6	30.9	34.4
Other parties			
Soc. and Dem. Lab. Party	0.4	0.5	0.5
Plaid Cymru	0.4	0.4	0.5
Scottish National Party	1.1	1.3	1.9
Sinn Fein	0.3	0.3	
Ulster Popular Unionist Party	0.1		
Ulster Unionists	0.8		
Dem. Unionist Party	0.5		
(All 3)		1.2	1.2
Others	1.0	0.5	1.8
Total vote for mainstream parties	**95.4**	**95.8**	**94.2**
Source	EWY-86	EWY-90	EWY-95

United States   Popular vote for President

	1980	1984	1988	1992
Mainstream parties				
Democrats	41.0	40.5	45.6	42.9
Republicans	50.8	58.8	53.4	37.5
Others				
John Anderson	6.6			
Ross Perot				18.9
Others	1.6	0.7	1.0	0.8
Total vote for mainstream parties	**91.8**	**99.3**	**99.0**	**80.4**
Source	EWY-81	EWY-88	EWY-90	EWY-94

Summary of Contents of Volumes I and III

Throughout this volume, reference has been made to the themes presented in volume I (published by Blackwell Publishers in 1996) and volume III (to be published in 1997). An outline of their contents is given below:

Volume I: *The Rise of the Network Society*

Prologue: The Net and the Self
1 The Information Technology Revolution
2 The Informational Economy and the Process of Globalization
3 The Network Enterprise: the Culture, Institutions, and Organizations of the Informational Economy
4 The Transformation of Work and Employment: Networkers, Jobless, and Flexitimers
5 The Culture of Real Virtuality: the Integration of Electronic Communication, the End of the Mass Audience, and the Rise of Interactive Networks
6 The Space of Flows
7 The Edge of Forever: Timeless Time
Conclusion: The Network Society

Volume III: *End of Millennium*

A Time of Change
1 The Crisis of Industrial Statism and the Collapse of the Soviet Union
2 The Rise of the Fourth World: Informational Captalism, Poverty, and Social Exclusion
3 The Perverse Connection: the Global Criminal Economy

References

Abelove, Henry, Barale, Michele Aina and Halperin, David M. (eds) (1993) *The Lesbian and Gay Studies Reader*, New York: Routledge.

Abramson, Jeffrey B., Artertone, F. Christopher and Orren, Cary R. (1988) *The Electronic Commonwealth: The Impact of New Media Technologies in Democratic Politics*, New York: Basic Books.

Adler, Margot (1979) *Drawing Down the Moon: Witches, Druids, Goddess-worshippers, and Other Pagans in America Today*, Boston: Beacon.

Aguirre, Pedro et al. (1995) *Una reforma electoral para la democracia. Argumentos para el consenso*, Mexico: Instituto de Estudios para la transicion democratica.

Akhmatova, Anna (1985) *Selected Poems*, trans. D. M. Thomas, London: Penguin.

Al-Azmeh, Aziz (1993) *Islams and Modernities*, London: Verso.

Alberdi, Ines (ed.) (1995) *Informe sobre la situacion de la familia en Espana*, Madrid: Ministerio de Asuntos Sociales.

Albo, Xavier (1993) *Y de Kataristas a MNRistas? La soprendente y audaz alianza entre Aymaras y neoliberales en Bolivia*, La Paz: CEDOIN-UNITAS.

Alexander, Herbert E. (1992) *Financing Politics. Money, Elections, and Political Reform*, Washington, DC: CQ Press.

Allen, Thomas B. (1987) *Guardian of the Wild. The Story of the National Wildlife Federation, 1936-1986*, Bloomington, Ind.: Indiana.

Alley, Kelly D. et al. (1995) "The historical transformation of a grass-roots environmental group", *Human Organization*, 54 (4): 410–16.

Alonso Zaldivar, Carlos (1996) *Variaciones sobre un mundo en cambio*. Madrid: Alianza Editorial.

— and Castells, Manuel (1992) *Espana fin de siglo*, Madrid: Alianza Editorial.

Ammerman, Nancy (1987) *Bible Believers: Fundamentalists in the Modern World*, New Brunswick, NJ: Rutgers University Press.

Anderson, Benedict (1983) *Imagined Communities: Reflections on the Origin and Spread of Nationalism*, London: Verso (read in the 2nd edn, 1991).

Anderson, P. and Comiller, P. (eds) (1994) *Mapping the West European Left*, London: Verso.

Ansolabehere, Stephen and Iyengar, Shanto (1994) "Riding the wave and claiming ownership over issues: the joint effects of advertising and news coverage in campaigns", *Public Opinion Quarterly*, 58: 335–57.

— et al. (1993) *The Media Game: American Politics in the Television Age*, New York: Macmillan.

Anthes, Gary H. (1993) "Government ties to Internet expand citizens' access to data", *Computerworld*, 27, (34): 77.

Anti-Defamation League (1994) *Armed and Dangerous*, New York: Anti-Defamation League of B'nai B'rith.

Anti-Defamation League (1995) *Special Report: Paranoia as Patriotism: Far-Right Influence on the Militia Movement*, New York: Anti-Defamation League of B'nai B'rith.

Aoyama, Yoshinobu (1991) *Riso Shakai: kyosanto sengen kara shinri'e (The Ideal Society: from Communist Manifesto to Truth)*, Tokyo: AUM Press.

Appiah, Kwame Anthony and Gates, Henry Louis, Jr (eds) (1995) *Identities*, Chicago: The University of Chicago Press.

Archondo, Rafael (1991) *Compadres al microfono: la resurreccion metropolitana del ayllu*, La Paz: Hisbol.

Ardaya, Gloria and Verdesoto, Luis (1994) *Racionalidades democraticas en construccion*, La Paz: ILDIS.

Arlachi, Pino (1995) "The Mafia, Cosa Nostra, and Italian institutions", in Sechi (ed.): 153–63.

Armond, Paul (1995) "Militia of Montana meeting at the Maltby Community Center", *World Wide Web*, MOM site, February 11.

Armstrong, David (1995) "Cyberhoax!", *Columbia Journalism Review*, September/October.

Arquilla, John and Rondfeldt, David (1993) "Cyberwar is coming!", *Comparative Strategy*, 12 (2): 141–65.

Arrieta, Carlos G. et al. (1991) *Narcotrafico en Colombia. Dimensiones politicas, economicas, juridicas e internacionales*, Bogota: Tercer Mundo Editores.

Asahara, Shoko (1994) *Metsubo no Hi (The Doomsday)*, Tokyo: AUM Press.

— (1995) *Hi Izuru Kuni Wazawai Chikashi (Disasters Come Close to the Nation as the Rising Sun)*, Tokyo: AUM Press.

Astrachan, Anthony (1986) *How Men Feel: Their Response to Women's*

Demands for Equality and Power, Garden City, NY: Anchor Press/Doubleday.

Athanasiou, Tom (1996) *Divided Planet: The Ecology of Rich and Poor*, Boston: Little, Brown.

Awakening (1995) Special issue, no. 158–1961, Taipei (Chinese language).

Axford, Barrie et al. (1992) "Image management, stunts, and dirty tricks: the marketing of political brands in television campaigns", *Media, Culture, and Society*, 14 (4): 637–51.

Azevedo, Milton (ed.) (1991) *Contemporary Catalonia in Spain and Europe*, Berkeley: University of California, Gaspar de Portola Catalonian Studies Program.

Bachr, Peter R. and Gordenker, Leon (1994) *The UN in the 1990s*, New York: St Martin's Press.

Badie, Bertrand (1992) *L'etat importe: essai sur l'occidentalisation de l'ordre politique*, Paris: Fayard.

Bakhash, Shaul (1990) "The Islamic Republic of Iran, 1979-1989", *Middle East Focus*, 12 (3): 8–12, 27.

Balta, Paul (ed.) (1991) *Islam: Civilisations et sociétés*, Paris: Editions du Rocher.

Balz, Dan and Brownstein, Ronald (1996) *Storming the Gates: Protest Politics and the Republican Revival*, Boston: Little, Brown.

Barber, Benjamin R. (1993) "Letter from America, September 1993: the rise of Clinton, the fall of democrats, the scandal of the media", *Government and Opposition*, 28 (4): 433–43.

Barker, Anthony (1992) *The Upturned Stone: Political Scandals in Twenty Democracies and their Investigation Process"*, Colchester: University of Essex, Essex Papers in Politics and Government.

Barnett, Bernice McNair (1995) "Black women's collectivist movement organizations: their struggles during the 'doldrums'", in Ferree and Martin (eds), pp. 199–222.

Barone, Michael and Ujifusa, Grant (1995) *The Almanac of American Politics 1996*, Washington: National Journal.

Barron, Bruce and Shupe, Anson (1992) "Reasons for growing popularity of Christian reconstructionism: the determination to attain dominion", in Misztal and Shupe (eds), pp. 83-96.

Bartholet, E. (1990) *Family Bonds, Adoption and the Politics of Parenting*, New York: Houghton Mifflin.

Bartz, Steve (1996) "Environmental organizations and evolving information technologies", Berkeley: University of California, Department of Sociology, unpublished seminar paper for SOC 290.2, May.

Baylis, John and Rengger, N.J. (eds) (1992) *Dilemmas of World Politics. International Issues in a Changing World*, Oxford: Clarendon Press.

Beccalli, Bianca (1994) "The modern women's movement in Italy", *New Left Review*, 204, March/April: 86-112.

Bellah, Robert N., Sullivan, William M., Swidler, Ann and Tipton, Steven M. (1985) *Habits of the Heart. Individualism and Commitment in American Life*, Berkeley: University of California Press (cited in the Perennial Library edition from Harper and Row, New York, 1986).

Bellers, Jurgen (ed.) (1989) *Politische Korruption*, Munster: Lit.

Bennett, David H. (1995) *The Party of Fear: the American Far Right from Nativism to the Militia Movement*, New York: Vintage Books.

Bennett, William J. (1994) *The Index of Leading Cultural Indicators: Facts and Figures on the State of American Society*, New York: Touchstone.

Berdal, Mats R. (1993) *Whither UN Peacekeeping?: An Analysis of the Changing Military Requirements of UN Peacekeeping with Proposals for its Enhancement*, London: Brassey's for International Institute of Strategic Studies.

Berins Collier, Ruth (1992) *The Contradictory Alliance. State-Labor Relationships and Regime Changes in Mexico*, Berkeley: University of California, International and Area Studies.

Berlet, Chips and Lyons, Matthew N. (1995) "Militia nation", *The Progressive*, June.

Berman, Jerry and Weitzner, Daniel J. (1995) "Abundance and user control: renewing the democratic heart of the First Amendment in the age of interactive media", *Yale Law Journal*, 104, (7) 1619–37.

Bernard, Jessie (1987) *The Female World from a Global Perspective*, Bloomington, Ind.: Indiana University Press.

Berry, Sebastian (1992) "Party strategy and the media: the failure of Labour's 1991 election campaign", *Parliamentary Affairs*, 45, (4): 565–81.

Betts, Mitch (1995) "The politicizing of cyberspace", *Computerworld*, 29 (3): 20.

Bilbao La Vieja Diaz, Antonio, Perez de Rada, Ernesto and Asturizaga, Ramiro (1996) "CONDEPA movimiento patriotico", La Paz: Naciones Unidas/CIDES, unpublished research monograph.

Birnbaum, Lucia Chiavola (1986) *Liberazione della donna: Feminism in Italy*, Middletown, Conn.: Wesleyan University Press.

Black, Gordon S. and Black, Benjamin D. (1994) *The Politics of American Discontent: How a New Party Can Make Democracy Work Again*, New York: John Wiley and Sons.

Blakely, Edward and Goldsmith, William (1993) *Separate Societies: Poverty and Inequality in American Cities*, Philadelphia: Temple University Press.

Blas Guerrero, Andres (1994) *Nacionalismos y naciones en Europa*, Madrid: Alianza Editorial.

Blossfeld, Hans-Peter (ed.) (1995) *The New Role of Women: Family Formation in Modern Societies*, Boulder, Colo.: Westview Press.

Blum, Linda (1991) *Between Feminism and Labor: The Politics of the Comparable Worth Movement*, Berkeley: University of California Press.

Blumberg, Rae Lesser, Rakowski, Cathy A. Tinker, Irene and Monteon, Michael (eds) (1995) *EnGENDERing Wealth and Wellbeing*, Boulder, Colo.: Westview Press.

Blumenfield, Seth D. (1994) "Developing the global information infrastructure", *Federal Communications Law Journal*, 47(2): 193–6.

Blumstein, Philip and Schwartz, Pepper (1983) *American Couples: Money, Work, Sex*, New York: William Morrow.

Boardmann, Robert (1994) *Post-socialist World Orders: Russia, China, and the UN system*, New York: St Martin's Press.

Bobbio, Norberto (1994) *Destra e sinistra: ragioni e significati di una distinzione politica*, Roma: Donzelli editore.

Borja, Jordi (1988) *Estado y ciudad*, Barcelona: Promociones y Publicaciones Universitarias.

— and Castells, Manuel (1996) *Local and Global: The Management of Cities in the Information Age*, London: Earthscan.

— et al. (1992) *Estrategias de desarrollo e internacionalizacion de las ciudades europeas: las redes de ciudades*, Barcelona: Consultores Europeos Asociados, Research Report.

Bouissou, Jean-Marie (1991) "Corruption à la Japonaise", *L'Histoire*, 142, March: 84–7.

Bramwell, Anna (1989) *Ecology in the 20th Century: A History*, New Haven: Yale University Press.

— (1994) *The Fading of the Greens: The Decline of Environmental Politics in the West*, New Haven: Yale University Press.

Brenner, Daniel (1994) "In search of the multimedia grail", *Federal Communications Law Journal*, 47 (2), pp: 197–203.

Broadcasting & Cable (1995) "Top of the week", May.

Brown, Helen (1992) *Women Organising*, London: Routledge.

Brown, Michael (1993) "Earth worship or black magic?", *The Amicus Journal*, 14 (4): 32–4.

Brubaker, Timothy H. (ed.) (1993) *Family Relations: Challenges for the Future*, Newbury Park, Calif.: Sage.

Bruce, Judith, Lloyd, Cynthia B. and Leonard, Ann (1995) *Families in Focus: New Perspectives of Mothers, Fathers, and Children*, New York: Population Council

Brulle, Robert J. (1996) "Environmental discourse and social movement organizations: a historical and rhetorical perspective on the development of US environmental organizations", *Sociological Inquiry*, 66 (1): 58–83.

Buci-Glucksman, Christine (1978) *Gramsci et l'état*, Paris: Grasset.

Buckler, Steve (1993) *Dirty Hands: the Problem of Political Morality*, Brookfield: Averbury.

Buckley, Peter (ed.) (1994) *Cooperative Forms of Transnational Corporation Activity*, London and New York: Routledge.

Buechler, Steven M. (1990) *Women's Movement in the United States*, Brunswick, NJ: Rutgers University Press.

Bull, Hedley (1977) *The Anarchical Society*, London: Macmillan.

Burgat, Francois and Dowell, William (1993) *The Islamic Movement in North Africa*, Austin, Texas: University of Texas Center for Middle Eastern Studies.

Burnham, David (1983) *The Rise of the Computer State*, New York: Vintage.

Business Week (1995a) "The future of money", June 12.

Business Week (1995b) "Hot money", March 20.

Business Week (1995c), "Mexico: Salinas is fast becoming a dirty word", December 25: 54–5.

Business Week (1995d) "The new populism", March.

Business Week (1995e) "Power to the states", August: 49–56.

Buss, David M. (1994) *The Evolution of Desire: Strategies of Human Mating*, New York: Basic Books.

Butler, Judith (1990) *Gender Trouble: Feminism and the Subversion of Identity*, New York: Routledge.

Cabre, Anna (1990) "Es compatible la proteccion de la familia con la liberacion de la mujer?", in Instituto de la Mujer (ed.), *Mujer y Demografia*, Madrid: Ministerio de Asuntos Sociales.

— and Domingo, Antonio (1992) "La Europa despues de Maastrich: reflexiones desde la demografia", *Revista de Economia*, 13: 63–9.

Cacho, Jesus (1994) *MC: un intruso en el laberinto de los elegidos*, Madrid: Temas de hoy.

Caipora Women's Group (1993) *Women in Brazil*, London: Latin American Bureau.

Calabrese, Andrew and Borchert, Mark (1996) "Prospects for electronic democracy in the United States: rethinking communication and social policy", *Media, Culture, and Society*, 18: 249–68.

Calderon, Fernando (1995) *Movimientos sociales y politica*, Mexico: Siglo XXI.

— and Laserna, Roberto (1994) *Paradojas de la modernidad*, La Paz: Fundacion Milenio.

— et al. (1996) *Esa esquiva modernidad: desarrollo, ciudadania y cultura en America Latina y el Caribe*, Caracas: Nueva Sociedad/UNESCO.

Calhoun, Craig (ed.) (1994) *Social Theory and the Politics of Identity*, Oxford: Blackwell.

Camilleri, J.A. and Falk, K. (1992) *The End of Sovereignty*, Aldershot: Edward Elgar.

Campbell, B. (1992) "Feminist politics after Thatcher." In H. Hinds, et al. (eds) *Working Out: New Directions for Women's Studies*, London: Taylor and Francis: 13–17.

Campbell, Colin and Rockman, Bert A. (eds) (1995) *The Clinton Presidency: First Appraisals*, Chatham, NJ: Chatham House.

Campo Vidal, Manuel (1996) *La transicion audiovisual*, Barcelona: B Ediciones.

Cardoso de Leite, Ruth (1983) "Movimientos sociais urbanos: balanco critico." In *Sociedade e politica no Brasil pos-64*, Sao Paulo: Brasiliense.

Carnoy, Martin (1984) *The State and Political Theory*, Princeton, NJ: Princeton University Press.

— (1993) "Multinationals in a changing world economy: whither the nation-state?", in Carnoy et al. (eds), pp. 45–96.

— (1994) *Faded Dreams: The Politics and Economics of Race in America*, New York: Cambridge University Press.

—, Castells, Manuel, Cohen, Stephen S. and Cardoso, Fernando H. (1993) *The New Global Economy in the Information Age*, University Park, PA: Penn State University Press.

Carre, Olivier (1984) *Mystique et politique: Lecture revolutionnaire du Coran by Sayyed Qutb*, Paris: Editions du Cerf-Presses de la Fondation Nationale des Sciences Politiques.

Carrere d'Encausse, Helene (1987) *Le grand defi: Bolcheviks et nations, 1917–1930*, Paris: Flammarion.

— (1993) *The End of the Soviet Empire: The Triumph of Nations*, New York: Basic Books (original French edition 1991).

Castells, Manuel (1981) "Local government, urban crisis, and political change", in *Political Power and Social Theory: A Research Annual*, Greenwich, CT: JAI Press, 2, pp. 1–20.

— (1983) *The City and the Grassroots: A Cross-cultural Theory of Urban Social Movements*, Berkeley: University of California Press, and London: Edward Arnold.

— (1992a) "Four Asian tigers with a dragon head: a comparative analysis of the state, economy, and society in the Asian Pacific rim", in Appelbaum, Richard, and Henderson, Jeffrey (eds) *States and Development in the Asian Pacific Rim*, Newbury Park, CA: Sage, pp. 33–70.

— (1992b) *La nueva revolucion rusa*, Madrid: Sistema.

— (1992c) "Las redes sociales del SIDA." Keynote address delivered at the Social Sciences Symposium, World Congress on AIDS research, Madrid, May 1992.

— (1996) "El futuro del estado del bienestar en la sociedad informacional", *Sistema*, 131, March: 35–53.

— and Murphy, Karen (1982) "Cultural identity and urban structure: the spatial organization of San Francisco's gay community", in

Fainstein, Norman I., and Fainstein, Susan S. (eds) *Urban Policy Under Capitalism*, Urban Affairs Annual Reviews, vol. 22, Beverly Hills, Calif.: Sage: 237–60.

—, Yazawa, Shujiro and Kiselyova, Emma (1996) "Insurgents against the global order: a comparative analysis of the Zapatistas in Mexico, the American Militia and Japan's Aum Shinrikyo", *Berkeley Journal of Sociology*, 40: 21–60.

Castells, Nuria (forthcoming) "Environmental policies and international agreements in the European Union: a comparative analysis", Amsterdam: University of Amsterdam, Economics Department, unpublished doctoral dissertation.

Chatterjee, Partha (1993) *The Nation and its Fragments: Colonial and Postcolonial Histories*, Princeton, NJ: Princeton University Press.

Chesnais, François (1994) *La mondialisation du capital*, Paris: Syros.

Cheung, Peter T.Y. (1994) "Relations between the central government and Guandong", in Y.M. Yeung and David K.Y. Chu (eds), *Guandong: Survey of a Province Undergoing Rapid Change*, Hong Kong: The Chinese University Press, pp. 19–51.

Cho, Lee-Jay and Yada, Moto (eds) (1994) *Tradition and Change in the Asian Family*, Honolulu: University of Hawaii Press.

Chodorow, Nancy (1978) *The Reproduction of Mothering: Psychoanalysis and the Sociology of Gender*, Berkeley: University of California Press.

— (1989) *Feminism and Psychoanalytical Theory*, New Haven: Yale University Press.

— (1994) *Feminities, Masculinities, Sexualities: Freud and Beyond*, Lexington, Ky: University Press of Kentucky.

Chong, Rachelle (1994) "Trends in communication and other musings on our future", *Federal Communications Law Journal*, 47 (2): 213–19.

Choueri, Youssef M. (1993) *Il fondamentalismo islamico: Origine storiche e basi sociali*, Bologna: Il Mulino.

Coalition for Human Dignity (1995) *Against the New World Order: the American Militia Movement*, Portland, Oregon: Coalition for Human Dignity Publications.

Coates, Thomas J. et al. (1988) *Changes in Sex Behavior of Gay and Bisexual Men since the Beginning of the AIDS Epidemics*, San Francisco: University of California, Center for AIDS Prevention Studies.

Cobble, Dorothy S. (ed.) (1993) *Women and Unions: Forging a Partnership*, New York: International Labour Review Press.

Cohen, Roger (1996) "Global forces batter politics", *The New York Times*, Sunday November 17, s. 4: 1–4.

Cohen, Stephen (1993) "Geo-economics: lessons from America's mistakes", in Carnoy et al. (eds), pp. 97–148.

Cohen, Jeffrey E. (1986) "The dynamics of the 'revolving door' on the FCC", *American Journal of Political Science*, 30 (4).

Coleman, Marilyn and Ganong, Lawrence H. (1993) "Families and marital disruption", in Brubaker (ed.), pp. 112–28.

Coleman, William E. Jr and Coleman, William E., Sr (1993) *A Rhetoric of the People: the German Greens and the New Politics*, Westport, Conn.: Praeger.

Collective Author (1996) *La seguridad humana en Bolivia: percepciones politicas, sociales y economicas de los bolivianos de hoy*, La Paz: PRON-AGOB-PNUD-ULDIS.

Collier, George A. (1995) *Restructuring Ethnicity in Chiapas and the World*, Stanford University, Department of Anthropology, Research Paper (published in Spanish in Nash et al. (eds), pp. 7–20).

— and Lowery Quaratiello, Elizabeth (1994) *Basta! Land and the Zapatista Rebellion in Chiapas*, Oakland, California: Food First Books.

Conquest, Robert (ed.) (1967) *Soviet Nationalities Policy in Practice*, New York: Praeger.

Contreras Basnipeiro, Adalid (1991) "Medios multiples, pocas voces: inventario de los medios de comunicacion de masas en Bolivia", *Revista UNITAS*, pp. 61–105.

Cook, Maria Elena et al. (eds) (1994) *The Politics of Economic Restructuring: State-society Relations and Regime Change in Mexico*, La Jolla: University of California at San Diego, Center of US–Mexican Studies.

Cooke, Philip (1994) *The Cooperative Advantage of Regions*, Cardiff: University of Wales, Centre for Advanced Studies.

Cooper, Jerry (1995) *The Militia and the National Guard in America since Colonial Times: a Research Guide*, Westport, Conn.: Greenwood Press.

Cooper, Marc (1995) "Montana's mother of all militias", *The Nation*, May 22.

Corn, David (1995) "Playing with fire", *The Nation*, May 15.

Costain, W. Douglas and Costain, Anne N. (1992) "The political strategies of social movements: a comparison of the women's and environmental movements", in *Congress and the Presidency*, 19 (1): 1–27.

Cott, Nancy (1989) "What's in a name? The limits of 'social feminism'; or, expanding the vocabulary of women's history", *Journal of American History*, 76: 809–29.

Couch, Carl J. (1990) "Mass communications and state structures", *The Social Science Journal*, 27, (2): 111–28.

CQ Researcher (1992) Special Issue: "Politicians and privacy", 2 (15), April 17.

Dalton, Russell J. (1994) *The Green Rainbow: Environmental Groups in Western Europe*, New Haven: Yale University Press.

— and Kuechler, Manfred (1990) *Challenging the Political Order: New Social and Political Movements in Western Democracies*, Cambridge: Polity Press.

Daniel, Donald and Hayes, Bradd (eds) (1995) *Beyond Traditional Peacekeeping*, New York: St Martin's Press.

Davidson, Osha Grey (1993) *Under Fire: the NRA and the Battle for Gun Control*, New York: Henry Holt.

Davis, John (ed.) (1991) *The Earth First! Reader*, Salt Lake City: Peregrine Smith Books.

Dees, Morris, and Corcoran, James (1996) *Gathering Storm: America's Militia Network*, New York: Harper-Collins.

Dekmejian, R. Hrair (1995) *Islam in Revolution: Fundamentalism in the Arab World*, Syracuse, NY: Syracuse University Press.

Delcroix, Catherine (1995) "Algeriennes et Egyptiennes: enjeux et sujets de societes en crise", in Dubet and Wieviorka (eds), pp. 257–72.

DeLeon, Peter (1993) *Thinking about Political Corruption*, Armonk, NY: M.E. Sharpe.

Delphy, Christine (ed.) (1984) *Particularisme et universalisme*, Paris: Nouvelles Questions Feministes, n. 17/17/18.

D'Emilio, John (1980/1993) "Capitalism and gay identity", in Abelove et al. (eds), pp. 467–76.

— (1983) *Sexual Politics, Sexual Communities: the Making of a Homosexual Minority in the United States, 1940–1970*, Chicago: University of Chicago Press.

DeMont, John (1991) "Frontline fighters", *Mclean's*, 104 (50): 46–7.

Dentsu Institute for Human Studies (1994) *Media in Japan*, Tokyo: DataFlow International.

Deutsch, Karl (1953) *Nationalism and Social Communication: an Inquiry into the Foundations of Nationality* (consulted in the 1966 edition, Cambridge, Mass.: MIT Press).

De Vos, Susan (1995) *Household Composition in Latin America*, New York: Plenum Press.

Diamond, Irene and Orenstein, Gloria (1990) *Reweaving the World: the Emergence of Ecofeminism*, San Francisco: Sierra Club Books.

Diani, Mario (1995) *Green Networks: a Structural Analysis of the Italian Environmental Movement*, Edinburgh: Edinburgh University Press.

Dickens, Peter (1990) "Science, social science and environmental issues: Ecological movements as the recovery of human nature", paper prepared for the meeting of the British Association for the Advancement of Science, University of Swansea, August.

Dietz, Thomas and Kalof, Linda (1992) "Environmentalism among nation-states", *Social Indicators Research*, 26: 353–66.

Di Marco, Sabina (1993) "Se la televisione guarda a sinistra", *Ponte*, 49 (7): 869–78.

— (1994) "La televisione, la politica e il cavaliere", *Ponte*, 50 (2): 9–11.

Dionne, E.J. (1996) *They Only Look Dead: Why Progressives Will Dominate the Next Political Era*, New York: Simon and Schuster.

Dobson, Andrew (1990) *Green Political Thought: an Introduction*, London: Unwin Hyman.

— (ed.) (1991) *The Green Reader: Essays toward a Sustainable Society*, San Francisco: Mercury House.

Doyle, Marc (1992) *The Future of Television: a Global Overview of Programming, Advertising, Technology and Growth*, Lincolnwood, Ill.: NTC Business Books.

Drew, Christopher (1995) "Japanese sect tried to buy US arms, technology, Senator says", *New York Times*, October 31: A5.

Dubet, François, and Wieviorka, Michel (eds) (1995) *Penser le sujet*, Paris: Fayard.

Duffy, Ann and Pupo, Norene (eds) (1992) *Part-time Paradox: Connecting Gender, Work and Family*, Toronto: The Canadian Publishers.

Dulong, Rene (1978) *Les regions, l'état et la société locale*, Paris: Presses Universitaires de France.

Dunaher, Kevin (ed.) (1994) *50 Years is Enough: the Case against the World Bank and the IMF*, Boston: South End Press.

Ebbinghausen, Rolf and Neckel, Sighard (eds) (1989) *Anatomie des politischen Skandals*, Frankfurt: Suhrkamp.

Ehrenreich, Barbara (1983) *The Hearts of Men: American Dreams and the Flight from Commitment*, Garden City, NY: Anchor Press/Doubleday.

Eisenstein, Zillah R. (1981/1993) *The Radical Future of Liberal Feminism*, Boston: Northeastern University Press.

Ejercito Zapatista de Liberacion Nacional (1994) *Documentos y comunicados*, Mexico: Ediciones Era (with preface by Antonio Garcia de Leon, and chronicles by Elena Poniatowska and Carlos Monsivais).

—/Subcomandante Marcos (1995) *Chiapas: del dolor a la esperanza*, Madrid: Los libros de la catarata.

Eley, Geoff, and Suny, Ronald Grigor (eds) (1996) *Becoming National: a Reader*, New York: Oxford University Press.

Elliott, J.H. and de la Pena, J.F. (1978) *Memoriales y cartas del Conde-Duque de Olivares*, Madrid: Alfaguara.

Epstein, Barbara (1991) *Political Protest and Cultural Revolution: Nonviolent Direct Action in the 1970s and 1980s*, Berkeley: University of California Press.

— (1995) "Grassroots environmentalism and strategies for social change", *New Political Science*, 32: 1–24.

Ergas, Yasmine (1985) *Nelle maglie della politica: femminismo, instituzione e politiche sociale nell'Italia degli anni settanta*, Milan: Feltrinelli.

Espinosa, Maria and Useche, Helena (1992) *Abriendo camino: historias de mujeres*, Bogota: FUNDAC.

Esposito, John L. (1990) *The Iranian Revolution: its Global Impact*, Miami: Florida International University Press.

Esprit (1994) "Editorial: face à la telecratie", 5: 3–4.

Etzioni, Amitai (1993) *The Spirit of Community: Rights, Responsibilities, and the Communitarian Agenda*, New York: Crown.

Evans, Sara (1979) *Personal Politics: the Roots of Women's Liberation in Civil Rights Movement and the New Left*, New York: Knopf.

Eyerman, Ron and Jamison, Andrew (1989) "Environmental knowledge as an organizational weapon: the case of Greenpeace", *Social Science Information*, 28 (1): 99–119.

Fackler, Tim and Lin, Tse-Min (1995) "Political corruption and presidential elections, 1929–1992", *The Journal of Politics*, 57 (4): 971–93.

Faison, Seth (1996) "Chinese cruise Internet, wary of watchdogs", *New York Times*, February 5, p. A1.

Falk, Richard (1995) *On Humane Governance: Towards a New Global Politics*, University Park, PA: Pennsylvania State University Press.

Fallows, James (1996) *Breaking the News: How the Media Undermine American Democracy*, New York: Pantheon.

Faludi, Susan (1991) *Backlash: the Undeclared War on American Women*, New York: Crown.

Farnsworth Riche, Martha (1996) "How America is changing – the view from the Census Bureau, 1995", in *The World Almanac and Book of Facts*, 1996: 382–83.

Fassin, Didier (1996) "Exclusions, underclass, marginalidad: figures contemporaines de la pauvreté urbaine en France, aux Etats-Unis et en Amerique Latine", *Revue Française de Sociologie*, 37: 37–75.

Ferraresi, Franco and Kemeny, Pietro (1977) *Classi sociali e politica urbana*, Rome: Officina Edizioni.

Ferrater Mora, Josep (1960) *Les formes de la vida catalana*, Barcelona: Editorial Selecta.

Ferree, Myra Marx and Hess, Beth B. (1994) *Controversy and Coalition: the New Feminist Movement across Three Decades of Change*, New York: Maxwell Macmillan.

— and Martin, Patricia Yancey (eds) (1995) *Feminist Organizations: Harvest of the Women's Movement*, Philadelphia: Temple University Press.

Ferrer i Girones, F. (1985) *La persecucio politica de la llengua catalana*, Barcelona: Edicions 62.

Financial Technology International Bulletin (1995) "A lawless frontier", 12 (12): 10.

Fischer, Claude S. (1982) *To Dwell among Friends: Personal Networks in Town and City*, Chicago: University of Chicago Press.

— et al. (1995) *Inequality by Design*, Princeton, NJ, Princeton University Press.

Fisher, Robert and Kling, Joseph (eds) (1993) *Mobilizing the Community: Local Politics in the Era of the Global City*, Thousand Oaks, CA: Sage.

Fitzpatrick, Mary Anne and Vangelisti, Anita L. (eds) (1995) *Explaining Family Interactions*, Thousand Oaks, CA: Sage.

Fooner, Michael (1989) *Interpol: Issues in World Crime and International Criminal Justice*, New York: Plenum Press.

Foucault, Michel (1976) *La volonté de savoir: histoire de la sexualité*, vol. I, Paris: Gallimard.

— (1984a) *L'usage des plaisirs: histoire de la sexualité*, vol. II, Paris: NRF.

— (1984b) *Le souci de soi: histoire de la sexualité*, vol. III, Paris: NRF.

Frankel, J. (1988) *International Relations in a Changing World*, Oxford: Oxford University Press.

Frankland, E. Gene (1995) "The rise, fall, and recovery of Die Grunen", in Richardson and Rootes (eds), pp. 23–44.

Franklin, Bob (1994) *Packaging Politics: Political Communications in Britain's Media Democracy*, London: Edward Arnold.

Freeman, Michael (1994) "Polls set spending record", *Mediaweek*, 4(44): 6.

Friedland, Lewis A. (1996) "Electronic democracy and the new citizenship", *Media, Culture, and Society*, 18: 185–211.

Friedrich, Carl J. (1966) "Political pathology", *Political Quarterly*, 37: 74.

Fujita, Shoichi (1995) *AUM Shinrikyo Jiken [The Incidents of AUM Shinrikyo]*, Tokyo: Asahi-Shinbunsha.

Funk, Nanette and Mueller, Magda (eds) (1993) *Gender Politics and Post-Communism: Reflections from Eastern Europe and the Former Soviet Union*, New York: Routledge.

Fuss, Diana (1989) *Essentially Speaking: Feminism, Nature, and Difference*, London: Routledge.

Ganley, Gladys G. (1991) "Power to the people via personal electronic media", *The Washington Quarterly*, Spring: 5–22.

Gans, Herbert J. (1995) *The War against the Poor: the Underclass and Anti-poverty Policy*, New York: Basic Books.

Garaudy, Roger (1990) *Integrismes*, Paris: Belfont.

Garber, Doris A. (1984) *Mass Media in American Politics*, 2nd edn, Washington DC: CQ Press.

— (1996) "The new media and politics – what does the future hold?", *Political Science and Politics*, 29 (1): 33–6.

Garcia Cotarelo, Ramon (1995) *La conspiracion*, Barcelona: Ediciones B.

Garcia de Leon, Antonio (1985) *Resistencia y utopia: memorial de agravios y cronica de revueltas y profecias acaecidas en la provincia de Chiapas durante los ultimos quinientos anos de su historia*, vol 2, Mexico: Ediciones Era.

Garcia-Ramon, Maria Dolors and Nogue-Font, Joan (1994) "Nationalism and geography in Catalonia", in Hooson (ed.), pp. 197–211.

Garment, Suzanne (1991) *Scandal: the Culture of Mistrust in American Politics*, New York: New York Times Books.

Garramone, Gina M. et al. (1990) "Effects of negative political advertising on the political process", *Journal of Broadcasting and Electronic Media*, 34 (3): 299–311.

Gates, Henry Louis, Jr (1996) "Parable of the talents", in Gates and West (eds), pp. 1–52.

— and West, Cornel (eds) (1996) *The Future of the Race*, New York: Alfred Knopf.

Gelb, Joyce and Lief-Palley, Marian (eds) (1994) *Women of Japan and Korea: Continuity and Change*, Philadelphia: Temple University Press.

Gellner, Ernest (1983) *Nations and Nationalism*, Ithaca, NY: Cornell University Press (originally published by Blackwell, Oxford).

Gerami, Shahin (1996) *Women and Fundamentalism: Islam and Christianity*, New York: Garland.

Gerbner, George, Mowlana, Hamid and Nordenstreng, Kaarle (eds) (1993) *The Global Media Debate: its Rise, Fall, and Renewal*, Norwood, NJ: Ablex.

Giddens, Anthony (1985) *A Contemporary Critique of Historical Materialism*, vol. II: *The Nation-state and Violence*, Berkeley: University of California Press.

— (1991) *Modernity and Self-identity: Self and Society in the Late Modern Age*, Cambridge: Polity Press.

— (1992) *The Transformation of Intimacy: Sexuality, Love and Eroticism in Modern Societies*, Stanford: Stanford University Press.

Gil, Jorge et al. (1993) "La red de poder mexicana: el caso de Miguel Aleman", *Revista Mexicana de Sociologia*, 3/95: 103–20.

Ginsborg, Paul (ed.) (1994) *Stato dell'Italia*, Milano: Il Saggiatore.

Giroux, Henry A. (1996) *Fugitive Cultures: Race, Violence and Youth*, New York: Routledge.

Gitlin, Todd (1980) *The Whole World is Watching: Mass Media in the Making and Unmaking of the New Left*, Berkeley: University of California Press.

Gleason, Nancy (1995) "Freenets: cities open the electronic door", *Government Finance Review*, 11 (4): 54–5.

Godard, Francis (ed.) (1996) *Villes*, Special issue of *Le Courrier du CNRS*, Paris: Centre National de la Recherche Scientique.

Gohn, Maria da Gloria (1991) *Movimientos sociais e luta pela moradia*, Sao Paulo: Edicoes Loyola.

Golden, Tim (1995) "A cocaine trail in Mexico points to official corruption", *New York Times*, April 19, pp. 1, 8.

Goldsmith, M. (1993) "The Europeanisation of local government", *Urban Studies*, 30: 683–99.

Gole, Nilufer (1995) "L'emergence du sujet islamique", in Dubet and Wieviorka (eds), pp. 221–34.

Gonsioreck, J.C. and Weinrich, J.D. (1991) *Homosexuality: Research Implications for Public Policy*, Newbury Park, CA: Sage.

Goode, William J. (1993) *World Changes in Divorce Patterns*, New Haven: Yale University Press.

Gottlieb, Robert (1993) *Forcing the Spring: the Transformation of the American Environmental Movement*, Washington DC: Island Press.

Graf, James E. (1995) "Global information infrastructure first principles", *Telecommunications*, 29 (1): 72–3.

Graham, Stephen (1995) "From urban competition to urban collaboration? The development of interurban telematic networks", *Environment and Planning C: Government and Policy*, 13: 503–24.

Granberg, A. (1993) "The national and regional commodity markets in the USSR: trends and contradictions in the transition period", *Papers in Regional Science*, 72: 1.

— and Spehl, H. (1989) *Regionale Wirstchaftspolitik in der UdSSR und der BRD*, Report to the Fourth Soviet–West German Seminar on Regional Development, Kiev, 1–10 October 1989.

Greenberg, Stanley B. (1995) *Middle Class Dreams: The Politics of Power of the New American Majority*, New York: Times Books.

Gremion, Pierre (1976) *Le pouvoir peripherique*, Paris: Seuil.

Grier, Peter (1995) "Preparing for the 21st century information war", *Government Executive*, 28 (8): 130–2.

Griffin, Gabriele (ed.) (1995) *Feminist Activism in the 1990s*, London: Francis and Taylor.

— et al. (eds) (1994) *Stirring It: Challenges for Feminism*, London: Francis and Taylor.

Grosz, Elizabeth (1995) *Space, Time, and Perversion*, London: Routledge.

Grubbe, Peter (1993) *Selbstbedienungsladen: vom Verfall der Demokratischen Moral*, Wuppertal: Hammer.

Guehenno, Jean Marie (1993) *La fin de la democratie*, Paris:

Flammarion. Read in the Spanish translation, Barcelona: Paidos, 1995 (quotations are my own translation into English).

Gumbel, Andrew (1994) "French deception", *New Statesman and Society*, 7, 328: 24.

Gunlicks Arthur B. (ed.) (1993) *Campaign and Party Finance in North America and Western Europe*, Boulder, Colo.: Westview Press.

Habermas, Jurgen (1973) *Legitimation Crisis*, Boston: Beacon Press.

Hacker, Kenneth L. (1996) "Missing links and the evolution of electronic democratization", *Media, Culture, and Society*, 18: 213–323.

Hadden, Jeffrey and Shupe, Hanson (1989) *Fundamentalism and Secularization Reconsidered*, New York: Paragon House.

Hage, Jerald, and Powers, Charles (1992) *Postindustrial Lives: Roles and Relationships in the 21st Century*, London: Sage.

Halperin, David M., Winkler, John J. and Zeitlin, Froma I.(eds) (1990) *Before Sexuality: the Construction of Erotic Experience in the Ancient Greek World*, Princeton, NJ: Princeton University Press.

Halperin Donghi, Tulio (1969) *Historia contemporanea de America Latina*, Madrid: Alianza Editorial.

Handelman, Stephen (1995) *Comrade Criminal: Russia's New Mafiya*, New Haven: Yale University Press.

Hay, Colin (1994) "Environmental security and state legitimacy", *Capitalism, Nature, Socialism*, 1: 83–98.

Heard, Alex (1995) "The road to Oklahoma City", *The New Republic*, May 15.

Heidenheimer, Arnold J., Johnston, Michael and LeVine, Victor T. (eds) (1989) *Political Corruption: a Handbook*, New Brunswick, NJ: Transaction.

Held, David (1991) "Democracy, the nation-state and the global system", *Economy and Society*, 20 (2): 138–72.

— (ed.) (1993) *Prospects for Democracy*, Cambridge: Polity Press.

Heller, Karen S. (1992) "Silence equals death: discourses on AIDS and identity in the gay press, 1981–1986", unpublished PhD dissertation, San Francisco: University of California.

Helvarg, David (1995) "The anti-enviro connection", *The Nation*, May 22.

Hempel, Lamont C. (1996) *Environmental Governance: the Global Challenge*, Washington DC: Island Press.

Herek, Gregory M. and Greene, Beverly (eds) (1995) *HIV, Identity and Community: the HIV Epidemics*, Thousand Oaks, CA: Sage.

Hernandez Navarro, Luis (1995) *Chiapas: la guerra y la paz*, Mexico: ADN Editores.

Hester, Marianne, Kelly, Liz and Radford, Jill (1995) *Women, Violence, and Male Power: Feminist Activism, Research and Practice*, Philadelphia: Open University Press.

Hicks, L. Edward (1994) *Sometimes in the Wrong, but Never in Doubt: George S. Benson and the Education of the New Religious Right*, Knoxville: University of Tennessee Press.

High Level Experts Group (1996) *The Information Society in Europe*, Report to the European Commission, Brussels: Commission of the European Union.

Himmelfarb, Gertrude (1995) *The De-moralization of Society: from Victorian Virtues to Modern Values*, New York: Alfred Knopf.

Hirkett, Mervyn (1992) *Some to Mecca Turn to Pray. Islamic Values in the Modern World*, St Albans: Claridge Press.

Hiro, Dilip (1989) *Holy Wars: The Rise of Islamic Fundamentalism*, New York: Routledge.

Hirst, Paul and Thompson, Grahame (1996) *Globalization in Question: the International Economy and the Possibilities of Governance*, Cambridge: Polity Press.

Hobsbawm, Eric J. (1990) *Nations and Nationalism since 1780*, Cambridge: Cambridge University Press.

— (1992) *Naciones y nacionalismo desde 1780*, Barcelona: Critica (expanded and updated version of original 1990 English publication).

— (1994) *The Age of Extremes: a History of the World, 1914–1991*, New York: Pantheon Books.

Hochschild, Jennifer L. (1995) *Facing up to the American Dream: Race, Class, and the Soul of the Nation*, Princeton, NJ: Princeton University Press.

Holliman, Jonathan (1990) "Environmentalism with a global scope",*Japan Quarterly*, July–September: 284–90.

hooks, bell (1989) *Talking Back: Thinking Feminist, Thinking Black*, Boston: South End Press.

— (1990) *Yearning: Race, Gender, and Cultural Politics*, Boston: South End Press.

— (1993) *Sisters of the Yaw: Black Women and Self-Recovery*, Boston: South End Press.

Hooson, David (1994a) "Ex-Soviet identities and the return of geography", in Hooson (ed.), pp. 134–40.

— (ed.) (1994b) *Geography and National Identity*, Oxford: Blackwell.

Horsman, M. and Marshall, A. (1994) *After the Nation State*, New York: Harper-Collins.

Horton, Tom (1991) "The green giant", *Rolling Stone*, September 5: 43–112.

Hsia, Chu-joe (1996) Personal communication.

Hsing, You-tien (1996) *Making Capitalism in China: the Taiwan Connection*, New York: Oxford University Press.

Hughes, James (1994) "The 'Americanization' of Russian politics:

Russia's first television election, December 1993", *The Journal of Communist Studies and Transition Politics*, 10 (2): 125–50.

Hulsberg, Werner (1988) *The German Greens: a Social and Political Profile*, London: Verso.

Hunter, Robert (1979) *Warriors of the Rainbow: a Chronicle of the Greenpeace Movement*, New York: Holt, Rinehart and Winston.

— "Issues, candidate image and priming: the use of private polls in Kennedy's 1960 presidential campaign", *American Political Science Review*, 88 (3): 527–40.

Inoguchi, Takashi (1993) "Japanese politics in transition: a theoretical review", *Government and Opposition*, 28 (4): 443–55.

Irigaray, Luce (1977/1985) *Ce sexe qui n'en est pas un*, read in the English translation (1985), Ithaca, NY: Cornell University Press.

— (1984/1993) *Ethique de la difference sexuelle*, read in the English translation (1993), Ithaca, NY: Cornell University Press.

Irving, Larry et al. (1994) "Steps towards a global information infrastructure", *Federal Communications Law Journal*, 47 (2): 271–9.

Ivins, Molly (1995) "Fertilizer of hate", *The Progressive*, June.

Jacobs, Lawrence R. and Shapiro, Robert Y. (1995) "The rise of presidential polling: the Nixon White House in historical perspective", *Public Opinion Quarterly*, 59: 163–95.

Janowitz, Morris (1976) *Social Control of the Welfare State*, Chicago: University of Chicago Press.

Jaquette, Jane S. (ed.) (1994) *The Women's Movement in Latin America. Participation and Democracy*, Boulder, Colo.: Westview Press.

Jarrett-Macauley, Delia (ed.), (1996) *Reconstructing Womanhood, Reconstructing Feminism: Writings on Black Women*, London: Routledge.

Jelen, Ted (ed.) (1989) *Religion and Political Behavior in America*, New York: Praeger.

— (1991) *The Political Mobilization of Religious Belief*, New York: Praeger.

Johansen, Elaine R. (1990) *Political Corruption: Scope and Resources: an Annotated Bibliography*, New York: Garland.

Johnson, Chalmers (1982) *MITI and the Japanese Miracle*, Stanford, Stanford University Press.

— (1995) *Japan: Who Governs? The Rise of the Developmental State*, New York: W.W. Norton.

Johnston, R.J, Knight, David and Kofman, Eleanore (eds) (1988) *Nationalism, Self-determination, and Political Geography*, London: Croom Helm.

Jordan, June (1995) "In the land of white supremacy", *The Progressive*, June.

Judge, David, Stokes, Gerry and Wolman, Hall (1995) *Theories of Urban Politics*, Thousand Oaks, CA: Sage.

Juergensmayer, Mark (1993) *The New Cold War? Religious Fundamentalism Confronts the Secular State*, Berkeley: University of California Press.

Jutglar, Antoni (1966) *Els burgesos catalans*, Barcelona: Fontanella.

Kahn, Robert E. (1994) "The role of government in the evolution of the Internet", *Communications of the ACM*, 37 (8): 15–19.

Kahne, Hilda and Giele, Janet Z. (eds). (1992) *Women's Work and Women's Lives: The Continuing Struggle Worldwide*, Boulder, Colo.: Westview Press.

Kaid, Lynda Lee and Holtz-Bacha, Christina (eds). (1995) *Political Advertising in Western Democracies*, Thousand Oaks, CA: Sage.

Kaminiecki, Sheldon (ed.) (1993) *Environmental Politics in the International Arena: Movements, Parties, Organizations, Policy*, Albany: State University of New York Press.

Kanagy, Conrad L. et al. (1994) "Surging environmentalisms: changing public opinion or changing publics", *Social Science Quarterly*, 75 (4): 804–19.

Katznelson, Ira (1996) *Liberalism's Crooked Circle: Letters to Adam Michnik*, Princeton, NJ: Princeton University Press.

Kazin, Michael (1995) *The Populist Persuasion: an American History*, New York: Basic Books.

Keating, Michael (1995) *Nations against the State: the New Politics of Nationalism in Quebec, Catalonia, and Scotland*, New York: St Martin's Press.

Keen, Sam (1991) *Fire in the Belly: on Being a Man*, New York: Bantam Books.

Kelly, Petra (1994) *Thinking Green: Essays on Environmentalism, Feminism, and Nonviolence*, Berkeley: Parallax Press.

Kepel, Gilles (1995) "Entre société et communauté: les musulmans au Royaume-Uni et au France aujourd'hui", in Dubet and Wieviorka (eds), pp. 273–88.

Khazanov, Anatoly M.(1995) *After the USSR: Ethnicity, Nationalism, and Politics in the Commonwealth of Independent States*, Madison: University of Wisconsin Press.

Khosrokhavar, Farhad (1995) "Le quasi-individu: de la neo-communauté à la necro-communauté", in Dubet and Wieviorka (eds), pp. 235–56.

Khoury, Philip and Kostiner, Joseph (eds) (1990) *Tribes and State Formation in the Middle East*, Berkeley: University of California Press.

Kim, Marlene (1993) "Comments", in Cobble (ed.), pp. 85–92.

King, Anthony (1984) "Sex, money and power: political scandals in Britain and the United States", Colchester, University of Essex, Essex Papers in Politics and Government.

King, Joseph P. (1989) "Socioeconomic development and corrupt campaign practices in England", in Heidenheimer et al. (eds), pp. 233–50.

Kiselyova, Emma and Castells, Manuel (1997) *The New Russian Federalism in Siberia and the Far East*, Berkeley: University of California, Center for Eastern European and Slavic Studies/Center for German and European Studies, Research Paper.

Klanwatch/Militia Task Force (KMTF) (1996) *False Patriots. The Threat from Antigovernment Extremists*, Montgomery, Alabama: Southern Poverty Law Center.

Klinenberg, Eric and Perrin, Andrew (1996) "Symbolic politics in the Information Age: the 1996 presidential campaign in cyberspace", Berkeley: University of California, Department of Sociology, Research Paper for Soc 290.2, unpublished.

Kolodny, Annette (1984) *The Land before Her: Fantasy and Experience of the American Frontiers, 1630–1860*, Chapel Hill: University of North Carolina Press.

Kozlov, Viktor (1988) *The Peoples of the Soviet Union*, Bloomington, Ind.: Indiana University Press.

Kraus, K. and Knight, A. (1995) *State, Society, and the UN System: Changing Perspectives on Multilateralism*, New York: United Nations University Press.

Kuppers, Gary (ed.) (1994) *Companeras: Voices from the Latin American Women's Movement*, London: Latin American Bureau.

Kuttner, Robert (1995) "The net as free-market utopia? Think again", *Business Week*, September 4, p. 24.

Lamberts-Bendroth, Margaret (1993) *Fundamentalism and Gender: 1875 to Present*, New Haven, CT: Yale University Press.

Langguth, Gerd (1984) *The Green Factor in German Politics: from Protest Movement to Political Party*, Boulder, Colo.: Westview Press.

Lasch, Christopher (1980) *The Culture of Narcissism*, London: Abacus, 1980.

Laserna, Roberto (1992) *Productores de democracia: actores sociales y procesos politicos*, Cochabamba: Centro de Estudios de la Realidad Economica y Social.

Lash, Scott and Urry, John (1994) *Economies of Signs and Space*, London: Sage.

Laumann, Edward O. et al. (1994) *The Social Organization of Sexuality: Sexual Practices in the United States*, Chicago: University of Chicago Press.

L'Avenc: Revista d'Historia (1996) Special issue: "Catalunya- Espanya", no. 200, February.

Lavrakas, Paul J. et al. (eds) (1995) *Presidential Polls and the New Media*, Boulder, Colo.: Westview Press.

Lawton, Kim A. (1989) "Whatever happened to the Religious Right?", *Christianity Today*, December 15: 44.

Leal, Jesus et al. (1996) *Familia y vivienda en Espana*, Madrid: Universidad Autonoma de Madrid, Instituto de Sociologia, Research Report.

Lechner, Frank J. (1991) "Religion, law, and global order", in Robertson and Garrett (eds), pp. 263–80.

Lesthaeghe, R. (1995) "The second demographic transition in Western countries: an interpretation", in Mason and Jensen (eds), pp. 17–62.

Levin, Murray B. (1987) *Talk Radio and the American Dream*, Lexington, MA: Heath.

Levine, Martin (1979) "Gay ghetto", in Martin Levine (ed.), *Gay Men*, New York: Harper and Row.

Lewis, Bernard (1988) *The Political Language of Islam*, Chicago: University of Chicago Press.

Lewis, Peter H. (1996a) "Judge temporarily blocks law that bars indecency on Internet", *New York Times*, February 16, pp. C1–C16.

— (1996b) "Judges turn back law to regulate Internet decency", *New York Times*, June 13, p. A1.

Leys, Colin (1989) "What is the problem about corruption?", in Heidenheimer et al. (eds), pp. 51–66.

L'Histoire (1993) Special dossier "Argent, politique et corruption: 1789-1993", May, 166: 48 ff.

Li, Zhilan (1995) "Shanghai, Guandong ruheyu zhongyang zhouxuan (How did Shanghai and Guandong negotiate with the central government?)", *The Nineties Monthly*, December, 311: 36–9.

Lienesch, Michael (1993) *Redeeming America: Piety and Politics in the New Christian Right*, Chapel Hill: University of North Carolina Press.

Lipschutz, Ronnie D. and Coca, Ken (1993) "The implications of global ecological interdependence", in Ronnie D. Lipschutz and Ken Coca (eds), *The State and Social Power in Global Environmental Politics*, New York: Columbia University Press.

Lipset, Seymour M. (1996) *American Exceptionalism: a Double-edged Sword*, New York: Norton.

— and Raab, Earl (1978) *The Politics of Unreason: Right-wing Extremism in America, 1790–1970*, New York: Harper and Row.

Lloyd, Gary A. and Kuselewickz J. (eds.) (1995) *HIV Disease: Lesbians, Gays, and the Social Services*, New York: Haworth Press.

Lodato, Saverio (1994) *Quindici anni di Mafia*, Milan: Biblioteca Universale Rizzoli.

Longman (1990) *Political Scandals and Causes Célèbres since 1945*, London: Longman's International Reference Compendium.

Lowi, Theodore J. (1988) "Foreword", in Markovits and Silverstein (eds), pp. vii–xii.

Luecke, Hanna (1993) *Islamischer Fundamentalismus – Rueckfall ins Mittelalter oder Wegbereiter der Moderne?*, Berlin: Klaus Schwarz Verlag.

Lyday, Corbin (ed.) (1994) *Ethnicity, Federalism and Democratic Transition in Russia: A Conference Report*, Report of a Conference sponsored by the Berkeley-Stanford Program in Soviet and Post-Soviet Studies held at Berkeley on November 11–17, 1993.

Lyon, David (1994) *The Electronic Eye: the Rise of Surveillance Society*, Cambridge: Polity Press.

MacDonald, Greg (1990) *The Emergence of Multimedia Conglomerates*, Geneva: ILO, Multinational Enterprises Program, Working Paper 70.

McDonogh, Gary W. (ed.) (1986) *Conflict in Catalonia*, Gainsville: University of Florida Press.

McGrew, Anthony G. (1992a) "Global politics in a transitional era", in McGrew et al. (eds) pp. 312–30.

— (1992b) "Military technology and the dynamics of global militarization", in McGrew et al. (eds), pp. 83–117.

— Lewis, Paul G., et al. (1992) *Global Politics: Globalization and the Nation State*, Cambridge: Polity Press.

McInnes, Colin (1992) "Technology and modern warfare", in Baylis and Rengger (eds), pp. 130–58.

— and Sheffield, G.D. (eds) (1988) *Warfare in the 20th Century: Theory and Practice*, London: Unwin Hyman.

McLaughlin, Andrew (1993) *Regarding Nature: Industrialism and Deep Ecology*, Albany: State University of New York Press.

Macy, Joanna (1991) *World as Lover, World as Self*, Berkeley: Parallax Press.

Magleby, David B. and Nelson, Candice J. (1990) *The Money Chase: Congressional Campaign Finance Reform*, Washington DC: Brookings Institution.

Maheu, Louis (1995) "Les mouvements sociaux: plaidoyer pour une sociologie de l'ambivalence", in Dubet and Wieviorka (eds), pp. 313–34.

Mainichi Shinbun (1995), May 1.

Manes, Christopher (1990) *Green Rage: Radical Environmentalism and the Unmaking of Civilization*, Boston: Little, Brown.

Mansbridge, Jane (1995) "What is the feminist movement?", in Ferree and Martin (eds), pp. 27–34.

Markovits, Andrei S. and Silverstein, Mark (eds) (1988a) *The Politics of Scandal: Power and Process in Liberal Democracies*, New York: Holmes and Meier.

— and — (1988b) "Power and process in liberal democracies", in Markovits and Silverstein (eds), pp. 15–37.

Marquez, Enrique (1995) *Por que perdio Camacho*, Mexico: Oceano.

Marsden, George M. (1980) *Fundamentalism and American Culture: the Shaping of the 20th Century Evangelicalism, 1870–1925*, New York: Oxford University Press.

Martinez Torres, Maria Elena (1994) "The Zapatista rebellion and identity", Berkeley: University of California, Program of Latin American Studies, research paper (unpublished).

— (1996) "Networking global civil society: the Zapatista movement. The first informational guerrilla", Berkeley: University of California, seminar paper for CP 229 (unpublished).

Marty, Martin E. (1988) "Fundamentalism as a social phenomenon", *Bulletin of the American Academy of Arts and Sciences*, 42: 15–29.

— and Appleby, Scott (eds) (1991) *Fundamentalisms Observed*, Chicago: University of Chicago Press.

Masnick, George, S. and Ardle, Nancy M. (1994) *Revised US Households Projections: New Methods and New Assumptions*, Cambridge, Mass.: Harvard University, Graduate School of Design/ John F. Kennedy School of Government, Joint Center for Housing Studies, Working Papers Series.

— and Kim, Joshua M. (1995) *The Decline of Demand: Housing's Next Generation*, Cambridge, Mass.: Harvard University, Joint Center for Housing Studies, Working Papers Series.

Mason, Karen O. and Jensen, An-Magritt (1995) *Gender and Family Change in Industrialized Countries*, New York: Oxford University Press.

Mass, Lawrence (1990) *Dialogues of the Sexual Revolution*, New York: Haworth Press.

Massolo, Alejandra (1992) *Por amor y coraje: Mujeres en movimientos urbanos de la Ciudad de Mexico*, Mexico: El Colegio de Mexico.

Mattelart, Armand (1991) *La communication-monde: histoire des ideés et des strategies*, Paris: La Decouverte.

Matthews, Nancy A. (1989) "Surmounting a legacy: the expansion of racial diversity in a local anti-rape movement", *Gender and Society*, 3: 519–33.

Maxwell, Joe and Tapia, Andres (1995) "Guns and Bibles", *Christianity Today*, 39 (7): 34.

Mayer, William G. (1994) "The polls – poll trends: the rise of the new media", *Public Opinion Quarterly*, 58: 124–46.

Mayorga, Fernando (1993) *Discurso y politica en Bolivia*, La Paz, ILDIS-CERES.

Mejia Barquera, Fernando et al. (1985) *Televisa: el quinto poder*, Mexico: Claves Latinoamericanas.

Melchett, Peter (1995) "The fruits of passion", *New Statesman and Society*, April 28: 37–8.

Melucci, Alberto (1995) "Individualisation et globalisation: au-delà de la modernité?", in Dubet and Wieviorka (eds), pp. 433–48.

Meny, Yves (1992) *La corruption de la Republique*, Paris: Fayard.

Merchant, Carolyn (1980) *The Death of Nature: Women, Ecology, and the Scientific Revolution*, New York: Harper and Row.

Mesa, Carlos D. (1986) "Como se fabrica un presidente", in *Cuarto Intermedio*, pp. 4–23.

Michelson, William (1985) *From Sun to Sun: Daily Obligations and Community Structure in the Lives of Employed Women and their Families*, Totowa, NJ: Rowman and Allanheld.

Mikulsky, D.V. (1992) *Ideologicheskaya kontseptsiya Islamskoi partii vozrozhdeniya (Ideological Concept of Islamic Revival Party)*, Moscow: Gorbachev-Fund.

Minc, Alain (1993) *Le nouveau Moyen Age*, Paris: Gallimard.

Misztal, Bronislaw and Shupe, Anson (1992a) "Making sense of the global revival of fundamentalism", in Bronislaw and Shupe (eds), pp. 3–9.

— and — (eds) (1992b) *Religion and Politics in Comparative Perspective: Revival of Religious Fundamentalism in East and West*, Westport, Conn.: Praeger.

Mitchell, Juliet (1966) "Women: the longest revolution", *New Left Review*, 40, November/December.

Miyadai, Shinji (1995) *Owarinaki Nichijo of Ikiro (Live in Endless Everyday Life)*, Tokyo: Chikuma-Shobo.

Moen, Matthew C. (1992) *The Transformation of the Christian Right*, Tuscaloosa: University of Alabama Press.

— and Gustafson, Lowell S. (eds) (1992) *The Religious Challenge to the State*, Philadelphia: Temple University Press.

Mokhtari, Fariborz (ed.) (1994) *Peacemaking, Peacekeeping and Coalition Warfare: the Future of the UN*, Washington DC: National Defense University.

Monnier, Alain and de Guibert-Lantoine, Catherine (1993) "La conjoncture démographique: l'Europe et les pays développés d'outre-mer", *Population*, 48 (4): 1043–67.

Moog, Sandra (1995) "To the root: the mobilization of the culture concept in the development of radical environmental thought", Berkeley: University of California, Department of Anthropology, Seminar Paper for Anthro. 250X (unpublished).

— (1996) "Electronic media and informational politics in America", Berkeley: University of California, Department of Sociology, Research Paper for Soc 290.2 (unpublished).

Moore, David W. (1992) *The Superpollsters: How They Measure and*

Manipulate Public Opinion in America, New York: Four Walls Eight Windows.

Moreau Deffarges, Philippe (1993) *La mondialisation: vers la fin des frontieres?*, Paris: Dunod.

Moreno Toscano, Alejandra (1996) *Turbulencia politica: causas y razones del 94*, Mexico: Oceano.

Morgen, Sandra (1988) "The dream of diversity, the dilemmas of difference: race and class contradictions in a feminist health clinic" in J. Sole (ed.), *Anthropology for the Nineties*, New York: Free Press.

Morin, Edgar and Kern, Anne B. (1993) *Terre-Patrie*, Paris: Seuil.

Morris, Stephen D. (1991) *Corruption and Politics in Contemporary Mexico*, Tuscaloosa: The University of Alabama Press.

Moscow Times (1996), "Style beats substance in ad campaigns", May 30, p. 1.

Moser, Leo (1985) *The Chinese Mosaic: the Peoples and Provinces of China*, London: Westview Press.

Mouffe, Chantal (1995) "The end of politics and the rise of the radical right", *Dissent*, Fall: 488.

Mundy, Alicia (1996) "Taking a poll on polls", *Media Week*, 6 (8): 17–20.

Murray, Charles and Herrnstein, Richard (1994) *The Bell Curve: Intelligence and Class Structure in American Life*, New York: Free Press.

Nair, Sami (1996) "La crisis argelina", in *Claves*, April: 14–17.

Nakazawa, Shinichi et al. (1995) "AUM Jiken to wa Nandatta no ka (Was AUM an incident?)", in *Kokoku Hihyo*, June.

Nash, June et al. (1995) *La explosion de comunidades en Chiapas*, Copenhagen: International Working Group on Indian Affairs, Document IWGIA n. 16.

Navarro, Vicente (1994) *The Politics of Health Policy: The US Reforms, 1980–1994*, Oxford: Blackwell.

— (1995) "Gobernabilidad, desigualdad y estado del bienestar. La situacion en Estados Unidos y su relevancia para Europa", Barcelona: Paper delivered at the International Symposium on Governability, Inequality, and Social Policies, organized by the Institut d'Estudis Socials Avancats, 23–25 November (unpublished).

Negroponte, Nicholas (1995) *Being Digital*, New York: Alfred Knopf.

Norman, E. Herbert (1940) *Japan's Emergence as a Modern State: Political and Economic Problems of the Meiji Period*, New York: Institute of Pacific Relations.

Nunnenkamp, Peter et al. (1994) *Globalisation of Production and Markets*, Tubingen: Kieler Studien, J.C.B. Mohr.

OECD (1993–95) *Employment Outlook*, Paris: OECD.

OECD (1994a) *The OECD Jobs Study*, Paris: OECD.

OECD (1994b) *Women and Structural Change: New Perspectives*, Paris: OECD.

OECD (1995) *Labour Force Statistics*, Paris: OECD.

Offen, Karen (1988) "Defining feminism: a comparative historical approach", *Signs*, 14 (11): 119–57.

Ohama, Itsuro (1995) "AUM toiu Danso (AUM as an attempt to disconnect themselves from history)", in *Seiron*, July.

Orr, Robert M. (1995) "Home-grown terrorism plagues both the US and Japan", *Tokyo Business*, July.

Orstrom Moller, J. (1995) *The Future European Model: Economic Internationalization and Cultural Decentralization*, Westport, Conn.: Praeger.

Osawa, Masachi (1995) "AUM wa Naze Sarin ni Hashitakka (Why did AUM use sarin)?", in *Gendai*, October.

Ostertag, Bob (1991) "Greenpeace takes over the world", *Mother Jones*, March-April: 32–87.

Oumlil, Ali (1992) *Islam et etat national*, Casablanca: Editions Le Fennec.

Oversight of the IMF and the World Bank (1995) *A Meeting of a Multinational Group of Parliamentarians Involved in Oversight of the IMF and the World Bank*, Washington, DC: US Government Printing Office.

Page, Benjamin I. and Shapiro, Robert Y. (1992) *The Rational Public: Fifty Years of Trends in American's Policy Preferences*, Chicago: University of Chicago Press.

Pagano, Michael A. and Bowman, Ann O'M. (1995) "The state of American federalism, 1994-95", *Publius: The Journal of Federalism*, 25 (3): 1–21.

Panarin, Alexander S. (1994) "Rossia v evrazii: geopolitisichie vyzovy i tsivilizatsionnye otvety", Voprosy filosofii, 12: 19–31 (read from *Russian Social Science Review: A Journal of Translations*, May–June 1996: 35-53).

Pardo, Mary (1995) "Doing it for the kids: Mexican American community activists, border feminists?", in Ferree and Martin (eds), pp. 356–71.

Partido Revolucionario Institucional (1994) *La reforma del PRI y el cambio democratico en Mexico*, Mexico: Editorial Limusa.

Patterson, T. E. (1993) *Out of Order: How the Decline of the Political Parties and the Growing Power of the News Media Undermine the American Way of Electing Presidents*, New York: Alfred Knopf.

Pattie, Charles et al. (1995) "Winning the local vote: the effectiveness of constituency campaign spending in Great Britain, 1983–1992", *American Political Science Review*, 89 (4): 969–85.

Perez-Argote, Alfonso (ed.) (1989) *Sociologia del nacionalismo,* Vitoria: Argitarapen Zerbitzua Euskal Herriko Unibertsitatea.
Perez Fernandez del Castillo, German, et al. (1995) *La voz de los votos: un analisis critico de las elecciones de 1994,* Mexico: Miguel Angel Porrua Grupo Editorial.
Perez Iribarne, Eduardo (1993a) *La opinion publica al poder,* La Paz: Empresa Encuestas y Estudios.
— (1993b) "La television imposible", *Fe y Pueblo,* 3: 67–84.
Perez-Tabernero, Alfonso et al. (1993) *Concentracion de la comunicacion en Europa: empresa comercial e interes publico,* Barcelona: Generalitat de Catalunya, Centre d'Investigacio de la Comunicacio.
Phillips, Andrew (1992) "Pocketbook politics: Britain's Tories face a tough fight against Labour Party rivals in an April election", *Maclean's,* 105 (12): 22–25.
Philo, Greg (1993) "Political advertising, popular belief and the 1992 British general election", *Media, Culture, and Society,* 15 (3): 407–18.
Pi, Ramon (ed.) (1996) *Jordi Pujol: Cataluna, Espana,* Madrid: Espasa Hoy.
Pinelli, Antonella (1995) "Women's condition, low fertility, and emerging union patterns in Europe", in Mason and Jensen (eds), pp. 82–104.
Pipes, Richard (1954) *The Formation of the Soviet Union: Communism and Nationalism, 1917–23,* Cambridge, Mass.: Harvard University Press.
Piscatori, James (1986) *Islam in a World of Nation-states,* Cambridge: Cambridge University Press.
Pi-Sunyer, Oriol (1991) "Catalan politics and Spanish democracy: the matter of cultural sovereignty", in Azevedo (ed.), pp. 1–20.
Plant, Judith (1991) "Ecofeminism", in Dobson (ed.), pp. 100–4.
Po, Lan-chih (1996) "Feminism, identity, and women's movements: theoretical debates and a case study in Taiwan", Berkeley: University of California, Department of City and Regional Planning, research paper (unpublished).
Poguntke, Thomas (1993) *Alternative Politics: the German Green Party,* Edinburgh: Edinburgh University Press.
Pollith, Katha (1995) "Subject to debate", *The Nation,* 260 (22): 784.
Porrit, Jonathan (1994) *Seeing Green: the Politics of Ecology Explained,* Oxford: Blackwell.
Portes, Alejandro et al. (eds.) (1989) *The Informal Economy,* Baltimore: Johns Hopkins University Press.
Poulantzas, Nicos (1978) *L'etat, le pouvoir, le socialisme,* Paris: Presses Universitaires de France – Politiques.
Prat de la Riba, Enric (1906) *La nacionalitat catalana,* Barcelona: Edicions 62, republished in 1978.
Price, Vincent and Hsu, Mei-Ling (1992) "Public opinion about AIDS

policies: the role of misinformation and attitudes towards homo-sexuals", *Public Opinion Quarterly*, 56 (1).

Puiggene i Riera, Ariadna et al. (1991) "Official language policies in contemporary Catalonia", in Azevedo (ed.), pp. 30–49.

Putnam, Robert (1995) "Bowling alone: America's declining social capital", *Journal of Democracy*, 6 (1): 65–78.

Reigot, Betty Polisar and Spina, Rita K. (1996) *Beyond the Traditional Family. Voices of Diversity*, New York: Springer Verlag.

Rich, Adrienne (1980/1993) "Compulsory heterosexuality and lesbian existence", in Abelove et al. (eds), pp. 227–54.

Richardson, Dick and Rootes, Chris (eds) (1995) *The Green Challenge: The Development of Green Parties in Europe*, London: Routledge.

Riechmann, Jorge and Fernandez Buey, Francisco (1994) *Redes que dan libertad: introduccion a los nuevos movimientos sociales*, Barcelona: Paidos.

Riesebrodt, Martin (1993) *Pious Passion: the Emergence of Modern Fundamentalism in the United States and Iran*, Berkeley: University of California Press.

Roberts, Marilyn and McCombs, Maxwell (1994) "Agenda setting and political advertising: origins of the news agenda", *Political Communication*, 11: 249–62.

Robertson, Roland and Garrett, William R. (eds) (1991) *Religion and Global Order*, New York: Paragon House.

Rochester, J. Martin (1993) *Waiting for the Millennium: the UN and the Future of World Order*, Columbia, SC: University of South Carolina Press.

Rodgers, Gerry (ed.) (1994) *Workers, Institutions and Economic Growth in Asia*, Geneva: International Institute of Labour Studies.

Rojas, Rosa (1995) *Chiapas: la paz violenta*, Mexico: Ediciones La Jornada.

Rokkan, Stein and Urwin, Derek W. (eds) (1982) *The Politics of Territorial Identity*, London: Sage.

Roman, Joel (1993) "La gauche, le pouvoir, les medias: à-propos du suicide de Pierre Beregovoy", *Esprit*, 6: 143–6.

Rondfeldt, David (1995) "The battle for the mind of Mexico", electronically published in June 1995 at RAND Corporation home page. Available at: http://www.eco.utexas.edu/homepages/faculty/cleaver/chiapas95/netawars.

Roper Center of Public Opinion and Polling (1995) "How much government, at what level?: change and persistence in American ideas", *The Public Perspective*, 6 (3).

Rosenau, J. (1990) *Turbulence in World Politics*, London: Harvester Wheatsheaf.

Ross, Loretta J. (1995) "Saying it with a gun", *The Progressive*, June.

Ross, Shelley (1988) *Fall from Grace: Sex, Scandal, and Corruption in American Politics from 1702 to present*, New York: Ballantine.

Roth, Jurgen and Frey, Marc (1992) *Die Verbrecher Holding: das vereinte Europa im Griff der Mafia*, Piper and Co. (read in the Spanish translation, Madrid: Anaya/Mario Muchnik, 1995).

Rovira i Virgili, A. (1988) *Catalunya: Espanya*, Barcelona: Edicions de la Magrana (originally published in 1912).

Rowbotham, Sheila (1974) *Hidden from History: Rediscovering Women in History from the 17th Century to the Present*, New York: Pantheon Books.

— (1989) *The Past is Before Us: Feminism and Action since the 1960s*, London: Pandora.

— (1992) *Women in Movement: Feminism and Social Action*, New York: Routledge.

Rowlands, Ian H. (1992) "Environmental issues and world politics", in Baylis and Rengger (eds), pp. 287–309.

Rubert de Ventos, Xavier (1994) *Nacionalismos: el laberinto de la identidad*, Madrid: Espasa-Calpe.

Rubin, Rose M. and Riney, Rose (1994) *Working Wives and Dual- earner Families*, Westport, Conn.: Praeger.

Ruiz-Cabanas, Miguel (1993) "La campana permanente de Mexico: costos, beneficios y consecuencia", in Smith (ed.), pp. 207–20.

Rupp, Leila J. and Taylor, Verta (1987) *Survival in the Doldrums: the American Women's Rights Movement, 1945 to the 1960s*, New York: Oxford University Press.

Sabato, Larry J. (1991) *Feeding Frenzy: How Attack Journalism has Transformed American Politics*, New York: Free Press.

Saboulin, Michel and Thave, Suzanne (1993) "La vie en couple marie: un modele qui s'affaiblit", in INSEE, *La société française: données sociales*, Paris: INSEE.

Salaff, Janet (1981) *Working Daughters of Hong Kong*, Cambridge: Cambridge University Press.

— (1988) *State and Family in Singapore: Restructuring a Developing Society*, Ithaca: Cornell University Press.

— (1992) "Women, family and the state in Hong Kong, Taiwan and Singapore", in Richard Appelbaum and Jeffrey Henderson (eds), *States and Development in the Asian Pacific Rim*, Newbury Park, CA: Sage Publications.

Salmin, A. M. (1992) *SNG: Sostoyanie i perspektivy razvitiya*, Moscow: Gorbachev Fund.

Salrach, Josep M. (1996) "Catalunya, Castella i Espanya vistes per si mateixes a l'edad mitjana", *L'Avenc*, 200: 30–7.

Saltzman-Chafetz, Janet (1995) "Chicken or egg? A theory of relationship between feminist movements and family change", in Mason and Jensen (eds), pp. 63–81.

Salvati, Michele (1995) "Italy's fateful choices", *New Left Review*, 213: 79–96.

Sanchez, Magaly and Pedrazzini, Yves (1996) *Los malandros: la culture de l'urgence chez les jeunes des quartiers populaires de Caracas*, Paris: Fondation Humanisme et Developpement.

Sanchez Jankowski, Martin (1991) *Islands in the Street: Gangs and American Urban Society*, Berkeley: University of California Press.

Santoni Rugiu, Antonio (1994) "La bisciopedagogia", *Ponte*, 50 (2): 20–5.

Saravia, Joaquin and Sandoval, Godofredo (1991) *Jach'a Uru: la esperanza de un pueblo?*, La Paz: CEP-ILDIS.

Savigear, Peter (1992) "The United States: superpower in decline?", in Baylis and Rengger (eds), pp. 334–53.

Scammell, Margaret and Semetko, Holli A. (1995) "Political advertising on television: the British experience", in Kaid and Holtz-Bacha (eds), pp. 19–43.

Scanlan, J. (ed.) (1990) *Surviving the Blues: Growing up in the Thatcher Decade*, London: Virago.

Scarce, Rik (1990) *Eco-warriors: Understanding the Radical Environmental Movement*, Chicago: Noble Press.

Schaeffer, Francis (1982) *Time for Anger: the Myth of Neutrality*, Westchester, Ill.: Crossway Books.

Scharf, Thomas (1994) *The German Greens: Challenging the Consensus*, Oxford: Berg.

Scheer, Leo (1994) *La democratie virtuelle*, Paris: Flammarion.

Scheff, Thomas (1994) "Emotions and identity: a theory of ethnic nationalism", in Calhoun (ed.), pp. 277–303.

Schlesinger, Philip (1991) "Media, the political order and national identity", *Media, Culture, and Society*, 13: 297–308.

Schneir, Miriam (ed.), (1994) *Feminism in our Time: The Essential Writings, World War II to the Present*, New York: Vintage Books.

Scott, Allen (1995) *From Silicon Valley to Hollywood: Growth and Development of the Multimedia Industry in California*, Los Angeles, UCLA's Lewis Center for Regional Policy Studies, Working Paper no. 13, November 1995.

Scott, Beardsley et al. (1995) "The great European multimedia gamble", *McKinsey Quarterly*, 3: 142–61.

Sechi, Salvatore (ed.) (1995) *Deconstructing Italy: Italy in the Nineties*, Berkeley: University of California, International and Area Studies, Research Series.

Sengenberger, Werner and Campbell, Duncan (eds) (1994) *Creating Economic Opportunities: The Role of Labour Standards in Industrial*

Restructuring, Geneva: ILO, International Institute of Labour Studies.

Sennett, Richard (1978) *The Fall of Public Man*, New York: Vintage Books.

— (1980) *Authority*, New York: Alfred Knopf.

Servon, Lisa and Castells, Manuel (1996) *The Feminist City: a Plural Blueprint*, Berkeley: University of California, Institute of Urban and Regional Development, Working Paper.

Shabecoff, Philip (1993) *A Fierce Green Fire: The American Environmental Movement*, New York: Hill and Wang.

Shaiken, Harley (1990) *Mexico in the Global Economy: High Technology and Work Organization in Export Industries*, La Jolla, CA: University of California at San Diego, Center for US–Mexican Studies.

Shapiro, Jerrold L. et al, (eds) (1995) *Becoming a Father: Contemporary Social, Developmental, and Clinical Perspectives*, New York: Springer Verlag.

Sheps, Sheldon (1995) "Militia – History and Law FAQ", World Wide Web, September.

Shimazono, Susumu (1995) *AUM Shinrikyo no Kiseki (Trajectory of AUM Shinrikyo)*, Tokyo: Iwanami-Shoten.

Simpson, John H. (1992) "Fundamentalism in America revisited: the fading of modernity as a source of symbolic capital", in Misztal and Shupe (eds), pp. 10–27.

Singh, Tejpal (1982) *The Soviet Federal State: Theory, Formation, and Development*, New Delhi: Sterling.

Sisk, Timothy D. (1992) *Islam and Democracy: Religion, Politics, and Power in the Middle East*, Washington DC: United States Institute of Peace Press.

Siune, Karen and Truetzschler, Wolfgang (eds). (1992) *Dynamics of Media Politics. Broadcast and Electronic Media in Western Europe*, London: Sage.

Sklair, Leslie (1991) *The Sociology of the Global System*, London: Harvester/Wheatsheaf.

Slezkine, Yuri (1994) "The USSR as a communal apartment, or how a Socialist state promoted ethnic particularism", *Slavic Review*, 53 (2): 414–52.

Smith, Anthony D. (1986) *The Ethnic Origins of Nations*, Oxford: Blackwell.

— (1989) "The origins of nations", *Ethnic and Racial Studies*, 12 (3): 340–67 (quoted from Eley and Suny (eds) (1996), p. 125).

Smith, Michael P. (1991) *City, State and Market: The Political Economy of Urban Society*, Oxford: Blackwell.

Smith, Peter H.(ed.) (1993) *El combate a las drogas en America*, Mexico: Fondo de Cultura Economica.

Sole-Tura, Jordi (1967) *Catalanisme i revolucio burgesa: la sintesi de Prat de la Riba*, Barcelona: Edicions 62.

Spalter-Roth, Roberta and Schreiber, Ronnee (1995) "Outsider issues and insider tactics: strategic tensions in the women's policy network during the 1980s", in Ferree and Martin (eds), pp. 105–27.

Spence, Jonathan D. (1996) *God's Chinese Son: the Taiping Heavenly Kingdom of Hong Xiuquan*, New York: Norton.

Spitz, Glenna (1988) "Women's employment and family relations: a review", *Journal of Marriage and the Family*, 50: 595–618.

Spivak, Gayatri Chakravorty (1990) *The Postcolonial Critique: Interviews, Strategies, Dialogues* (ed. Sarah Harasym), New York: Routledge.

Spragen, William C. (1995) *Electronic Magazines: Soft News Programs on Network Television*, Westport, Conn.: Praeger.

Spretnak, Charlene (ed.) (1982) *The Politics of Women's Spirituality: Essays on the Rise of Spiritual Power within the Women's Movement*, New York: Anchor.

Spruyt, Hendrik (1994) *The Sovereign State and its Competitors*, Princeton, NJ: Princeton University Press.

Stacey, Judith (1990) *Brave New Families: Stories of Domestic Upheaval in Late Twentieth Century America*, New York: Basic Books.

Staggenborg, Susan (1991) *The Pro-choice Movement*, New York: Oxford University Press.

Stallings, Barbara (1992) "International influence on economic policy: debt, stabilization, and structural reform", in Stephan Haggard and Robert Kaufman (eds), *The Politics of Economic Adjustment*, Princeton, NJ: Princeton University Press, pp. 41–88.

Standing, Guy (1990) "Global feminization through flexible labor", *World Development*, 17 (7): 1077–96.

Stanley, Harold W. and Niemi, Richard G. (1992) *Vital Statistics on American Politics*, 3rd edn, Washington DC: CQ Press.

Starovoytova, Galina (1994) "Lecture at the Center for Slavic and East European Studies", University of California at Berkeley, 23 February.

Stebelsky, Igor (1994) "National identity of Ukraine", in Hooson (ed.), pp. 233–48.

Sterling, Claire (1994) *Thieves' World: the Threat of the New Global Network of Organized Crime*, New York: Simon and Schuster.

Stern, Kenneth S. (1996) *A Force upon the Plain: the American Militia Movement and the Politics of Hate*, New York: Simon and Schuster.

Stevens, Mark (1995) "Big boys will be cow boys", *The New York Times Sunday Magazine*, November 19: 72–9.

Streeck, Wolfgang and Schmitter, Philippe C. (1991) "From national corporatism to transnational pluralism: organized interests in the single European market", *Politics and Society*, 19 (2), pp. 133–63.

Strobel, Margaret (1995) "Organizational learning in the Chicago Women's Liberation Union", in Ferree and Martin (eds), pp. 145–64.

Summers, Lawrence (1995) "Ten lessons to learn", *The Economist,* December 23, pp. 46–8.

Sun Tzu (c.505-496 BC) *On the Art of War,* trans. with critical notes by Lionel Giles, Singapore: Graham Brash, 1988 (first published in English in 1910).

Suny, Ronald Grigor (1993) *The Revenge of the Past: Nationalism, Revolution, and the Collapse of the Soviet Union,* Stanford: Stanford University Press.

Susser, Ida (1982) *Norman Street: Poverty and Politics in an Urban Neighborhood,* New York: Oxford University Press.

— (1991) "The separation of mothers and children", in John Mollenkopf and Manuel Castells (eds), *Dual City: Restructuring New York,* New York: Russell Sage, pp. 207–24.

— (1996) "The construction of poverty and homelessness in US cities", *Annual Reviews of Anthropology,* 25: 411–35.

— (forthcoming) "The flexible woman: re-gendering labor in the informational society", *Critique of Anthropology.*

Swan, Jon (1992) "Jennifer", *Columbia Journalism Review* 31 (4): 36.

Szasz, Andrew (1994) *EcoPopulism: Toxic Waste and the Movement for Environmental Justice,* Minneapolis: University of Minnesota Press.

Szmukler, Monica (1996) *Politicas urbanas y democracia: la ciudad de La Paz entre 1985 y 1995,* Santiago de Chile: ILADES.

Tanaka, Martin (1995) "La participacion politica de los sectores populares en America Latina", *Revista Mexicana de Sociologia,* 3: 41–65.

Tarrow, Sydney (1978) *Between Center and Periphery,* New Haven, Conn.: Yale University Press.

Tello Diaz, Carlos (1995) *La rebelion de las canadas,* Mexico: Cal y Arena.

Temas (1995) Special issue "Prensa y poder", 5: 18–50.

The Economist (1994), "Feeling for the future: special survey of television", February 12.

The Economist (1995a) "The future of democracy", June 17: 13–14.

The Economist (1995b), "The Mexican connection", December 26: pp. 39–40.

The Economist (1995c) "Mexico: the long haul", August 26: pp. 17–19.

The Economist (1996) "Satellite TV in Asia: a little local interference", February 3.

The Gallup Poll Monthly (1995) April, 355: 2.

The Nation (1995) Editorial, May 15.

The New Republic (1995a) "An American darkness", May 15.

The New Republic (1995b) "TRB from Washington", May 15.

The New York Times (1995) "Where cotton's king, trouble reigns", October 9: A6.

The New York Times Sunday (1995a) "The rich: a special issue", November 19.

The New York Times Sunday (1995b) "The unending search for demons in the American imagination", July 23: 7.

The Progressive (1995) "The far right is upon us", June.

The World Almanac of Books and Facts, 1996 (1996) New York: Funk and Wagnalls Corporation, World Almanac Books.

Thompson, Dennis F. (1995) *Ethics in Congress: from Individual to Institutional Corruption*, Washington DC: The Brookings Institution.

Thurman, Joseph E. and Trah, Gabriele (1990) "Part-time work in international perspective", *International Labour Review*, 129 (1): 23–40.

Thurow, Lester (1992) *Head to Head: the Coming Economic Battle between Japan, Europe, and the United States*, New York: Morrow.

Tibi, Bassam (1988) *The Crisis of Modern Islam: a Pre-industrial Culture in the Scientific-technological Age*, Salt Lake City: Utah University Press.

— (1992a) *Die fundamentalische Herausforderung: der Islam und die Weltpolitik*, Munich: Beck Press.

— (1992b) *Religious Fundamentalism and Ethnicity in the Crisis of the Nation-state in the Middle-East: Superordinate Islamic and Pan-Arabic Identities and Subordinate Ethnic and Sectarian Identities*, Berkeley: University of California, Center for German and European Studies, Working Paper.

Tilly, Charles (ed.) (1975) *The Formation of Nation States in Western Europe*, Ann Arbor: University of Michigan Press.

— (1995) "State-incited violence, 1900–1999", *Political Power and Social Theory*, 9: 161–79.

Time (1995) "Hell raiser: a Huey Long for the 90s: Pat Buchanan wields the most lethal weapon in Campaign 96: scapegoat politics", November 6.

Tirado, Ricardo and Luna, Matilde (1995) "El Consejo Coordinador Empresarial de Mexico: de la unidad contra el reformismo a la unidad para el Tratado de Libre Comercio (1975–1993)", *Revista Mexicana de Sociologia*, 4: 27–60.

Toner, Robin (1996) "Coming home from the revolution", *The New York Times*, Sunday November 10, s. 4: 1.

Tonry, Michael (1995) *Malign Neglect: Race, Crime, and Punishment in America*, New York: Oxford University Press.

Touraine, Alain (1965) *Sociologie de l'action*, Paris: Seuil.

— (1966) *La conscience ouvrière*, Paris: Seuil.

— (1988) *La parole et le sang: politique et société en Amerique Latine*, Paris: Odile Jacob.

— (1992) *Critique de la modernité*, Paris: Fayard.
— (1994) *Qu'est-ce que la democratie?* Paris: Fayard.
— (1995a) "La formation du sujet", in Dubet and Wieviorka (eds), pp. 21–46.
— (1995b) *Lettre à Lionel, Michel, Jacques, Martine, Bernard, Dominique . . . et vous*, Paris: Fayard.
— et al. (1996) *Le grand refus: reflexions sur la grève de decembre 1995*, Paris: Fayard.
Tranfaglia, Nicola (1992) *Mafia, Politica e Affari, 1943-91*, Roma: Laterza.
Trejo Delarbre, Raul (1994a) *Chiapas: la comunicacion enmascarada. Los medios y el pasamontanas*, Mexico: Diana.
— (ed.) (1994b) *Chiapas: La guerra de las ideas*, Mexico: Diana.
Trend, David (ed.) (1996) *Radical Democracy: Identity, Citizenship, and the State*, New York and London: Routledge.
Trias, Eugenio (1996) "Entrevista: el modelo catalan puede ser muy util para Europa", *El Mundo*, June 30: 32.
Tsuya, Noriko O. and Mason, Karen O. (1995) "Changing gender roles and below-replacement fertility in Japan", in Mason and Jensen (eds), pp. 139–67.
Twinning, David T. (1993) *The New Eurasia: a Guide to the Republics of the Former Soviet Union*, Westport, Conn.: Praeger.
Ubois, Jeff (1995) "Legitimate government has its limits", *Midrange Systems*, 8 (22): 28.
United Nations (1970–1995) *Demographic Yearbook*, various years, New York: United Nations.
— (1995) *Women in a Changing Global Economy: 1994 World Survey on the Role of Women in Development*, New York: United Nations.
United Nations Commission on Global Governance (1995) *Report of the Commission*, New York: United Nations.
United Nations, Economic and Social Council (1994) "Problems and Dangers Posed by Organized Transnational Crime in the Various Regions of the World", Background Document for World Ministerial Conference on Organized Transnational Crime, Naples, 21–23 November (unpublished).
US Bureau of the Census (1994) *Diverse Living Arrangements of Children*, Washington DC: US Bureau of the Census.
US Bureau of the Census (1996) *Composition of American Households*, Washington DC: Department of Commerce, Bureau of the Census.
US Department of Commerce, Economics and Statistics Administration, Bureau of the Census, Current Population Reports Washington DC: Bureau of the Census:
— (1989) *Singleness in America: Single Parents and their Children. Married-couple Families with their Children.*

— (1991) *Population Profile of the United States, 1991*, Series P23, no. 173.

— (1992a) *Households, Families, and Children: a 30-year Perspective*, P23–181.

— (1992b) *When Households Continue, Discontinue, and Form* by Donald J. Hernandez, P23, no. 179.

— (1992c) *Marriage, Divorce, and Remarriage in the 1990s*, by Arthur J. Norton and Louisa F. Miller, P23-180.

— (1992d) *Population Trends in the 1980s*, P-23, no. 175.

Vajrayana Sacca (1994), August, no. 1. Tokyo: Aum Press.

Valdes, Teresa and Gomariz, Enrique (1993) *Mujeres latinoamericanas en cifras*, Madrid: Ministerio de Asuntos Sociales, Instituto de la Mujer.

Vedel, Thierry and Dutton, William H. (1990) "New media politics: shaping cable television policy in France", *Media, Culture, and Society*, 12 (4): 491–524.

Vicens Vives, Jaume (1959) *Historia social y economica de Espana y America*, Barcelona: Ariel.

— and Llorens, Montserrat (1958) *Industrials i Politics del Segle XIX*, Barcelona: Editorial Teide.

Vilar, Pierre (1964) *Catalunya dins l'Espanya Moderna*, Barcelona: Edicions 62.

— ed. (1987–90) *Historia de Catalunya*, Barcelona: edicions 62, 8 vols.

Vogler, John (1992) "Regimes and the global commons: space, atmosphere and oceans", in McGrew et al. (eds), pp. 118–37.

Wacquant, Loic J.D. (1994) "The new urban color line: the state and fate of the ghetto in postfordist America", in Calhoun (ed.), pp. 231-76.

Walter, David (1994) "Winner takes all: the incredible rise – and could it be fall – of Silvio Berlusconi", *Contents*, 23, (4/5): 18–24.

Wapner, Paul (1995) "Politics beyond the state: environmental activism and world civic politics", *World Politics*, April: 311-40.

— (1996) *Environmental Activism and World Civic Politics*, Albany, NY: State University of New York Press.

Weinberg, Steve (1991) "Following the money", *Columbia Journalism Review*, 30 (2): 49–51.

Weisberg, Jacob (1996) *In Defense of Government: the Fall and Rise of Public Trust*, New York: Scribner.

Wellman, Barry (1979) "The community question", *American Journal of Sociology*, 84: 1201–31.

WEPIN Store (1995), "Michigan Militia T-shirt", World Wide Web, West El Paso Information Network.

West, Cornel (1993) *Race Matters*, Boston: Beacon Press.

— (1996) "Black strivings in a twilight civilization", in Gates and West (eds), pp. 53–112.

West, Darrell M. (1993) *Air Wars: Television Advertising in Election Campaigns, 1952–1992*, Washington DC: CQ Press.

Whisker, James B. (1992) *The Militia*, Lewiston, NY: E. Mellen Press.

Whittier, Nancy (1995) *Feminist Generations: the Persistence of the Radical Women's Movement*, Philadelphia: Temple University Press.

Wideman, Daniel J. and Preston, Rohan B. (eds) (1995) *Soulfires: Young Black Men on Love and Violence*, New York: Penguin.

Wiesenthal, Helmut (1993) *Realism in Green Politics: Social Movements and Ecological Reform in Germany*, ed. John Ferris, Manchester: Manchester University Press.

Wieviorka, Michel (1988) *Sociétés et terrorisme*, Paris: Fayard.

— (1993) *La democratie à l'épreuve: nationalisme, populisme, ethnicité*, Paris: La Decouverte.

Wilcox, Clyde (1992) *God's Warriors: the Christian Right in 20th century America*, Baltimore: Johns Hopkins University Press.

Wilensky, Harold (1975) *The Welfare State and Equality: Structural and Ideological Roots of Public Expenditures*, Berkeley: University of California Press.

Williams, Lance and Winokour, Scott (1995) "Militia extremists defend their views", San Francisco Examiner, April 23.

Wilson, William Julius (1987) *The Truly Disadvantaged: the Inner City, the Underclass, and Public Policy*, Chicago: University of Chicago Press.

Winerip, Michael (1996) "An American place: the paramilitary movement. Ohio case typifies the tensions between Militia groups and law", *The New York Times*, June 23, p. A1.

Wittig, Monique (1992) *The Straight Mind*, Boston: Beacon Press.

Woldenberg, Jose (1995) *Violencia y politica*, Mexico: Cal y Arena.

Woodward, Bob (1994) *The Agenda: Inside the Clinton White House*, New York: Simon and Schuster.

WuDunn, Sheryl (1996) "Uproar over a debt crisis: does Japan's mob bear part of the blame?", *The New York Times*, February 14, p. C1.

Yazawa, Shujiro (forthcoming) *Japanese Social Movements since World War II*, Boston: Beacon Press.

Yoshino, Kosaku (1992) *Cultural Nationalism in Contemporary Japan*, London: Routledge.

Zaller, John and Hunt, Mark (1994) "The rise and fall of candidate Perot: unmediated versus mediated politics, part I", *Political Communication*, 11: 357–90.

Zaretsky, Eli (1994) "Identity theory, identity politics: psychoanalysis, marxism, post-structuralism", in Calhoun (ed.), pp. 198–215.

Zeskind, Leonard (1986) *The Christian Identity Movement: Analyzing its*

Theological Rationalization for Racist and Anti-semitic Violence, Atlanta, GA: National Council of the Churches of the Christ in the USA, Center for Democratic Renewal.

Ziccardi, Alicia (ed.) (1991) *Ciudades y gobiernos locales en la America Latina de los noventa*, Mexico: Miguel Angel Porrua Grupo Editorial.

— (ed.) (1995) *La tarea de gobernar: gobiernos locales y demandas ciudadanas*, Mexico: Miguel Angel Porrua Grupo Editorial.

Zisk, Betty H. (1992) *The Politics of Transformation: Local Activism in the Peace and Environmental Movements*, Westport, Conn.: Praeger.

Zook, Matthew (1996) "The unorganized militia network: conspiracies, computers, and community", Berkeley: University of California, Department of Sociology, Seminar paper for SOC 290.2 (unpublished).

Index

Page numbers in italics denote information in figures or tables.